Albert S. Cook

A First Book in Old English

Elibron Classics
www.elibron.com

A FIRST BOOK IN OLD ENGLISH

GRAMMAR, READER, NOTES, AND VOCABULARY

BY

ALBERT S. COOK

PROFESSOR OF THE ENGLISH LANGUAGE AND LITERATURE
IN YALE UNIVERSITY

THIRD EDITION

LONDON

9, St. Martin's Street, Leicester Square

GINN & COMPANY, PUBLISHERS

The Athenæum Press

GINN & COMPANY · PRO-
PRIETORS · BOSTON · U.S.A.
·

PREFACE TO FIRST EDITION.

THE present volume is an attempt to be of service to those who are beginning the study of our language, or who desire to acquaint themselves with a few specimens of our earliest literature. It has seemed to the author that there were two extremes to be avoided in its compilation — the treatment of Old English as though it consisted of wholly isolated phenomena, and the procedure upon a virtual assumption that the student was already acquainted with the cognate Germanic tongues and with the problems and methods of comparative philology. The former treatment robs the study of its significance and value, which, like that of most other subjects, is found in its relations; the latter repels and confounds the student at a stage when he is most in need of encouragement and attraction.

How well the author has succeeded must be left to the judgment of others — the masters whom he follows at a distance, and the students whose interests he has constantly borne in mind. Of one thing, however, he can assure such as may care to inspect his book — that he has spared no pains in treading the path which seemed to be thus marked out for him in advance. Errors there doubtless are — errors of judgment, and errors of fact; but for both he must plead the best excuse ever offered for similar imperfections, that of King Alfred in the last sentence on page 162 of this volume.

The selections have been made with reference to giving a fairly just, though necessarily incomplete, view of the surroundings, occupations, problems, ideals, and sentiments of our English ancestors. The earlier pieces of both prose and poetry are short; the longer ones that follow either have more sustained interest, or are supported by their reference to preceding ones; but they, too, fall into natural subdivisions, partially indicated in the printing, so that they may be read as successions of short extracts.

It may be objected that Latin and Greek have been too freely used for illustration. The reply to such an objection is twofold: that the book is likely to fall into the hands of some who possess at least an elementary acquaintance with one or both of these languages, and that to these the disclosure of the relations involved in a comparison with the ancient tongues will materially increase their pleasure and their gain; and, secondly, that the book may be intelligently read, from cover to cover, without the slightest knowledge of either Greek or Latin.

The passages from Bede have been taken from Miller's edition; the portion of Ælfric's Colloquy from the Wright-Wülker Vocabularies; the extracts from Wulfstan from Napier's edition; the selections from Beowulf and Andreas are based upon the Grein-Wülker edition of the Bibliothek derAngelsächsischen Poesie; that from the Judith upon my own edition. The originals of the others are either indicated, or will be patent to scholars.

The normalization of the texts to an Early West Saxon basis — Cosijn's Altwestsächsische Grammatik being the chief authority for norms — will doubtless be criticised by some scholars whose judgment is entitled to respect; but here again the author has had in mind the beginner, for whose especial use the book is intended. If he welcomes this introduction on account of its greater ease, and is yet not led astray by it; if he becomes solidly grounded in the elements, so that further progress is facilitated, while yet he has nothing to unlearn in the future; the author will be consoled by his approbation for the censure of those who entertain a different opinion on this head.

To the normalization of the texts exception has been made in the case of the poetry. For this there are two reasons. In spite of the greater difficulty of the poetry, the student should have had sufficient practice in reading, and particularly in parsing — the importance of which cannot be too much insisted upon — to proceed in the poetry without great obstruction from the retention of manuscript forms, especially as the cross-references of the Vocabulary will furnish him with the necessary assistance; and, secondly, the normalization of the poetry would sometimes have been attended with considerable uncertainty, an uncertainty which is decidedly less in the case of the prose. Besides, such profit as accrues to the student from the inspection of the irregular orthography of the manuscripts may, by the literal reproduction of the orthography, be gained from this part.

The device noted on page 202 is presented with some

persuasion of its utility, though frankly as an experiment on which the author would gladly take, after sufficient trial, the judgment of his colleagues.

The Grammar is the merest outline. Its condensation has been largely effected by confining the treatment almost entirely to Old English itself, excluding all references to the theoretical Primitive Germanic. This method is accompanied with some loss; but, again, it is the beginner whom the author has had in view. More doubtful, perhaps, is the expediency of an empirical classification of nouns, instead of the scientific arrangement according to stems; many of us have unquestionably found, however, that the more purely scholarly classification occasions not a little trouble in practice, and that its theoretical advantages are dearly purchased at this stage, before there is any adequate conception of comparative philology and its postulates. The author is not so clear with regard to the probable utility of paragraphs 12–14, on original and derivative vowels; criticism on this point will be especially welcome.

The Appendixes include illustrative matter for which there was no natural place elsewhere, or materials and hints for those who would prosecute their researches a little further. The first three of them carry their meaning on their face; the last is provided in order to facilitate the beginning of dialectic study. It — Appendix IV. — has cost more thought than is likely to appear on the surface. The dialects have as yet been but imperfectly discriminated; it is easier to say what is non-West-Saxon than what is Mercian or Kentish; the residuum of demonstrably pure Northumbrian forms in Cædmon's Hymn, for example, turns out to be surprisingly small.

Care has been devoted to the unification of the book — to making its parts mutually coherent; the illustrations of syntax are therefore taken from the texts printed in the Reader, and the Vocabulary contains copious references to the Grammar. It is hoped that this plan will prevent distraction on the part of the student, and conduce to a nearly absolute mastery of the matter here presented. The book ought to occupy at least a semester, and could readily be used for a longer time. The author believes that the history of the English language may most profitably begin with such a manual, studied under a competent teacher and with access to a few good reference books. Thus used, it might advantageously be introduced into the earlier part of College courses, and perhaps into the better sort of High Schools and Academies.

In conclusion, it is a pleasure to the author to acknowledge his indebtedness to Miss Elizabeth Deering Hanscom, graduate student of Yale University and American Fellow of the Association of Collegiate Alumnæ, who has rendered material assistance in the preparation of the Vocabulary.

YALE UNIVERSITY, December 11, 1893.

PREFACE TO SECOND EDITION.

THE favorable reception accorded to the first edition has encouraged the author, besides correcting several small errors, to amplify Appendix I., and to add a new Appendix, numbered V. The provision of a brief bibliography has been so generally welcomed that it has seemed desirable to append a list of books of a more advanced character, while retaining the former one essentially unchanged. No attempt at completeness has been made, but perhaps not many books of primary value have been omitted. The illustration of umlaut from Gothic, suggested by a reviewer, now constitutes Appendix V.

Certain teachers having expressed a wish that the Vocabulary should give the gender of nouns, the author thinks it proper to state the principle upon which the designation of gender was omitted. This principle was that the Grammar should be in constant use. The cardinal use of a knowledge of the gender is with reference to declension; given the declension, and the gender follows. Now the references to the Grammar under nouns primarily indicate the declensions. If, then, the student recognizes the meaning of such references as **43**, **47**, etc., it is a proof that he is sufficiently acquainted with the paradigms they indicate; if not, it is a clear sign that he ought to refer to them, and that a mere knowledge of the gender would not suffice. This is the author's opinion, but he holds himself prepared to defer to the expressed wish of his colleagues, when he can believe that that wish is at all general among those who have given the book a fair trial.

The author hopes soon to issue a small companion volume of exercises in Old English, designed chiefly to facilitate drill on inflections. These exercises will consist of brief sentences for translation into Old English, based upon the successive prose selections of the Reader, together with an English-Old English Vocabulary.

A final word to those who use this book — a word based upon experience with it: *Look up carefully every foot-note, and constantly refer from the Vocabulary to the Grammar, with reference to the speedy mastery of the latter, supplementing this process by the committal to memory of paradigms.*

YALE UNIVERSITY, December 31, 1894.

PREFACE TO THIRD EDITION.

In this edition Appendix I. has again been revised and amplified; Appendix VI. has been added, as Appendix IV. was in the second edition; and a few minor errors have been corrected.

Certain kindly critics have desired changes which would virtually mean the introduction of a larger element of comparative Germanics, but I have not seen my way clear to satisfy them, for the reasons stated on p. viii; such persons can always find what they desire in Sievers' *Old English Grammar*, in Bülbring's *Altenglisches Elementarbuch*, or in my *Phonological Investigation of Old English*. Any curiosity about the general appearance of the other Germanic tongues may now be gratified by a glance at Appendix VI.

The *Exercises in Old English*, based principally upon the earlier prose texts of this book, has proved its utility as a means of securing grammatical drill with a comparatively small expenditure of effort and time, and may therefore be commended to teachers with some confidence.

YALE UNIVERSITY, December 20, 1902.

SUPPLEMENTARY NOTE

For a new impression of this book I now have the opportunity of consulting Krapp's edition of the *Andreas*, and have conformed a few readings to his, besides emending *sēce* to *sęcge* (216. 5).

YALE UNIVERSITY, June 28, 1906.

CONTENTS.

GRAMMAR.

INTRODUCTION.

Dialects and Periods.

1. Old English (sometimes called Anglo-Saxon) is the name of the Germanic language spoken in England between the middle of the fifth and the middle of the twelfth century. Its literature extends from the eighth to the twelfth century, and there are no Old English words found in documents earlier than the seventh century. The principal prose texts date from the period of King Alfred (871–901 A.D.), or from that of Abbot Ælfric (pronounced Alfric), who flourished about the year 1000 A.D. The poetical pieces are mostly of uncertain dates, ranging from the eighth to the tenth or eleventh century.

There are four dialects of Old English, the Northumbrian, Mercian, Kentish, and West Saxon; of these the Mercian is intermediate in its characteristics between the Northumbrian and West Saxon. The Northumbrian dialect formed the basis of modern Scotch and Northern English, the Mercian of standard literary English. The literature of Old English is chiefly extant in West Saxon, though the poetry,

3

and some of the prose, contains forms from other dia.
lects, chiefly from the Northumbrian.

Since the remains of the other dialects are comparatively small, West Saxon is the principal existing
representative of Old English, and hence the two
terms are often used interchangeably. West Saxon
is divided into Early West Saxon (EWS.) and Late
West Saxon (LWS.). The former is the language as
written in King Alfred's time, the latter as in that
of Abbot Ælfric and his successors. A hundred years
made some changes in the language, but rather with
respect to syntax, euphony, and style in general than
to the forms of words, though these also underwent
some modification.

In this work, the forms are those of Early West
Saxon, which is assumed as the standard, even when
the selections are from Late West Saxon.

PHONOLOGY.

2. Alphabet. — The Old English alphabet has the letters of Modern English, with the exception of *j*, *k*, *q*, *v*, and *z*, and with the addition of ð and þ, both of which represent the modern *th*. Of these, *j* and *v* are never used, being represented by **g** (or **i**) and **f**, respectively; *k*, *q*, and *z* but rarely, *k* being commonly represented by **c**, *ks(cs)* by **x**, *q(u)* by **c(w)**, and *z* by **ts**. The two unfamiliar characters ð and þ are pronounced *eth* (*eth* in *brethren*) and *thorn*, respectively; they are used interchangeably in the manuscripts; in this book ð will, in general, stand for both.

3. Vowels and diphthongs. — The vowel-letters are those of Modern English, with the addition of æ. Modern editors employ ę and ǫ to denote respectively an **e** and **o** which sprang from an original **a** (but ę occasionally from **o**; **17, 25**). The vowels may be either short or long.

The diphthongs are represented by **ea**, **eo**, and **ie**, both short and long. The second vowel sound in each diphthong is scarcely heard in pronunciation, the first element being the one which receives the stress.

5

The vowel of every syllable is to be pronounced, but in an unstressed syllable the sound is less distinct (**23**).

4. Quantity. — Long vowels and diphthongs must be carefully distinguished from short ones. In normalized texts, length is indicated by the acute accent (´) or the macron (¯), placed over a vowel or the first element of a diphthong. For instance, OE. **god** is Mod. Eng. *god*, but OE. **gód** or **gōd** is Mod. Eng. *good;* so **for**, *for*, but **fōr**, *went;* **bær**, *bare*, but **bǣr**, *bier;* **ac**, *but*, but **āc**, *oak;* **geat**, *gate*, but **gēat**, *poured;* **is**, *is*, but **īs**, *ice;* **man**, *man*, but **mān**, *crime;* **tol**, *toll*, but **tōl**, *tool;* **węnde**, *went*, but **wēnde**, *weened.* Beginners should never fail to note whether the radical vowel of each word is long or short, and should no more confound **a** with **ā** than **a** with **y**.

The length of a syllable must be distinguished from that of a vowel. Every syllable containing a long vowel is itself long, but so is also one which contains a short vowel followed by any two consonants or a double consonant. In the latter case, the syllable is said to be long by position; in the former, by nature.

5. Pronunciation of vowels and diphthongs. — The pronunciation of the vowels and diphthongs can only be mastered by ignoring their pronunciation in Modern English. Any modern language, or Latin or Greek as pronounced by the Continental method, would be a safer guide.

The exact pronunciation of the Old English vowels and diphthongs can be but imperfectly represented. The learner will not be far astray if he follows the pronunciation indicated in this table: —

a	as in	last (not *a* in man)	**habban**
ā	"	far	**ān**
æ	"	man	**æt**
ǣ	"	care	**ǣr**
e, ę	"	men	**help, męnn**
ē	"	they	**hē**
i	"	fin	**in**
ī	"	machine	**wīn**
o, ǫ	"	broad (but shorter)	**god**
ō	"	tone	**gōd**
u	"	full	**full**
ū	"	rune	**dūn**
y	"	{ dünn (Germ.) { din (less accurate)	**dynn**
ȳ	"	{ grün (Germ.) { green (less accurate)	**hȳd**
ea	=	æ + ŭh	**eall**
ēa	=	ē + ah	**nēah**
eo	=	e + o	com
ēo	=	ē + o	**frēond**
ie	=	i + ĕh	**fierd**
īe	=	ī + ĕh	**nīed**

NOTE. — The true sounds of **y** and **ȳ** are most readily produced by placing the lips in the position for pronouncing long *oo*, and, while retaining the lips in this position, pronouncing respectively the *i* in *it*, and the *ee* in *deem*.

6. Consonants. — The consonants are divided into —

labials, **w, m, p, b, f.**

dentals, **r, l, n, t, d, ð, s.**

gutturals (sometimes *palatals*), **(ng), c, g, h.**

7. Pronunciation of consonants. — **w** was pronounced as in Mod. Eng., also distinctly in the combinations **wr, wl**; **m, p,** and **b** as in Mod. Eng.; **f** as *f* and as *v* (**2**).

r and **l** were pronounced nearly as in Mod. Eng. (but see **21**); **n, t, d,** as in Mod. Eng.; **ð** as *th* in *thin* and in *the;* **s** as *s* and as *z*.

ng was pronounced like Mod. Eng. *ng* in *finger;* when palatal (**10**) it resembled *ng* in *singe*. **c** was pronounced like Mod. Eng. *k*, or, when palatal, like English *ch* in *child*, and was distinctly heard as *k* in the combination **cn**; **cg** like *dg* in Mod. Eng. *bridge* (see **11**). **g** was pronounced as *g* (but see **9**) and as *y* (**10**). **h** was pronounced as in English, even in the combinations **hl, hn, hr, hw**; when final, and in the combinations **ht, hð,** and **hh**, it had the sound of German *ch*, as in *ach* or in *ich*. **hs** was pronounced like Mod. Eng. *x* (cf. **2**).

When **c** was pronounced as *k*, **g** as *g*, and **h** as German *ch* in *ach*, these letters are to be regarded as gutturals; when as *ch* in *child*, *y*, and *ch* in *ich* respectively, as palatals (**10**).

8. Surds and sonants. — The consonants **p, t, c,** together with **f, s, ð** when pronounced like Mod. Eng. *f*, *s*, *th* in *thin*, are called surds. All the other consonants, and all the vowels and diphthongs, are called sonants.

f, s, and **ð** are surds when beginning a syllable, or following a surd at the end of a syllable; they are sonants, that is, are pronounced like *v*, *z*, and *th* in *the*, when they occur between two sonants, or follow a sonant at the end of a syllable. To the foregoing rule there may be some exceptions; in case of doubt, the analogy of Modern English may be followed.

9. Spirants and stops. — Spirants are consonantal sounds producible by a continuous emission of breath. Stops are momentary or explosive. The spirants are **f, s, ð,** and **h** (properly also **g**); to **f** and **ð** correspond the surd stops **p** and **t,** and the sonant stops **b** and **d.**

10. Gutturals and palatals. — The consonants **c, g, h,** are gutturals when occurring before consonants or the vowels **a, ā, ē, o, ǫ, ō, u, ū, y,** and **ȳ** (and sometimes **æ**). They are palatals when occurring before, and sometimes after, the palatal vowels **æ, e, ę, i, ī, ea, ēa, eo, ēo, ie, ie** (sometimes **æ**); **c** and **g** medially (that is, in the middle of a word), when they are or may be followed by **e** or **i; c** likewise in the combination **sc** (pronounced almost like **sh**); **g** in the medial combination **cg;** and **c(cc, nc), g(ng)** often medially and finally after a palatal vowel, but at least **ng** not always: *e.g.*, **ęngel, Englisc** have not **ng** = *nj*. For the pronunciation of these consonants as palatals see **7.**

11. Double consonants. — Double consonants must not be pronounced as in Mod. Eng., except at the end of a syllable. When medial, each consonant is pronounced separately : **sunnum** as *sun-num*, the *n*'s as in Mod. Eng. *penknife.*

Double **f**, when sonant, is always represented by **bb**, and double **g** is usually written **cg**. The only consonant never doubled is **w**.

Effects and Relations of Sounds.

12. Original and derivative vowels. — Of the vowels and diphthongs of Old English, some are original, in the sense of being more directly an inheritance from the Parent Germanic tongue, while others are derivative, or result from modifications of those that we call original.

The original vowels and diphthongs are the following : —

a, ā, æ, ǣ (sometimes), **e, ē** (rarely), **i** (sometimes), **ī, o, ō, u** (regularly), **ū, ēa, ēo** (sometimes).

The derivative vowels and diphthongs are : —

æ (sometimes), **ǣ** (sometimes), **ę, ē** (usually), **i** (sometimes), **ǫ, u** (occasionally), **y, ȳ, ea, eo, ēo** (sometimes), **ie, īe**. Though **ea, eo, ie** when short are all derivatives, **ie** may be called a derivative of the second order, since it arises from one of the two others.

13. Relation of original to derivative vowels. — The relations between original and derivative vowels may thus be shown (see **17, 18, 20, 21, 25**) : —

ORIGINAL.	DERIVATIVE.
a	æ, ę, ǫ, ea, ie
ā	ǣ
e	i, eo, ie, o
i	eo, u
ę	ę
o	ę, eo
ō	ē, ēo
u	y
ū	ȳ
ēa	ie
ēo	ie

14. **Relation of derivative to original vowels.** — Reversing the order of the last table, we obtain : —

DERIVATIVE.	ORIGINAL.
æ	a
ǣ	ā
ę	a, ǫ, o
ē	ō
i	e
ǫ	a
y	u
ȳ	ū
ea	a (æ)
ēa (rarely)	ǣ
eo	e, i, o
ēo .	ō
ie	a (ea), ę, e (eo), i (eo)
ie	ēa, ēo

Occasionally (**28, 29, 30**) ǣ is derived from æ, ē from e, ī from i, ō from o or a, ū from u, ȳ from y, ēa from ea, and ēo from eo. Rarely are o and u derived from e and i (**26**).

It must be observed that not every vowel standing in the column of derivatives belongs exclusively there. Thus **i**, *for example, is sometimes original* (**12**).

15. Umlaut. — Umlaut is a change effected in the vowel of a stressed syllable by the vowel of a following, usually the next following, syllable.

There are two chief kinds of umlaut, the **i**-umlaut (pron. *ĭh'-oom'-lowt*), and the **u**- or **o**-umlaut (*oo*- or *ŏh*-).

16. The i-umlaut. — **i**-umlaut is a change effected in a vowel or diphthong by palatalization, such palatalization consisting in an approximation of the umlauted vowel or diphthong to the sound of **i** (*ĭh*). The cause of **i**-umlaut was in all cases an **i** or a **j** (pronounced like Mod. Eng. *y*) of a following syllable, but the **i** or **j** usually disappeared before the period of historic Old English, or was turned into e. When the word umlaut is used without qualification, **i**-umlaut is to be understood. See Appendix V.

17. Illustrations of i-umlaut. — The effect of **i**-umlaut will be shown by the following table: —

ORIGINAL VOWEL.	UMLAUT VOWEL.
a	ę (æ)
ā	ǣ
e	i
ǫ	ę
o	ę
ō	ē̆
u	y

Original Vowel.	Umlaut Vowel.
ū	ȳ
ea (from a)	ie
ēa	īe
eo (from e)	ie
ēo	īe

Examples are: **mann** (*man*), **menn** (*men*); **lār** (*lore*), **lǣran** (*teach*); **helpan** (*help*), **hilpð** (*helps*); **monn** (*man*), **menn** (*men*); **oxa** (*ox*), **exen** (*oxen*); **dōm** (*doom*), **dēman** (*judge*); **wulle** (*wool*), **wyllen** (*woollen*); **brūcan** (*use*), **brȳcð** (*uses*); **eald** (*old*). **ieldu** (*age*); **hēah** (*high*), **hīehra** (*higher*); **weorpan** (*throw*), **wierpð** (*throws*); **hrēowan** (*rue*), **hrīewð** (*rues*).

Sometimes two words are so related that **y** seems to be i-umlaut of **o**, like **gold** (*gold*), **gylden** (*golden*); but in such cases the **o** came from an earlier **u**.

The umlaut of **a** is generally **e**, but in some words **æ** is found.

Strictly speaking, **i** is not the umlaut of **e**, but the phenomenon, though resulting from a somewhat different cause, is virtually the same.

18. Palatal influence. — Initial **g**, **c**, and **sc**, change **æ** (from a) to **ea**, **ǣ** to **ēa**, and **e**, **e** to **ie**; and **sc** sometimes changes **a** to **ea**, **ā** to **ēa**, **o** to **eo**, and **ō** to **ēo**. Examples: **gæf** (*gave*), **geaf**; **gǣfon** (*gave*, plur.), **gēafon**; **sceppan** (*create*), **scieppan**; **gefan** (*give*), **giefan**; **scacan** (*shake*), **sceacan**; **scādan**

(*separate*), scēadan; scop (*poet*), sceop; scōh (*shoe*), scēoh. Even ēo from ū: scēor, from scūr, *shower*.

In the following words, the **ge** represents original **j** (pron. *y*): **geoc,** *yoke* (orig. **joc**); **geond,** *through* (orig. **jond**); **geong,** *young* (orig. **jung**); **geoguð,** *youth* (orig. **juguð**); **gēomor,** *grief* (orig. **jōmor**); **gēa,** *yea* (orig. **jā**); **gēar,** *year* (orig. **jār**); **gē,** *ye* (orig. **jē**). Perhaps better scēadan, geōmor, etc.

The **i** found in the present stem of some weak verbs (**116**) stands for original **j** (pron. *y*), and, as **g** represents this **j** in the words just instanced, so it often appears in the endings of these weak verbs, sometimes alone, sometimes followed by **e,** sometimes in one of these two forms preceded by **i.** Thus **nęrian,** save, occurs also as **nęrgan, nęrigan, nęrigean,** etc.; the ind. pres. 1st sing. **nęrie** as **nęrge, nęrige,** etc.

Wherever in or just preceding the inflectional ending of a word, **c** or **g** is followed by **e** before another vowel, the **e** must be understood to indicate an original **j** (pron. *y*), and an alternative form without **e** also exists. Thus **sēcean** and **sēcan,** seek; **męnigeo** and **męnigo,** multitude. Similarly, the **i** and **g** in the inflectional endings of nouns like **hęre,** *army* (**44.** 2) represent original **j** (pron. *y*).

19. y and ȳ for ie and īe. — **y** and **ȳ** properly represent the i-umlaut of **u** and **ū**, but are also frequently found for **ie** and **īe.** Sometimes, again, the latter are represented by **i** and **ī**. Hence, in looking for words containing these letters, it is never safe to confine the search to any one of the three. From **eald**, *old*, is formed by means of **i**-umlaut the noun **ieldu**, *age* (**17**); but the latter might occur in a text or glossary as **yldu**. Contrariwise, on finding **yldu** in a .text or glossary, it would not be safe to conclude that the **y** represented the **i**-umlaut of **u**, since, as we have just seen, it really goes back to **ea** and **a**. Again, were the word to be found as **ildu**, it should not be inferred that the **i** is either original or derived from **e** (**17**), for the reason just adduced.

Remember that **y** *or* **i**, *short or long*, may *stand for* **ie**, *short or long*.

20. The u- or o-umlaut. — This umlaut is a change effected in the vowels **a**, **e**, or **i** by a **u** or **o** of the following syllable. By it **a** is converted to **ea**, and **e** or **i** to **eo** (sometimes **i** to **io**). Examples : **caru**, *care*, becomes **cearu** ; **weruld**, *world*, becomes **weoruld** ; **miluc**, *milk*, becomes **meoloc** or **mioloc**. The change of vowel is, however, not invariable in these circumstances, and, on the whole, may be regarded as exceptional.

The explanation of this phenomenon is that the vowel sound of the following syllable is anticipated, as it were. The vocal organs, while pronouncing the **a** (properly **æ**) of **caru** (**cæru**), are already shaping themselves to pronounce the **u**; hence the result is **cæuru**, very nearly, which is further modified into **cearu**. For **weoruld** the explanation is similar, but easier.

21. Breakings. — Before **r** + consonant, **l** + consonant, and **h** + consonant or **h** final, **a** is regularly converted into **ea**, and **e** or **i** frequently into **eo**. This change is called *breaking*, because the one vowel is, as it were, *broken* into two. Examples: —

a) **a** to **ea**: **arm** (*arm*), **earm**; **ald** (*old*), **eald**; **ahta** (*eight*), **eahta**.

b) **e** or **i** to **eo** (**io** sometimes from **i**): **erðe** (*earth*), **eorðe**; **elh** (*elk*), **eolh**; **fehtan** (*fight*), **feohtan**; **Piht** (*Pict*), **Pioht, Peoht.**

It must be remembered that the sound of **e** in **ea** differs materially from that of the same letter in **eo** (**5**; cf. **20**).

The explanation of breaking lies in the fact that the vowels which experienced · breaking were formed with a position of the vocal organs quite different from that concerned in the production of **r**, **l**, and **h**, as pronounced in Old English. These consonants, at the time when they caused breaking, were gutturals; the vowels that underwent breaking were palatals (strictly speaking, when we say that **a** was broken, we should rather say that it was **æ**). In the production of these consonants, the back part of the mouth was chiefly concerned; in that of the vowels it was the forward part. Hence, in passing from the vowel position to that of the consonant, an intermediate vowel sound or glide was produced, akin in position and sound to the consonant which it preceded. Although these consonants have at present a pronunciation which cannot be called guttural, yet it is possible to pronounce a sentence like ' What ails you?' in so drawling a manner, especially as regards ' ails,' that this word shall have nearly the sound of *ā-uls*. The obscure *ŭh*-sound thus developed may be compared to the second element of the diphthong in **ea** and **eo**. Here may be adduced Shakespearian lines such as —

> Strikes his breast *hard* (hah-urd), and anon he casts.
> — HEN. VIII. 3. 2. 117.

> Look how he makes to Cæsar, *mark* (mah-urk) him.
> — JUL. CÆS. 3. 2. 18.

> My *lord* (law-urd), will it please you pass along.
> — RICH. III. 3. 1. 136.

In all these, metre seems to demand that the italicized words shall be pronounced as disyllabic (Abbott's *Shakespearian Grammar*, § 485).

22. Ablaut. — Ablaut (pron. *ahp'lowt*) is a prehistoric relation existing between the vowels of different tense-stems derived from the same verbal root. Thus the relation of *i*, *a*, and *u*, in the Mod. Eng. *sing, sang, sung,* is an ablaut relation, and so is the relation of

i, o, i in the Mod. Eng. *drive, drove, driven.* In Old
English the tense-stems of these verbs would be **sing-,
sang, sung-, sung-** (104); **drīf-, drāf, drif-, drif-** (102).
In the former, **i, a, u, u** stand in an ablaut relation ;
in the latter, **ī, ā, i, i.**

It must be observed that the verbal stems concerned
sometimes appear in nouns and adjectives, as well as
in verbs. Thus the vowel of the Mod. Eng. noun
song stands in an ablaut relation with those of the tense-
stems *sing* and *sung.* Again, in Old English, the **i**
of the noun **bite,** *bite,* stands in an ablaut relation
with the other vowels of the tense-stems of **bītan,**
bite. The latter are **bīt-, bāt, bit-, bit-** (102), and
hence the radical vowel of the noun is identical with
that of the third and fourth stems.

*Ablaut is not to be confounded with umlaut. Um-
laut admits of explanation; ablaut must, so far as Old
English is concerned, be merely accepted as a fact.*

23. Stress, and the vowels of unstressed syllables. —
The stressed syllable is the principal one, and usually
the first one of the word, except in compounded verbs,
and nouns or adjectives with the prefixes **be-, ge-,** and
sometimes **for-** ; these stress the root syllable. The
laws relating to vowels hold only of stressed syllables.
In unstressed syllables, especially in the second syllable of trisyllabic words, the vowel is liable to pass into
a neutral sound, often represented by **e,** or to disappear

altogether. When the vowel disappears, the trisyllabic word of course becomes disyllabic: ęngel, *angel*,
gen. ęngles (instead of ęngeles); hēafod, *head*, gen.
hēafdes (instead of hēafodes). Syncope, as such disappearance is termed, is most apt to occur after a long
syllable (4).

**24. Representation of Old English vowels in Modern
English.** — The same Old English vowel letter is not
always represented by the same Mod. Eng. letter, nor
its sound by the same Mod. Eng. sound; yet there is
a certain uniformity, differing in degree with different
vowels, in the representation of both sound and letter.
Some of the more regular correspondences are given
in the subjoined table, though it must be understood
that exceptions are numerous. The Mod. Eng. sound
or letter that is first given is the commonest; the
second is often comparatively rare. The figuration
of the Mod. Eng. vowel sounds is that of Webster's
Dictionary. For details, see Mayhew's *Synopsis of Old
English Phonology.*

	OE. LETTERS.	MOD. E. LETTERS.	MOD. E. SOUNDS.	ILLUSTRATIONS.
	a	a	ā, ă	**nama**, name ; **land**, land
But	ag	aw	a̤	**haga**, haw
	ā	o, oa	ō; ò before r	**hām**, home ; **ār**, oar
	æ	a	ă, ä	**glæd**, glad ; **fæder**, father
But	æg	ai, ay	ā	**brægn**, brain ; **dæg**, day
	ǣ	ea, ee, e	ē, ĕ	**dǣl**, deal ; **sǣd**, seed ; **flǣsc**, flesh

OE. LETTERS.	MOD. E. LETTERS.	MOD. E. SOUNDS.	ILLUSTRATIONS.
e, ę	e, ea	ĕ, ē	feðer, feather; twęlf, twelve; spere, spear
But eg	ai, ay, a	ā	regn, rain; weg, way; ðegn, thane
ē	ee, e	ē (seldom ĕ)	cwēn, queen; hēr, here; (blētsian, bless)
i	i	ĭ; ī before ht, nd, ld	fisc, fish; miht, might; blind, blind; cild, child
But ig	i	ī	nigon, nine
ī	i	ī, ĭ	rīm, rime; wīsdōm, wisdom
o, ǫ	o, oa	ŏ, ō; ô before r	bodig, body; lǫng, long; bolla, bowl; hord, hoard
ō	oo, o	ōō, ŭ, o͝o	hrōf, roof; ōðer, other; bōc, book
But ōw	ow	o	blōwan, blow
u	u, o	ŭ, o͝o	lufu, love; wulf, wolf
But und	ound	ound	hund, hound
ū	ou, ow, u	ou, ŭ	hlūd, loud; būr, bower; būtan, but
y	i, u, o	ĭ, û	cyning, king; byrðen, burthen; wyrm, worm
ȳ	i	ī, ĭ	brȳd, bride; fȳst, fist
ea	a	ă, ä, a̤	weaxan, wax; heard, hard; eall, all
But eald (Anglian āld)	old	ōld	beald, bold
ēa	ea	ē, ĕ	bēacen, beacon; dēad, dead
But ēaw	ew	ū	dēaw, dew
eo	ea, e, u	ĉ, û	eorðe, earth; beorg, berg; ceorl, churl
But eor	ar, ear	ar	heorot, hart; heorte, heart
ēo	ee, ie, e	ē, ĕ	dēop, deep; fēond, fiend; dēofol, devil
But ēow	ew	ū	blēow, blew
ie	e, ie	ĕ, ē	hierde, herd; gieldan, yield
īe	See ē		

25. Influence of nasals. — The nasals **m** and **n** change a preceding **a** to **ǫ**. Usage is not uniform; some texts have **a** in this position, and others **ǫ**.

When a word cannot be found under **a**, *look for it under* **ǫ**, *and conversely.*

26. Influence of w. — In cases where **e** or **i** has become **eo** or **io** (20, 21), a preceding **w** is apt to change **eo** to **o** or **u**, and **io** to **u**. For example, **weruld** (*world*) becomes **weoruld** through the influence of u-umlaut (**20**), and this may then become **woruld**. Similarly, **widuwe** (*widow*) becomes **wioduwe**, and then **wuduwe**. For the **o** and **u** thus produced, **y** is sometimes found.

When **o**, **u**, *or* **y** *immediately follows* **w**, *it may be suspected, though it must not be assumed, that the vowel was once* **eo** *or* **io**, *originally* **e** *or* **i**.

Consonantal Loss and Change.

27. Loss or vocalization of w. — Some words ending in a long vowel or diphthong originally ended in **w**, and the **w** is still found in the *oblique* cases of these words. Thus, nom. **cnēo** (*knee*), gen. **cnēowes**, etc., and occasionally in the nominative, **cnēow** (**47. 3**).

At the end of a word, and following a short syllable which ends in a consonant, **u** often stands for original **w**, the latter having undergone vocalization in that position. When an inflectional syllable is added beginning with a vowel, the **w** reappears. Thus, nom. **gearu** (*ready*), gen. **gearwes**, etc. (**57**. 5).

There is frequent loss of initial **w** in the negative forms of the verbs **wesan**, *be*, **witan**, *know*, **willan**, *will:* **næs**, *was not*, **nāt**, *knows not*, **nolde**, *would not*, etc. It also disappears in **nā(u)ht** for **nāwiht**, *naught*, **cuc** for **cwic**, *alive*, and a few other words.

28. Loss or replacement of g. — Before **d** and **n** (and before **ð** in the word **tīðian**, *grant*), **g** is often lost, the preceding vowel being lengthened by way of compensation: **mægden** and **mǣden**, *maiden;* **ðegn** and **ðēn**, *thane*. Properly speaking, the palatal **g**, already in such cases pronounced almost like a vowel, becomes indistinguishable from **i** or **y** in pronunciation, and by this time its effect is simply to lengthen the vowel which precedes. In a similar manner, **ig** may be contracted into **ī**, sometimes shortened to **i**: **hungrig** and **hungri**, *hungry;* **ligeð** and **līð**, *lies* (from **licgan**); **stīgrāp** and **stīrāp**, *stirrup*. The above losses are *regular* only after palatal vowels (**10**).

After a guttural vowel (**10**), after **r**, or (especially in LWS.) before -**st** and -**ð**, endings respectively of the 2d and 3d sing. pres. ind., **g** frequently becomes **h**, occasionally **gh**: **genōg** and **genōh**, *enough;* **burg** and **burh**, *city;* **stīgð** and **stīhð**, *climbs*.

29. Loss of h. — Certain words ending in **h** lose the **h** before an inflectional ending beginning with a vowel, at the same time lengthening the vowel of the stem, if short: **feorh**, *life*, gen. **fēores**; **feoh**, *property*, gen. **fēos**. There are besides a number of contract verbs (**101**) in which an original **h** has been lost before vowels (**100**); **gefēon**, *rejoice*, orig. **gefehan**.

The initial **h** of certain indefinite pronouns, and of the various forms of **habban**, *have*, is frequently lost after **ne**, *not:* **nāwðer**, **nāðer** (**27**) for **ne āhwæðer**, *neither;* **næfde**, *had not*.

30. Loss of m and n. — Before the spirants **f, s,** and **ð** there has been in some words the loss of an original **m** or **n**, with a lengthening of the preceding vowel: **ōsle**, *ousel*, orig. **amsala**; **ūs**, *us*, orig. **uns**. When the resulting vowel is **ō**, or its umlaut **ē** (**17**), the original vowel was **a** (**ǫ** before nasal, **25**): **gōs**, *goose*, orig. **gans**; **ēst**, *favor*, orig. **ansti**.

31. Metathesis of r. — In some words in which a vowel was originally preceded by **r**, the **r** has changed places with the vowel. Thus **burna**, *fountain, brook* (cf. Scottish *burn*), was originally **brun(n)a** (cf. Germ. *Brunnen*); **hors**, *horse*, orig. **hros** (cf. Germ. *Ross*).

32. Metathesis of sc. — After a vowel, **sc** frequently becomes **cs**, often represented by **hs** or **x** (**2**). Thus **āscian**, *ask* (cf. Germ. (*h*)*eischen*) becomes **ācsian**, **āhsian**, **āxian** (dial. Mod. Eng. *axe*).

33. Change of d to t.— When **d** either precedes or follows a surd (8) in the same word, it regularly becomes **t**. Thus from **bindan**, *bind*, the ind. pres. 2d sing. is formed by adding -st (though sometimes -est), thus, **bindst**; but, in accordance with this principle, **bindst** becomes **bintst**. So from **īecan**, *increase*, the ind. pret. 3d sing. is formed by adding -**de**, thus, **īecde**; but **īecde** becomes **īecte**.

34. Changes of ð in conjunction with other dentals.— Whenever **d** or **t** comes to stand immediately before **ð**, the combination becomes **tt**, which is sometimes simplified to **t** (35). Thus **bindeð**, ind. pres. 3d sing. of **bindan**, becomes **bindð** by elision of the **e** in an unstressed syllable (23); but **bindð** invariably appears as **bint**; **bīdð** and **bītð**, respectively from **bīdan**, *await*, and **bītan**, *bite*, both become **bītt** or **bīt**.

By a somewhat similar change, **sð** often becomes **st**. For **ðs** is usually found **ss**, which may be simplified to **s** (35).

Suspect that **t** *near the end of a verb may stand for* **d** *or* **ð**, *or be the result of contraction.*

35. Gemination simplified.— Double consonants are of frequent occurrence, especially before an inflectional syllable beginning with a vowel. Thus **swimman**, *swim*, **bedde**, *to a bed*, etc. But gemination is frequently simplified, or, in other words, the second consonant is dropped, (*a*) at the end of a word, (*b*) before another consonant, (*c*) in certain other situations. Thus: —

(*a*) **mannes**, gen. sing., but **mann** or **man**, *man*, nom. sing.; (*b*) **ealles**, gen. sing. of **eal(1)**, *all*, but **ealne**, acc. sing. masc.; (*c*) **ōðer**, *other*, with gen. plur. ending **ōðerra**, but usually **ōðera**, **ōðra**.

36. Gemination pointing to original j. — In many words which contain a double consonant, especially those whose stem vowel is ę, the stem was originally followed by **j** (pron. *y*), and the consonant was not geminated, but single: **sęllan**, *give*, orig. **saljan**. This was always the case with words containing **cg**, which, it will be remembered, is the representative of **gg (11)**: **sęcgan**, *say*, orig. **sagjan**; **hrycg**, *back*, orig. **hrugjo-**.

37. Grammatical change. — As between certain related words, there is an interchange of **ð** and **d**, **s** and **r**: inf. **cēosan**, *choose*, past part. **coren**; inf. **cweðan**, *say*, past part. **cweden** (cf. the noun **cwide**, *discourse*). This is technically known as grammatical change. Under similar circumstances, there is a like change between **h** and **g**, and **h** and **w**, but owing to a partial disappearance of the **h** (cf. **100**) this is less noticeable: **sliehð**, *strikes* (inf. **slēan**), **slōg**, *struck;* **siehð**, *sees* (inf. **sēon**), **sāwon** (*they*) *saw*.

INFLECTION.

Declension of Nouns.

38. Gender of nouns. — Nouns are either masculine, feminine, or neuter. Names of males are masculine, and those of females feminine, except **mægden, mǣden (28)**, *girl*, **wīf**, *wife*, and **bearn, cild**, *child*, which are neuter. The gender of most nouns must be learned from the dictionary; but all nouns ending in -**a** are masculine, and belong to the weak declension (**53**); all ending in -**dōm**, -**els**, -**ere**, -**hād**, and -**scipe**, and most in -**end**, with *names of persons* in -**ing** and -**ling**, are strong masculines; those ending in -**estre**, -**nes**, -**rǣden**, -**ð(u)** (-**ðo**), -**ung**, most in -**u**, and a few *abstracts* in -**ing**, are strong feminines.

Compound nouns take the gender of their last component; thus **wīfman**, *woman*, is masculine, because **man(n)** is masculine.

39. Strong and weak nouns. — According to their declension, all nouns are either strong or weak. The nominative of weak nouns always ends in a vowel, either -**a** or -**e**, but not all nouns ending in -**e** are weak.

40. Cases of nouns and adjectives. — Old English has six cases, though in general only four are distinguished. These four are the nominative, genitive, dative, and accusative; the two additional are the vocative, the case of direct address, and the instrumental, which is virtually indistinguishable from the dative, except in adjectives.

The nominative is used as in English. The genitive is the case denoting possessor, source, or cause; its sign is *of*. The dative denotes the indirect object of an action; its sign is *to* or *for*. The accusative denotes the direct object; it has no sign. The instrumental denotes the means by which an action is performed; its sign is *by*.

The instrumental of nouns is included in the declensions under the dative.

41. Uniform case endings. — All nouns, whatever their declension, end in -**um** in the dative plural. The genitive plural always ends in -**a**, either appended directly to the stem, or with -**en**- (rarely -**r**-) interposed (**43. 6**); accordingly the genitive plural, to speak more strictly, always ends in -**a** or -**ena** (very rarely -**ra**).

Instead of -**um** is occasionally found -**un**, -**on**, or -**an**, and in later Old English these endings grow common.

42. Strong masculine endings. — All strong masculines, except umlaut masculines (**46**) and those in -**u** (**45**), take the following as regular endings (for exceptions

see **43.** 5-9; **44.** 4), where — represents the form of
the nominative singular: —

SINGULAR.	PLURAL.
N.V.A. —	-as
G. -es	-a
D. -e	-um

43. Masculines ending in a consonant. — The greater
number of strong masculines are declined like **fisc,**
fish : —

SINGULAR.	PLURAL.
N.V.A. fisc	fiscas
G. fisces	fisca
D. fisce	fiscum

1. A very few words ending in **-cg** may insert **-e**
before the endings of the plural: **secgeas,** etc. (**18**).

2. If the radical vowel of the nominative is **æ** before
a single consonant, this is changed in the plural to **a:**
dæg, *day,* but plur. **dagas, daga, dagum.**

3. Nouns ending in **h** lose this consonant before a
case ending, and in so doing lengthen the radical
vowel or diphthong. Thus **fearh,** *swine,* but **fēares,**
etc. (**29**). If the **h** is preceded by a vowel, the vowel
of the ending is lost: **scōh,** *shoe,* but nom. plur. **scōs,**
not **scōas.**

4. Disyllabic nouns generally lose the vowel of the
second syllable before all endings, when the stem is
long by nature or position (**4, 23**), if the second syllable
is not long by position. Otherwise the vowel of the

second syllable is regularly preserved. Examples are
as follows : —

a. Stem long by nature, and second syllable short:
ēðel, *country*, gen. ēðles, not ēðeles.

b. Stem long by position, and second syllable long
by position : **hęngest**, *stallion*, dat. **hęngeste**, not
hęngste.

c. Stem long by position (vowel before two consonants), and second syllable short: **dryhten**, *lord*, gen.
dryhtnes, not **dryhtenes.**

d. Stem short by nature, and second syllable short:
heofon, *heaven*, dat. **heofone**, not **heofne.**

Occasional exceptions are found: **dryhtenes, heofne.**
The retention or loss of the vowel is in part dependent
upon the date of the particular text.

5. In a few words there is an occasional gen. and
dat. sing. and nom. plur. in -**a**: **feld**, *field*, **ford**, *ford*,
winter, *winter*, **sumer**, *summer*, and a few others of
rare occurrence.

6. Nouns in -**end**, originally present participles (**143**),
take the gen. plur. in -**ra**, instead of -**a**, and the plur.
nom. voc. acc. in -**e**, or without ending, as well as in
-**as**, the latter being rare. Thus nom. plur. **hǣlend**,
hǣlende, as well as **hǣlendas**; gen. **hǣlendra.**

7. A single word, **bearu**, *grove*, has the nom.
sing. in -**u**, and takes **w** instead of the -**u** before all
inflectional endings: nom. sing. **bearu**, gen. **bearwes**,
etc. (**27**).

8. The noun **fæder**, *father*, frequently omits the terminations of the sing. gen. and dat.

9. **Hæleð**, *hero*, and **mōnáð**, *month*, sometimes omit the termination of the nom. acc. plur.

44. Masculines in -e. — The declension of strong masculines in -e is almost identical with that of **fisc.** The sing. nom. acc. voc. takes **-e**; other exceptions will be noted below. **Ende**, *end*, is thus declined: —

	SINGULAR.	PLURAL.
N.V.A.	ende	endas
G.	endes	enda
D.	ende	endum

1. Here belong important classes of nouns ending in **-ere (143)** and **-scipe**, besides some others. They are much less numerous, however, than those of the preceding declension.

2. The noun **here**, *army*, sometimes takes **-g-** or **-ig-** before the endings of the singular, and the same, or **-ige-**, before the endings of the plural: **her(i)ges**, etc. Two words sometimes have the gen. plur. in **-ig(e)a**, **-ia**: **wine**, *friend*, **Dene**, *Danes*, gen. plur. **winigea, Deniga, Denia (18)**.

3. Nouns ending in **-ce** may retain the **-e** before the endings of the plural: **lǣce**, *physician*, nom. plur. **lǣceas**, as well as **lǣcas (18)**.

4. A few masculine nouns in **-e** occasionally take the nom. acc. plur. in **-e**, instead of **-as**: **wine**, or

winas, *friend.* The following are found in the plural only: **lēode** (also **lēoda**), *people,* **ielde,** *men,* **ielfe,** *elves,* and the proper nouns **Ęngle,** *Angles,* **Seaxe,** *Saxons,* **Mierce,** *Mercians.*

45. Masculines in -u. — Here belong the words **sunu,** *son,* **wudu,** *wood,* **me(o)du,** *mead,* **magu,** *boy,* **bre(o)go,** *prince,* **heoru,** *sword,* **lagu,** *lake,* **si(o)du,** *custom,* **spitu,** *spit.* **Sunu** is thus declined: —

	SINGULAR.	PLURAL.
N.V.A.	sunu	suna
G.	suna	suna
D.	suna	sunum

1. The ending of the nom. sing. -u (sometimes -o) is liable to intrude everywhere except in the dat. plur. and gen. sing. and plur.

2. Besides **sunu** and **wudu,** the nouns above given are scarcely found except in the nom. acc. sing.

3. In later Old English these words begin to assume the endings of **fisc (43):** gen. **sunes,** nom. plur. **sunas,** etc.

46. Umlaut masculines. — Here belong **fōt,** *foot,* **tōð,** *tooth;* **man(n),** *man;* **fēond,** *enemy,* **frēond,** *friend,* **(142);** **brōðor,** *brother.* These take umlaut of the radical vowel **(17)** in the dat. sing. and nom. voc. acc. plur., and have no ending in those cases. **Fōt** is thus declined: —

	SINGULAR.	PLURAL.
N.V.A.	fōt	fēt
G.	fōtes	fōta
D.	fēt (fōte)	fōtum

1. **Brōðor** is irregular, forming its nom. voc. acc. plur. as **brōðor** or **brōðru**, instead of **brēðer**.

2. Occasionally there is found a plur. **fōtas, tōðas,** instead of **fēt, tēð**.

3. **Fēond** and **frēond** usually have dat. sing. **fēonde, frēonde,** sometimes plur. **fēond, frēond,** or even **fēondas, frēondas**.

47. Strong neuters. — In general, the chief distinction between the declension of masculines and that of neuters is in the plur. nom. acc. Where the masculine has -**as**, the neuter, if its radical syllable be short, has -**u,** or sometimes -**o** ; *if long, has no ending whatever* (cf. **23,** and especially its final sentence). When the *radical syllable is short,* the paradigm accordingly is (**hof,** *dwelling*) : —

	SINGULAR.	PLURAL.
N.A.	hof	hofu
G.	hofes	hofa
D.	hofe	hofum

With a *long radical syllable* (**4**), the paradigm is (**word,** *word*) : —

	SINGULAR.	PLURAL.
N.A.	word	word
G.	wordes	worda
D.	worde	wordum

1. Disyllables are sometimes without ending in the nom. acc. plur., and sometimes take -u: **wǣp(e)n** and **wǣpnu**, *weapons;* but usually **mægenu**, *forces,* **nīetenu,** *cattle,* **earfoðu,** *labors,* **wæt(e)ru,** *waters,* **hēafdu,** *heads,* **wundor,** *wonders.*

2. Occasionally the nom. acc. plur. takes -o or -a instead of -u.

3. **Trēo,** *tree,* and **cnēo,** *knee,* take -w before all case endings, and sometimes in the nom. sing.: **trēowes,** etc. (**27**). Nom. acc. plur. **trēowu, cnēowu.**

4. For a change in the radical vowel of the plural, see **43. 2**: **fæt,** *vessel,* but **fatu, fata, fatum.**

5. For the loss of final **h**, see **43. 3**: **feoh,** *money, fee,* gen. **fēos.**

6. For the loss (syncopation) of the vowel of the second syllable, see **43. 4**: **hēafod,** *head,* nom. plur. **hēafdu,** not (usually) **hēafodu**; **tungol,** *star,* nom. plur. **tunglu,** not **tungolu**; **wæter,** *water,* gen. **wæteres,** not (regularly) **wætres.** Syncopation is, however, less constant in the nom. acc. plur. of neuters, in cases corresponding to **43. 4.** *a.*

7. Neuters ending in -en and -et sometimes double the final consonant before a case ending: **æfen,** *even* (*-ing*), gen. **æfenes** or **æfennes,** etc. These nouns retain the -e of the second syllable.

48. Neuters in -e. — These are declined like **word,** except that the sing. nom. voc. acc. has -e, and the plur. nom. voc. acc. has -**u**.   Paradigm (**wīte**, *punː ishment*) :

	SINGULAR.	PLURAL.
N.V.A.	wīte	wītu
G.	wītes	wīta
D.	wīte	wītum

1. If the -**e** of the nom. sing. is preceded by **c** or **g**, the endings of the plural *may* be preceded by **i** (or **e**) : **rīcu** or **rīciu**, **rīca** or **rīcia**, etc. (**18**).

49. Neuters in -u. — These are declined like **bearu** (**43. 7**), except that they take -**u** in the plur. nom. acc., instead of -**as**.   There are only half a dozen in all, and these are not of common occurrence : **bealu**, *evil*, gen. **bealwes**, etc.

50. Irregular neuters. — The three words **lamb**, *lamb*, **cealf**, *calf*, **ǣg**, *egg*, and sometimes **cild**, *child*, are declined regularly in the singular, but take **r** in the plural before the endings -**u**, -**a**, -**um** : **lamb**, gen. **lambes**, but nom. plur. **lambru**.

In LWS. the regular forms, without **r**, occur.

51. Strong feminines. — Feminine disyllables ending in -**u**, and having a short radical syllable, belong here ; monosyllables with a long radical syllable, and most disyllables, discard the -**u** of the nom. sing. Abstracts, though long, follow *a*.

a) Paradigm of the short stems, **giefu**, *gift:* —

	SINGULAR.	PLURAL.
N.V.	giefu, -o	giefa, -e
G.	giefe	giefa (-ena)
D.	giefe	giefum
A.	giefe	giefa, -e

Occasionally the ending **-u** or **-o** is found in the oblique cases of the singular and in the nom. acc. plural. **Duru**, *door*, has **-a** in the gen. dat. sing., and in the whole plural except the dative. Two or three nouns in **-u** take **-w** before the ending in the oblique cases: **beadu**, *battle*, gen. **beadwe**, etc.

b) Paradigm of the long stems and polysyllables, **glōf**, *glove:* —

	SINGULAR.	PLURAL.
N.V.	glōf	glōfa, -e
G.	glōfe	glōfa
D.	glōfe	glōfum
A.	glōfe	glōfa, -e

1. A few nouns discard the **-e** of the acc. sing.: **dǣd**, *deed*, **tīd**, *time*, **woruld** (**20, 26**), *world*.

2. Only rarely does the gen. plur. of long stems take **-(e)na**.

3. Disyllables in **-ung** often have **-a** instead of **e** in the dat. sing., and sometimes in the gen. acc. sing.: **leornung**, *learning*, dat. **leornunga**. The words **hand**, *hand*, **flōr**, *floor*, and **woruld**, *world*, occasionally make the same change.

4. Disyllables syncopate the vowel of the second

syllable according to **43. 4** : sāwol, *soul*, gen. **sāwle,** etc.

5. Polysyllables in -nes, -en, -el, and -et double the final consonant when a syllable is added, and retain the preceding -e : gen. dat. acc. sing. **ēaðmōdnesse,** *humility*, **byrðenne,** *burden*, etc.

52. Umlaut feminines. — These modify the root vowel by umlaut in the dat. sing. and nom. voc. acc. plur., and often in the gen. sing., that is, change **ā** to **ǣ**, **o** to **ę**, **ō** to **ē**, **u** to **y**, and **ū** to **ȳ**. The gen. sing., and occasionally the dat. sing., is sometimes formed regularly, without umlaut, and with the ending -e. Paradigm, (**gōs,** *goose*) : —

	SINGULAR.	PLURAL.
N.V.A.	gōs	gēs
G.	gēs, gōse	gōsa
D.	gēs	gōsum

The principal nouns which belong here are : **āc,** *oak*, **gāt,** *goat;* **bōc,** *book*, **brōc,** *trousers*, **gōs,** *goose*, **wlōh,** *fringe;* **burg,** *castle, city*, **furh,** *furrow*, **sulh,** *plough*, **turf,** *turf;* **cū,** *cow*, **grūt,** *grout, grits*, **lūs,** *louse*, **mūs,** *mouse*, **ðrūh,** *trough;* **ēa,** *river;* **niht,** *night*.

1. The dat. (gen.) sing. of **burg** is usually **byrig,** not **byrg.**

2. **Mōdor,** *mother*, and **dohtor,** *daughter*, are declined like **brōðor (46. 1)**, except that **mōdor** has only the nom. acc. plur. **mōdru, -a,** and both may have an umlaut gen. sing. in LWS. (but usually **mōdor, dohtor**).

3. **Sweostor**, *sister*, is without umlaut in any case; it remains **sweostor** in every case except the gen. plur. **sweostra** and dat. plur. **sweostrum**.

53. Weak nouns. — Masculines end in -a, feminines and neuters in -e; but the neuters may be conveniently disregarded, only **ēage**, *eye*, and **ēare**, *ear*, belonging to this declension. Paradigms (**mōna**, *moon*, **tunge**, *tongue*) : —

	MASCULINE.	FEMININE.
Sing. N.V.	mōna	tunge
G. D. A.	mōnan	tungan
Plur. N.V.A.	mōnan	tungan
G.	mōnena	tungena
D.	mōnum	tungum

1. The number of feminines thus declined is comparatively small. The commonest are perhaps **eorðe**, *earth*, **heorte**, *heart*, **lufe**, *love*, **cirice**, *church*, **tunge**, *tongue*, **hearpe**, *harp*, **sunne**, *sun*, **nǣdre**, *viper*, and **ælmesse**, *alms*. The masculines are, on the contrary, very numerous.

2. The declension of the neuters **ēage** and **ēare** differs from that of the feminines only in the acc. sing., which is like the nom. Their gen. plur. is often **ēagna**, **ēarna**.

3. The weak feminine **heofone**, *heaven*, should be distinguished from the strong masculine **heofon**. Besides the weak **lufe**, there is also a strong **lufu**, *love* (**51.** *a*).

54. Proper names. — Native names are declined like
common nouns, except that feminines ending in **-burg**
take the dative in **-e** and are without umlaut. Foreign
names are sometimes naturalized, and sometimes take
their original case endings, but not always with entire
consistency. The words **Cęnt, Cęrt, Ī, Tęnet,** and
Wiht are indeclinable, except that **Wiht** has the gen.
Wihte.

Declension of Adjectives.

55. Weak and strong adjectives. — Adjectives are declined weak when in the comparative, and usually when
in the superlative; when ordinals (except **ōðer,** *second,*
78, 80); when preceded by a demonstrative; when used
as masculine or feminine nouns preceded by the definite
article ; in direct address ; sometimes when preceded
by a possessive pronoun ; and exceptionally in poetry
in place of the strong adjective. Otherwise adjectives
are always used in the strong form.

56. Strong declension of adjectives. — Here it is necessary to distinguish between long monosyllables on the
one hand, and short monosyllables (comparatively few)
and disyllables on the other.

57. Disyllables and short monosyllables. — Paradigm,
glæd, *glad :* —

MASCULINE.	NEUTER.	FEMININE.
Sing. N.V. **glæd**	**glæd**	**gladu**
G. **glades**		*glœdre*

	MASCULINE.		NEUTER.	FEMININE.
D.		*gladum*		*glœdre*
A.	*glœdne*		**glæd**	**glade**
I.		**glade**		
Plur. N.V.A.	*glade*	.	**gladu, -e**	**glada, -e**
G.			*glœdra*	
D.			**gladum**	

1. Italicized words indicate differences from the noun declension; cf. these with the pronominal declensions (**81, 84, 85**).

2. When the radical vowel is æ, it is changed as in the paradigm. Otherwise it remains unchanged.

3. Disyllables take the same endings as in the paradigm, but frequently syncopate the vowel of the second syllable before an ending beginning with a vowel, as in ·**ēadig**, *blessed*, gen. **ēadges** (**23**; cf. **43**. 4), and sometimes conform the nom. sing. fem. to the masc. and neut., and the neut. plur. nom. voc. acc. to the sing.: **hālig**, *holy*, not **hāl(i)gu**.

4. For the ending -**u** sometimes occurs -**o**, and for -**um** the LWS. -**on**, -**an** (cf. **41**).

5. Adjectives ending in -**u** (-**o**) change the **u** to **w** before vowels (**27**): **gearu**, *ready*, gen. **gearwes**, etc.

58. Long monosyllables. — The only difference between the declension of the long and that of the short monosyllables is that the ending -**u** of the latter is dropped, and that the radical vowel always remains unchanged. Paradigm, **gōd**, *good*: —

	MASCULINE.	NEUTER.	FEMININE.
Sing. N.	gōd	gōd	gōd
Plur. N.	gōde	gōd	gōde, -a

1. Adjectives ending in **h** drop the **h** in disyllabic forms, and lengthen the radical vowel or diphthong (**29**): ðweorh, *transverse*, gen. ðwēores; but hēah, *high,.* often assimilates the final **h** to a following consonant: hēanne, hēarra, etc. In LWS. the **h** is often changed to **g** before a vowel: hēagum, etc.

2. Words ending in a double consonant usually retain this only before a vowel (**35**).

59. Adjectives in -e. — These are quite numerous. They are declined like the short monosyllables, except that *they always retain their -e when no other ending is provided, but lose it before an ending.* Paradigm, **grēne**, *green :* —

	MASCULINE.	NEUTER.	FEMININE.
Sing. N.V.	grēne	grēne	grēnu
G.	grēnes		grēnre
Plur. N.V.A.	grēne	grēnu, -e	grēna, -e

From an acc. masc. sing., like **grēnne**, **bliðne**, for example, it is therefore *not* safe to infer a dictionary form **grēn**, **bliÐ**.

In consulting the lexicon, care should be taken to distinguish adjectives in -e from such as end in a consonant.

60. Weak declension of adjectives. — This is the same as that of nouns, except that the gen. plur. is regularly formed in **-ra** (only exceptionally **-a** or the regular weak ending **-ena**). Paradigm, **gōda**, *the good*: —

	MASCULINE.	NEUTER.	FEMININE.
Sing. N.V.	gōda	gōde	gōde
G.		gōdan	
D.		gōdan	
A.	gōdan	gōde	gōdan
Plur. N.V.A.		gōdan	
G.		gōdra	
D.		gōdum	

1. In LWS. **-um** frequently becomes **-an**.

2. When, in consequence of contraction, too many **r**'s or **n**'s are brought together, one of them is rejected. Thus **gearu**, *ready*, forms a comparative **gearura**. This comparative, in turn, would form a gen. plur. **gearurara**. By contraction this would reduce to **gear(u)-r(a)ra**; but the three **r**'s are simplified to two, and the resulting gen. plur. stands as **gearra**.

61. The present participle. — The present participle in **-ende** is not to be confounded with the noun in **-end** (for which see **43. 6**). It is declined like **grēne** (59). When used in the predicate as nom. or acc. it is generally uninflected. The present participle, like the adjective, is also declined weak.

62. The past participle. — The past participle has the double declension of the adjective, both strong and weak. When used in the predicate it is generally indeclinable, or ends like the strong masculine.

Comparison of Adjectives.

63. Regular comparison. — The comparative is formed by adding -**ra** to the stem of the positive, and the superlative by adding -**osta** (-**esta**); with the latter cf. Greek -ιστος. The final -**a** represents the masculine termination of the weak adjective (**60**), and undergoes all the replacements of the weak declension. More rarely the superlative is found in -**ost** (-**est**), which is then regarded as strong. A final -**e** of the positive is dropped in comparison (*e.g.* ēaðe, *easy*, comp. īeðra, not īeðera) and a radical **æ** becomes **a** in the superlative (*e.g.* smæl, *small*, superl. smalost, not smælost; cf. **43**. 2).

64. Comparison without umlaut. — This is the usual mode: —

POSITIVE.	COMPARATIVE.	SUPERLATIVE.
heard, *hard*	heardra	heardost, -esta
lēof, *dear*	lēofra	lēofost, -esta
rīce, *powerful*	rīcra	rīcost, -esta
smæl, *small*	smælra	smalost, -esta

65. Comparison with umlaut. — This is followed by a few adjectives. The superlative generally ends in -**esta**: —

POSITIVE.	COMPARATIVE.	SUPERLATIVE.
eald, *old*	ieldra	ieldesta
lang, *long*	lęngra	lęngesta
geong, *young*	giengra	giengesta
sceort, *short*	sciertra	sciertesta
hēah, *high*	hīehra (hīerra)	hīeh(e)sta
grēat, *great*	grīetra	grīetesta
ēaðe, *easy*	īeðra	īeðesta

1. For some of these, unumlauted forms are also found: **hēahra, hēahsta,** etc.

2. Syncope of **e** in the superlative occurs in LWS.: **lęngsta,** etc.; in **hīehsta** this is also EWS.

3. For -ost may occur -ust.

66. Different stems in comparison. — In the following the comparative and superlative are not formed from the same stem as the positive: —

POSITIVE.	COMPARATIVE.	SUPERLATIVE.
gōd, *good*	{ bęt(e)ra { sēlla, sēlra	bętst(a) sēlest(a)
yfel, *bad*	**wiersa**	wier(re)st(a)
micel, *great*	**māra**	mǣst(a)
lȳtel, *small*	**lǣssa**	lǣst(a)

67. Comparison defective. — In four cases the positive is wanting as an adjective, but may be supplied as an adverb or preposition: —

POSITIVE.	COMPARATIVE.	SUPERLATIVE.
(**feor,** *far*)	**fierra**	**fierrest(a)**
(**nēah,** *near*)	**nēarra**	**nīehst(a)**
(**ǣr,** *earlier*)	**ǣrra**	**ǣrest(a)**
(**fore,** *before*)	**furðra**	**fyrst(a)**

68. Superlatives in -ma. — Besides the superlative in **-est,** there is one in **-ma** (cf. Lat. pri-*mus*). Two examples are found: **forma,** *the first;* **hindema,** *the hindmost.*

69. Superlatives in -ma + -esta = -mest(a). — These double superlatives, as they may be called, are chiefly formed from adverbs and prepositions. The comparative is peculiar in being *generally* formed in -**erra**, instead of -**ra**: —

POSITIVE.	COMPARATIVE.	SUPERLATIVE.
(sīð, *late*)	sīðra	sīðemest
(læt, *late*)	lætra	lætemest
(inne, *within*)	innerra	innemest
(ūte, *without*)	ūterra, ȳterra	ūtemest, ȳtemest
(ufan, *above*)	uferra, yferra	ufemest, yfemest
(niðan, *below*)	niðerra	niðemest
(fore, *before*)	furðra	fyrmest
(æfter, *after*)	æfterra	æftemest
(mid, *mid*)		midmest
(norð, *northward*)	norðerra, nyrðerra	norðmest
(sūð, *southward*)	sūðerra, sȳðerra	sūðmest
(ēast, *eastward*)	ēasterra	ēastmest
(west, *westward*)	westerra	westmest

Formation and Comparison of Adverbs.

70. Adverbs formed from adjectives. — Adverbs are formed from adjectives by the addition of -**e**, -**lice**, and -**unga** or -**inga**. Examples are: **wīd**, *wide*, **wīde**, *widely;* **swīð**, *strong*, **swīðe**, *very;* **sōð**, *true*, **sōðlice**, *truly;* **eall**, *all*, **eallunga**, **eallinga**, *entirely*. Occasionally -**unga**, -**inga** is employed to form adverbs from other parts of speech.

71. Adjectives in the genitive as adverbs. — The ending -**es** of the gen. sing. neut. is employed to form a few adverbs from adjectives: **ealles**, *altogether:* **ðweores** (58. 1), *perversely*, etc.

72. Adjectives in the dative plural as adverbs. — Examples are : **miclum,** *very;* **lȳtlum,** *little.*

73. Adjectives in the accusative as adverbs. — Examples are : **full,** *fully;* **genōg,** *enough.*

74. Adverbs from nouns. — From the genitive: **dæges,** *by day;* **nīedes,** *needs;* etc.   From the instrumental: **sāre,** *sore,* etc.   From the dative plural : **dropmǣlum,** *drop by drop,* etc. (cf. *piecemeal*).

75. Adverbs of place. — These are of three classes, according as they answer the question, *Where? Whither?* or *Whence?*   Examples are : —

WHERE ?	WHITHER ?	WHENCE ?
ᚦǣr	ᚦider	ᚦǫnan
hwǣr	hwider	hwǫnan
hēr	hider	heonan

76. Comparison of adverbs. — Adverbs from adjectival stems are regularly compared by adding **-or** for the comparative and **-ost** for the superlative.   Example: **strangor,** *more strongly,* **strangost,** *most strongly* (cf. **65**).

77. Irregular comparison of adverbs. — A few adverbs have no termination in the comparative.   They are always monosyllabic, and have usually undergone umlaut.   Such are **bęt,** *better;* **mā, mǣ,** *more;* **nēar,** *nearer;* etc.

Numerals.

78. Numerals. — The numerals are as follows: —

CARDINAL.	ORDINAL.
1 . . . ān	forma, ǣresta
2 . . . twēgen, twā (tū)	ōðer, æfterra
3 . . . ðrīe, ðrēo	ðridda
4 . . . fēower	fēorða
5 . . . fīf	fīfta
6 . . . siex	siexta
7 . . . seofon	seofoða
8 . . . eahta	eahtoða
9 . . . nigon	nigoða
10 . . . tīen	tēoða
11 . . . endlefan	endlefta
12 . . . twęlf	twęlfta
13 . . . ðrēotīene	ðrēotēoða
14 . . . fēowertīene	fēowertēoða
15 . . . fīftīene	fīftēoða
16 . . . siextīene	siextēoða
17 . . . seofontīene	seofontēoða
18 . . . eahtatīene	eahtatēoða
19 . . . nigontīene	nigontēoða
20 . . . twēntig	twēntigoða
21 . . . ān and twēntig	ān and twēntigoða
30 . . . ðrītig	ðrītigoða
40 . . . fēowertig	fēowertigoða
50 . . . fīftig	fīftigoða
60 . . . siextig	siextigoða
70 . . . hundseofontig	hundseofontigoða
80 . . . (hund)eahtatig	hundeahtigoða
90 . . . hundnigontig	hundnigontigoða
100 . . . hund, hundred, hundtēontig	
110 . . . hundendlefantig	hundendleftigoða
120 . . . hundtwęlftig	hundtwęlftigoða
200 . . . twā hund, tū hund	
1000 . . . ðūsend	

1. Other ordinals for 1 are **fyresta, fyrmesta.**

2. Another form of ordinal for 21 is **ān ēac twēntigum.**

3. **Endlefan** and **twęlf** probably stand for **ānlif** and **twalif** (representing **twālif**). The **-lif** may mean *left*. After counting on the fingers up to 10, *one left* (**ānlif**) would be 11; *two left* (**twālif**), 12. The final **-an (-on)** of **endlefan** may have been added after the analogy of **seofon, nigon,** etc.

4. Fractions are usually formed by the help of **dǣl,** *part:* **ðridda dǣl,** *one-third;* **seofoða dǣl,** *one-seventh.* For *one and a half* occurs **ōðer healf** (cf. Germ. *anderthalb*); so **ðridde healf,** *two and a half;* in other words, the OE. ordinal indicates the cardinal from which $\frac{1}{2}$ must be subtracted.

5. Interesting forms, which actually occur, are: **19, ān lǣs twēntig; 39, ān lǣs fēowertig; 59, ānes wana siextig** (cf. Greek ἑνὸς δέοντες εἴκοσι); **450, fīftig and fēower hund, fīfte healf hund; 482, fēower hund and twā and hundeahtatig**: **100,000, ān hund ðūsenda; 1,500,000, fīftīene hund ðūsend.** Note also **fīftīena sum,** *one of fifteen,* i.e. *with fourteen companions.*

79. Declension of cardinals. — **Ān** is declined like **gōd (58),** but with acc. sometimes **ænne,** inst. **ǣne.** When declined weak, **āna,** it signifies *alone.* **Twēgen** is declined thus: —

	MASCULINE	NEUTER.	FEMININE.
N.A.	twēgen	twā, tū	twā
G.		twēg(r)a	
D.		twǣm, twām	

So also is declined **bēgen**, *both*. **Ðrīe, ðrēo** is declined: —

	MASCULINE.	NEUTER.	FEMININE.
N.A.	**ðrīe**	**ðrēo**	**ðrēo**
G.		**ðrēora**	
D.		**ðrīm**	

The cardinals between 3 and 20 are usually indeclinable. Those ending in **-tig** are sometimes treated as neuter nouns (in which case they are followed by a partitive genitive), sometimes as adjectives, and are sometimes uninflected. **Hund** and **ðūsend** are sometimes undeclined, but there is also a plural of **hund**, nom. **hunde**, dat. **hundum**; and of **ðūsend**, nom. **ðūsendu**, gen. **-da, -dra**, dat. **-dum**. These numerals are always followed by the genitive.

80. Declension of ordinals. — All are declined like weak adjectives (**60**), except **ōðer**, *second*, which is strong.

Pronouns.

81. Personal pronouns. —

	FIRST PERSON.	SECOND PERSON.
Sing. N.	**ic**	**ðū**
G.	**mīn**	**ðīn**
D.	**mē**	**ðē**
A.	**mē**	**ðē**

	FIRST PERSON.	SECOND PERSON.
Dual N.	wit	git
G.	uncer	incer
D.	unc	inc
A.	unc	inc
Plur. N.	wē	gē
G.	ūre	ēower
D.	ūs	ēow
A.	ūs	ēow

THIRD PERSON.

	MASCULINE.	NEUTER.	FEMININE.
Sing. N.	hē	hit	hēo
G.	his		hi(e)re
D.	him		hi(e)re
A.	hi(e)ne	hit	hi(e)
Plur. N.A.		hī(e)	
G.		hi(e)ra, heora	
D.		him	

1. Less common forms are: in the accusative, **mec**, **ðec**, **ūsic**, **ēowic**; **hī(e)** for **hēo**, and conversely. **Hīo** is frequent, parallel with **hēo**, and **ūser** is found for **ūre**.

82. Reflexive pronouns. — In place of the reflexive, which does not exist as an independent form, is used the personal pronoun (**81**).

83. Possessive pronouns. — Two sorts of possessives must be distinguished, the declinable and the indeclinable. All of these are identical in form with the genitive of the personal pronoun, except **sīn**, which is formed from a lost reflexive. The declinable pos-

sessives are **mĭn**, *my*, **ðīn**, *thy*, **ūre**, *our*, **ēower**, *your*,
sīn, *his*, and the seldom used **uncer**, *of us two*, and
incer, *of you two*. These follow the strong declension of adjectives (**57, 58**). The *indeclinables* are **his**,
his, **hi(e)re**, *her*, and **hi(e)ra**, *their*, the genitives of
the *third* personal pronoun.

84. The demonstrative 'that.' — The pronoun se, sēo,
ðæt, is at once the equivalent of Mod. Eng. *that*
and of the article. Like *that*, it is employed in a
relative as well as a demonstrative sense, and frequently does duty for the third personal pronoun.
The demonstrative pronouns have an instrumental
case, as does the neuter of the interrogative **hwæt**.

	MASCULINE.	NEUTER.	FEMININE.
Sing. N.	se (emphatic sē)	ðæt	sēo
G.	ðæs		ðǣre
D.	ðǣm (ðām)		ðǣre
A.	ðone	ðæt	ðā
I.	ðȳ, ðon		
Plur. N.A.		ðā	
G.		ðāra (ðǣra)	
D.		ðǣm (ðām)	

1. The *conjunction* **ðæt**, and the *adverb* **ðā** (= *there*,
then, etc.), must not be confounded with the *pronoun*.

2. Parallel with se, sēo, is a rare **ðe**, **ðēo**, which
eventually supplants the former.

3. **Ðǣm**, **ðām** becomes **ðan**, **ðon** in such words
as **sĭððan**, *since* (= **sĭð ðām**).

4. The forms of this pronoun should be carefully distinguished from those of the next.

85. The demonstrative ' this.' — Mod. Eng. *this* is represented by the demonstrative ðes, ðēos, ðis.

	MASCULINE.		NEUTER.	FEMININE.
Sing. N.	ðes		ðis	ðēos
G.		ðis(s)es		ðisse
D.		ðis(s)um		ðisse
A.	ðisne		ðis	ðās
I.		ðȳs		
Plur. N.A.			ðās	
G.			ðissa	
D.			ðis(s)um	

1. Alternative or occasional forms are nsf. ðīos ; gsf. dsf. ðis(se)re ; dat. ðiosum (20).

86. Minor demonstratives. — Less important demonstratives are **ilca,** *same*, which is declined weak, and **self,** *self*, which takes both declensions.

87. Relative pronouns. — The office of the relative is assumed :

a) by the demonstrative **se, sēo, ðæt,** the reference being rendered explicit by the case form.

b) by the demonstrative **se, sēo, ðæt,** with the particle ðe appended.

c) by the indeclinable ðe, the reference being rendered explicit by an appended personal pronoun in the proper case form.

d) by the particle **ðe** alone, representing all numbers, genders, and cases, the reference being much
less explicit.

Illustrations of each of these modes would be: —

a)	Se stān, ðone	ðā wyrhtan	āwurpon.
	(*The stone, which*	*the builders*	*rejected.*)
b)	Se stān, ðone ðe ðā wyrhtan āwurpon.		
c)	Se stān, ðe hine ðā wyrhtan āwurpon.		
d)	Se stān, ðe	ðā wyrhtan āwurpon.	

88. Interrogative pronouns. — The most important is
hwā, *who?* of both genders, with its neuter **hwæt**,
what? what sort of a?

	MASC. FEM.	NEUTER.
N.	hwā	hwæt
G.	hwæs	
D.	hwǣm (hwām)	
A.	hwone	hwæt
I.		hwȳ, hwon

Hwilc, *which?* **hwæðer,** *which of two?* and **hūlic,** *of
what sort?* are declined like strong adjectives (**57, 58**).

89. Indefinite pronouns. — The indefinites are: —

a) **ān, sum,** *a, a certain,* **ǣnig,** *any,* **nān, nǣnig,**
no, none, **ǣlc, gehwilc,** *each,* **ǣgðer, āhwæðer,** *either,*
nāhwæðer, *neither,* **ōðer,** *other,* **swilc,** *such,* are declined like strong adjectives.

b) **āwiht, ōht,** *anything,* and **nāwiht, nōht,** *nothing,*
with the compounds of -**hwega** (**hwæthwega,** *anything,* etc.) are indeclinable.

c) **hwā,** *any one* (and its compounds) is declined like the interrogative.

d) Indefinite relatives are formed from the interrogatives by **swā-swā**: **swā-hwā-swā,** *whoever,* etc.

e) **man** (originally **mann**), *one* (cf. French *on,* Ger. *man*), is used only in the nom. sing.

Verbs.

90. Classification of verbs. — Verbs are either strong (**92**) or weak (**96**); besides which there are two small classes of important verbs, called respectively preteritive presents (**124** ff.) and anomalous (**137** ff.). Weak verbs are in general derivative; and the stem can usually be detected as existing in some other independent word, often a noun or adjective, or the pret. sing. tense-stem of a strong verb.

91. The present stem. — The present stem of a verb is what remains after cutting off the infinitive ending **-an** or **-ian** (in contract verbs, **-n**). The radical vowel is the vowel of this stem; and the consonant or consonants which terminate the stem are, when such exist, called stem-finals. The stem as obtained above is one of the four tense-stems of strong verbs, or of he three tense-stems of weak verbs.

92. Tense-stems of strong verbs. — Strong verbs change the radical vowel to form the different tense-stems, like

the verbs called irregular in Modern English. As in
Modern English the verb *drive* has the preterit *drove*
and past participle *driven*, so in Old English the same
verb has the pret. sing. **drāf** and past participle **drifen**.
However, instead of the three tense-stems of Modern
English, there are four in Old English for strong
verbs, the preterit being subdivided into preterit singular and preterit plural.

The four stems of **drīfan**, *drive*, are : —

PRESENT.	PRET. SING.	PRET. PLUR.	PAST PART.
drīf-	drāf	drif-	drif-

93. Forms derived from each stem. — From the present
stem are formed the whole of the present indicative and
optative, the imperative singular and plural, the infinitive, the gerund, and the present participle — in all
seventeen forms.

From the pret. sing. stem are formed only the 1st
and 3d persons singular — two forms.

From the pret. plur. stem are formed the whole pret.
plur. of indicative and optative, the whole pret. sing.
of the optative, and the 2d person singular indicative
— ten forms.

From the past participial stem is formed only the
past participle — one form.

94. Commonest forms of the verb. — From the present
stem the form in commonest use is the ind. pres. 3d
sing.; from the pret. sing. stem, the ind. pret. 3d sing.;

from the pret. plur. stem, the ind. pret. 3d plur.
Umlaut (17) and contraction (34) are apt to obscure
the origin of the first of these, but not of the other
two. Thus from **standan**, *stand* — whose principal
parts are **standan, stōd, stōdon, standen** — the ind.
pret. 3d sing. is **stōd**, the ind. pret. 3d plur. **stōdon**,
but the ind. pres. 3d sing. **stęnt** (instead of **standeð**).

◄ 95. Conjugation of a strong verb.—Types are: **bindan**,
bind; (for contracts) **fōn**, *seize:* —

	INDICATIVE.	OPTATIVE.
Pres. Sing. 1.	**binde; fō**	**binde; fō**
2.	**bind(e)st, bintst; fēhst**	**binde; fō**
3.	**bind(e)ð, bint; fēhð**	**binde; fō**
Plur.	**bindað, binde; fōð**	**binden; fōn**
Pret. Sing. 1.	**band; fēng**	**bunde; fēnge**
2.	**bunde; fēnge**	**bunde; fēnge**
3.	**band; fēng**	**bunde; fēnge**
Plur.	**bundon; fēngon**	**bunden; fēngen**

Imper. Sing. **bind; fōh**   Infin. **bindan; fōn**
    Plur. **bindað, binde; fōð**   Gerund **tō bindanne; tō fōnne**
Pres. Part. **bindende; fōnde**   Past Part. **(ge)bunden; (ge)fangen**

The 2d sing. pres. ind. is sometimes formed in -**sð**.
The **ð** is derived from the **ðū** of the personal pronoun,
the old ending having been s. This s, followed by the
personal pronoun, became **sð**, which *should* regularly
become **st** (34), but does not always.

NOTE. — The ind. and imper. (sometimes opt.) plur. **binde** is used
when the verb is immediately followed by a pronoun as subject: **binde
wē**, not **bindað wē**, *we bind, let us bind;* **binde gē**, not **bindað gē**,
bind ye; similarly, **dō wē, nolde gē**.

96. Conjugation of the weak verb. — Weak verbs form the preterit by the addition to the present stem of **-de** for the singular (ind. pret. 2d sing. **-dest**), and **-don** (**-den**) for the plural. A few verbs take **-e** before the **-de**, and many take **-o**. The vowel of the present stem is never changed before **-ede** and **-ode**, but in some verbs is changed before **-de**; a list of the latter is given in **114**.

The past participle of weak verbs is formed by the addition of **-ed** (**-od, -d**).

The **-d** of the endings **-de**, etc., and **-ed**, is changed to **-t** after certain stem-finals (**33**), and is lost in other situations; for details see **113** and **114**. Certain stem-finals also undergo change before the same endings; for details see **114**.

97. Classes of strong verbs. — Under strong verbs are included two principal divisions, according as their tense-stems were originally formed in one manner or another. Strong verbs are accordingly divided into Ablaut Verbs and Reduplicating Verbs. This distinction is mainly historical, and for practical purposes need not be insisted on at the outset.

98. Ablaut verbs. — Of these there are six principal classes, for which see **102–107**.

99. Vowels of the present stem. — To facilitate the assignment of verbs to their proper classes, the follow-

ing table may be useful, in conjunction with **101–110**.
The Ablaut Classes are distinguished by the Roman
numerals, and the Reduplicating Verbs by Red.

Short Radical Vowel.	Class.
a	VI, Red.
æ	VI
ę	VI
e + **r** or **l** (also **brecan**)	IV
e + any single cons. but **r** or **l**	V
e + two cons.	III
i followed by nasal	III, IV
i followed by non-nasal	III, V
ǫ, see **a**	
u in **cuman**	IV
u in other verbs	III
ea	VI, Red.
eo	III
ie	III, V, VI

Long Radical Vowel.	Class.
ā	Red.
ǣ	Red.
ē	Red.
ī	I
ō	Red.
ū	II
ēa	VI, Red.
ēo in contract verbs	I, II, V
ēo in other verbs	II

100. Contract verbs. — Contract verbs are strong verbs
whose stem-final was originally **h**. This h was lost
before vowels (**29**), and the preceding vowel was then

amalgamated with the following. The resultant diphthong (or vowel) is ēo in the case of ten verbs, ēa in
that of four, and ō in that of two. The ō-verbs belong
to the Reduplicating Class, the ēa-verbs to the Sixth
Ablaut Class, and the ēo-verbs to the First, Second,
and Fifth Ablaut Classes.

101. Contract verbs according to classes. — Distributed
according to classes, the contract verbs are as follows: —

I. **lēon** (orig. **līhan**), *lend;* **sēon,** *sift;* **tēon,** *censure;* **ðēon,**
thrive; **wrēon,** *cover.*

II. **flēon** (orig. **flēohan**), *flee;* **tēon,** *draw.*

V. **gefēon** (orig. **gefehan**), *rejoice;* **plēon,** *venture;* **sēon,** *see.*

VI. **flēan** (orig. **flahan**), *flay;* **lēan,** *blame;* **slēan,** *strike;*
ðwēan, *wash.*

Red. **fōn** (orig. **fanhan** > **fōhan**), *seize;* **hōn,** *hang.*

Of these the most important are **tēon,** *censure,* **ðēon,**
thrive, **wrēon,** *cover;* **flēon,** *flee,* **tēon,** *draw;* **gefēon,**
rejoice, **sēon,** *see;* **slēan,** *strike,* **ðwēan,** *wash;* **fōn,**
seize, and **hōn,** *hang.*

Tēon, *draw* (II), should be carefully distinguished
from **tēon,** *censure* (I); and likewise **sēon,** *see* (V),
from **sēon,** *sift* (I). The principal parts of **tēon,**
draw, are: —

tēon	**tēah**	**tugon**	**(ge)togen**

of **tēon,** *censure,* are: —

tēon	**tāh**	**tigon**	**(ge)tigen**

But there is a tendency on the part of contract verbs
like the latter of these (I) to assume throughout the
forms of the former (II).

Ðēon, *thrive* (102), has past part. ðigen and ðungen.

The imp. sing. always ends in h, and has a long
vowel in verbs of the First, Second, and Reduplicating Classes, a short vowel in the Fifth and Sixth.
Examples: (I) tēon, *censure*, imp. tīh; (II) tēon,
draw, imp. tēoh; (V) sēon, *see*, imp. seoh; (VI) slēan,
strike, imp. sleah; (Red.) fōn, *seize*, imp. fōh.

102. Strong verbs of the First Ablaut Class. —

Stem vowels (normally) ī, ā, i, i
Typical verb **drīfan**, *drive*
Four stems **drīfan drāf drifon drifen**

Like **drīfan** are conjugated all strong verbs with ī in
the present stem. Here belongs any strong verb with ā
in the first preterit stem, i in the second preterit stem, or
i in the past participial stem. Among the more common
are: **bīdan**, *remain;* **bītan**, *bite;* **rīdan**, *ride;* **(ā)rīsan**,
arise; **scīnan**, *shine;* **slītan**, *tear;* **stīgan**, *ascend;* **swīcan**, *abandon;* **(ge)wītan**, *go;* **wrītan**, *write.*

Umlaut does not affect the vowel of the present
stem (94).

The 2d and 3d sing. pres. ind. are thus formed
(33, 34): —

d-stems	bīdan	bītst, bīt(t)
t-stems	bītan	bītst, bīt(t)

s-stems	rīsan	rīst, rīst (rīsð́)
ð-stems	snīðan	snīst, snīð (ð́)
Contracts (101)	wrēon	wrīhst, wrīhð́
Others are normal	drīfan	drīfst, drīfð́

The second preterit and past participial stems of the verbs snīðan, *cut*, līðan, *go*, and scrīðan, *proceed*, take d instead of ð (37): snidon, sniden, etc. Other verbs in ð retain the ð.

103. Strong verbs of the Second Ablaut Class. —

Stem vowels	ēo or ū, ēa, u, o		
Typical verbs	bēodan, *offer;* brūcan, *enjoy*		
Four stems	bēodan	bēad	budon	boden
	brūcan	brēac	brucon	brocen

Like bēodan are conjugated all strong verbs having ēo in the present stem, except some contracts, and like brūcan all having ū. Here belongs any strong verb having ēa in the first preterit stem. Among the more common are: cēosan, *choose;* drēogan, *endure;* hrēosan, *fall;* (for)lēosan, *lose;* tēon, *draw;* būgan, *bow.*

Stems in s, ð, and contract vowel (37): —

cēosan	cēas	curon	coren
sēoðan	sēað	sudon	soden
tēon (101)	tēah	tugon	togen

Like cēosan are formed stems in s; like sēoðan, ābrēoðan, *frustrate;* like tēon, flēon, *flee.*

Umlaut changes the ēo of the present to īe (or ī),

and ū of the present to ȳ, in the 2d and 3d sing.
pres. ind.: **forlīest, brȳcð.**

The 2d and 3d sing. pres. ind. are thus formed
(33, 34): —

d-stems	bēodan	bīetst, bīet(t)
t-stems	gēotan	gīetst, gīet(t)
s-stems	forlēosan	forlīesꞇ, forlīest (-sð)
g-stems (28)	drēogan	drīegst (-hst), driegð (-hð)
Contracts (101)	tēon	tīehst, tīehð
Others are normal	crēopan	crīepst, crīepð

104. Strong verbs of the Third Ablaut Class. —

Stem vowels various, but all short

Typical verbs **bindan,** *bind;* **helpan,** *help;* **gieldan,** *yield;* **weorpan,**
throw; **berstan,** *burst*

Four stems	bindan	band	bundon	bunden
	helpan	healp	hulpon	holpen
	gieldan	geald	guldon	golden
	weorpan	wearp	wurpon	worpen
	berstan	bærst	burston	borsten

Like **bindan** are conjugated all strong verbs in **in**
or **im** + consonant, besides **iernan,** *run,* **beornan,**
burn, originally **rinnan, brinnan.**

Like **helpan** are conjugated all in **el** + consonant,
besides **fēolan,** *reach,* which is irregular.

Like **gieldan** are conjugated all in **iel** + consonant.

Like **weorpan** are conjugated all in **eor** or **eoh** +
consonant (21. *b*).

Like **berstan** are conjugated ðerscan, *thresh;* **bregd-**
an, *brandish;* **stregdan,** *strew;* besides **frignan,** *in-*

quire, which resembles it in all except the vowel of the present.

The stems of **weorðan**, *become*, are (**37**): —

> weorðan   wearð   wurdon   worden

Bregdan and **frignan** may drop g, and lengthen the preceding vowel (**28**): **brǣd, frīnan**.

Findan, *find*, likewise forms its 3d sing. pret. ind. as **funde**, which is indeed the usual form.

Among the more common verbs are: **drincan**, *drink;* **findan**, *find;* (on)**ginnan**, *begin;* **winnan**, *strive;* **limpan**, *happen;* **belgan**, *be angry;* **hweorfan**, *turn;* **feohtan**, *fight.*

Umlaut changes the **eo** of the present to **ie** in the 2d and 3d sing. pres. ind.: **wierpð**. A similar change, though not due to precisely the same cause (**17**), is found in presents in **e**, which is converted to **i** or **ie**: **hilpst, bierst.**

The 2d and 3d sing. pres. ind. are thus formed (**33, 34**): —

d-stems	**bindan**	**bintst, bint**
t-stems	**feohtan**	**fiehtst, fieht**
st-stems	**berstan**	**bierst, bierst**
ð-stems	**weorðan**	**wier(ð)st, wierð**
nn-stems	**winnan**	**winst, winð** (**35**, *b*)
Others are normal	**singan**	**singst, singð**

The stems of **fēolan**, *reach*, are: —

> fēolan   fealh   fulgon (fǣlon)   folen

Exceptional forms are the 3d sing. pres. ind. of **bregdan** and **stregdan**: **brītt, strēt(t)**.

105. Strong verbs of the Fourth Ablaut Class. —

Stem vowels	e	æ	ǣ	o
	i (u)	ō	ō	u
Typical verb	beran, *bear*			
Four stems	beran, bær, bǣron, boren			

Like **beran** are conjugated **teran**, *tear;* **scieran (18)**, *shear;* **cwelan**, *die;* **helan**, *conceal;* **stelan**, *steal;* **hwelan**, *roar;* **brecan**, *break.*

The two irregular verbs of this class are among the most important in the language: **niman**, *take,* and **cuman**, *come.* Their stems are: —

niman	nōm	nōmon	numen
cuman	c(w)ōm	c(w)ōmon	cumen (cymen)

Umlaut changes the **u** of **cuman** to **y** in the 2d and 3d sing. pres. ind.: **cymst, cymð**. A similar change, though not due to precisely the same cause (**17**), is found in the presents in **e**, which is changed to **i** or **ie**: **bi(e)rst, stilð**.

106. Strong verbs of the Fifth Ablaut Class. —

Stem vowels (normally) **e, æ, ǣ, e**

Typical verbs **sprecan**, *speak;* **cweðan**, *say;* **giefan**, *give;* **biddan**, *request;* **gefēon**, *rejoice*

Four stems	sprecan	spræc	sprǣcon	sprecen
	cweðan	cwæð	cwǣdon (37)	cweden
	giefan (18)	geaf	gēafon	giefen

Four stems	biddan	bæd	bǣdon	beden
	gefēon (101)	gefeah	gefǣgon	

Like **sprecan** are conjugated **etan**, *eat;* **tredan**, *tread;* **metan**, *measure;* **wrecan**, *pursue;* and a few others.

Like **cweðan** is conjugated no other verb.

Like **giefan** is conjugated **gietan**, *get* (**18**).

Like **biddan** are conjugated **licgan**, *lie;* **sittan**, *sit.*

Like **gefēon** is conjugated **sēon**, *see*, except that its pret. plur. is **sāwon**, and past participle **sewen, segen**.

Umlaut, or a change analogous to it (**17**), converts the **e** of the present to **i** in the 2d and 3d sing. pres. ind.: **cwið**; in contracts we have **ie**, not **īe**, since the vowel of the present was originally short: **siehð**.

The 2d and 3d sing. pres. ind. are thus formed (**33, 34**): —

d-stems	tredan	tritst, trit(t)
t-stems	gietan	gietst, giet(t)
ð-stems	cweðan	cwist, cwið
g-stems (**28**)	licgan	ligst (līst), ligð (līð)
Contracts (**101**)	sēon	siehst, siehð
Others are normal	sprecan	spricst, spricð

The vowel of the pret. sing. is sometimes long in verbs in **et**: **ǣt, mǣt**. Imp. sing. **bide** (cf. **107**).

107. Strong verbs of the Sixth Ablaut Class. —

Stem vowels (normally) **a, ō, ō, a**

Typical verbs **faran**, *go;* **slēan**, *strike;* **standan**, *stand;* **hebban**, *raise*

Four stems	faran	fōr	fōron	faren
	slēan (101)	slōg	slōgon (37)	slægen (slęgen)
	standan	stōd	stōdon	standen
	hębban (11)	hōf	hōfon	hafen

Like faran are conjugated sacan, *dispute*, wacan, *wake*, tōsc(e)acan, *depart*, and one or two others.

Like slēan are conjugated lēan, *blame*, ðwēan, *wash*.

Like standan is conjugated no other verb.

In the main like hębban are conjugated the following: —

hliehhan (36), *laugh*	hlōh	hlōgon (37)	
scieppan (18), *create*	scōp (scēop)	scōpon (scēopon)	sceapen
stæppan, *step*	stōp	stōpon	stapen
swęrian, *swear*	swōr	swōron	sworen

Umlaut changes the a of the present to ę (æ). and the ēa of the present (see 101) to ie (not īe), in the 2d and 3d sing. pres. ind.: stęnt, færst, sliehð.

The 2d and 3d sing. pres. ind. are thus formed (34): —

d-stems	standan	stęntst, stęnt
b-stems	hębban	hęfst, hęfð
Contracts (101)	slēan	sliehst, sliehð
Others are normal	faran	færst, færð

The verbs like hębban are peculiar in having umlaut in the present stem, which causes them, in so far, to resemble the Weak Verbs of the First Class (111). Like sęllan, etc., they have the imp. sing. in -e: hęfe, swęre, etc. (cf. 117). The umlaut is due to the fact that the stem of this group, unlike that of

most strong verbs, was followed by a **j** (**16**). Thus
the inf. **stæppau** stands for original **stapjau**; were it
not for the umlaut-causing **-j-**, the infinitive would
have been **stapan**; and so in the other four verbs.

108. Reduplicating verbs. — Stem vowels various.

A peculiarity of this class — shared, however, by a
very few verbs of the Sixth Ablaut Class (**107**) — is
that the vowels of the first and fourth stems are
identical (with two or three exceptions noted below),
and that those of the second and third stems are
likewise identical. The vowel (diphthong) of the
preterit is sometimes **ēo**, less frequently **ē**.

109. Reduplicating preterits in ēo. — The present
stem has **ea** (rarely **a**), **ā**, **ēa**, **ō**, or **ē**.

Typical verbs	feallan, *fall;* bannan, *summon;* cnāwan, *know;*		
	hēawan, *hew;* flōwan, *flow;* wēpan, *weep*		
Four stems	feallan	fēoll	fēollon	feallen
	bannan	bēonn	bēonnon	bannen
	cnāwan	cnēow	cnēowon	cnāwen
	hēawan	hēow	hēowon	hēawen
	flōwan	flēow	flēowon	flōwen
	wēpan	wēop	wēopon	wōpen

Like **feallan** are conjugated verbs in **eal** + consonant, besides **weaxan**, *grow* (originally of the Sixth
Ablaut Class, **107**): **healdan**, *hold;* **wealdan**, *govern*, etc.

Like **bannan** (very rare) is conjugated **gangan**, *go*
(but usually as **gān, 141**).

Like **cnāwan** are conjugated verbs in **āw**, besides **swāpan**, *sweep* : — **blāwan**, *blow ;* **sāwan**, *sow*, etc.

Like **hēawan** are conjugated verbs in **ēa** : **bēatan**, *beat ;* **hlēapan**, *leap.*

Like **flōwan** are conjugated verbs in **ō** : **blōwan**, *bloom* (not to be confounded with **blāwan**, *blow*) ; **grōwan**, *grow ;* **spōwan**, *thrive ;* **rōwan**, *row.*

Like **wēpan** is conjugated no other common verb ; in **wēpan** (orig. **wōpjan**) the stem vowel of the present is derived by umlaut from **ō**, the latter reappearing in the past participle. — Umlaut as in **94**.

110. Reduplicating preterits in ē. — The present stem has **ā**, **ǣ**, or **ō**. Umlaut as in **94**.

Typical verbs **lǣtan**, *let ;* **hātan**, *call ;* **fōn**, *seize*

Four stems			
lǣtan	**lēt**	**lēton**	**lǣten**
hātan	**hēt**	**hēton**	**hāten**
fōn (101)	**fēng**	**fēngon**	**fangen**

Like **lǣtan** are conjugated **drǣdan**, *dread ;* **rǣdan**, *consult, read* (usually weak) ; **slǣpan**, *sleep.*

Like **hātan** is conjugated **lācan**, *jump ;* **scādan**, **scēadan** (18), *separate.*

Like **fōn** is conjugated **hōn**, *hang* (3d sing. **fēhð**, **hēhð**).

111. Weak verbs of the First Class. — The stem vowel of the present always has umlaut (except that **ēo** sometimes persists, *i.e.*, does not become **īe**). The infinitive ends in **-an** or **-ian**, the latter being infrequent.

112. Weak infinitives in -an. — These take the preterit either (**113, 114**) in -de (-te) or (**115**) in -ede, the
past participle in -ed or in -d (-t).

**113. Weak preterits in -de (-te), with retention of the
stem vowel.** — Here belong verbs whose stem vowel is
long by nature (**4**), and a number in which the stem
syllable is long by position as a result of gemination
(**36**). The past participle is formed in -ed, contraction
taking place in **t**- and **d**- stems. The infinitive always
ends in -**an**. Simplified gemination by **35**.

Three stems			
	hīeran, *hear*	hīerde	(ge)hīered
	fyllan, *fill*	fylde (35)	(ge)fylled
	cyssan, *kiss*	cyste (33, 35)	(ge)cyssed
	sęttan, *set*	sętte (33)	(ge)sętt
	sęndan, *send*	sęnde	(ge)sęnd(ed)
	lǣdan, *lead*	lǣdde	(ge)lǣd(ed)
	īecan, *increase*	īecte (33)	(ge)īeced
	ēhtan, *persecute*	ēhte	(ge)ēht
	mētan, *find*	mētte	(ge)mēt(t)
	glerwan, *prepare*	gierede	(ge)gier(w)ed

Like **hīeran** are conjugated all verbs not belonging
to any of the following divisions.

Like **fyllan** are conjugated stems ending in a double
consonant, excepting those like **cyssan** and **sęttan**, and
under **114** and **115**.

Like **cyssan** are conjugated stems ending in **ff, pp,**
and **ss**.

Like **sęttan** are conjugated stems ending in **tt** (imp.
sing. **sęte**).

Like **sęndan** are conjugated stems ending in a consonant + **d**.

Like **lǣdan** are conjugated stems ending in a vowel + **d**.

Like **īecan** are conjugated stems ending in **c, p,** and **x**.

Like **ēhtan** are conjugated stems ending in a consonant + **t**.

Like **mētan** are conjugated stems ending in a vowel + **t**.

Like **gierwan** are conjugated stems ending in **rw** and **lw**. The forms of the present sometimes retain the **w**, sometimes not.

114. Irregular preterits and past participles. — Certain verbs, in other respects like those of the last paragraph, and whose stems end in **ll, cc, c** (**nc, rc**), or **g** (**cg, ng**), form their preterits and past participles from a stem without umlaut. In the case of the **ll-**, **cc-**, and simple **c**-verbs, to determine, from the present stem, what form the past stem will assume, find the original vowel corresponding to the umlaut vowel of the present, and consider what changes, if any, will be caused by breaking (**21**). The l-verbs take **-de** and **-d**, the **c-** and **g**-verbs **-te** and **-t**. The **c-** and **g**-verbs often insert **-e-** before the infinitive ending (**18**). Stems ending in **c** and **g** change these consonants to **h** before the **t** of the ending.

The list is as follows: —

ll-verbs	cwęllan, *kill*	cwealde	(ge)cweald
	dwęllan, *deceive*		
	sęllan, *give*		
	stęllan, *place*		
	tęllan, *count*		
cc-verbs	cwęcc(e)an, *shake*	cweahte	(ge)cweaht
	dręcc(e)an, *vex*		
	lęcc(e)an, *moisten*		
	ręcc(e)an, *expound*		
	stręcc(e)an, *stretch*		
	ꝥęcc(e)an, *cover*		
	w(r)ęcc(e)an, *wake*		
	læcc(e)an, *seize*	læhte	(ge)læht
c-verbs	rǣc(e)an, *reach*	rǣhte	(ge)rǣht
	tǣc(e)an, *teach*	tǣhte	(ge)tǣht
	rēc(e)an, recc(e)an, *reck*	rōhte	(ge)rōht
	sēc(e)an, *seek*	sōhte	(ge)sōht
nc-verbs	ꝥęnc(e)an, *think*	ꝥōhte	(ge)ꝥōht
	ꝥync(e)an, *seem*	ꝥūhte	(ge)ꝥūht
rc-verb	wyrc(e)an, *work*	worhte	(ge)worht
cg-verb	bycg(e)an, *buy*	bohte	(ge)boht
ng-verb	bringan, *bring*	brōhte	(ge)brōht

The preterit and past participle of **rǣc(e)an** and **tǣc(e)an** should properly have **ā**: **rāhte**, etc. This does, indeed, sometimes occur, but is much less common than the **ǣ**.

115. Infinitives in -an, with preterit in -ede. — Here belong two groups of verbs whose infinitives end in -**an** (exceptionally -**ian**).

(*a*) The first group comprises the following verbs with stems ending in a double consonant (cf. **11**);

frẹmman, *perform;* grẹmman, *provoke;* trymman, *confirm;* ðẹnnan, *extend;* wẹnnan, *accustom;* dynnan, hlynnan, *resound;* cnyssan, *beat;* scẹððan, *injure* (sometimes strong); swẹbban, *quiet;* wẹcg(e)an, *agitate;* ðicg(e)an, *receive* (sometimes strong). Occasionally these verbs take an infinitive in -ian (116).

(*b*) The second group comprises stems ending in a consonant + either l, n, or r. This group is somewhat irregular, occasionally having preterits like hyngerde, instead of the more regular hyngrede, nẹmde for nẹmn(e)de, *named,* and ẹfnde for ẹfnede, *performed.*

Typical verbs (*a*) frẹmman, *perform*   **frẹmede**   **(ge)frẹmed**
             (*b*) hyngran, *hunger*   **hyngrede**   **(ge)hyngred**

NOTE. — Lẹcg(e)an, *lay,* is irregular in the preterit and past part.: lẹgde (lēde), (ge)lẹgd (-lēd), instead of lẹgede, (ge)lẹged.

116. Infinitives in -ian with preterit in -ede. — Here belong a few weak verbs of the First Class. They have a short stem ending in r, or occasionally in l, m, n, or one of the spirants. The vowel of the stem is usually ẹ (ie) or y. Examples are: nẹrian, *save;* hẹrian, *praise;* byrian, *pertain;* hẹlian, *conceal;* trymian, *confirm* (see 115. *a*).

Three stems   **nẹrian**   **nẹrede**   **(ge)nẹred**

117. Paradigms of the First Class. — For the conjugation of weak verbs of the First Class we may choose: hīeran, *hear* (113); sęllan, *give* (114, 36); fręmman, *perform* (115); nęrian, *save* (116).

PRESENT.

INDICATIVE.

Sing. 1.	hīere	sęlle	fręmme	nęrie
2.	hīerst (23)	sęl(e)st	fręmest	nęrest
3.	hierð	sęl(e)ð	fręmeð	nęreð
Plur.	hīeraða	sęllað	fręmmað	nęriað

OPTATIVE.

Sing.	hīere	sęlle	fręmme	nęrie
Plur.	hīeren	sęllen	fręmmen	nęrien

IMPERATIVE.

Sing.	hīer (23)	sęle	fręme	nęre
Plur.	hīerað	sęllað	fręmmað	nęriað

INFINITIVE.

hīeran	sęllan	fręmman	nęrian

PARTICIPLE.

hīerende	sęllende	fręmmende	nęriende

PRETERIT.

INDICATIVE.

Sing. 1.	hīerde	sealde	fręmede	nęrede
2.	hīerdest	sealdest	fręmedest	nęredest
3.	hīerde	sealde	fręmede	nęrede
Plur.	hīerdon	sealdon	fręmedon	nęredon

OPTATIVE.

Sing.	hīerde	sealde	fręmede	nęrede
Plur.	hīerden	sealden	fręmeden	nęreden

PARTICIPLE.

Sing.	hīered	seald	fręmed	nęred
Plur.	hīer(e)de	sealde	fręmede	nęrede

118. Weak verbs of the Second Class. — These are very numerous. Many are formed from nouns and adjectives (cf. **90**). The infinitive always ends in -ian, or its equivalent -ig(e)an (**18**). Though the i of an ending usually causes umlaut, it does not in these verbs, because of its comparatively late origin, the older termination having been -ōjon (that is, -ō-yon), which was incapable of causing umlaut, since it was -ō-, rather than -j- (that is, -y-), which immediately followed the stem.

Hence it is easy to distinguish verbs of this Class from verbs in -ian of the First Class (**116**): —

1. Of those verbs there are but few; of these, many.

2. Of those the vowels are always umlauted (usually ę or y); of these, rarely, and only when the verb was formed from a noun or adjective whose vowel was already umlauted.

3. Of those the stem usually ends in r; of these, in any consonant or consonant combination.

119. Paradigm of the Second Class. — As a typical verb we may select **lufian**, *love*.

	PRESENT.	
INDICATIVE.	OPTATIVE.	IMPERATIVE.
Sing. 1. **lufie**		Sing. **lufa**
2. **lufast**	**lufie**	Plur. **lufiað**
3. **lufað**		
Plur. **lufiað**	**lufien**	
Infin. **lufian**		Part. **lufiende**

PRETERIT.

	INDICATIVE.	OPTATIVE.
Sing. 1.	lufode	
2.	lufodest	lufode
3.	lufode	
Plur.	lufedon, -odon	lufoden, -eden
Part.	(ge)lufod	

In the endings, **ig(e)** or **g** is frequently found for i (**18**).

Sometimes, instead of **-ode**, the ending is **-ade**, **-ude**, or even **-ede**; but **-ode** is normal.

120. Weak verbs of the Third Class. — These comprise **habban**, *have;* **libban** (**lifian**), *live;* **sęcg(e)an**, *say;* **hycg(e)an**, *think.* These are conjugated partly according to the First Class (**117**), and partly according to the Second (**119**).

121. Conjugation of habban, have. — **Habban**, *have;* **nabban**, *have not* (**29**).

	INDICATIVE.	OPTATIVE.
Pres. Sing. 1.	hæbbe	hæbbe
2.	hæfst (hafast)	hæbbe
3.	hæfð (hafað)	hæbbe
Plur.	habbað (hæbbað)	hæbben
Pret. Sing.	hæfde, etc.	hæfde
Plur.	hæfdon	hæfden
Imper. Sing.	hafa	
Plur.	habbað	Infin. habban
Pres. Part.	hæbbende	Past Part. (ge)hæfd

	INDICATIVE.		OPTATIVE.
Pres. Sing. 1.	næbbe		næbbe
2.	næfst (nafast)		næbbe
3.	næfð (nafað)		næbbe
Plur.	nabbað		næbben
Pret. Sing.	næfde, etc.		næfde
Plur.	næfdon		næfden
Imper. Sing.	nafa	Infin.	nabban
Plur.	nabbað		
Pres. Part.	næbbende	Past Part.	(ge)næfd

122. Conjugation of libban, *live.* —

	INDICATIVE.		OPTATIVE.
Pres. Sing. 1.	libbe		libbe, lifie, etc.
2.	leofast (20)		
3.	leofað		
Plur.	libbað, lifiað		libben, lifien
Pret. Sing.	lifde, etc.		lifde
Plur.	lifdon		lifden
Imper. Sing.	leofa (20)	Infin.	libban, lifian
Plur.	libbað, lifiað		
Pres. Part.	libbende, lifiende	Past Part.	(ge)lifd

123. Conjugation of sęcg(e)an, *say.* —

	INDICATIVE.		OPTATIVE.
Pres. Sing. 1.	sęcge		sęcge, etc.
2.	sægst, sęgst, sagast		
3.	sægð, sęgð, sagað		
Plur.	sęcg(e)að		sęcgen
Pret. Sing.	sægde, sǣde (28), etc.		sægde, sǣde
Plur.	sægdon, sǣdon		sægden, sǣden
Imper. Sing.	saga, sęge	Infin.	sęcg(e)an
Plur.	sęcg(e)að		
Pres. Part.	sęcgende	Past Part.	(ge)sægd, (ge)sǣd

124. Conjugation of hycg(e)an, *think.* —

		INDICATIVE.	OPTATIVE.
Pres. Sing.	1.	hycge	hycge, etc.
	2.	hygst, hogast	
	3.	hygð, hogað	
	Plur.	hycg(e)að	hycgen
Pret. Sing.		hog(o)de, etc.	hog(o)de
	Plur.	hog(o)don	hog(o)den
Imper. Sing.		hoga	Infin. hycg(e)an
	Plur.	hycg(e)að	
Pres. Part.		hycgende	Past Part. (ge)hog(o)d

PRETERITIVE PRESENTS.

125. Preteritive presents. — A small group of verbs have strong preterits with present meaning (the old presents being lost), and form new weak preterits from these. They are: **witan,** *know;* **āgan,** *own;* **dugan,** *avail;* **unnan,** *grant;* **cunnan,** *know;* **ðurfan,** *need;* **durran** (?), *dare;* **sculan,** *shall;* **munan,** *intend;* **mugan** (?), *can;* **nugan** (?), *suffice;* **mōtan** (?), *may.*

126. Conjugation of witan, *know.* — Ind. pres. sing. 1. 3. **wāt,** 2. **wāst;** plur. **wi(e)ton;** pret. **wiste (wisse),** etc. Opt. pres. **wi(e)te,** etc.; pret. **wiste (wisse),** etc. Imper. **wite.** Infin. **wi(e)tan.** Pres. part. **witende;** past part. **(ge)witen.**

For **wi(e)tan,** etc., is found **wiotan,** etc.

Like **witan** is conjugated **nytan,** *not to know:* **nāt,** etc. Wherever, in the forms of **witan,** i (ie, io) occurs, **y** is here to be substituted.

127. Conjugation of **āgan,** *possess.* — Ind. pres. sing. 1. 3. **āh,** 2. **āhst;** plur. **āgon;** pret. **āhte,** etc. Opt. pres. **āge,** etc.; pret. **āhte.** Imper. **āge.** Infin. **āgan.** Pres. part. **āgende;** past part. **āgen,** *own (adj.).*

So **nāgan,** *not to possess.*

128. Conjugation of **dugan,** *avail.* — Ind. pres. sing. 1. 3. **dēah;** plur. **dugon;** pret. **dohte,** etc. Opt. pres. **dyge, duge,** etc. Infin. **dugan.** Pres. part. **dugende.**

129. Conjugation of **unnan,** *grant.* — Ind. pres. sing. 1. 3. **an(n);** plur. **unnon;** pret. **ūðe.** Opt. pres. **unne,** etc.; pret. **ūðe,** etc. Imper. **unne.** Infin. **unnan.** Pres. part. **unnende;** past part. **(ge)unnen.**

130. Conjugation of **cunnan,** *know.* — Ind. pres. sing. 1. 3. **can(n), canst;** plur. **cunnon;** pret. **cūðe,** etc. Opt. pres. **cunne,** etc.; pret. **cūðe, cȳðe,** etc. Infin. **cunnan.** Past part. **(ge)cunnen,** and **cūð** *(adj.).*

131. Conjugation of **ðurfan,** *need.* — Ind. pres. sing. 1. 3. **ðearf,** 2. **ðearft;** plur. **ðurfon;** pret. **ðorfte,** etc. Opt. pres. **ðyrfe, ðurfe,** etc.; pret. **ðorfte,** etc. Infin. **ðurfan.** Pres. part. **ðearfende.**

132. Conjugation of **durran,** *dare.* — Ind. pres. sing. 1. 3. **dearr,** 2. **dearst;** plur. **durron;** pret. **dorste,** etc. Opt. pres. **dyrre, durre,** etc.

133. Conjugation of sculan, *shall.* — Ind. pres. sing. 1. 3. **sceal,** 2. **scealt**; plur. **sculon**; pret. **sc(e)olde,** etc. Opt. pres. **scyle, scule,** etc. Infin. **sculan.**

134. Conjugation of munan, *intend.* — Ind. pres. sing. 1. 3. **man,** 2. **manst**; plur. **munon (munað)**; pret. **munde.** Opt. pres. **myne, mune,** etc. Imper. sing. **mun**; plur. **munað.** Infin. **munan.** Pres. part. **munende**; past part. **(ge)munen.**

135. Conjugation of mugan, *can.* — Ind. pres. sing. 1. 3. **mæg,** 2. **meaht**; plur. **magon**; pret. **mealhte,** etc. Opt. pres. **mæge,** etc.

136. Conjugation of nugan, *suffice.* — Ind. pres. sing. 3. **neah**; plur. **nugon**; pret. **nohte,** etc. Opt. pres. **nuge,** etc.

137. Conjugation of mōtan, *may.* — Ind. pres. sing. 1. 3. **mōt,** 2. **mōst**; plur. **mōton**; pret. **mōste,** etc. Opt. pres. **mōte,** etc.

ANOMALOUS VERBS.

138. Conjugation of wesan, bēon, *be.* —

INDICATIVE.	OPTATIVE.
Pres. Sing. 1. eom; bēo	sīe; bēo, etc.
2. eart; bist	
3. is; bið; neg. nis	
Plur. sind, -t; sindon; bēoð	sīen; bēon

INDICATIVE.	OPTATIVE.
Pret. Sing. 1. wæs; neg. næs	wǣre; neg. nǣre
wǣre; neg. nǣre	wǣre; neg. nǣre
wæs; neg. næs	wǣre; neg. nǣre
wǣron; neg. nǣron	wǣren; neg. nǣren
Imper. Sing. wes; bēo	Infin. wesan; bēon
Plur. wesað; bēoð	Pres. Part. wesende; bēonde

139. Conjugation of willan, *will.* —

INDICATIVE.   OPTATIVE.

Pres. Sing. 1. wil(l)e; neg. ne(l)le, ny(l)le ⎰ wille, etc.; neg. nelle, ⎱ nylle, etc.

2. wilt; neg. nelt, nylt

3. wil(l)e; neg. nel(l)e, nyl(l)e

Plur. willað; neg. nellað, nyllað ⎰ willen; neg. nellen, ⎱ nyllen

Pret. Sing. wolde, etc.; neg. nolde, etc.   wolde; neg. nolde

Plur. woldon; neg. noldon   wolden; neg. nolden

Imper. Plur. neg. nellað, nyllað   Infin. willan

Pres. Part. willende

140. Conjugation of dōn, *do.* —

INDICATIVE.	OPTATIVE.
Pres. Sing. 1. dō	dō, etc.
2. dēst	
3. dēð	
Plur. dōð	dōn
Pret. Sing. dyde, dydest, dyde	dyde
Plur. dydon	dyden
Imper. Sing. dō	Infin. dōn
Plur. dōð	
Pres. Part. dōnde	Past Part. (ge)dōn

141. Conjugation of gān, *go.* —

	INDICATIVE.	OPTATIVE.
Pres. Sing. 1.	**gā**	**gā**, etc.
2.	**gǣst**	
3.	**gǣð**	
Plur.	**gāð**	**gān**
Pret. Sing.	**ēode**, etc.	**ēode**
Plur.	**ēodon**	**ēoden**
Imper. Sing.	**gā**	Infin. **gān**
Plur.	**gāð**	
Pres. Part.	**gānde**	Past Part. (**ge**)**gān**

FORMATION OF WORDS.

142. Prefixes. — Many Old English prefixes are self-explanatory. Others, with their meanings, are as follows: —

ā-   (1) = 'up,' 'out' (Ger. er-): **āfyllan,** *fill up,* **āscēotan,** *shoot out.*

    (2) representing **on**: **āweg** = **on weg,** *away.*

    (3) = 'any': **āhwǣr,** *anywhere.*

    (4) practically meaningless: **ābīdan,** *await.*

æf-, see **of-**.

ǣg- = 'any,' 'each': **ǣghwā,** *any one.*

æt- (1) = 'at,' 'to' (Lat. ad-): **ætwītan,** *twit,* **ætgædere,** *together.*

    (2) = 'from,' 'away': **ætwindan,** *escape from.*

and-, ǫnd- is found as the prefix of a few nouns; for its meaning see **on-**.

be- (Ger. be-):

    (1) = 'about': **besorgian,** *be anxious about.*

    (2) makes an intransitive verb transitive: **behycgan,** *think about, consider.*

    (3) privative: **beniman,** *take from, deprive,* **behēafdian,** *behead.*

(4) practically meaningless : **bebēodan**, *command*.

ed-   (1) = 'counter-,' 're-' (Lat. re-): **edlēan**, *recompense*.

(2) occasionally for æt-: **edwītan**, *twit*.

for- (Ger. ver-, für-, vor-) :

(1) = 'away,' 'up,' 'utterly,' 'very,' denoting destruction effected by the action of the simple verb: **fordōn**, *destroy*.

(2) negative : **forbēodan**, *forbid*.

(3) = 'falsely' : **forswęrian**, *forswear*.

(4) = 'down upon' : **forsēon**, *despise*.

(5) = 'in behalf of' : **forstandan**, *stand up for*.

(6) = 'fore-' : **forscēawian**, *foresee*.

fore- = 'fore-' (Lat. præ-): **foresēon**, *foresee, provide*.

ge- (Ger. ge-, Lat. con-) :

(1) = 'together' : **gefēra**, *companion*.

(2) = 'attain by' the action of the simple verb: thus, **winnan**, *fight*, but **gewinnan**, *gain by fighting, conquer*.

(3) usual sign of past participle, when the verb lacks any other prefix : **gegān**, *gone*.

(4) practically meaningless : **gebed**, *prayer*.

mis- = 'mis-' : **miswęndan**, *pervert*.

n- (for **ne-**) = 'not' : **nā** (= **ne** + **ā**, *not ever*), *not at all;* **nis**, *is not*.

of-   (1) = 'off,' 'from' (Lat. de-, ab-, pro-, ex-): **of-spring**, *offspring*.

(2) = 'upon': **ofsittan,** *sit upon, oppress.*

(3) denoting offence, injury, death (Lat. ob-):
ofðyncan, *displease,* **ofstingan,** *stab to death.*

(4) = 'attain by' the action of the simple verb:
offaran, *catch up with,* **ofāscian,** *learn by asking.*

(5) intensive: **ofhyngrod,** *very hungry.*

ofer- (1) = 'over': **oferbrǣdan,** *overspread.*

(2) negative: **ofergietan,** *forget.*

on- (1) = 'on,' 'of': **ondrincan,** *drink of.*

(2) = 'from,' 'out of': **onspringan,** *burst forth.*

(3) = 'un-': **onlūcan,** *unlock.*

(4) intensive: **onstyrian,** *agitate.*

or- = 'without': **orsorg,** *without anxiety,* **orwēne,** *without hope, desperate.*

ōð- = 'away' (Lat. ex-, ab-, de-): **ōðflēon,** *flee away.*

tō- (1) = 'to': **tōcyme,** *advent.*

(2) = 'asunder' (Ger. zer-, Lat. dis-): **tōteran,** *tear apart,* **tōcnāwan,** *discern.*

un- (1) = 'un-': **unforht,** *fearless,* **unrīm** (*unnumber*), *multitude.*

(2) = 'bad': **undǣd,** *ill deed.*

wiðer-(1) = 'again': **wiðertrod,** *return.*

(2) = 'against': **wiðersaca,** *adversary.*

ymb- = 'around' (Lat. circum-): **ymbgang,** *circuit,* **ymbsittan,** *besiege.*

143. Suffixes of masculine nouns. — The more important are **-end**, **-ere**, **-ing**, **-ling**, besides the originally independent words **-dōm**, **-hād**, and **-scipe**. The first four denote persons; the last three, qualities or abstractions. Besides these, there is a masculine suffix **-els**, denoting things.

-end (orig. **-ende**, forming present participles) = '-er,' '-or': **scieppend**, *creator.* Contract nouns with this ending are **fēond**, *enemy*, **frēond**, *friend.*

-ere = '-er': **hearpere**, *harper*, **bōcere**, *scribe.*

-ing (1) = 'son of': **Æðelwulfing**, *son of Athelwulf*, **Adaming**, *son of Adam.*

(2) more generally: **Cęnting**, *inhabitant of Kent*, **cyning**, *king*, **pęning**, *penny.* The **i** sometimes causes umlaut, sometimes not.

-ling: **geongling**, *youngling*, **hȳrling**, *hireling.*

-dōm (Ger. **-thum**) = '-dom,' '-ity,' '-ism,' '-ship,' '-acy': **Crīstendōm**, *Christianity*, **cynedōm**, *kingship.*

-hād (Ger. **-heit**, **-keit**) = '-hood,' '-head,' '-ity': **cildhād**, *childhood*, **mægdenhād**, *virginity.*

-scipe (Ger. **-schaft**) = '-ship,' '-hood,' '-ness,' '-ity': **frēondscipe**, *friendship*, **fēondscipe**, *enmity.*

-els: **byrgels**, *tomb*, **rǣdels**, *riddle.*

144. Suffixes of feminine nouns. — The chief are **-estre**, **-nes**, **-ð**, **-ðu** (**-ðo**), **-ung** (**-ing**), and the originally independent **-rǣden.**

-estre = '-tress': **lǣrestre**, *instructress.*

-nes (Ger. -nis) = '-ness,' '-ity,' forms abstracts from
the present and past participial stems of verbs,
but especially from adjectives: ēhtnes, *persecution*,
forsewennes, *contempt*, hālignes, *holiness*.

-ð, -ðu, -ðo = '-th': hǣlð, *health*, strengðu, *strength*.
This ending was originally -iða, the -i of which
caused umlaut.

-ung (occasionally -ing) = '-ing,' '-ation,' forms nouns
from the present stem of (usually weak) verbs:
blētsung, *blessing*, costung, *temptation*.

-rǣden = '-red,' '-ship,' '-ity': hierdrǣden, *guardian-
ship, guard.*

145. **Suffixes of neuter nouns.** — The two principal, -lāc
and -rīce, were originally independent words: —

-lāc (Mod. Eng. -lock, -ledge): brȳdlāc, *wedding*.

-rīce = 'rule,' 'realm,' 'region': biscoprīce, *bishopric*,
heofonrīce, *kingdom of heaven*.

146. **Adjective suffixes.** — The principal are -en, -ig, -iht,
-isc, and -ol, besides the originally independent -bǣre,
-cund, -fæst, -feald, -full, -lēas, -lic, -mōd, -sum, -weard,
-wende, -weorð, -wierðe, and -wīs. The first four sometimes cause umlaut, sometimes not.

-en (Lat. -inus) = '-en': līnen, *linen*, gylden, *golden*.

-ig (Ger. -ig) = '-y': ēadig, *blessed*, grǣdig, *greedy*.

-iht (Ger. -icht) = '-y': hrēodiht, *reedy*, stǣniht, stān-
iht, *stony*.

-**isc** (Ger. -isch) = '-ish': forms adjectives from common, but especially from proper nouns: **hǣðenisc**, *heathenish*, **Englisc**, *English*.

-**ol** (Lat. -ulus) = 'disposed to': **swicol**, *deceitful*.

-**bǣre** (Ger. -bar, Lat. -ferus, -fer, -ger): **cwealmbǣre**, *deadly*, **lustbǣre**, *agreeable*.

-**cund** = '-ly': **heofondcund**, *heavenly*.

-**fæst** (Ger. -fest) = 'possessing,' 'firm in': **stędefæst**, *possessing, or firm in, one's place, steadfast*, **ārfæst**, *merciful, pious*.

-**feald** (Ger. -falt) = '-fold': **fēowerfeald**, *fourfold*.

-**full** (Ger. -voll) = '-ful': **gelēaffull**, *faithful*, **synfull**, *sinful*.

-**lēas** (Ger. -los) = '-less': **ārlēas** (Ger. ehrlos), *infamous*.

-**lic** (Ger. -lich) = '-ly,' '-al': **cynelic**, *royal*, **eorðlic**, *terrestrial*.

-**mōd** (cf. Ger. -müthig) = '-minded': **ānmōd** (cf. Ger. einmüthig), *unanimous*, **ēaðmōd**, *humble*.

-**sum** (Ger. -sam) = '-full,' '-some,' '-able': **lufsum**, *lovable*, **wynsum**, *winsome*.

-**weard** (cf. Ger. -wärts) = '-ward': **hāmweard**, *homeward, on the way home*, **andweard**, *present*.

-**węnde** = '-ary': **hālwęnde**, *salutary*.

-**weorð**, -**wurð** = '-worthy': **ārweorð**, **ārwurð**, *venerable*.

-**wierðe**, -**wyrðe** (cf. Ger. -würdig) = '-worthy': **nytwierðe**, *useful*.

-**wīs** = '-wise': **gescēadwīs**, *intelligent*, **rihtwīs**, *righteous*.

147. Composition. — Compounds are numerous in Old English. In this respect it resembles German and Greek, while Modern English has allowed this power of forming compounds to fall into disuse, largely through the influence of Latin and French. For this reason it would often be easier to make an idiomatic translation into Old English from Greek than from Latin; in its plastic and pictorial quality a page of Old English poetry suggests Homer or Pindar rather than Virgil or Horace, and among Roman poets the earlier, such as Lucretius.

The relation of the first element of compounds to the second should always be noted. The first limits or defines the second, and for this reason takes the stress; but the precise relation of the two elements is now of one sort, now of another. Sometimes it may be expressed by a preposition, sometimes by the sign of a case, sometimes by an adjective: **gærs-hoppa, gærs-stapa,** *grasshopper, hopper in or through the grass;* **han-crēd,** *cock's-crowing;* **hēah-ęngel,** *high-angel, archangel;* **gim-stān,** *gem-stone, jewel.*

Although compounds should be studied with reference to the meaning and relation of their components, they should frequently be translated by a simple Modern English word. Thus **gærshoppa** may sometimes be translated by *locust;* **gimstān** should never be translated *gemstone;* and **hēahfæder** should always be rendered by *patriarch* or *father.*

SYNTAX.

148. Object of this sketch. — The object of the present sketch is not to present a complete view of Old English syntax, even in outline, but rather to call attention to such peculiarities as are most likely to cause difficulty. Many constructions common to all the cultivated European languages, especially to the inflected ones, will either be passed over without notice or but briefly touched upon.

Nouns.

149. Subject. — The subject of a finite verb is in the nominative case. For that of an infinitive, see **169**.

150. Predicate nominative. — A predicate noun (or adjective), denoting the same person or thing as its subject, agrees with it in case. Examples: **ic eom Apollonius; ðæt ic gewurde wǣdla.**

151. Apposition. — A noun annexed to another noun, and denoting the same person or thing, agrees with it in case. Examples: **and wēnde ðæt hēo Diana wǣre, sēo gyden**; Arcestrates (gen.) **dohtor ðæs cyninges.**

Note **hīe sume** = *some of them.*

152. Vocative. — The vocative, which is identical in form with the nominative, is used in direct address. It may be preceded by an interjection, the second personal pronoun, or a possessive pronoun; this possessive pronoun, when followed by an adjective, usually takes before the latter the demonstrative pronoun **se**. Examples: **ðū sǣ Neptune; mīn se lēofesta fæder.**

153. Genitive with nouns. — The genitive is distinctively an adnominal case; that is, its principal function is to limit the meaning of a noun. Its sign is *of*. It denotes various relations, not all of which can be strictly defined.

a) Relationship: **ūre ealra mōdor.**

b) Source: **sunnan and mōnan lēoman; ðǣre hearpan swēg; frẹmdra ðēoda ungeðwǣrnes.**

c) Subject. The noun in the genitive stands for the *author* of the action denoted by the noun upon which the genitive is dependent. Example: **ðīnra halgena earnungum.**

d) Object. This may be known by the possibility of turning the noun upon which it is dependent into a cognate verb, when the noun in the genitive will become the *object* of that verb; for example, in **Frēan ẹgesan, Frēan** is an obj. gen., because, if we substitute for the noun **ẹgesa**, *fear*, the verb *fear*, the noun *Lord* becomes the object of the verb. Examples: **ðæs dæges līehtinge; līfes tilungum; unscẹðð igra beswīcend; lǣswe scēapa and nēata; hyht hǣle.**

e) Cause (denoted by *for*): **lēan ꝺissa swǣs-enda.**

f) Characteristic: **meregreotan ǣlces hīwes; trēowum missenlicra cynna;** setl his **mǣgenꝺrymnesse.** Here, perhaps, belongs: **werhādes** and **wīfhādes hē gescēop hīe.**

g) Specification of time: **ānes mōnꝺes fierst.**

h) Specification of place: **gārsecges īgland** (Latin influence).

i) Unclassified: **ꝺǣre nēowolnesse brādnes; ꝺæt mægen lufe; ꝺǣre sprǣce ęnde.**

154. Partitive genitive. — The genitive denotes the whole, with words denoting a part.

a) With nouns: **unrīm ceastra; fela gēara; lȳthwōn cwicera cynna.**

b) With pronouns: **manna ǣnigne; hiera nān; hwilc ēower; gumena gehwæne; hwæthwugu swilces; sē manna.** Note the peculiar **ānra gehwilc,** *each one.*

c) With numerals: **eahta fōta; fēower hund wintra.**

d) With superlatives: **bēacna beorhtost.** Similarly, with a cognate noun, to denote eminence: **dryhtna Dryhten.**

155. Genitive with adjectives. — The genitive is used to define an adjective with respect to the part or relation in which the quality is conceived. Such adjectives are frequently akin to verbs which take the genitive (**156**), and sometimes correspond to Latin adjectives of inclination in -*ax*. They may be roughly classified as follows: —

a) Want: **dǣllēas mīnes rēnes; īdel and unnyt gōda** (154. *b*) **gehwilces.**

b) Fulness: **berende** (Lat. *ferax*) **missenlicra fugla.**

c) Desire: **ǣtes georn.**

d) Retentiveness: **fæsthafol** (Lat. *tenax*) **mīnra gōda.**

e) Knowledge: **wordes wīs.**

156. Genitive with verbs. — The genitive is used with many verbs, mostly such as denote mental action, but also with those of cessation and refusal, and some others. Frequently the underlying notion is a *partitive* one; that is, the object is conceived as affected *in part*.

a) Desire: **friðes wilnedon.**

b) Request: **biddende mīnra gōda.**

c) Rejoicing: **þæs se hlanca gefeah.**

d) Experiment: **wǣda cunnedan.**

e) Use: **eardes brūcað.**

f) Care: **gīemden ðæs dæges.**

g) Supposition or belief: **nōhtes ęlles wēndon; ðæs gelīefan.**

h) Fear: **ne ondrǣd ðū ðē ǣniges ðinges.**

i) Granting: **āra unnan.**

j) Refusal: **tīðe forwierndest.**

k) Cessation: **geswāc his weorces.**

l) Awaiting: **ðæs wordes bād.**

m) Approaching: **cēoles nēosan.**

n) Producing: **gāsta strēonan.**

157. Adverbial genitive. — Certain adverbial relations may be expressed by the genitive (cf. **71**). Example: **hine gewęnde ðæs weges.**

1. The demonstrative **ðæt** is frequently used in the genitive in various adverbial senses. Thus of time, **ðæs (ðe)** = *from the time that, after, afterwards;* of manner, = *as far as, as;* of cause, = *for this, because;* etc.

158. Genitive with prepositions. — The genitive is occasionally used with certain prepositions, such as **wið, tō,** and **wana.** Examples: **wið ðæs fæstengeates; tō ðæs; ānes wana siextig (78. 5).**

159. Genitive with other cases. — Verbs which take a genitive denoting the thing, may also take a dative or accusative of the person.

a) With dative (including reflexives, **184**): **him (164.** *a*) **ne ūðe (156.** *i*) **God lęngran līfes; nolde gē mē (dat.) wǣda tīðian (156.** *i*)**; gē mē (dat.) ǣtes forwierndon (156.** *j*)**; Apollonius**

hiere (164. *c*) ðæs ðancode; ne ondrǣd (156. *h*)
ðū ðē (161. 1) ǣniges ðinges.

b) With accusative (including impersonals, **190**):
ðē (acc.) ōhtes āxian; hine **fultumes** bǣdon;
ðē twēonie ðǣre sprǣce; męreliðendum (161)
miltsa biddan wuldres Āldor (acc.); ðegnas
ðearle gelyste (190) gārgewinnes.

160. Dative in general. — The dative denotes the
indirect object, usually the person *to* or *for* or *with
reference to* whom something is done. When used
with verbs (**164**), the general notion of the verb may
often be regarded as implying some sort of *giving* (or
its opposite), if this term be employed in its widest
sense.

1. The dative is sometimes used for the instrumental (**174**): **cleopode micelre stefne.**

161. Dative of benefit or interest. — The sign of this
dative is *for.* Examples: **scipu ēow eallum ic
wyrce.** Perhaps also: **ðīnre eorðan ne rīnð.**

1. Akin to this is the *reflexive dative* (**184**): **ðæt
hīe him** (*for themselves*) **wǣpnu worhten.**

2. Similar, too, is the *dative of possession*, which,
without much change in the sense, might be replaced
by the genitive: **him fēollon tēaras of ðǣm ēagum**
(so Ger. *ihm fielen Thränen von den Augen*); **him
mǫn feaht on lāst; wulfum tō willan.**

162. Dative of deprivation. — Some verbs of deprivation (cf. 177) take the dative of the object removed,
sometimes with an accusative of the person *from
whom*. Examples: hē hine unscrȳdde ᚦǣm healfan sciccelse; ᚦingum ongierede and genacodode.

163. Dative of resemblance or approach. — This is
self-explanatory.

a) With verbs: geflit cymᚦ ᚦǣm behealdendum.

b) With adjectives (cf. 165): fugole gelīcost.

164. Dative with various verbs. — Such are verbs
of (160) —

a) Giving or imparting: ᚦearfum dǣlan.

b) Speaking: hiere ārealite; him gecȳᚦan.

c) Thanking: Gode ᚦanciende.

d) Promising: behēt mīnum lārēowe.

e) Serving and benefiting: hē him ᚦēnode;
fremme gehwilc ōᚦrum; him fēng God on
fultum; manigum genyhtsumian.

f) Obeying and following: gehīersumian mīnum
willan; ᚦe hiere folgode.

g) Pitying: gemiltsa mē.

h) Requiting: forgieldan ǣghwilcum.

i) Ruling: ᚦēodum racian. Similarly, ȳᚦum
stilde.

j) Receiving: onfēng ᚦǣre wununge.

k) Pleasing and suiting: **h im e a l l u m līcode; ꝺē gedafenaꝺ.**

l) Seeming: **m ē ꝺyncꝺ.**

m) Opposing: **w o r u l d e wiꝺsacan.**

n) Betraying or deserting: **swīcaꝺ ꝺ ē.**

o) Using (rare): **notaꝺ c r æ f t e mīnu m.**

165. Dative with adjectives. — The dative is chiefly employed with adjectives signifying *dear, generous, useful, obedient*, etc., and their opposites.   Examples: **lidwērigụm ēste; Gode ꝺone lēofan fæder** (*the father dear to God*); **behēfe ic eom cyninge; folcum fracoꝺ.**

1. The dative of want or deprivation (cf. **162**) is also found here: **Gode orfeorme.**

166. Dative with prepositions. — The dative is by far the commonest case with prepositions.   Examples would be superfluous.

1. After the preposition **on (in)**, certain adjectives, like **mid** and **ufanweard**, agree with the following noun, instead of being treated like nouns governing it in the genitive, as are their counterparts in Mod. Eng.   Examples: **on midre ꝺ ære s æ** (so Lat. *in medio mari*, but Mod. Eng. *in the midst* of *the sea*); **on ꝺ æm fæstene ufanweardum.**

167. Dative absolute. — A noun and a participle, not involved in the main construction of the sentence,

may stand by themselves in the dative, and constitute an adverbial clause, most frequently of time.
This construction is imitated from the Latin ablative
absolute. Examples: **onfangenre his blētsunge;
ðisum eallum ðus gedōnum.**

168. Accusative after transitive verbs. — The direct
object of a transitive verb is put in the accusative.
Examples: **hē swang ðone top; ealne norðdæl
genōmon.**

1. A special case of the foregoing is the cognate
accusative, in which the object is etymologically akin
to the verb: **libbað hiera līf.**

169. Subject accusative. — The subject of an infinitive is put in the accusative. Examples: **geseah hē
sumne fiscere gān; hē gehīerde ðone blisse-
sang ūpāstīgan.**

170. Accusative of extent. — The accusative may denote extent of time or space. Example: **wæs se
storm ealne ðone dæg swīðe micel and strang.**

171. Accusative after impersonals. — Impersonals (**190**)
of appetite or passion govern an accusative of the
person suffering. Example: **mē hyngrede.**

172. Accusative after prepositions. — Some prepositions always govern the accusative, others only under

certain circumstances. Those of the former class
are **geond, ōꝺ, ꝺurh,** and **ymb(e)**; of the latter,
a large number that more frequently take the
dative **(166).**

1. Of the second class, **on (in)** is perhaps the commonest representative, taking the *dative* when denoting
rest in, the *accusative* when denoting *motion towards;*
this distinction, however, is not invariably observed.
Examples of accusative: **inēode on ꝺæt bæꝺ; in
ꝺæt mynster ēode.**

Exceptions to the rule are: **on ꝺone seofoꝺan
dæg; mid ꝺone bisceop.**

173. Two accusatives. — Verbs signifying *to make, to
name, to regard,* and the like, may take a predicate
accusative besides the object accusative. Examples:
God hine (obj. acc.) **geworhte wundorlicne and
fægerne; God gecīegde ꝺā drȳgnesse** (obj. acc.)
eorꝺan; hwonne gesāwon wē ꝺē (obj. acc.) **hungrigne?**

174. Instrumental in general. — The instrumental,
which in form is sometimes (especially in the plural)
indistinguishable from the dative (see **160.** 1), denotes
manner, means, instrument, or *material.* Its sign is *by*
or *with.* Examples: **geseah blīꝺum andwlitan;
gestaꝺolade strangum mihtum; gefæstnade
folmum; gefrætwade foldan scēatas leomum
and lēafum.**

This case is more common in poetry than in prose, where its place is often taken by **mid** with the dative; even in poetry, the simple instrumental sometimes alternates with the dative accompanied by **mid**, *e.g.* (*Andreas*, 320) **sārcwide** occurs in the same construction as **mid oferhygdum.** Occasionally the instrumental is employed where Modern English would use an accusative: **mundum brugdon,** *they waved (with) their hands.*

The instrumental being one of the more difficult cases to master, a few of its regular combinations are separately appended: —

a) With verbs of journeying and transporting, where its sign may almost be regarded as *in:* **cēolum līðan; fæðmum fęrian; sīðe gesōhte.** So with **libban: drēamum lifdon.**

b) With verbs of speaking, to indicate voice or language (see also **160. 1**): **wordum cwæð; ondsweorodon gēncwidum.**

c) With past participles, generally preceding the latter (common in poetry): **sweordum gehēawen; hilde gesǣged; dōme gedȳrsod.**

d) With adjectives (generally in poetry), to denote *in what respect,* or sometimes *instrumentality:* **feðerum hręmig; ęcgum gecoste; mundum frēorig; synnum wunde.** These last two afford the metrical combinations exhibited in **217. 1** — among the commonest in Old English.

175. **Instrumental with prepositions.** — **Mid**, which frequently takes the dative, is sometimes found with the
instrumental, especially in the Anglian dialect; so
occasionally **for**. Examples: **mid ealle; mid micle
sige; mid ðȳ rēadestan gōdwębbe; for hwȳ.**

176. **Adverbial instrumental.** — The instrumental may
denote adverbial relations, especially *time when.* Examples: **sume dæge; ðȳ seofoðan dæge; ælce
gēare; word stunde āhōf.**

1. It may also denote the *number of times:* **siextīene sīðum.**

2. The instrumental may denote *the way:* **ðȳ ilcan
wege.**

177. **Instrumental of deprivation.** — Some verbs of
deprivation may take an object *of which* in the
instrumental (cf. **162**). Examples: **māðmum bedǣled; ǣhtum benǣmde.**

178. **Instrumental of difference.** — The instrumental
denotes the measure of difference. Examples: **micle
lęngran; ðȳ bealdran; þon cymlicor; stręngre
eallum ðǣm ǣrgedōnum.**

Adjectives.

179. **Agreement of adjectives.** — Adjectives agree with
their nouns in gender, number, and case. This applies
also to demonstrative, possessive, and indefinite pro-

nouns, and to participles, when used as adjectives. When used predicatively, however, participles may be uninflected.

180. Strong and weak adjectives. — For the distinction in the use of strong and weak adjectives, see **55**.

181. Adjectives as nouns. — An adjective may be used as a noun (see **55**). Examples: **ðā ymbsittendan; hwā giefð ðǣm uncūðan līfes fultum.**

Adverbs.

182. Use of adverbs. — Adverbs qualify verbs, adjectives, and other adverbs.

183. Two negatives. — Two or more negatives strengthen the negation, instead of making an affirmative. Example: **ðīn nis nān wiht.**

Pronouns.

184. Reflexive pronouns. — The reflexive pronoun (**82**), in the dative (**161. 1**; cf. **159**) or accusative, is used with certain verbs whose counterparts in Mod. Eng. would not necessarily require it.

a) Dative: **worhton him hōcas; bǣr him eaxe on handa; him land curon; gewāt him; far ðē; cierde wē ūs.**

b) Accusative: hē gerḗste **h i n e**; ᶞæt trēow **brǣt h i t**; bewḗnde **h i n e**; **h i n e** gemḗngde; ēow fȳsan.

185. Relative pronouns. — For these see **87.**

Verbs.

186. Forms of the verb. — Old English verbs are either transitive or intransitive. They have two voices, — active and passive; three moods, — indicative, optative, and imperative — besides the infinitive, gerund, and participles; and five tenses, — present, preterit, perfect, pluperfect, and future. The uses of these forms correspond, in general, to those of the same forms in other languages.

187. Voices. — The forms of the active voice are given in **95**; those of the passive are formed by adding the past participle to the appropriate tense of **wesan (bēon)**, *be,* or **weorᶞan,** *become.*

188. Tenses. — Only two independent tenses are distinguished by their stems, — the present and the preterit. The present may also be used for the future; the preterit, for any of the three past tenses. Otherwise the distinctions of tense are indicated by means of auxiliaries, as in Modern English: the future being formed by the infinitive with **sculan,** *shall* (**133**), and willan, *will* (139); the perfect and pluperfect, by the past participles with the appropriate tenses of **hab-ban**, *have* (121), in the case of transitive verbs, and of **wesan**, *be* (138), in the case of intransitives.

189. **Agreement.** — A finite verb agrees with its subject in number and person. Exceptions are : —

1. When the subject consists of two nouns denoting essentially the same thing, united by a conjunction, the verb in agreement may be in the singular: **sīe sibb and geðwærnes betweoh ūs.**

2. A collective noun may take a verb in the plural: **sēo cnēoris wāgon and læddon.**

3. A plural verb, with a predicate in the plural, may be introduced by a neuter singular: **ðæt wæron ẹngla gāstas; hit ðonne wæron mīne wæteru.**

NOTE. — The subject is sometimes to be supplied (cf. 190): **hēt ðæt lēoht Dæg.**

190. **Impersonals.** — Impersonal verbs are those whose subject is an implied **hit**, *it*. They are often transitive, taking an object in the dative or accusative (**164. k, l; 171**). Examples: **mē ðyncð; mē hyngrede; swā gesælde īu; hū hyre æt beaduwe gespēow.** Sometimes they take two cases: **þegnas gelyste gārgewinnes (159. b).**

191. **Indicative.** — The indicative has the functions common to it in most languages.

192. Optative in general. — The optative, sometimes called the subjunctive, is used to express an action or state simply as conceived by the mind. It is employed either in independent sentences or in subordinate clauses. Of these subordinate clauses there are two principal kinds, — substantive or noun clauses, and adverbial clauses. Of these, the noun clauses, generally introduced by ðæt, are the more important. Whenever the conjunction ðæt can be translated *in order that* or *so that*, it introduces an adverbial clause; otherwise, a noun clause. Other adverbial clauses are those of *place, time,* and *manner.* Less frequent are *adjective clauses*, introduced by or implying a *relative pronoun.*

193. Optative in independent clauses. — Under this head falls the use of the optative (*a*) to express a command or an emphatic wish; (*b*) in doubtful questions implying a negative answer; and (*c*) in hypothetical sentences.

a) Command: **bēo nū lēoht; ādl ðē fornime; gān wē sēcean.**

b) Question: **hwæt ðonne mē fręmede gedeorf mīn?**

c) Hypothesis: **sīe ðæt ðū sīe.**

194. Optative in noun clauses. — The noun clause takes the place either of the subject (or predicate nominative) or of the object of a principal clause.

The object clause is commonest after verbs of knowledge, affirmation, command, and desire, such as *know, say, order, wish*, etc.

a) Subject clause : līcaꝺ ꝺē ꝺæt Apollonius ꝺus heonan fare; wēn is ꝺæt ꝺū gemēte sumne.

b) Object clause : gewite hwæt se geonga mann sīe; ne meahte findan hwilc hiera forliden wǣre; ic ꝺē bebēode ꝺæt ꝺū ꝺæt nǣnigum menn cȳꝺe; ic wȳsce ꝺæt ic eft forlidennesse gefare.

NOTE. — Certainty is rendered by the indicative : ic oncnāwe ꝺæt ꝺū eart wel gelǣred.

195. Optative by attraction. — This is a name given to the optative found in clauses following another optative. Examples : sprytte (193. *a)* sēo corꝺe trēow, ꝺæs sǣd sīe on him selfum; wēn is ꝺæt ꝺū gemēte (194. *a)* sumne ꝺæt ꝺē gemiltsie; ꝺæs-ꝺe ꝺū geare forwite (196. *f*) hwǣm ꝺū gemiltsie; ꝺæt sum gestrēon ic mē begiete (196. *f*), ꝺanan ic mē āfēde.

196. Optative in adverbial clauses. — These are clauses of place (*where*), of time (*before, until, when, while*), of manner (*as if*), conditional (*if*), concessive (*though*), final (*in order that*), and consecutive (*so that*). Hypothetical or indefinite character in some measure attaches to the optative in each.

a) Place: ðæt ðū wer gecēose ðǣr ðū self wille.

b) Time: ǣr se dæg cume; bīd ōð-ðæt hē cume.

c) Manner: swilce hē cuma wǣre.

d) Conditional: gif ðū ne finde nænne, wend ðonne hider ongēan; swā hit ðē ne mislīcie. But sometimes indicative: gif ðū mē gelīefst.

e) Concessive: ðēah ðū stille sīe.

f) Final: and gesette hīe on ðǣre heofonan, ðæt hīe scinen ofer eorðan. So with ðæs-ðe: ðæs-ðe ðū geare forwite. Negative: ðȳ-lǣs-ðe ðē twēonie.

g) Consecutive: ādl ðē fornime, ðæt ðū ne bēo hāl.

197. Optative in adjective clauses. — Whenever a sentence introduced by an actual or virtual relative implies an element of doubt, it may take the optative. Examples: gecēose ænne, hwilcne ðū wille (hwilcne is a virtual relative); swā-hwæt-swā ðū wille.

198. Imperative. — The imperative is used in commands, sometimes with the second personal pronoun, sometimes without. Examples: bēo blīðe mid ūs; wite ðū; gē efthwerfað tō ciricean

199. Infinitive. — The infinitive is construed as a neuter noun, the subject or object of a finite verb.

When the object, it may itself have a subject noun
or pronoun in the accusative (**169**).

a) Subject (or pred. nom., **150**): **micel hienð and
sceamu hit is nellan.**

b) Object: **nellan wesan; hēt hyre ðīnenne
hēafod onwrīðan.**

1. An object infinitive is sometimes used for purposes of specification. With verbs of motion this
may often be translated by the present participle,
occasionally by the infinitive of purpose (= *in order
to*). Examples: **cōmon līðan; gewāt him gangan;
fēran gāsta strēonan** (purpose).

200. Gerund. — The gerund may usually be translated by the Mod. Eng. infinitive, in a variety of
senses. Examples: **cōmon mīnre dohtor tō biddanne; land swīðe feorr tō gesēceanne; ðā
ēstas him beforan lęgde ðe hē him tō bēodanne
hæfde.**

Prepositions.

201. Cases governed. — For the cases governed by
prepositions, see **158, 166, 172, 175**.

1. The preposition sometimes follows its object, or
immediately precedes the verb, and at times is difficult to distinguish from an adverb, or a prefix of the
verb. Examples: **ðe (87.** *c*) **ðū æfter āxodest; ðe
ðū swā wel wið gedēst.**

Conjunctions.

202. Correlatives. — Some of the more common correlatives are the following : —

a)	ge . . . . ge,		*both* . . . . . *and.*
b)	ꝺe . . . . ꝺe,		*whether* . . . *or.*
c)	nē . . . . nē,		*neither.* . . . *nor.*
d)	ꝺā-ꝺā . . . . . ꝺā			
	ꝺā . . . . ꝺā	},	*when* . . . . . *(then).*
	ꝺonne . . . . ꝺonne			
e)	ꝺēah . . . . . ꝺēah,		*though* . . . . *(yet).*
f)	swā-swā . . . swā,		*so* . . . . . . *as.*
g)	swā . . . . . . swā,		*the* . . . . . . *the.*

PROSODY.

—◆◇◆—

203. Old English verse stichic. — Old English verse is
rarely strophic, but almost without exception stichic;
that is, consists of ungrouped lines, following each
other as in Modern English blank verse.

204. The line and the hemistich. — The line of poetry
consists of two hemistichs, separated ‚by the cæsura.
Example : —

> **bord and brād swyrd,   brūne helmas.**

The hemistich may be either normal or expanded.
A normal hemistich contains two metrical feet. Example : —

> **cēne under cumblum.**

An expanded hemistich contains three metrical feet.
Example : —

> **swiŏmōd sinces āhte.**

205. The foot. — A metrical foot is a portion of a
line containing one primary stress. The syllable receiving the primary stress may or may not be followed or preceded by one or more lighter or slurred
syllables.

Of the lighter syllables following or preceding a primary stress, one may, under certain circumstances, receive a secondary stress (**23**). A syllable which receives neither primary nor secondary stress is called unstressed.

206. Stressed and unstressed syllables. — The primary stress nearly always falls upon a long syllable; this long syllable may, however, be represented by two syllables, of which the first is short, and the second so light as to admit of syncopation. The substitution of two such short syllables for a single long one is called resolution.

A long syllable is one which contains a long vowel or diphthong, or a short vowel followed by two consonants. A short syllable is one which contains a short vowel followed by a single consonant (**4**). Long and short syllables, when stressed, are represented in metrical schemes by the macron, —, and the breve, ◡, respectively. Stressed syllables are indicated by the acute or grave accent, according as the stress is primary or secondary. Unstressed syllables, whether short or long, are represented by the oblique cross, ✕.

The syllable which receives the primary stress is usually the root syllable of a word, while the lighter or slurred syllables comprise the terminations, enclitics, and proclitics; occasionally, however, the second element of a compound word is reckoned as a slurred syllable, though usually it takes a secondary stress.

207. Classification of feet. — The terms *iambic, trochaic,* etc., are used analogically, with reference to stress, and not, as in Greek and Latin prosody, with primary reference to quantity. This being understood, Old English metrical feet may be classified as follows: —

1. Monosyllabic: The monosyllabic foot regularly consists of a long syllable under the primary stress, $\angle$. This foot is never found except in conjunction with one of the dactylic type having a secondary stress (1. *h* to 1. *k*, **216**).

2. Disyllabic: The disyllabic foot may be either trochaic, $\angle \times$, or iambic, $\times \angle$. In the trochaic foot, the unstressed syllable may be replaced by a long syllable under the secondary stress. The dactyl formed by the resolution of the trochee may be called the light dactyl, to distinguish it from the heavy or normal dactyl, in which the first syllable is long.

3. Trisyllabic: The trisyllabic foot is either dactylic, $\angle \times \times$, or anapæstic, $\times \times \angle$. If dactylic, either the second or third syllable has in some cases secondary stress.

4. Polysyllabic: If tetrasyllabic, this foot resembles either a first pæon, $\angle \times \times \times$, or a fourth pæon, $\times \times \times \angle$. If it contains a greater number of syllables, it is still essentially dactylic or anapæstic in effect, $\angle \times \times \times ...$, or $... \times \times \times \angle$.

In any of the foregoing feet, resolution may take place, thus apparently increasing the number of typical syllables.

208. Anacrusis. — Before hemistichs beginning with a primary stress, one or more unstressed syllables may occur. These unstressed syllables constitute what is known as the anacrusis. It is rare at the beginning of the second hemistich, but more frequent before the first.

209. Expanded hemistichs. — These are formed by prefixing a foot of the form $\angle \times ...$ (less frequently $\angle$, and rarely in the first hemistich $\times \angle$) to a regular hemistich of two stresses. Expanded lines are employed in passages of peculiar elevation and solemnity, or expressive of unwonted agitation. The expanded hemistich has three stresses, instead of the normal two, since the prefixed portion differs from the anacrusis in having a primary stress. As a rule, the first and second stresses of the first hemistich, when expanded, take alliteration, while in the second hemistich the place of the alliterative syllable is unchanged, coinciding normally with the (new) second stress. Example: —

bēaga and beorhtra māðma,   hī þæt þǣre beorhtan ídese.

210. Alliteration. — Alliteration is a poetical ornament which is a distinctive feature of Old English verse. It consists in the employment of the same or similar sounds at the beginning of two or more syllables which receive the primary stress. The second hemistich contains one such alliterative syllable, as a rule that which

has the first primary stress; the first hemistich has regularly two, though frequently only one. The alliterative sound must be the same throughout, if consonantal;
if vocalic, it is usually different in the three syllables.
Examples are : —

   a)   *g*rame *g*ūðfrecan,   *g*āras sẹndon.

   b)   on ðæt *d*ægred sylf,   *d*ynedan scildas.

   c)   *ea*rn *ǣ*tes georn,   *ū*rigfeðera.

In expanded lines, the additional foot frequently
takes alliteration, thus removing it from one of its
normal positions.

211. Alliteration in relation to stress. — The accentual
principles observed by Old English poets in their man-
agement of alliteration virtually reduce themselves to
one : that the most important syllables of the most important words should receive primary stress. It must
be borne in mind, however, that the stress is sometimes
rhetorical, that is, depends not so much upon the intrinsic weight of the word as upon that which belongs to
it in virtue of its relation to other words in the same
sentence. For example, a preposition might be expected to have less intrinsic weight than a following
noun, yet instances occur where the preposition allit-
erates.

One general rule is that if a noun and a verb are
found in the same hemistich, it is the noun that allite-
rates.

212. Difference between the two hemistichs. — The first hemistich frequently differs from the second, not only in the number of its alliterative syllables, but also in that of the unstressed syllables admitted between two primary stresses, or in the form of anacrusis.

213. Rime. — Rime and various forms of assonance are occasionally employed by Old English poets, sometimes for the purpose of uniting more closely the two halves of the same line, less frequently to associate the second half of a line with the first or second half of the following line, rarely in formulas or compounds within the same hemistich.

214. Masculine and feminine rime. — Masculine or monosyllabic rime is perfect when the riming vowels are identical, and are followed by the same consonants or consonant combinations. Example (from *Bēowulf*): —

> ēode yrremōd: him of ēagum stōd.

Feminine or polysyllabic (usually disyllabic) rime is perfect when the first riming syllables are perfect masculine rimes and the following syllables are identical. Example: —

> scildburh scǣron,   scēotend wǣron.

There are also various sorts of imperfect rime.

215. Kennings. — A characteristic ornament of Old English, as well as of early Teutonic poetry in general, are the kennings. This term, which is of Norse origin, designates those synonyms or periphrastic phrases which are employed to diversify the expression of a thought, or to avoid the repetition of the same word, usually a noun. Many of these are striking metaphors, but by no means all; some, though metaphorical in their origin, were undoubtedly so familiar to the poet and audience that their peculiar significance was overlooked, and they were regarded as stereotyped and convenient synonyms. Examples of kennings for God are: **ārfæst Cyning, mihtig Dryhten, Metod, Frēa ælmihtig.**

216. Ordinary sequences of long and short syllables.[1] — Before proceeding to examine the metrical constitution of the hemistich, it is desirable to consider the ordinary sequences of long and short syllables in Old English, and particularly in Old English poetry.

1. Long syllables followed by short or slurred syllables. A long stressed syllable may be followed: —

a) by a derivative or inflectional syllable: **scūras**   ∠×

b) by a monosyllabic proclitic: **eft tō**   ∠×

c) by a monosyllabic prefix: **mōd ā(réted)**   ∠×

d) by a derivative or inflectional syllable + a monosyllabic prefix or proclitic: **cēnra tō**   ∠××

e) by a disyllabic proclitic or prefix: **fȳnd ofer(wunnen)**   ∠××

---

[1] This section is designed only for reference.

f) by a monosyllabic proclitic + a monosyllabic prefix: for𝖽 on ge(rihte) ∠××

g) by two monosyllabic words: him 𝖽ā se ∠××

h) by two syllables, derivative or inflectional: mōdigre ∠˯×

i) by the second element of a compound word, with
or without a derivative syllable interposed: —

    (*a*) scīrmǣled ∠˯×

    (*β*) hildeleō𝖽 ∠×˯

j) by a disyllabic word, with the stress upon its second
syllable: nēar ætstōp (*Bēow.*) ∠×˯

k) by a derivative or inflectional syllable + a monosyllabic word: ēa𝖽e mæg ∠×˯

2. Long syllables preceded by short or slurred syllables. A long stressed syllable may be preceded: —

a) by a monosyllabic prefix: gefēoll ×∠

b) by a monosyllabic proclitic: 𝖽urh mīn(e) ×∠

c) by a derivative or inflectional syllable: (frym)𝖽a
God ×∠

d) by a derivative or inflectional ending + a monosyllabic prefix or proclitic: (hlanc)a gefeah ××∠

e) by a disyllabic ending: (lār)ena gōd (*Bēow.*)
××∠

f) by a disyllabic proclitic: sy𝖽𝖽an frym𝖽(e) ××∠

g) by two monosyllabic words: 𝖽ā 𝖽e hwīl(e) ××∠

3. Long syllables followed by long or stressed syllables. In addition to the cases instanced under 1. *h* and
i, which belong under the head of secondary stress,

stressed syllables proper are here to be considered. A long syllable may be followed: —

a) by a monosyllabic word: **brād swyrd**   ∠∠(∠‿)

b) when a monosyllable, by the first syllable of a disyllabic word: **dōm āg(on)**   ∠∠(∠‿)

c) when a monosyllable, by the first syllable of a trisyllabic word: **sang hild(eleoð)**   ∠∠(∠‿)

d) when the second syllable of a disyllabic word, by the first syllable of a disyllabic word: **(ge)gān hæfd(on)**

∠∠(∠‿)

e) when the first syllable of a polysyllabic word (often a compound), by the second syllable of the same word: **niðheard, burhlēod(um)**   ∠∠(∠‿)

4. Short stressed syllables followed by short or slurred syllables. A short, stressed syllable may be followed: —

a) by a single unstressed syllable, forming with it two metrical syllables: **cyning**   ⌣×

b) by an unstressed syllable, forming with it the metrical equivalent of a single long syllable, and capable of being substituted for the latter in every position: **æðe(le)**

⌣×(=∠)

Compounds are metrically regarded, for the most part, as composed of two independent words, but their length, taken in connection with the invariability of their typical forms, restricts the employment of certain compounds to particular metrical schemes. Thus, compounds like **hildenædran** are adapted to hemistichs of the trochaic type, $\angle\times\mid\angle\times$; those like **burhlēodum** to the type $\angle\mid\angle\overset{\times}{}\times$.

217. Constitution of the hemistich. — There are five normal types of the hemistich, which may be called respectively (cf. **207**) the 1) trochaic (dactylic), 2) the iambic (anapæstic), 3) the iambic-trochaic, 4) the monosyllabic-bacchic (or -cretic), and the 5) bacchic-monosyllabic. Types 4 and 5 occasionally become trochaic-bacchic and bacchic-trochaic respectively.

Every hemistich ends either in a stressed syllable, or in a stressed syllable followed by a single short syllable (exceptionally by two short syllables, as in **216. 4.** *b*).

Occasionally a greater number of unstressed syllables than three occur together, but without destroying the character of the verse as belonging to one of the foregoing types.

218. Constitution of the various types. — 1. The first or trochaic (dactylic) type is formed by the union of two feet like those found in 1. *a* to 1. *g* above.   Thus: —

biddan wylle	$\angle\times\mid\angle\times$
cwicera cynna	$\angle\overset{\times}{}\times\mid\angle\times$
ealde ge geonge	$\angle\times\times\mid\angle\times$

With anacrusis (**208**): —

oððe sundoryrfes	$\times\times\mid\angle\times\mid\angle\times$

Occasionally, by the introduction of two consecutive long syllables, as in 3. *e*, there occur hemistichs of these forms: —

| scildburh scǣron | ∠ ⟍ | ∠ × |
| helmas and hupseax | ∠ × × | ∠ ⟍ |

A short stressed syllable is rare : —

| ārfæst cyning | ∠ × | ᴗ × |

2. The second or iambic (anapæstic) type is formed by the union of two feet like those found in 2. *a* to 2. *g* above. Thus : —

se hȳhsta dǣl	× ∠	× ∠
beraꝺ linde forꝺ	× × ∠	× ∠
nū ic gumena gehwæne	× × ᴗ ×	× × × ᴗ ×

With extra unstressed syllables in the *first* foot (**207.** 4) : —

| þæt hē in þæt būrgeteld | × × × × ∠ | × ∠ |

3. The third or iambic-trochaic type is formed by the union of two feet like those found in 1. *a* to 1. *g* and 2. *a* to 2. *g* respectively. Thus : —

and compwīge	× ∠	∠ ×
and gē dōm āgon	× × ∠	∠ ×
on ꝺām sigewonge	× × ᴗ ×	∠ ×

Rarely a short stressed syllable : —

| of hornbogan | × ∠ | ᴗ × |
| æt ꝺām æscplegan | × × ∠ | ᴗ × |

With extra unstressed syllables in the *first* foot : —

| þe hīe ofercuman mihton | × × × × ᴗ × | ∠ × |

It will be observed that where two long syllables meet in the middle of the hemistich there is such a sequence as in 3. *a* to 3. *e*.

4. The fourth or monosyllabic-bacchic type is formed by the union of a monosyllabic foot with such as are found in 1. *h* and 1. *i* (*a*). Thus: —

<blockquote>
mægð mōdigre $\angle \mid \angle \,\underline{\,\,}\times$
hæleð higerōfe $\smile\times\mid\smile\times\,\underline{\,\,}\times$
</blockquote>

Similarly, the monosyllabic-cretic takes groups like 1. *i* (*β*), 1. *j*, and 1. *k* for the second foot: —

<blockquote>
sang hildelēoð $\angle \mid \angle \times \,\underline{\,\,}$
</blockquote>

An example of the trochaic-bacchic type (found only in first hemistichs) is: —

<blockquote>
stōpon styrnmōde $\angle \times \mid \angle \,\underline{\,\,}\times$
</blockquote>

Where two long syllables belonging to different feet come together in the pure type, we have various cases under 3, the one above being under *c*.

5. The fifth or bacchic-monosyllabic type is formed by the union of such feet as are found in 1. *h* and 1. *i* (*a*) with a monosyllabic foot. Thus: —

<blockquote>
scīrmæled swyrd $\angle \,\underline{\,\,}\times\mid\angle$
sigerōfe hæleð $\smile\times\,\underline{\,\,}\times\mid\smile\times$
</blockquote>

219. Frequency of the various types. — The relative frequency of the various types is indicated by their order in the last paragraph, though Types 2 and 3 are not far from equal. Thus, in the poem of *Judith*, the percentages are, in round numbers, as follows, not counting expanded lines, which mostly belong to Type 1 (209): —

	FIRST HEMISTICH.	SECOND HEMISTICH.
TYPE 1	47	47
TYPE 2	14	26
TYPE 3	19	19
TYPE 4	15	5
TYPE 5	5	3

220. A specimen of scansion. — The following passage (*Judith* 164–175), accompanied by the scheme of its scansion, will serve to illustrate the metrical principles contained in the foregoing paragraphs: —

```
ðreatum and ðrymmum      þrungon and urnon
ongēan ðā þeodnes mægð   þūsendmǣlum,
ealde ge geonge ;        ǣghwylcum wearð
męn on ðǣre.medobyrig    mōd ārēted,
syððan hīe ongēaton      þæt wæs Iūdith cumen
ęft tō ēðle,      and ðā ofostlīce
hīe mid ēaðmēdum      in forlēton.
þā sēo glēawe hēt,      golde gefrætewod,
hyre ðīnenne      þancolmōde
þæs hęrewǣðan      hēafod onwrīðan,
and hyt tō bēhðe      blōdig ætȳwan
þām burhlēodum,      hū hyre æt beaduwe gespēow.
```

	First Hemistich		Second Hemistich	
1.	∠××∣∠×	‖	∠××∣∠×	1.
2.	×××∠∣×∠	‖	∠×∣∠×	1.
1.	∠××∣∠×	‖	∠⌣×∣∠	5.
1.	∠×××∣⌣⌣×⌣×	‖	∠×∣∠×	1.
1.	∠×××∣∠×	‖	××∠∣×⌣⌣×	2.
1.	∠×∣∠×	‖	××⌣⌣×∣∠×	3.
3.	××∠∣∠×	‖	∠×∣∠×	1.
2.	××∠∣×∠	‖	∠××∣⌣⌣×	1.
3.	××∠∣∠×	‖	∠×∣∠×	1.
3.	×⌣⌣×∣∠×	‖	∠××∣∠×	1.
1.	∠××∣∠×	‖	∠××∣∠×	1.
3.	×∠∣∠×	‖	××××⌣⌣×∣×∠	2.

I.

THE CREATION OF THE WORLD.

(Ælfric's Translation of Genesis, I.-II. 3.)

[In the earlier pages, references will be made to the forms of words as they occur in the Vocabulary, whenever there might be difficulty in discovering the latter. Other references are self-explanatory.

The student should by all means be familiar, before beginning this first selection, with the declension of the third personal pronoun (81), the demonstrative se (84), the first seven ordinals (78), the conjugation of **wesan** (138) and **weorðan** (95, 104), the prepositions æfter, bufan, fram, ofer, on, tō, and under, the particle ðe (87. *d*), and the distinction between the two ðā's (84. 1) and the two ðæt's.]

On anginne gesceop [1] God [2] heofonan [3] and eorðan. Sēo [4] eorðe sōðlice [5] wæs [6] īdlu and æmtigu ; and ðīestru [7] wæron [8] ofer [8] ðære [4] nēowolnesse [9] brādnesse [10]; and Godes gāst wæs [6] gefēred [11] ofer wæteru. [12] God cwæð [13] ðā, "Geweorðe [14] lēoht "; and lēoht wearð [15] geworht. [16] God geseah [17] ðā ðæt hit [18] gōd

---

[1] See **gescieppan**, and **18**.

[2] The order is probably determined by the Latin: *creavit Deus*.

[3] **53**. 3.

[4] See **se**.

[5] Lat. *autem*.

[6] See **wesan**.

[7] Plural, like Lat. *tenebræ*.

[8] Governs **brādnesse**.

[9] Genitive, dependent on **brādnesse** (**153**. *i*).

[10] See **166**.

[11] **wæs gefēred** = Lat. *ferebatur*. See **geferian**.

[12] See **wæter**, and **47**. 1, 6.

[13] See **cweðan**.

[14] See **geweorðan**, and **193**. *a*.

[15] See **weorðan**.

[16] **Wearð geworht** = *facta est.* See **gewyrcean**.

[17] See **gesēon**

[18] See **hē**.

123

wæs[1]; and hē gedǣlde[2] ðæt[3] lēoht fram ðǣm[3] ðīestrum.[4]
And hēt[5] ðæt[3] lēoht Dæg, and ðā[3] ðīestru[4] Niht.   Ðā wæs[1]
geworden[6] ǣfen and morgen ān dæg.[7]

God cwæð[8] ðā ęft,[9] "Geweorðe[10] nū fæstnes tōmiddes
5 ðǣm[3] wæterum,[11] and tōtwǣme[12] ðā[3] wæteru[11] fram ðǣm
wæterum." And God geworhte ðā fæstnesse, and tōtwǣmde
ðā wæteru ðe[13] wǣron under ðǣre fæstnesse fram ðǣm ðe[13]
wǣron bufan ðǣre fæstnesse; hit wæs ðā swā gedōn.[14]   And
God hēt ðā fæstnesse Heofonan.[15]   And wæs ðā geworden
10 ǣfen and morgen ōðer[16] dæg.

God ðā sōðlice[17] cwæð, "Bēon[18] gegaderode[19] ðā wæteru
ðe[13] sind[1] under ðǣre heofonan, and ætēowie[20] drȳgnes[21]";
hit wæs ðā swā gedōn.   And God gecīegde[22] ðā drȳgnesse
Eorðan[23]; and ðǣra[3] wætera gegaderunga[24] hē hēt Sǣs[25];
15 God geseah ðā ðæt hit gōd[26] wæs.   And cwæð,[27] "Sprytte[28]
sēo eorðe grōwende[29] gærs,[30] and sǣd wyrcende,[31] and æppel-

---

[1] See **wesan**.   [2] See **gedǣlan**.
[3] See **se**.   [4] See p. 123, note 7.
[5] See **hātan**, and **189**, note.
[6] **Wæs geworden** = *factum est*.   See **geweorðan**.
[7] Lat. *dies unus*.
[8] See **cweðan**.
[9] Lat. *quoque*.
[10] See **geweorðan**, and **193**. *a*.
[11] See **wæter**, and **47**. 1, 6.
[12] See **tōtwǣman**.
[13] See **87**. *d*.
[14] Past part. of **gedōn**.
[15] See **173**.
[16] Lat. *secundus*.
[17] Lat. *vero*.
[18] See **193**. *a*.

[19] See **gegaderian**, and **62**.
[20] See **ætēowian**.
[21] Lat. *arida*, Gr. ξηρά.
[22] See **geciegan**.
[23] See **173**.
[24] Acc. plur.
[25] Acc. plur.; see **sǣ**.
[26] See **4**.
[27] Cf. Mod. Eng. *quoth*.
[28] See **spryttan**, and **193**. *a*.
Lat. *germinet*.
[29] See **grōwan**, and **61**.
[30] See **31**.
[31] See **wyrcean**, and **61**.   **Grōwende gærs and sǣd wyrcende** = *herbam virentem et facientem semen*.

bǣre[1] trēow, wǣstm[2] wyrcende æfter his cynne,[3] ðæs sǣd
sīe[4] on him[5] selfum[6] ofer eorðan"; hit wæs ðā swā gedōn.
And sēo eorðe forðātēah[7] grōwende wyrt and sǣd berende[8]
be hiere[9] cynne, and trēow wǣstm wyrcende, and gehwilc[10]
sǣd[11] hæbbende æfter his hīwe[12]; God geseah ðā ðæt hit   5
gōd wæs.   And wæs geworden ǣfen and mergen[13] se ðridda[14]
dæg.

God cwæð ðā sōðlice,[15] "Bēon nū lēoht on[16] ðǣre heofonan[17]
fæstnesse, and tōdǣlen[18] dæg and niht, and bēon tō[16] tāc-
num,[19] and tō tīdum,[20] and tō dagum,[21] and tō gēarum.[22]   And   10
hīe scīnen[23] on ðǣre heofonan fæstnesse, and ālīehten ðā
eorðan"; hit wæs ðā swā geworden.   And God geworhte
twā[24] miclu[25] lēoht; ðæt māre[26] lēoht tō ðæs dæges līehtinge,[27] and ðæt lǣsse lēoht tō ðǣre niht[28] līehtinge; and
steorran hē geworhte.   And gesette[29] hīe on ðǣre heofonan,   15

---

[1] Lat. *pomiferum*, Gr. κάρ-
πιμον.   See **146**.

[2] Acc. sing., after **wyrcende**.

[3] See **cynn**.

[4] See **195**.

[5] Dat. sing.

[6] See **self**.

[7] Lat. *protulit*.

[8] Agrees with **wyrt**.   See
beran.

[9] Why **hiere**, instead of **his**?

[10] Nom. sing.

[11] Acc. sing.

[12] Lat. *speciem*.   See **hiw**.

[13] Note the different form, —
mergen instead of **morgen**.

[14] See **78**.

[15] Lat. *autem*.

[16] See **166**.

[17] Gen. sing.

[18] See **tōdǣlan**.

[19] See **tācen**, and **24**.

[20] See **tīd**, and **24**.

[21] See **dæg**, and **24**.

[22] See **gēar**, and **24**.

[23] See **193**. *a*.   Write the opt.
pret. plur. of this verb.

[24] See **twēgen**.

[25] See **micel**.

[26] See **66**.

[27] What is the relation of the
stem-vowel to that of **lēoht**?

[28] For **niht**, instead of **nieht**,
see **19**.   See **153**. *d*.

[29] See **gesettan**, and **189**, note.

ðæt hīe scinen[1] ofer eorðan, and gīemden ðæs dæges[2] and
ðǣre niht, and tōdǣlden lēoht and ðīestru; God geseah ðā
ðæt hit gōd wæs.   And wæs geworden ǣfen and mergen se
fēorða[3] dæg.

5   God cwæð ēac swilce,[4] "Tēon nū ðā wæteru forð[5] swim-
mendu cynn cucu[6] on līfe,[7] and flēogendu[8] cynn ofer eorðan
under ðǣre heofonan fæstnesse."   And God gescēop ðā[9] ðā
miclan hwalas,[10] and eall libbendu fisccynn and styriend-
licu,[11] ðe[12] ðā[13] wæteru tugon[14] forð[15] on hiera hīwum, and
10 eall flēogendu cynn æfter hiera cynne; God geseah ðā ðæt
hit gōd wæs.   And blētsode[16] hīe, ðus cweðende,[17] "Weaxað,[18]
and bēoð gemanigfielde,[19] and gefyllað[20] ðǣre sǣ wæteru, and
ðā fuglas bēon[21] gemanigfielde ofer eorðan."   And ðā wæs
geworden ǣfen and mergen se fīfta dæg.

15 God cwæð ēac swilce, "Lǣde[22] sēo eorðe forð[23] cucu nīetenu[24] on hiera cynne, and crēopendu[25] cynn and dēor æfter
hiera hīwum"; hit wæs ðā swā geworden.   And God geworhte
ðǣre eorðan dēor æfter hiera hīwum, and ðā nīetenu and eall
crēopendu cynn on hiera cynne; God geseah ðā ðæt hit gōd

---

[1] Opt. pret. = Lat. *lucerent.*
What would be the opt. pres. ?

  [2] See **156.** *f.*

  [3] See **78.**

  [4] **Ēac swilce** = *etiam.*

  [5] *Producant* = **tēon . . . forð.**

  [6] See **cucu.**

  [7] See **līf.**

  [8] See **flēogan**, and **61.**

  [9] Adverb; see **84. 1.**

  [10] See **hwæl.**

  [11] Lat. *motabilem.*

  [12] Acc.

[13] Nom. plur.

[14] See **tēon.**

[15] **Tugon forð** = *produxerunt.*

[16] See **blētsian**, and **33.**

[17] See **cweðan.**

[18] See **weaxan**, and **24.**

[19] Past part. in nom. plur.

[20] See **gefyllan.**

[21] See **193.** *a.*

[22] See **lǣdan.**

[23] **Lǣde . . . forð** = *producat.*

[24] See **nīeten.**

[25] See **crēopan.**

wæs. And cwæð, "Uton[1] wyrcean mann tō andlīcnesse and tō ūrre[2] gelīcnesse, and hē sīe[3] ofer ðā fiscas,[4] and ofer ðā fuglas, and ofer ðā dēor, and ofer ealle gesceafta,[5] and ofer eall ðā crēopendan ðe styriað[6] ofer eorðan." God gescēop ðā mann tō his andlīcnesse, tō Godes andlīcnesse hē gescēop hine; werhādes[7] and wīfhādes hē gescēop hīe.

And God hīe blētsode, and cwæð, "Weaxað, and bēoð gemanigfielde, and gefyllað ðā eorðan and gewieldað[8] hīe, and habbað[9] on ēowrum[10] gewealde ðǣre sǣ fiscas, and ðǣre lyfte fuglas, and eall nīetenu ðe styriað ofer eorðan." God cwæð ðā, "Efne ic forgeaf[11] ēow[12] eall gærs and wyrta sǣd[13] berenda ofer eorðan, and eall trēowu, ðā-ðe[13a] habbað sǣd on him selfum hiera āgnes cynnes, ðæt hīe bēon ēow[14] tō mǫte; and eallum nīetenum and eallum fugolcynne and eallum ðǣm ðe styriað on eorðan, on ðǣm-ðe[15] is libbende[16] līf,[17] ðæt hīe hæbben him tō[18] gereordianne"; hit wæs ðā swā gedōn. And God geseah eall ðā ðing[19] ðe hē geworhte, and hīe wǣron swīðe gōd. Wæs[20] ðā geworden ǣfen and mǫrgen se siexta dæg.

---

[1] = Let us.
[2] See 83. Ūrre properly belongs to both nouns; Lat. ad imaginem et similitudinem nostram.
[3] See wesan.
[4] See fisc.
[5] See gesceaft.
[6] See styrian.
[7] See 153. f.
[8] What is the relation of the stem diphthong to that of geweald?
[9] See habban.
[10] See 83.
[11] See forgiefan.
[12] See ðū, and 164. a.
[13] See 24.   [13a] See 87. b.
[14] See 161. 2. Auth. Vers.: 'to you it shall be for meat.'
[15] = whom.
[16] See libban.
[17] Libbende līf = anima viva.
[18] See gereordian, and 200.
[19] Acc. plur. Why like the singular?
[20] See 189. 1.

Eornostlice[1] ðā wǣron fullfrẹmede[2] heofonas and eorðe and eall hiera frætwung.[3]   And God ðā gefylde[4] on ðone seofoðan dæg[5] his weorc[6] ðe hē geworhte, and hē gerẹste[7] hine[8] on ðone seofoðan dæg fram eallum ðǣm weorce ðe hē

5 gefrẹmede.   And God geblētsode ðone seofoðan dæg and hine gehālgode,[9] for-ðon-ðe hē on ðone dæg geswāc[10] his weorces[11] ðe hē gescēop[12] tō wyrceanne.[13]

[1] Lat. *igitur.*

[2] See **fullfrẹmman.** Lat. *perfecti.*

[3] Lat.   *ornatus,* Gr. κόσμος ; *array,* or *splendid array,* would perhaps express the original sense.

[4] Lat. *complevit.*

[5] Acc. where we should expect dat.; Lat. *die septimo.* See **172.** 1.

[6] Sing., as the Latin shows.

[7] See **gerẹstan.** Why but one **t** in the preterit ?

[8] See **184.** *b.*

[9] See **gehālgian.** From **hālig** ; for loss of **i** see **23.** The root is **hāl** ; after umlaut of the stem vowel, what would this syllable become, and in what words is it found ?

[10] See **geswīcan.**

[11] **His weorces** = *ab omni opere suo.* See **156.** *k.*

[12] **gescēop tō wyrceanne** = *creavit ut faceret ;* Marg. of Auth. Vers., 'created to make.' See **200.**

[13] **Wyrc-** not umlaut of **weorc-**. The relation here is an ablaut one (**22**) : **werc** and **wurc** (**worc**); cf. Gr. ἔργον and ὄργανον.

II.

TRADES AND OCCUPATIONS.

(From Ælfric's Colloquy, probably prepared, like his Grammar, for the instruction of English youths in Latin. There are two MSS. — one in the British Museum, the other at Oxford. The Oxford MS. has the rubric: *Hanc sententiam Latini sermonis olim Alfricus abbas composuit, qui meus fuit magister, sed tamen ego, Ælfric Bata, multas postea huic addidi appendices.* This is virtually Ælfric Bata's sole title to fame. The Old English, like the Latin, is probably of the late tenth century.)

The Merchant and his Merchandise.

Teacher. Hwæt sægst[1] ðū, mangere[2]?

Merchant. Ic sęcge ðæt behēfe[3] ic eom ge[4] cyninge[5] and ·aldormannum,[6] and weligum, and eallum folce.

[1] See **123**.

[2] Lat. *mercator.* Other Old English terms for *merchant* are **cīepa** and **cīepmann**. From a collateral form of the latter, **cēapmann**, without umlaut, is derived Mod. Eng. *chapman.* How is *chap-* related to *cheap?* See the *New English Dictionary (New Eng. t.)* under these words.

[3] Lat. *utilis.* Cf. the Mod. Eng. noun *behoof.*

[4] **ge . . . and** = Lat. *et . . . et.*

[5] Carlyle (*Sartor Resartus*, Bk. 3, Chap. 7) has the following:

"*König* (King), anciently *Kön-ning*, means Ken-ning (Cunning), or which is the same thing, Can-ning. Ever must the Sovereign of Mankind be fitly entitled King." On the other hand Gummere (*Germanic Origins,* p. 270): "At the head of the family we found, of course, the father; and at the head of the state we naturally look for the king. The word 'king' means the child or son of the tribe, its representative or even creation; man of race, man of rank. Gradually the king ceases to be re-

[6] Lat. *ducibus.*

Teacher. And hū?

Merchant. Ic āstīge mīn scip mid hlæstum[1] mīnum, and rōwe[2] ofer sælice[3] dǣlas,[4] and cīepe[5] mīn ðing, and bycge ðing[6] dēorwierðu,[6] ðā on ðisum lande ne bēoð ācęnnede, and ic hit tōgelǣde[7] ēow hider mid miclum plihte[8] ofer sǣ, and hwīlum forlidennesse ic ðolie mid lyre ealra ðinga mīnra, unēaðe[9] cwic[9] ætberstende.[9]

Teacher. Hwilc ðing gelǣtst ðū ūs?

Merchant. Pællas[10] and sīdan,[11] dēorwierðe gimmas and gold, seldcūð[12] rēaf[13] and wyrtgemang,[14] wīn and ęle, elpes[15] bān[15] and mæsling,[16] ǣr[17] and tin, swefel and glæs, and ðyllices[18] fela.

---

garded as a creation of his race; his ancestry is pushed back to the gods, and his right is quite above all sanctions of popular choice or approval." Which of these views is confirmed by etymology?

[1] Lat. *mercibus.*

[2] Lat. *navigo.*

[3] Lat. *marinas.*

[4] Lat. *partes.*

[5] Lat. *vendo.*

[6] Lat. *res pretiosas.*

[7] Lat. *adduco.*

[8] Lat. *periculo.* Mod. Eng. form of **pliht**?

[9] Lat. *vix vivus evadens.* Note the love for alliteration, even in the Latin.

[10] Lat. *purpurum.* Cf. Spenser (*F. Q.* 2. 9. 37): "In a long *purple pall.*"

[11] Lat. *sericum.* From this Latin word (indicating what country?) comes OE. **seol(o)c.** What Mod. Eng. word from the latter (or the equivalent Old Norse (ON.) *silki*)? Cf. Skeat's *Principles of English Etymology* (I.), p. 440 (Skeat, *Prin.*). Other words in which Eng. *l* = Lat. *r* (through OE.) are *plum* = Lat. *prunus; purple* = Lat. *purpura; turtle* = Lat. *turtur.*

[12] Lat. *varias,* but this looks like a mistake. *Varius* usually = **mis(sen)lic** or **manigfeald.**

[13] Lat. *vestes.*

[14] Lat. *pigmenta.* Translate, *spice.*

[15] Lat. *ebur.*

[16] Lat. *aurichalcum.*

[17] Lat. *aes.*

[18] See **154.** *a.*

Teacher. Wilt[1] ðū sęllan ðing ðīn hēr eall[2] swā[2] ðū hīe gebohtest ðēr?

Merchant. Ic nelle. Hwæt ðonne mē fręmede[3] gedeorf[4] mīn? Ac ic wille hīe cīepan hēr luflicor[5] ðonne ic gebycge ðēr, ðæt[6] sum gestrēon[7] mē[8] ic begiete,[9] ðanan ic mē āfēde,[10] 5 and mīn wīf, and mīnne sunu.

The Choice of Occupations.

Teacher. Hwæt sægst ðū, wīsa? Hwilc cræft[11] ðē is[12] geðūht[13] betweox ðās furðra[14] wesan?

Counsellor. Ic sęcge ðē, mē is[15] geðūht[15] Godes ðēowdōm[16] betweoh ðās cræftas ealdorscipe[17] healdan, swā-swā hit is[12] 10 gerǣd on godspelle, "Fyrmest sēceað rīce Godes, and riht-wīsnesse[18] his, and ðās ðing eall bēoð tōgeīecte[19] ēow."

Teacher. And hwilc ðē is[12] geðūht betweox woruldcræftas[20] healdan ealdordōm?[17]

Counsellor. Eorðtilð,[21] for-ðām se ierðling[22] ūs ealle fēt.[23] 15

---

[1] See **139**.

[2] = *just as.*

[3] See **193**. *b.*

[4] Lat. *labor.*

[5] Lat. *carius.* Possibly mis-written for **lēoflicor**. A literal translation, not regarding the sense; **dēorra** or **dīerra,** from **dēore** or **dīere,** *dear,* would be more normal.

[6] See **84**. 1.

[7] Lat. *lucrum.* Acc. sing.

[8] See **161**. 1.

[9] Lat. *adquiram.* See **196**. *f.*

[10] See **195**.

[11] Lat. *ars.*

[12] Conjectural; not in the MSS.

[13] See **ðyncean.**

[14] Lat. *prior.* Nom. sing.

[15] Lat. *videtur.*

[16] See **143** and **149**.

[17] Lat. *primatum.*

[18] See **144**.

[19] Lat. *adjicientur.* See **tōge-īecan,** and **62**.

[20] Lat. *artes seculares.* MS. **cræftas woruld.**

[21] Lat. *agricultura.* See **147**.

[22] Lat. *arator.*

[23] See **fēdan.**

Se smið sœgð :

Hwanan ðæm ierðlinge sulhscear[1] oððe culter,[2] ðe nā gāde[3] hæfð būtan of cræfte mīnum ?   Hwanan fiscere[4] angel, oððe scēowyrhtan æl, oððe sēamere nædl ?   Nis hit of mīnum

5 geweorce ?

Se geðeahtend[5] andswarað :

Sōð, witodlice, sægst ðū[6]; ac eallum ūs lēofre is wīcian[7] mid ðæm ierðlinge ðonne mid ðē, for-ðām se ierðling sęleð ūs hlāf[8] and dręnc.   Ðū, hwæt sęlest ðū[6] ūs on smiððan

10 ðīnre būtan īserne[9] fȳrspearcan,[9] and swēginga[10] bēatendra[11] slęcgea[12] and blāwendra bęlga?

Se trēowwyrhta[13] sœgð :

Hwilc ēower[14] ne notað[15] cræfte[16] mīnum — ðonne hūs,[17] and mislicu fatu, and scipu ēow[18] eallum ic wyrce[19] ?

15 *Se smið[20] andwyrt:*

Ēalā trēowwyrhta, for[21] hwȳ[21] swā spricst ðū, ðonne[22]

1 MS. **sylanscear.**

2 Lat. *culter.*

3 See **24.**

4 See **161.**

5 Lat. *consiliarius.*

6 Not in MS.

7 Lat. *hospitari;* see **199.** *a.*

8 Lat. *panem.*   **Brēad,** which is found in Old English, scarcely has any other sense than that of 1) *fragment,* 2) *broken bread.* Later it acquires its modern meaning. See *New Eng. Dict.,* s.v. *bread.*

9 Lat. *ferreas scintillas.*

10 Lat. *sonitus.*   .

11 Lat. *tundentium.*

12 Lat. *malleorum.*

13 Lat. *lignarius.*   See **147.**

14 See **154.** *b.*

15 Lat. *utitur.*

16 See **164.** *o.*

17 Lat. *domos.*

18 See **161.**

19 Lat. *fabrico.*

20 Lat. *ferrarius.*   MS. **golsmið** (*sic*).

21 Lat. *cur;* see **175.**

22 Lat. *cum.*   Other temporal conjunctions used to denote cause are **nū** and **ðā.** Has Mod. Eng. any similar idiom ?

ne furðum[1] ān ðȳrel būtan cræfte mīnum ðū ne[2] meaht[3] dōn[4]?

Se geðeahtend sægð:

Ēalā, gefēran[5] and gōde wyrhtan! Uton tōweorpan hwætlicor[6] ðās geflitu,[7] and sīe[8] sibb and geðwærnes[9] be- 5 tweoh ūs, and fremme[10] ānra[11] gehwilc[11] ōðrum[12] on cræfte his, and geðwærien[13] simle mid ðǣm ierðlinge, ðǣr[14] wē bigleofan[15] ūs, and fōdor horsum ūrum habbað. And ðis geðeaht ic selle eallum wyrhtum, ðæt ānra[16] gehwilc cræft his geornlice begange,[17] for-ðām sē, ðe cræft[18] his forlǣt, hē[19] 10 bið forlǣten fram ðǣm cræfte. Swā-hwæðer[20] ðū sīe — swā[21] mæsseprēost,[22] swā munuc,[23] swā ceorl,[24] swā cempa[25] — begā[26] ðē selfne on ðisum, and bēo ðæt ðū eart; for-ðām micel hīenð[27] and sceamu hit is menn nellan[28] wesan ðæt hē is and ðæt hē wesan sceal.[29] 15

---

[1] Lat. *saltem.*

[2] See **183**.

[3] Lat. *vales.*

[4] Lat. *facere.*

[5] Lat. *socii;* see **152**.

[6] Lat. *citius;* used almost in the sense of the positive; see **76**.

[7] Lat. *contentiones.*

[8] See **189. 1**.

[9] Lat. *concordia.*

[10] Lat. *prosit.*

[11] Lat. *unusquisque.* MS. **urum gehwylcum.**

[12] See **160**.

[13] Lat. *conveniamus.*

[14] Lat. *ubi.*

[15] Lat. *victum.*

[16] See **154. b**.

[17] See **194. b**.

[18] Acc. sing.

[19] Lat. *ipse.*

[20] Lat. *sive.*

[21] **Swā . . . swā** = Lat. *sive . . . seu.*

[22] Lat. *sacerdos.*

[23] Lat. *monachus,* from which the OE. word is derived. For the **u** cf. OE. **munt** = Lat. *montem.*

[24] Lat. *laicus.*

[25] Lat. *miles.*

[26] MS. **bega oþþe behwyrf.** Lat. *exerce.*

[27] Lat. *damnum.*

[28] MS. **nelle.** See **199. a**.

[29] Lat. *debet.*

III.

THE DAY OF JUDGMENT.

(From Ælfric's Homilies, vol. 2, pp. 106–108; being a paraphrase of Matt. 25:31–46.)

Witodlice[1] Mannes Bearn cymð[2] on his mægenðrymme, and ealle ꝭnglas[3] samod mid him tō ðǣm miclan[4] dōme.[5] Þonne sitt[6] hē on ðǣm setle his mægenðrymnesse,[7] and bēoð gegaderode ætforan him ealle ðēoda,[8] and hē tōscǣt[9] hīe on twā, swā-swā scēaphierde[10] tōscǣt scēap[11] fram gātum.[12]   Þonne gelōgað hē ðā scēap on his swīðran[13] hand, and ðā gǣt[14] on his winstran.   Þonne cwið[15] se Cyning Crīst tō ðǣm ðe on his swīðran hand standað, "Cumað gē blētsode[16] mīnes Fæder,[17] and geāgniað ðæt

[1] Lat. *autem.*

[2] See **cuman.**

[3] See **ꝭngel.** What is the history of this word before it entered Old English ?

[4] See **55.**

[5] In what modern compound does this meaning of **dōm** persist?

[6] See **sittan.**

[7] See **153.** *f.*

[8] Nom. plur.

[9] See **tōscēadan.** Account for the vowel **ǣ.**

[10] In compound words, the vowel of the first syllable is apt to be shortened in Mod. Eng., the more general principle being that shortening is apt to occur before an accumulation of consonants.   Besides **scēaphierde,** *shepherd,* note *e.g.* **wīsdōm,** *wisdom.*

[11] Plural ; account for the form.

[12] See **24.**

[13] See **swīð.**

[14] See **52.**

[15] See **cweðan.** What is the ind. pret. 3d sing. ?

[16] Past part. in nom. plur.

[17] See **43. 8.**

rīce[1] ðe ēow[2] gegearcod wæs fram frymðe middangeardes. Mē[3] hyngrede,[4] and gē mē gereordedon; mē[3] ðyrste, and gē mē[5] scęncton; ic wæs cuma,[6] and gē mē underfēngon[7] on ēowrum giesthūsum; ic wæs nacod, and gē mē scrȳddon[8]; ic wæs geuntrumod, and gē mē genēosedon; ic wæs on cwearterne, and gē cōmon tō mē and mē gefrēfredon.[9] " 5

Ðonne andswariað ðā rihtwīsan[10] Crīste[11] and cweðað, "Dryhten, hwonne gesāwe[12] wē ðē hungrigne, and wē ðē gereordedon? oððe ðurstigne, and wē ðē scęncton? oððe hwonne wǣre ðū cuma,[13] and wē ðē underfēngon? oððe 10 hwonne gesāwe[13a] wē ðē untrumne oððe on cwearterne, and wē ðē genēosedon?" Ðonne andwyrt se Cyning ðǣm rihtwīsum ðisum wordum,[14] "Sōð[15] ic ēow sęcge, swā[16] lange swā[17] gē dydon ānum, ðisum lǣstan,[18] on mīnum

---

[1] Still found as the last syllable of bishopric.

[2] See 81.

[3] See 190.

[4] What is the relation of the stem-vowel to that of hungrig? See 90.

[5] Dat.

[6] Lat. hospes.

[7] See underfōn.

[8] What peculiar senses has the verb shroud in Spenser, Shakespeare, or Milton? What form would scrȳdan most naturally assume in Mod. Eng. (24)? How can the Mod. Eng. form of the verb shroud be accounted for?

[9] What is the relation of the stem-vowel to that of frōfor? See 90.

[10] Nom. plur. See 181.

[11] Dat.

[12] See gesēon.

[13] See 150.   [13a] See 95, note.

[14] See 174. b.

[15] Lat. amen, Eng. verily.

[16] = so.

[17] = as. Notice this early use of so long as (= Lat. quamdiu) in the sense of inasmuch as.

[18] The WS. translation of the Gospel has ānum of ðisum mīnum lǣstum gebrōðrum, which is much more literal. In Ælfric's version we must understand lǣstan to be in apposition with ānum. See 66.

naman, gē hit dydon mē selfum.[1]" Đonne cwið hē ęft
tō ðǣm synfullum, ðe on his winstran healfe standað,
"Gewītað fram mē, gē āwiergdan, intō ðǣm ēcean fȳre,
ðe is gegearcod ðǣm dēofle[2] and his āwiergdum gāstum.
5 Mē hyngrede, and gē mē ǣtes[3] forwierndon; mē ðyrste,
and gē mē drincan ne sealdon; ic wæs cuma, and gē mē
underfōn noldon; ic wæs nacod, nolde[4] gē mē wǣda[5]
tīðian[6]; ic wæs untrum and on cwearterne, nolde[4] gē
mē genēosian." Đonne andswariað[7] ðā unrihtwīsan mān-
10 fullan,[8] "Lā lēof, hwonne gesāwe[4] wē ðē hungrigne,[9] oððe
ðurstigne, oððe cuman, oððe nacodne, oððe geuntrumodne,
oððe on cwearterne, and wē ðē noldon ðēnian[6]"? Đonne
andwyrt se Cyning him, and cwið, "Sōð ic ēow sęcge,
swā lange swā gē forwierndon ānum of ðisum lȳtlum,
15 and noldon[10] him on mīnum naman tīðian, swā lange[11]
gē mē selfum his[3] forwierndon." Đonne farað ðā uncyst-
gan[12] and ðā unrihtwīsan intō ēcre cwicsūsle, mid dēofle
and his āwiergdum ęnglum; and ðā rihtwīsan gecierrað
fram ðǣm dōme intō ðǣm ēcean līfe.

---

[1] **Not** = *myself;* **self** agrees
with **mē.** The Latin has no original here for **self**; Ælfric adds it
to strengthen the expression.

    [2] See 161.

    [3] See 159.

    [4] See 95, note.

    [5] See 159. What is the Mod.
Eng. form of this word ?

    [6] See 28 ; 164. e.

[7] How is the **and-** of this
word related to the *anti-* of
Eng. *antiphon?*

    [8] See 4.

    [9] See 173.

    [10] See 139.

    [11] Correlative with the **swā
lange swā** of the preceding
clause.

    [12] See 55 ; 57. 3 ; 181.

IV

BEDE'S DESCRIPTION OF BRITAIN.

(Eccl. Hist., Bk. I., Chap. I.)

[Ælfric testifies to a translation of Bede's History having been made by Alfred, and so does William of Malmesbury; besides, the MS. of the Cambridge University Library twice has this couplet,—

> Historicus quondam fecit me Beda latinum,
> Ælfred rex Saxo transtulit ille pius.

On the other hand, it has such undoubted Anglian peculiarities that it has been suggested (by Miller, its latest editor) that "the version may have been executed by Mercian scholars under orders from the king," and that it was possibly made at Lichfield.

The distinction between English idiom and imitation of the Latin should be remarked, wherever possible. Moberly's edition of the Ecclesiastical History, which contains scholarly and interesting notes, may profitably be compared.]

Breoton[1] is gārsecges[2] īgland, ðæt wæs īu gēara Albion hāten.... Hit is welig—ðis īgland—on wæstmum and on trēowum missenlicra cynna,[3] and hit is gescrēpe on læswe sceapa[4] and nēata[5]; and on sumum stōwum wīngeardas

Britannia oceani insula, cui quondam Albion nomen fuit. ... Opima frugibus atque arboribus insula, et alendis apta pecoribus ac jumentis; vineas etiam quibusdam in locis germinans: sed et avium ferax terra marique gene-

---

[1] Moberly says: "This description of Britain is pieced from the accounts of Plinius, Solinus, Orosius, Dio Cassius, and Gildas."

[2] See **153.** *h.*

[3] See **153.** *f.*

[4] See **153.** *d.*

[5] What Mod. Eng. word represents this? What OE. noun-stem contains the umlaut of this one?

grōwað.   Swilce ēac ðēos eorðe is berende missenlicra fugla[1] and sǣwihta. . . .   And hēr bēoð oft fangene[1a] sēolas, and hranas, and męreswīn; and hēr bēoð oft numene[2] missenlicra[3] cynna weolocscielle[4] and muscule,

5 and on ðǣm bēoð oft gemētte[5] ðū bętstan[6] meregreotan[7] ǣlces hīwes.   And hēr bēoð swīðe genyhtsume weolocas, of ðǣm bið geworht se weolocrēada tęlg, ðone ne mæg sunne blǣcan[8] nē ne regn[9] wierdan; ac, swā hē bið ieldra,[10] swā hē fægerra bið.   Hit hæfð[11] ēac — ðis land

10 — sealtsēaðas; and hit hæfð hāt wæter, and hāt baðu,[12] ǣlcre ielde[13] and hāde, ðurh tōdǣleda stōwa,[14] gescrēpe.

ris diversi. . . .   Capiuntur autem sæpissime et vituli marini, et delphines, necnon et ballenæ: exceptis variorum generibus conchyliorum; in quibus sunt et musculæ, quibus inclusam sæpe margaritam, omnis quidem coloris optimam inveniunt. . . .   Sunt et cochleæ satis superque abundantes, quibus tinctura coccinei coloris conficitur, cujus rubor pulcherrimus nullo unquam solis ardore, nulla valet pluviarum injuria pallescere; sed quo vetustior est, eo solet esse venustior.   Habet fontes salinarum, habet et fontes calidos, et ex eis fluvios balnearum calidarum, omni ætati et sexui, per distincta loca, juxta suum cui-

[1] This genitive after a present participle is exceptional; cf. the Latin for an explanation (**155**).

[1a] See **fōn**.   [2] See **niman**.

[3] See p. 130, n. 12.   [4] Nom. plur.

[5] From what noun is the stem of **mētan** derived?   See **14**.

[6] See **66**.

[7] This word is adapted from the Latin, but simulates a compound of **męre**, *sea*, and **grēot**, *earth, gravel*.

[8] From what adjective is **blǣcan** derived (**17**)?

[9] To what might **regn** contract (**28**)?

[10] See **65**.

[11] See **121**.

[12] See **bæð**.

[13] Governed by **gescrēpe**.   See **165**.

[14] What does *-stow* mean in a proper name like *Chepstow*?

Swilce hit is ēac berende[1] on węcga ōrum — āres and
īsernes, lēades and seolfres.   Hēr bið ēac gemētt gagates;
sē stān bið blæc gimm; gif man[2] hine on fȳr dēð,[3] ðonne
flēoð ðær næddran[4] onweg.[5]   Wæs ðis īgland[6] ēac ge-
weorðod mid ðæm æðelestum ceastrum[7]—ānes wana ðrīt-   5
igum[8]— ðā-ðe[9] wæron mid weallum,[10] and torrum,[10] and
geatum, and ðæm trumestum locum getimbrede, būtan
ōðrum læssan[11] unrīme ceastra.

And for-ðām-ðe ðis īgland under ðæm selfum norðdæle
middangeardes nīehst līð,[12] and lēohte niht on sumera   10
que modum accommodos. . . .   Quæ etiam venis metal-
lorum, æris, ferri, et plumbi et argenti fæcunda, gignit et
lapidem gagatem plurimum optimumque: est autem nigro-
gemmeus et ardens igni admotus, incensus serpentes fugat.
. . .   Erat et civitatibus quondam viginti et octo nobilis-
simis insignita, præter castella innumera, quæ et ipsa muris,
turribus, portis, ac seris erant instructa firmissimis.

Et quia prope sub ipso septentrionali vertice mundi jacet,
lucidas æstate noctes habet; ita ut medio sæpe tempore

[1] Cf. the construction of this
word with that above, p. 138, l. 1.

[2] See **89. e.**   [3] See **140.**

[4] How did **næddre** become
adder? Cf. OE. **nafogār**, Mod.
Eng. *auger.*   See Skeat, *Prin.*,
p. 216.

[5] There is a parallel form,
āweg, already in OE. The **ā**-
is a contraction of **on.** Mention
other Mod. Eng. words in which
the *a-* represents *on.*

[6] How does the Mod. Eng.
island acquire its *s* ? See Skeat,
Prin., p. 380, and note 3, next page.

[7] From Lat. *castra.* Cf. the
-caster, *-chester*, of Lancaster,
Winchester, etc. Some of the
more important of these cities
were York, Colchester, Winchester, Canterbury, and Chester (see
Moberly, p. 7).

[8] Cf. **78. 5**; **158.** The number
does not correspond to the Latin.

[9] Does this relative have the
same antecedent as in the Latin?

[10] **Weall** is from Lat. *vallum*;
torr, from Lat. *turris.*

[11] Agrees with **unrīme.**

[12] See **licgan**, and **28.**

hæfð — swā ðæt oft on midre niht geflit cymð[1] ðǣm
behealdendum, hwæðer hit sīe ðe[2] æfenglōmung, ðe on
morgen dagung — is on ðǣm sweotol, ðæt ðis īgland[3]
hæfð micle[4] lęngran dagas on sumera,[5] and swā ēac niht[6]
5 on wintra,[5] ðonne ðā sūðdǣlas middangeardes.[7]

noctis in quæstionem veniat intuentibus, utrum crepus-
culum adhuc permaneat vespertinum, an jam advenerit
matutinum . . . : unde etiam plurimæ longitudinis habet
dies æstate, sicut et noctes contra in bruma.

[1] See **cuman**.

[2] Lat. *utrum* . . . *an* = ð̄e
. . . ð̄e (**202**. *b*).

[3] **Īg**- represents **īe**-, the umlaut
of **ēa**, *water*. **Ēa** goes back to
the same Indo-European root as
Lat. *aqua*.

[4] See **178**.

[5] See **43**. **5**.

[6] **Niht** belongs under **52**. It
has already experienced umlaut
in the nominative, and hence does
not change in the acc. plur.

[7] This last clause is supplied by
the translator.

V.

ÆTHELWALD CALMS THE SEA.[1]

(Bede, Eccl. Hist., Bk. V., Chap. I.)

Ic cōm mid twǣm[2] ōðrum brōðrum tō Farne,[3] ðǣm iglande. Wolde ic sprecan mid ðone[4] ārwierðan fæder Æðelwald. Mid-ðȳ ic ðā wæs mid his gesprece wel gerētt,[5] and mē blētsunge bæd, and wē hām[6] hwurfon,[7] ðā wē ðā wǣron on midre[8] ðǣre sǣ, ðā[9] wæs samninga heofones smyltnes tōsliten, ðǣre-ðe[10] wē ǣr lidon[11] ūt; and swā micel winter[12] ūs onhrēas,[13] and swā rēðe storm cōm, ðæt wē nē mid segle nē mid rōwnesse āwiht framgān[14] meahton, nē wē ūs nōhtes[15] elles wēndon nefne

[1] This story was related by Abbot Guthfrith to Bede. Æthelwald succeeded Cuthbert as the hermit of Farne, dwelling there from 687 to 699, when he died.

[2] See **79**.

[3] Two miles from Bamborough. One of the islands of the group was the scene of Grace Darling's heroism in 1858. That inhabited by Æthelwald was the largest.

[4] The acc. with **mid** is exceptional (**172. 1**). [5] See **113**.

[6] Acc. sing. as adv.; Lat. *domum*.

[7] Lat. *rediremus*.

[8] See **166. 1**.

[9] To **ūt** = *interrupta est serenitas qua vehebamur*.

[10] Translate *in* (or *with*) *which*. The Latin shows that the preposition is to be understood.

[11] See **līðan**, and **37**.

[12] Lat. *hiems*, but no doubt in the sense of *tempest*.

[13] See **onhrēosan**. What is the ind. pret. plur. ?

[14] Lat. *proficere*.

[15] See **156. g**.

dēaðes[1] selfes. Mid-ðȳ wē ðā swīðe lange wið ðǣm winde
and wið ðǣm sǣ hōlunga[2] campedon and wunnon,[3] ðā æt
nīehstan lōcedon wē on bæcling, hwæðer wēn[4] wǣre[4] ðæt
wē ǣnge[5] ðinga[5] furðum ðæt īgland gesēcean[6] meahton,
5 ðæt wē ǣr ūt of gangende[7] wǣron.[7] Cierde[8] wē ūs ðider
wē cierdon, gemētton[9] wē ūs ǣghwanan gelīce[10] storme[10]
foresętte and foretȳnde, and nǣnigne hyht[11] hǣle[12] in ūs
tō[13] lāfe[13] standan.[13] Ðā wæs æfter langum fæce ðæt wē
ūre gesihð feorr[14] ūpāhōfon, ðā gesāwon wē in Farne,
10 ðǣm īglande, Gode[15] ðone lēofan fæder Æðelwald of his
dīegelnessum[16] ūtgangende,[17] ðæt[18] hē[18] wolde[18] ūrne sīðfæt
scēawian, and gesēon hwæt ūs gelumpe,[19] for-ðon hē gehīerde ðæt gebrec ðǣra storma and ðæs weallendes sǣs.[20]
Mid-ðȳ hē ðā ūs ēac scēawode, and geseah in gewinne
15 and in ormōdnesse[21] gesętte bēon,[22] ðā bīegde hē his

[1] See **156**. *g*.

[2] Lat. *frustra*.

[3] See **winnan**.

[4] Lat. *forte*.

[5] Lat. *aliquo conamine*. For
ǣnige see **174**; for **ðinga** see
154. *b*.

[6] Lat. *repetere*.

[7] Lat. *egressi eramus*. The
pres. part. with the verb is sometimes used in OE. to denote the
simple past, as here, and not the
progressive.

[8] See **95**, note.

[9] To **foretȳnde** = Lat. *inve-
nimus nos undiqueversum pari
tempestate præclusos*.

[10] See **174**.

[11] Acc. sing., the subj. of
standan.

[12] See **153**. *d*.

[13] Lat. *restare*.

[14] Translate, *from a distance*.

[15] Governed by **lēofan**; =
amantissimum Deo. See **165**.

[16] Lat. *latibulis*.

[17] Translates the Latin past
part., *egressum*.

[18] Translate, *that he might, in
order to, to*. The Latin has the
infinitive.   [19] See **194**. *b*.

[20] Lat. *fragore procellarum ac
ferventis oceani*.

[21] Lat. *desperatione*.

[22] Supply **ūs** as subject acc.
(**169**).

cnēowu tō Fæder ūres Dryhtnes Hǽlendes Crīstes, and
wæs[1] gebiddende[1] for ūrre hǽle and for ūrum līfe. And
mid-ðȳ hē ðā ðæt gebed gefylde,[2] hē ðā samod ætgædere
ge ðone āðundnan[3] sǽ gesmylte ge ðone storm gestilde,
tō[4] ðon[4] ðætte[4] ðurh[5] eall[5] seo rēðnes ðæs stormes wæs[1] 5
blinnende,[1] and gesyndge[6] windas ðurh ðone smyltestan
sǽ ūs æt lande gebrōhton. Mid-ðȳ wē ðā ūp cōmon tō
lande, and ūre scip ēac[7] swilce[7] fram ðǽm ȳðum ūp
ābǽron, ðā sōna se ilca storm eft hwearf and cōm,[8] se-ðe
for[9] ūrum[9] intingan[9] medmicel fæc[10] gestilde, and ealne 10
ðone[11] dæg[10] swīðe micel and strang wæs, ðætte[12] menn
sweotollice ongietan meahton ðætte se medmicla fierst
ðǽre stilnesse, ðe ðǽr becōm, tō[13] bēnum[13] ðæs Godes[14]
weres[15] for intingan ūrre hǽle[16] heofonlice[17] forgiefen[18] wæs.

---

[1] See above, p. 142, n. 7.
[2] Lat. *compleret*.
[3] Lat. *tumida*.
[4] Lat. *adeo ut*, nearly = *so that*.
[5] Lat. *per omnia*, = *entirely*.
[6] Lat. *secundi*. What letter (sound) has been lost from the OE. form?
[7] Lat. *quoque*.
[8] Supply eft. Latin has only one verb, *rediit*.
[9] Lat. *nostri gratia*.
[10] See **170**.
[11] Lat. *illo*. Translate, *that*.
[12] From ðæt-ðe (34).
[13] Lat. *ad preces*. Cf. the Mod. Eng. phrase, 'bootless bene.'
[14] Dependent on **weres**.
[15] Dependent on **bēnum**.
[16] Lat. *evasionis*.
[17] Lat. *cælitus* = *from heaven*.
[18] Not *forgiven*, but *given*.

VI.

THE INVASION OF BRITAIN BY THE PICTS AND SCOTS.

(Bede, Eccl. Hist., Bk. I., Chaps. XI., XII.)

Of ðǣre tīde[1] Romane blunnon[2] rīcsian on Breotone. Hæfdon hīe Breotona rīce fēower hund wintra,[3] and, ðæs fīftan, hundseofontig,[4] ðæs-ðe[5] Gaius, ōðre naman Julius, se cāsere,[6] ðæt ilce īgland gesōhte. And ceastra, and
5 torras,[7] and strǣta,[8] and brycga on hiera rīce geworhte wǣron, ðā wē tō-dæg scēawian magon. Eardodon Bryttas binnan ðǣm dīce[9] tō sūðdǣle, ðe wē gemyngodon ðæt Severus,[10] se cāsere, hēt ðwīeres ofer ðæt īgland[11] gedīcian.

[1] Lat. *ex quo tempore* = Eng. *from this time forth.*

[2] See **blinnan.**

[3] See **154. c.**

[4] So the Latin: *post annos ferme quadringentos septuaginta.* But the best calculations make this to have been about sixty years earlier.

[5] Lat. *ex quo* = Eng. *from the time that.*

[6] Lat. *Gaius Julius Cæsar.*

[7] Lat. *farus,* for *pharos,* from Pharos, the name of an island near Alexandria in Egypt. The lighthouse built on this island gave its name to other light-houses (cf. Fr. *phare*). Here watch-towers are meant.

[8] Lat. *stratœ.* Are the two words connected? See Skeat, *Prin.,* pp. 68, 432.

[9] Lat. *intra vallum.* Mod. Eng. *ditch* is Southern English; *dike* probably Northern. Cf. Eng. *church* with Scotch *kirk.*

[10] This wall was between the Friths of Forth and Clyde (see

[11] Lat. *trans insulam.*

Đā[1] ongunnon twā ðēoda, Pihtas[2] norðan, and Scottas westan, hīe onwinnan, and hiera ǣhta niman and hęrgian; and hīe fela gēara iermdon and hīendon.   Đā, on ðǣre unstilnesse, onsęndon hīe ǣrendwrecan[3] tō Rome mid gewritum[4] and wēpendre bēne; him fultumes[5] bǣdon, 5 and him gehēton ēaðmōde hīernesse and singāle underðēodnesse,[6] gif hīe him gefultumoden ðæt hīe meahten

Moberly's Bede, p. 16), but Bede, following Orosius, is no doubt thinking of that between the Tyne and the Solway Frith, which was built by Hadrian (A.D. 120). Severus' wall was built A.D. 207-210.

[1] "[This account] is pieced together as an abridgment of Gildas, xi.-xvi.; but the turgidity of his style is chastened, and his faulty grammar in several places corrected" (Moberly, pp. 26, 27).

[2] On the Picts the last edition of *Chambers' Encyclopædia* remarks: "Four hypotheses have been formed in regard to the language and origin of the Picts. The first, started by Pinkerton and put by Sir Walter Scott into the mouth of the 'Antiquary,' is hat they were Teutons, speaking a Gothic dialect; the second, maintained by Dr. Skene, is that they were Gaelic-speaking Celts; . . . the third, due to Professor Rhys, is that the Picts were non-Aryans, whose language was overlaid by loans from Welsh and Irish; and the fourth, held by two of the most eminent Celtic scholars of the day, Professor Windisch and Dr. Whitley Stokes, is that they were Celts, but more nearly allied to the Cymry than to the Gael. . . . The conclusion to which we come is that the Picts,· whatever traces they show of a non-Aryan racial element, . . . spoke a Celtic language belonging to a branch of Celtic allied to the Cymric, . . . and that this dialect of the Gallo-Cymric stock was a wave of Celtic speech from the continent previous to the Gaulish which held England when Cæsar entered Britain."

[3] Lat. *legatos*.

[4] Lat. *epistolis*.

[5] See **156.** *b*.

[6] This pair of phrases renders *subjectionem continuam*. What parallel to the use of such synonymous terms may be found in the English Prayer-Book? How is it to be accounted for?

hiera fīend[1] oferwinnan. Ðā[2] onsęndon[3] hīe him micelne
hęre tō fultume, and, sōna ðæs-ðe hīe on ðis īgland cōmon,
ðā campedon hīe[4] wið hiera fēondum, and him micel wæl
ongeslōgon, and of hiera[5] gemǣrum ādrifon and āflīemdon[6];
5 and lǣrdon ðæt hīe fæsten[7] worhten him[8] tō gebeorge wið
hiera fēondum; and swā, mid micle sige,[9] hām fōron.[10]

Ðā[11] ðæt ðā ongēaton ðā ǣrran gewinnan,[12] ðæt se Roma-
nisca hęrc wæs onweg gewiten, ðā cōmon hīe sōna mid
sciphęre on hiera landgemǣru, and slōgon[13] ealle and cweald-
10 on[13] ðæt hīe gemētton, and swā-swā rīpe ierðe[14] fortrǣdon and
fornōmon, and hīe mid ealle[15] foriermdon. And hīe ðā ęft
sęndon ǣrendwrecan tō Rome, and wēpendre stefne him
fultumes bǣdon,[16] ðæt[17] se[17] earma ēðel mid ealle[15] ne
fordilgod ne wǣre, nē se nama ðǣre Romaniscan ðēode,[18]
15 se-ðe mid him swā lange scēan[19] beorhte,[19] fram fręmdra

---

[1] See 46.

[2] This may be anywhere between A.D. 388 and 420. See
Moberly, p. 27.

[3] This clause translates *Quibus
mox legio destinatur armata.* Note
the use of the active for the passive, which also appears in other
sentences of the context.

[4] The legionaries, apparently.

[5] Of the Britons; Lat. *socio-
rum finibus.*

[6] Lat. *expulit.* See above, p.
145, n. 6.

[7] Lat. *murum.*

[8] See 184. *a.*

[9] Lat. *triumpho.* See 175.

[10] A passage of the Latin is
here omitted in the translation,
describing the construction of
the (earthen) wall, between the
Friths of Forth and of Clyde.

[11] These three ðā's respectively
= *when, then,* and *the.*

[12] Lat. *inimici.*

[13] Lat. *cædunt.* See above, p.
145, n. 6.

[14] Lat. *segetem.*

[15] **Mid ealle** = *completely.* See
175.

[16] Lat. *implorantes.*

[17] MS. **ðæt.**

[18] Lat. *provinciæ.*

[19] Lat. *claruerat.* Is the Old
English to be translated as perfect
or as pluperfect? See **scīnan** (18).

ðēoda[1] ungeðwǣrnesse[2] fornumen and fordilgod bēon sceolde. Ðā wæs ęft hęre[3] hider sęnd,[4] se wæs cumende on ungewēnedre[5] tīde, on hærfeste. And hīe sōna wið hiera fēondum gefuhton, and sige hæfdon, and ealle ðā, ðe ðone[6] dēað[6] beswīcian[6] meahton, ofer ðone sǣ norð 5 āflīemdon, ðā-ðe ǣr, ǣlce gēare,[7] ofer ðone sǣ hlōðedon and hęrgedon. Ðā gesǣgdon Romane on ān[8] Bryttum ðæt hīe nō mā ne meahten for hiera gescieldnesse[9] swā gewinnfullicum[10] fierdum[11] swęncte[12] bēon.[12] Ac hīe manedon[13] and[13] lǣrdon[13] ðæt hīe him wǣpnu worhten,[14] 10 and mōdes stręngðe nōmen,[15] ðæt hīe campoden and wiðstōden hiera fēondum.[16] And hīe him ðā ēac tō rǣde and tō frōfre fundon ðæt hīe gemǣnelice fæsten geworhten him tō gescieldnesse — stǣnenne weall rihtre[17] stīge[17] fram ēastsǣ ōð westsǣ, ðǣr Severus,[18] se cāsere, 15 īu hēt dīcian and eorðweall gewyrcean; ðone man[19] nū tō-dæg scēawian mæg, eahta fōta[20] brādne, and twęlf fōta[20] hēahne.[21] Swilce ēac on ðæs sǣs wearoðe tō sūð-

---

[1] See 153. c.

[2] Lat. improbitate.

[8] Lat. legio.

[4] Past part.; see 113.

[5] Lat. inopinata.

[6] Lat. evadere, not mortem evadere.

[7] See 176.

[8] On ān = at once; it is the Mod. Eng. anon, which see in the New Eng. Dict.

[9] Lat. defensionem.

[10] Lat. laboriosis.

[11] Lat. expeditionibus.

[12] Lat. fatigari.

[18] Lat. monent. See above, p. 145, n. 6.

[14] See 194. b. [15] See niman.

[16] The translation here is very free, as is much of this selection.

[17] Lat. recto tramite; see 160. 1; 176. 2.

[18] This is wrong; it is Hadrian's wall that is meant. See p. 144, n. 10, and an article in the Quarterly Review for January, 1860.

[19] See 89. e. [20] See 154. c.

[21] A comparison of this sen-

dǣle, ðanan ðe hīe[1] sciphęre[2] on becōm, torras timbredon
tō gebeorge[3] ðæs sǣs. Ðā, sōna ðæs-ðe ðis fæsten geworht
wæs, ðā sealdon hīe him bȳsena[4] maniga hū hīe him wǣpnu
wyrcean sceolden, and hiera fēondum wiðstandan[5]; and
5 hīe ðā grētton, and him cȳðdon ðæt hīe nǣfre mā hīe
sēcean woldon; and hīe sigefæste ofer sǣ fērdon. Ðā[7]
ðæt ðā Pihtas and Scottas geāxedon, ðæt hīe hām gewitene
wǣron, and ēac ðæt hīe hider nō[8] ęft mā hīe sēcean ne[8]
woldon, ðā wǣron hīe ðȳ[9] bealdran gewordene, and sōna
10 ealne norðdǣl · ðises īglandes ōð ðone weall genōmon[10]
and[10] gesętton.[10] Wið ðisum stōd on ðǣm fæstene ufanweardum[11] se earga[12] fēða[13] Brytta, and ðǣr forhtiendre[14]
heortan[14] wunode dæges[15] and nihtes.[15] Ðā sōhton hiera
gewinnan him searwu, and worhton him· hōcas, and mid
15 ðǣm tugon hīe earmlice[16] ādūn of ðǣm wealle; and hīe
wǣron sōna dēade swā hīe eorðan gesōhton.[17] Hīe ðā
forlēton ðone weall and hiera byrig,[18] and flugon[19] onweg;

tence with the original will show
the translator's power and free-
dom.

[1] Acc. plur.; the Britons.
[2] Nom. sing.; of the enemy.
The Latin is different.
[3] Lat. *prospectum*.
[4] Lat. *monita*.
[5] Free translation.
[6] From this point to the end of
the sentence = Lat. *et valedicunt
sociis tanquam ultra non rever-
suri. Quibus ad sua remeantibus.*
Probably A.D. 418.
[7] From here to **woldon** = Lat.

*cognita Scotti Pictique reditus
denegatione.*
[8] See **183**.   [10] Lat. *capessunt.*
[9] See **178**.   [11] See **166. 1.**
[12] Lat. *segnis.*
[13] Lat. *acies.*
[14] Lat. *trementi corde.*   See
160. 1.
[15] See **74**.   **Nihtes** is formed
on the model of **dæges**, though
from a feminine **niht.**
[16] Lat. *miserrime.*
[17] The whole sentence is very
free.   [18] Acc. plur. (**52**).
[19] See **flēon.**

and hiera gewinnan hīe ēhton and slōgon,[1] and on wæl
fieldon. Wæs ðis gefeoht wælgrimre and strengre eallum[2]
ðæm ǣrgedōnum.[3] For-ðon swā-swā scēap[4] fram wulfum[5]
and[5] wildēorum[5] bēoð fornumene, swā ðā earman ceasterwaran tōslitene[6] and[6] fornumene[6] wǣron[6] fram hiera   5
fēondum, and hiera ǣhtum[7] benǣmde, and tō hungre
gesette.

[1] See **slēan**.   [2] See **178**.   [5] Lat. *feris.*

[3] Lat. *prioribus.*   [6] Lat. *discerpuntur.*

[4] See **47**. What is the modern plural?   [7] See **177**.

VII.

THE PASSING OF CHAD.[1]

(Bede, Eccl. Hist., Bk. IV., Chap. III.)

Cōm[2] hē[3] mid Æðelðrȳðe[4] of Ēastęnglum; and hē wæs hiere ðegna,[5] and hūses,[5] and hiere gefērscipes,[5] ofer eall ealdormann. Ðā Godes gelēafa ðā wēox, and hāt wæs, ðā

[1] Chad, Bishop of Lichfield, died March 2, 672. See the *Dict. Nat. Biog.*

[2] In 660.

[3] Ōwini. An interesting memorial of him was discovered, at the end of the last century, in the village of Haddenham, near Ely. It is a stone which appears to have formed the base of a cross, and on one of its sides is the following inscription : —

> ☩ LVCEM . TVAM . OVINO
> DA . DEVS . ET . REQVIĒ
> AMEN.

This is, according to Palgrave, perhaps one of the most venerable monuments of Saxon antiquity. It long served as a horse-block, but is now in the south aisle of Ely Cathedral. Dean Merivale of Ely has suggested that the words are meant for a pentameter line (the *m* in *lucem* being elided even before a consonant). For further particulars, see Mayor and Lumby's ed. of Bede, p. 429, and Bright's *Early English Church History*, p. 230.

[4] St. Etheldred, or Audrey (died 679), whose choice of the island of Ely as the site of a monastery led to the erection of the present cathedral. She was the daughter of Anna, king (not queen) of the East Anglians. What is the etymology of our modern word *tawdry ?*

[5] Dependent on **ealdormann.**

ðōhte hē ðæt hē sceolde worulde [1] wiðsacan, and ðæt
unāswundenlice swā gedyde; and hine middangeardes
ðingum tō ðon ongierede [2] and [2] genacodode [2] ðæt hē eall
forlēt ðā-ðe hē hæfde, nefne his ānfealdne gegierelan, and
cōm tō Læstinga īe, tō ðǣm mynstre [3] ðæs ārwierðan 5
bisceopes. [4] Bær him [5] æxe and adesan on handa; tāc-
node in [6] ðon ðæt hē nālæs tō īdelnesse, swā sume ōðre,
ac tō gewinne, in ðæt [7] mynster ēode; and ðæt selfe ēac
swilce mid dǣdum gecȳðde. And, for-ðon-ðe hē lȳt
genyhtsumode in smēaunge and in leornunge hāligra 10
gewrita, hē ðȳ [8] mā mid his handum wann, and [9] worhte
ðā ðing ðe nīedðearflicu wǣron. Ðæs [10] is tō tācne, ðæt
hē mid ðone bisceop in ðǣm foresprecenum wīcum [11] for
his ārwierðnesse and for his geornfulnesse [12] betweoh ðā
brōðor wæs hæfd. Ðonne [13] hīe inne [14] hiera leorňunge 15

[1] See **26**. The word is originally a compound, from **wer**,
man, and a hypothetical **ald**,
age (cf. the adj. **eald**, *old*).
From *age of man* to *generation*
= *the people living at one time*,
mankind; and from this to *inhabited earth*, the transitions are
not violent. The similar changes
in the meaning of the Lat. *sæculum* and Gr. *κόσμος*, especially in
Biblical usage, will be found sug-
gestive.

[2] Lat. *exuit;* two words for
one. See **162**.

[3] From what Latin word?
Has it the same meaning in
'York Minster'?

[4] From what Latin (Greek)
word?

[5] See **184**. *a.*

[6] Translate, *by.*

[7] Why the accusative?

[8] What is the form of this word
in Mod. Eng.? Wherein does it
differ from the other Mod. Eng.
word of the same form?

[9] This clause added by the
translator.

[10] Dependent on **tācne**.

[11] Lat. *mansione.*

[12] The double phrase translates
pro suæ reverentia devotionis.

[13] = *When.*

[14] Adverb; contrasted with **ūte**,
next line.

and hiera bēcrǣdinge[1] beēodon, ðonne wæs hē ūte wyrcende, swā-hwæt-swā ðearf gesegen[2] wæs.[2]

Ðā hē ðā sume[3] dæge[3] hwæthwugu swilces[4] ūte dyde,
and his gefēran tō byrig tō ciricean ēodon, swā hīe gelōm-
5 lice dydon, and se bisceop, āna in ðǣre ciricean,[5] oððe in
bēcrǣdinge oððe in gebedum geornfull wæs, ðā gehīerde
hē sęmninga, swā-swā hē ęft æfter ðon sægde, ðā swēt-
estan stefne[6] and ðā fægerestan, singendra and blissiendra,[7] of heofonum ōð eorðan āstīgan. Ðā stefne[8] and
10 ðone sang[8] hē cwæð, ðæt hē ǣrest gehīerde fram ēast-
sūðdǣle heofones, ðæt is fram hēanesse ðǣre winterlican
sunnan ūpganges; and ðanan tō him styccemǣlum[9] nēa-
lǣcton, ōð-ðæt hē[9a] becōm tō ðæcean[10] ðǣre ciricean ðe[11] se
bisceop in wæs; and, ingangende, eall[12] gefylde, and in
15 ymbhwyrfte ymbsealde. And hē ðā geornlice his mōd[13]
āðęnede[13] in ðā ðing ðe hē gehīerde. Ðā gehīerde hē
ęft swā-swā[14] healfre tīde fæce,[15] of hrōfe ðǣre ilcan
ciricean ūpāstīgan ðone ilcan blissesang,[16] and, ðȳ ilcan
wege[17] ðe hē ǣr cōm, ūp ōð heofonas mid unāsęcgendre[18]
20 swētnesse ęfthweorfan.[19]

[1] MS. becrædon.

[2] Lat. videbantur.

[3] See **176**.　　[4] See **154**. b.

[5] Lat. oratorio loci. The monks
had gone to the church. Cf. below,
p. 153, l. 7.

[6] See **169**. For this word see
Chaucer, Knight's Tale 1704.

[7] Lat. vocem suavissimam can-
tantium atque lætantium. What
adjective is concealed in **bliss-**
(see **34**)?

[8] Acc. after **gehīerde**.

[9] See **72**.　　[9a] **Se sang.**

[10] Lat. tectum, for which l. 17
has **hrōf.**

[11] Governed by **in**.

[12] Acc. sing.

[13] Lat. animum intenderet.

[14] Lat. quasi.　　[15] See **176**.

[16] Lat. lætitiæ canticum. See
169.　　[17] See **176**. 2.

[18] Lat. ineffabili.

[19] Lat. reverti.

Ða wunode hē ðǣr sum[1] fæc[1] tīde,[1] wundriende and
wafiende; and mid behygdigum mōde ðōhte and smēade
hwæt ðā ðing bēon sceolden. Ða ontȳnde se bisceop ðæt
ēagðȳrel[2] ðǣre ciricean, and mid his handa slōg tācen,
swā-swā his gewuna wæs gif hwilc mann ūte wǣre, ðæt 5
hē in tō him ēode. Ða ēode hē sōna in tō him. Cwæð
hē, se bisceop, him tō[3]: "Gang hraðe tō ciricean,[4] and
hāt[5] ūre seofon brōðor hider tō mē cuman; and ðū ēac
swilce mid wes.[6]" Ða hīe ðā tō him cōmon, ðā manode
hē hīe ǣrest ðæt hīe betwēonan him ðæt mægen[7] lufe[8] 10
and sibbe,[8] and betwēon[9] eallum Godes mannum geornlice
hēolden; and ēac swilce ðā gesetennesse ðæs regollican
ðēodscipes,[10] ðe hīe fram him geleornodon, and on him
gesāwon, oððe in ðǣra forðgelēoredra fædra dǣdum oððe
godcundum gemete, ðæt hīe ðā ungewērgedre[11] geornful- 15
nesse[11] fylgden and lǣsten.[12] Æfter ðon hē underðīedde,[13]
and him sægde ðæt se dæg swīðe nēah stōde his forðfōre,[14] and ðus cwæð: "Se lēofa[15] cuma and se lufiend-
lica,[15] se-ðe gewunode ūre brōðor nēosian, sē cōm swilce

---

[1] Lat. *aliquantulum horæ* (**170**).

[2] In what Mod. Eng. word is a
disguised form of -**ðȳrel** to be
found? What is the etymology
of *window*?

[3] See **201**. 1.

[4] What is the etymology of
church? From what language
is it originally derived?

[5] See **hātan**.

[6] Imper. sing. When followed
by the adj. **hǣl**, what Mod. Eng.
word does it give rise to?

[7] Lat. *virtutem*.

[8] See **153**. *i*.

[9] Lat. *ad* = *toward*, rather than
among.

[10] Lat. *instituta disciplinæ regularis*.

[11] See **174**; **160**. 1.

[12] How is this related to the
Mod. Eng. verb *last*, and to the
German *leisten*?

[13] Lat. *subjunxit*.

[14] Dependent on **dæg**.

[15] Lat. *amabilis*.

tō-dæg tō mē, and mē of worulde cīegde and laðode.
For-ðon gē ðonne nū ęfthweorfað[1] tō ciricean, and biddað[1]
ūre brōðor ðæt hīe mīne forðfōre mid hiera gebedum and
bēnum Dryhtne bebēoden[2]; and swilce ēac hiera selfra
5 forðfōre, ðǣre tīd is uncūð,[3] ðæt hīe gemynen[4] mid wæc-
cenum and gebedum and mid gōdum[5] forecuman.[6]

Mid-ðȳ hē ðā ðās word, and ðises gemetes manigu, tō
him sprecende wæs, and hīe, onfangenre[7] his blētsunge,[7]
swīðe unrōte fram him ēodon, ðā hwearf sē[8] āna[8] ęft[9] in
10 tō him se-ðe ðone heofonlican sang gehīerde, and hine
ēaðmōdlice on eorðan āstreahte fore ðone bisceop, and
ðus cwæð: "Mīn fæder, mōt[10] ic ðē ōhtes[11] āxian"?
Cwæð hē: "Āxa ðæs[11] ðū wille." Ðā cwæð hē: "Ic
ðē lā hālsie and bidde for Godes lufe ðæt ðū mē
15 gesęcge[12] hwæt se sang wǣre blissiendra ðe[13] ic gehīerde,
of heofonum cumendra[14] ofer ðās ciricean,[15] and, æfter
tīde,[16] ęfthweorfendra tō heofonum." Andswarode hē,
se bisceop: "Gif ðū sanges stefne gehīerde, and ðū
heofonlic weorod ongēate ofer ūs ēac cuman, ic ðē
20 bebēode on Dryhtnes naman ðæt ðū ðæt nǣnigum męnn

[1] Here are two independent
verbs, where the Latin has *rever-
tentes . . . dicite.*

[2] Lat. *commendent.*

[3] What change of meaning in
the modern word *uncouth ?* How
related to the ancient meaning ?

[4] See **134.**

[5] According to the Latin,
weorcum should be supplied.

[6] Dependent on **gemynen.**

[7] See **167.**

[8] Lat. *ipse solus*, meaning
Ōwini.

[9] Belongs with **hwearf**;
hwearf . . . ęft = Lat. *rediit.*

[10] See 137.

[11] See **156.**

[12] See **194.** *b.*

[13] Refers to **sang.**

[14] Belongs to **blissiendra.**

[15] Lat. *oratorium.* See above,
p. 152, n. 5.

[16] Lat. *tempus.*

cȳðe[1] nē[1] sęcge[1] ǣr mīnre forðfōre. Ic ðē sōðlice sęcge
ðætte ðæt wǣron[2] ęngla gāstas ðe ðǣr cōmon, ðā mē tō
ðǣm heofonlicum mēdum cīegdon and laðedon ðā ic simle
lufode and wilnode. And, æfter seofon dagum, hīe ęft-
hweorfende[3] and cumende[3] mē gehēton, and mē ðonne 5
mid him lǣdan woldon."

Ðæt wæs swā sōðlice mid dǣde gefylled swā him tō[4]
cweden wæs. Ðā wæs hē sōna gehrinen līchamlicre[5]
untrymnesse,[5] and sēo[6] dæghwǣmlice wēox and hęfigode;
and ðā, ðȳ seǫfoðan dæge,[7] swā him gehāten wæs, æfter- 10
ðon-ðe his forðfōre getrymede[8] mid onfangennesse ðæs
Dryhtenlican līchaman and blōdes, [ðætte[9]] sēo hālge
sāwl wæs onlīesed fram ðæs līchaman hęfignessum,[10] and
mid ęngla lāttēowdōme[11] and gefērscipe, swā riht[12] is tō
gelīefanne, ðā ēcean gefēan and ðā heofonlican ēadig- 15
nesse[13] gestāh and gesōhte. Is ðæt hwilc[14] wundor ðēah-
ðe hē ðone dæg his dēaðes, oððe mā,[15] ðone Dryhtnes
dæg, blīðe gesāwe, ðone hē simle sorgiende bād ōð-ðæt
hē cōme?

[1] Lat. *dicas*.

[2] See **189**. 3.

[3] These translate the Lat.
future part. *redituros*. Supply
would be in translation, or *would*
with the finite verb. The future
participle of the following clause,
adducturos, is translated by a
finite verb.

[4] Governs **him**, or may be regarded as belonging to the following verb (**201**. 1).

[5] See **174**; **160**. 1.

[6] Dem. pron. Translate by
that.

[7] See **176**.

[8] Supply **hē** as the subject.

[9] The MS. has **ðætte**, but the
sense does not require it.

[10] Lat. *ergastulo*.

[11] See **33** (**lād**-).

[12] Lat. *fas*.

[13] Acc. plur.

[14] Translate, *any*.

[15] Lat. *potius*.

VIII.

THE DANGERS OF GREATNESS.

(From Wulfstan's Homilies, No. 49.)

[Wulfstan — also known by his Latinized name, Lupus — was Bishop of Worcester and Archbishop of York from 1002 to 1023. This homily is one of those attributed to him, but, according to Napier, with insufficient reason, as a portion of it is found in the Blickling Homilies, the manuscript of which bears the date of 971.]

Ǣghwilc hēah ār, hēr on worulde, biþ mid frēcnessum[1] ymbseald[2]; efne swā[3] þā woruldgeþyngþa bēoþ māran, swā þā frēcnessa bēoþ swīþran. Swā wē magon, be þǣm, þā bȳsena oncnāwan and ongietan.[4] Đæt trēow, þonne, þe
5   wiext[5] on þǣm wudubearwe, þæt[6] hit hlīfaþ ūp ofer eall þā ōþru trēowu and brǣt[6a] hit,[7] þonne sęmninga storm[8] gestęnt, and se stranga wind,[9] þonne[10] biþ hit swīþlicor gewǣged and geswęnged þonne se ōþer wudu.[11] Swā biþ ēac gelīce be þǣm hēaclifum and torrum,[12] þonne hīe

¹ See **144**.   ² See **114**.
³ **Swā . . . māran, swā . . . swīþran** = *the greater, the fiercer.* Note the tendency to antithesis.
⁴ Observe the redundancy.
⁵ See **weaxan**.   ⁶ = *so that.*
⁶ᵃ See **brǣdan (34)**.
⁷ See **184.** *b.*
⁸ Note the alliteration.
⁹ Second subject of **gestęnt**.

¹⁰ Frequently the second correlative, in such pairs as **þonne . . . þonne, þā . . . þā**, need not be translated; it is frequently followed by an inverted order, as here, the verb preceding its subject. See **202**.
¹¹ **Se ōþer wudu** = *the rest of the forest,* not *the other wood.*
¹² Probably here = *crag.*

hlīfiað feorr ūp ofer ðā ōðre[1] eorðan, hīe ðonne sęmninga feallan onginnað,[2] and full ðearlice hrēosan[3] tō eorðan. Swilce[4] ēac be ðǣm hēagum[5] muntum and dūnum,[6] ðā-ðe hēah standað ofer ealne middangeard, ðā-hwæðre wīte habbað ðæs ealdordōmes, ðæt hīe bēoð geneahhe mid 5 heofonfȳre[7] geðrēade and geðrǣste, and mid līegum ge-

[1] See p. 156, n. 12.

[2] This resembles the use of *gin* in Chaucer, almost as an auxiliary tense-sign, like *do* in Mod. Eng., the latter not being thus used in OE. In Chaucer it usually occurs as the preterit *gan*, e.g. in the *Clerk's Tale*, 392: "til the sonne gan descende." See Lounsbury's *History of the English Language*. An interesting parallel is to be found in New Testament Greek, as, for example, Acts 1. 1: "The former treatise I made, O Theophilus, concerning all that Jesus *began* (ἤρξατο) both to do and to teach." According to Thayer, however (*Greek-English Lexicon of the New Testament*), there is in its employment always a sense of *beginning*, in its proper meaning.

[3] Dependent, like **feallan**, on **onginnað**. Give the ind. pret. plur.

[4] It would be interesting to know from what literary source these illustrations are ultimately derived. They remind one of Shakespeare (*Rich. III.*, 1. 3. 259–260): —

> They that stand high have many blasts to shake them;
> And if they fall, they dash themselves to pieces.

Cf. also *3 Hen. VI.*, 5. 2. 11–15. No doubt many Elizabethan parallels could be found; I have noted in Chapman, *Byron's Conspiracy*, Act 3, Scene 1 (p. 232 of Shepherd's ed.), and *Byron's Tragedy*, Act 5, Scene 1 (*Ib.*, p. 272). Perhaps the Elizabethans may have derived them from Seneca; cf. the Chorus in Act 4 of the *Hippolytus*, vv. 1123–1143; *Hercules Furens* 201; *Œdipus* 8–11. Seneca may have caught a suggestion from Sophocles, though the parallel is somewhat remote; see the latter's *Antigone*, vv. 712–717, and Horace, *C.* II. 10.

[5] See **58.** 1.

[6] Redundant. What is **dūn** in Mod. Eng. (24)? Whence is the adverb *down* derived?

[7] Note the poetical term.

slægene. Swā ðā hēan mihta[1] hēr on worulde hrēosað,
and feallað,[2] and tō lore weorðað, and ðisse[3] worulde[3]
welan weorðað tō sorge, and ðās eorðlican wundor
weorðað tō nāhte.[4]

5   Ðēah wē ðisse worulde wlęnca[5] tilien[6] swīðe, and in
wuldre[5] scīnen[6] swīðe; ðęah wē ūs gescierpen[6] mid ðȳ
rēadestan gōdwębbe,[5] and gefrætwien[6] mid[7] ðȳ beorht-
estan golde,[5] and mid[7] ðǣm dēorwierðestum gimmum[5]
ūtan ymbhōn[6]; hwæðre[8] wē sculon on nearonesse ęnde[9]

10 gebīdan. Ðēah-ðe ðā mihtigestan and ðā rīcestan hāten[6]
him[10] ręste gewyrcean of marmanstāne,[11] and mid gold-
frætwum and mid gimcynnum eall āstǣned, and mid
seolfrenum rūwum and gōdwębbe eall oferwrigen, and
mid dēorwierðum wyrtgemęngnessum eall gestrēd,[12] and

15 mid goldlēafum gestrēowod ymbūtan, hwæðre[8] se bitera
dēað ðæt tōdǣlð eall. Ðonne bið sēo glęng āgoten,[13] and
se ðrym tōbrocen, and ðā gimmas tōglidene, and ðæc
gold tōsceacen, and ðā līchaman tōhrorene[14] and tō dūste[15]
gewordene.

[1] This suggests Seneca (*Œdi-pus*, Act 1, v. 11): —

Imperia sic excelsa Fortunæ obja-
cent.

[2] Pleonastic.

[3] Genitive, dependent on **welan**.

[4] Cf. Mod. Eng. *come to naught*.

[5] Note the alliteration.

[6] In what mood and tense are these verbs, and why?

[7] **Mid** governs both the dative and the instrumental (**175**).

[8] This word might be omitted in translation; see p. 156, n. 10.

[9] Object of **gebīdan**.

[10] See **184**. *a*.

[11] Which part of this word is native, and which foreign?

[12] An instance of a strong verb (**104**; cf. **28**) which has already become weak in OE.

[13] Note the parallelism and the enumeration.

[14] From what verb (**37**)?

[15] See **24**.

IX

DUTIES OF THE RICH TOWARD THE POOR.

(From the same Homily as the last.)

Se Hǣlend cwæð tō ðǣm wlancan[1]: "For hwȳ wǣre
ðū swā fæsthafol mīnra gōda, ðe ic ðē sealde? Tō
hwon[2] rēcelēasodest ðū ðǣre giefe, ðe ic ðē geaf? Ic ðē
nū āfierre[3] fram mīnre sęlene, ðe ic ðē forgeaf; ðonne
bist[3] ðū wǣdla on woruldlīfe. For hwon[2] noldest[4] ðū 5
geðęncean ðæt ic wille[5] forgieldan ǣghwilcum męnn āne
gōde dǣd, ðe for mīnum naman mann gedēð? Mid
hundtēontigum ic hit him forgielde,[3] swā hit is on
mīnum godspelle gecweden and gesǣd,[6] 'Swā-hwæt-swā[7]
gē sęllað ānum of mīnum ðǣm lǣstum,[8] gē hit simle mē 10
sęllað,[9] and ic ēow wið[10] ðǣm gesęlle[3] ēcne drēam[11] on
heofonum.'

[1] From what OE. word is the
Mod. Eng. *rich* derived (see Skeat,
Prin., p. 61)? From what OE.
meaning is the modern signification derived?

[2] Note Wulfstan's use of **tō
hwon, for hwon**, in the sense
of *why*. See **88**.

[3] See **188**.   [4] See **139**.

[5] Why should not the preterit
be used here?

[6] Pleonastic.

[7] What portion of this is lost,
and how is it replaced, in the
Mod. Eng. *whatsoever* ?

[8] See **66**.

[9] Cf. the form of this sentence
with that on p. 135, l. 14.

[10] = *in return for*. How is this
to be reconciled with other senses
of **wið** ?

[11] Not *dream*, but *joy, bliss*.

Ðū mann, tō hwon eart ðū mē swā ungeðancfull mīnra[1]
giefena? Hwæt! ic ðē gescēop and gelīffæste, and æg-
hwæt[2] ðæs ðe ðū hæfst[3] ic ðē sealde. Mīn is eall ðæt
ðū hæfst, and ðīn nis nān wiht.[4] Ic hit eall āfierre
5 fram ðē; ðū leofa[5] būtan mē, gif ðū mæge.[6] Ðē ic hit
sealde, tō[7] ðon[7] ðæt[7] ðū hit sceoldest[12] ðearfum dǣlan. Ic
swęrie ðurh mē[8] selfne ðæt ic eom se ilca God ðe ðone
weligan and ðone hēanan geworhte mid mīnum handum.
Ðæt[9] ic wolde, ðæt ðū mīne ðearfan fēddest,[12] ðonne hīe
10 wǣron ðē biddende mīnra[10] gōda,[10] and ðū him simle
tīðe[11] forwierndest. For hwon noldest ðū hit[9] geðęncean,
gif ðū him mildheortnesse on gecȳðdest,[12] ðæt ðū ne
sceoldest[12] ðæs[13] nān ðing forlēosan, ðe[14] ðū him dydest,
nē mē on ðǣre sęlene ābelgan mīnes[15] āgnes[15]? Tō
15 hwon āgnodest ðū ðē ānum ðæt ic inc[16] bǣm[17] sealde?
Tō hwon fēddest ðū ðē ænne of ðǣm ðe ic inc[16] bǣm[17]
gescēop tō[18] welan, and tō[18] wiste, and tō[18] feorhnęre?
Tō hwon hēolde[19] ðū hit ðē ānum and ðīnum bearnum,
ðæt meahte manigum genyhtsumian[20]? Unīeðe ðē wæs

[1] See **155**.
[2] See **89**. *c*.   [3] See **121**.
[4] In what two Mod. Eng. words
does *wiht* appear? From what
OE. forms are *aught* and *naught*
derived?
[5] See **122** and **198**.
[6] = *canst*, not *mayst* (**135**).
[7] = *in order that*.
[8] What has this accusative become in Mod. Eng.?
[9] Anticipative of the following
noun-clause.

[10] See **156**. *b*.
[11] Not to be confounded with
tīde. See **156**. *j*.
[12] Optative more regular.
[13] See **154**. *a*.
[14] Refers to its antecedent
ðæs.
[15] Dependent on **sęlene**.
[16] Note this rare dual (**81**).
[17] See **79**.
[18] = *for, as*.
[19] From what infinitive?
[20] The sense is pluperfect.

ðæt ðū hit eall ne meahtest gefæstnian, nē mid inseglum
beclȳsan. Wēnst ðū ðæt hit[1] ðīu sīe ðæt sēo eorðe ðē
forðbringð? Hēo[2] ðē grēwð,[3] and blēwð,[3] and sǣd lǣt,[4]
and andlifan bringð. Ic nū āfierre mīnne fultum fram
ðē; hafa[5] ðū æt[6] ðīnum gewinne ðæt ðū mæge, and æt[6]   5
ðīnum geswince. Ic ðē[7] ætbrēde[8] mīne rēnas,[8] ðæt hīe
ðīnre eorðan[9] ne rīnen.[10] Ic āfierre fram ðē mīne mildheortnesse, and ðonne bið sōna gecȳðed ðīn iermðu, and
ætīewed.

Gif ðū wēne[11] ðæt hit ðīn bōcland[12] sīe ðæt ðū on   10
eardast, and on āgne ǣht[13] geseald, hit ðonne wǣron[1n]
mīne wæteru, ðā-ðe on heofonum wǣron, ðonne ic mīne
giefe eorðwarum dǣlde. Gif ðū miht hæbbe,[11] dǣl rēnas
ofer ðīne eorðan. Gif ðū strang sīe, sęle wǣstmas ðīnre
eorðan. Ic āhierde mīne sunnan, and hēo gebierht; ðonne   15
forbærnð[15] hēo ealle ðīne æceras, and ðonne bist[15] ðū dæl-
lēas[16] mīnes rēnes,[17] and ðē ðonne bið[15] ðīn eorðe īdel and
unnyt gōda[18] gehwilces.[19] Mīne ðearfan libbað be mē; gif
ðū mæge,[11] wuna būtan mē. Mīne ðearfan mē ealne[20] weg[20]
habbað, and ic hīe nǣfre ne forlǣte."   20

[1] Anticipative of ðæt.
[2] Refers to what?
[3] See 109.
[4] See lǣdan.
[5] See 121 and 198.
[6] = from; cf. at one's hands.
[7] See 164.   [8] See 28.
[9] See 161.   [10] MS. rinað.
[11] See 196. d.
[12] Land held by bōc or char-
ter, freehold estate; distinguished
from folcland, communal property. The term is explained by
the following clause.
[13] See 172. 1.
[14] See 189. 3.
[15] Are these presents or futures?
[16] See 146.
[17] See 155. a.
[18] Dependent on gehwilces.
See 154. b.
[19] Dependent on īdel and
unnyt. See 155. a.
[20] See 170. Mod. Eng. alway.

X.

ALFRED'S PREFACE TO BOETHIUS.

(Prefixed to his translation.)

Ælfred cyning wæs wealhstōd[1] ðisse bēc, and hīe of
Bōclǣdene[2] on Ẹnglisc wẹnde, swā hēo nū is gedōn.
Hwīlum hē sẹtte word be worde, hwīlum andgiet of
andgiete, swā-swā hē hit ðā sweotolost and andgiet-
5 fullicost gerẹccean meahte for ðǣm mislicum and manigfealdum woruldbisgum ðe hine oft ǣgðer ge on mōde
ge on līchaman bisgedon. Đā bisga[3] ūs sind swīðe
earfoðrīme ðe on his dagum on ðā rīcu becōmon ðe hẹ
underfangen hæfde, and ðēah, ðā hē ðās bōc hæfde
10 geleornod, and of Lædene tō Ẹngliscum spelle gewẹnd,
ðā geworhte hē hīe ẹft tō lēoðe, swā-swā hēo nū gedōn
is. And nū bitt[4] and for Godes naman hālsað ǣlcne
ðǣra ðe ðās bōc rǣdan lyste,[5] ðæt hē for hine gebidde,
and him ne wīte gif hē[6] hīe rihtlicor ongiete ðonne hē[7]
15 meahte; for-ðǣm-ðe ǣlc mann sceal be his andgietes
mǣðe, and be his ǣmettan, sprecan ðæt hē spricð, and
dōn ðæt-ðæt hē dēð.

---

[1] **Wealh**- signifies *foreign* (see
walnut), and sometimes *servant*,
orig. *Celtic, Celt* (cf. *Wales, Welsh,
Cornwall*), from *Volcæ*, the name
of a Celtic tribe (Cæsar, *Gallic
War*, Bk. VII.).

[2] Perhaps originally in contrast
to the Latin spoken in Britain.

[3] See **51.** *a.*

[4] Supply **hē.**   [5] See **190.**

[6] The reader.

[7] Alfred.

XI.

A PRAYER OF KING ALFRED.

(From the end of his translation of Boethius.)

Dryhten,[1] ælmihtiga God,[1] Wyrhta and Wealdend ealra
gesceafta, ic bidde ðē for ðīnre miclan mildheortnesse,
and for ðǣre hālgan rōde tācne,[2] and for Sanctæ Marian
mægðhāde, and for Sancti Michaeles gehīersumnesse, and
for ealra ðīnra hālgena[3] lufan and hiera earnungum, ðæt 5
ðū mē gewissie[4] bęt ðonne ic āworhte tō ðē; and gewissa
mē tō ðīnum willan, and tō mīnre sāwle ðearfe,[5] bęt ðonne
ic self cunne[6]; and gestaðela mīn mōd tō ðīnum willan and
tō mīnre sāwle ðearfe; and gestranga mē wið ðæs dēofles[3]
costnungum; and āfierr fram mē ðā fūlan gālnesse and ǣlce 10
unrihtwīsnesse; and gescield mē wið mīnum wiðerwinnum,
gesewenlicum and ungesewenlicum; and tǣc mē ðīnne willan[7] tō wyrceanne; ðæt ic mæge[8] ðē inweardlice lufian tō-
foran eallum ðingum, mid clǣnum geðance and mid clǣnum
līchaman. For-ðon-ðe ðū eart mīn Scieppend,[9] and mīn 15
Ālīesend, mīn Fultum, mīn Frōfor, mīn Trēownes, and
mīn Tōhopa. Sīe ðē lof and wuldor nū and ā ā ā, tō
worulde būtan ǣghwilcum ęnde. Amen.

---

[1] See 152. [4] See 194. b. [7] Object of **wyrceanne.**

[2] Governed by **for.** [5] See 166. [8] See 196. d.

[3] See 153. c. [6] Optative (130). [9] See 150.

XII.

APOLLONIUS OF TYRE.

[The Old English version of the *Romance of Apollonius*, from which our extract is taken, belongs, according to Wülker, to the second third of the eleventh century; according to Ebert, to its beginning; and according to Riese, most probably to the tenth. The original story was almost certainly written in Greek, probably in the third century of our era, and by an imitator of Xenophon of Ephesus. This is lost, and is only represented by a Latin version, which may have been made in the same century, and in any case not later than the sixth, by a writer of no great education, who introduced Christian terms and conceptions, added some things, and retrenched others. Over a hundred manuscripts of this Latin version are known, of which twelve are in England. Scarcely any two manuscripts agree, and the discrepancies are often great; still, for convenience, they have been grouped into three main classes. To the third of these, which is not the equal of the other two, the immediate original of our version must have belonged, resembling most nearly a manuscript of the Bodleian Library (Laud H. 39), and, at the next further remove, one of the British Museum (Sloan. 1619).

The popularity of the romance is attested not only by the number and variety of the Latin manuscripts, but no less by the mediæval and subsequent translations into almost every modern language. Thus, for example, there is in Old French a romance of *Jourdain de Blaic*, the scene being laid in the time of Charlemagne, and the temple of Diana being converted into a nunnery.

An abridgment of the Latin version found its way into the *Gesta Romanorum*, as No. 153 of that collection. In the twelfth century the story was incorporated into the *Pantheon* of Godfrey of Viterbo, whence it was turned into English verse by Gower, in his *Confessio Amantis* (Pauli's edition 3. 284 ff.; Morley's abridgment, in *The Carisbrooke Library*, pp. 410–431). From Gower it was borrowed by Shakespeare, or whoever was the author of the drama which passes under his name, as the groundwork of *Pericles, Prince of Tyre;* the name Pericles being perhaps adapted from the Pyrocles of Sidney's *Arcadia*. The scenes of *Pericles* which may be compared with our extract are the 1st, 2d, 3d, and 5th of Act II., and the 3d of Act V.

The Old English *Apollonius* was edited by Thorpe, in 1834, from MS. S. 18. 201 of Corpus Christi College, Cambridge; and to this edition the student is referred for the spelling and punctuation of the original. It is only a fragment, breaking off in the midst, and recommencing near the end of the tale, as we have indicated below. .

Further information will be found in Rohde, *Der griechische Roman*, Leipzig, 1876; Teuffel, *History of Latin Literature*, § 489; Singer, *Apollonius von Tyrus*, Halle, 1895 ; Zupitza's article on the OE. version in *Herrig's Archiv* 97. 17–35 ; Warton, *History of English Poetry* 2. 302–303 ; and Riese's edition of the Latin, which is the standard (Leipzig, 1871), and costs but a trifle.

Besides the Tudor versions, there is an English translation in Thorpe's edition, and another — of course not adhering closely to our text — in Swan's rendering of the *Gesta Romanorum* (Bohn Library)].

The Shipwreck.

Apollonius[1] hīe bæd ealle grētan,[2] and on scip āstāh.[3] Mid-ðȳ-ðe hīe ongunnon ðā rōwan,[4] and hīe forðweard wǣron on hiera weg, ðā wearð ðǣre sǣ smyltnes āwęnd fǣringa betweox twām tīdum,[5] and wearð miclu hrēohnes āweaht, swā ðæt sēo sǣ cnysede ðā heofonlican tunglu,[6] 5 and ðæt gewealc ðǣra ȳða hwaðerode mid windum. Ðǣr-tō-ēacan cōmon ēastnorðerne windas, and se angrīslica sūðwesterna wind him ongēan stōd,[7] and ðæt scip eall

[1] Apollonius, King of Tyre, has fled from the cruelty and treachery of Antiochus, King of Antioch, on a richly freighted vessel, and taken refuge with the citizens of Tarsus. Finding the citizens in extremity, on account of a prevalent famine, he relieves their necessities by liberal gifts, whereupon they erect a statue of him in the market-place. But notwithstanding the gratitude of his beneficiaries, he finds it expedient to leave them, and embarks for Cyrene, on the African coast. It is at this point that our selection begins.

[2] Observe the ellipsis, — *bade greet them all* — where the subject of the infinitive is to be supplied.

[3] See **28.**   [4] See **199.** *b.*

[5] Lat. *intra duas horas diei.*

[6] This seems to be a reminiscence of Virgil, *Æneid* I. 103.

[7] Lat. (verse): *Hinc Notus, hinc Boreas, hinc horridus Africus instat.*

tōbærst on ðisse ęgeslican hrēohnesse. Apollonius[1] gefēran
ealle forwurdon[2] tō dēaðe, and Apollonius āna[3] becōm mid
sunde tō Pentapolim ðǣm Cyreniscan lande, and ðǣr ūpēode
on ðǣm strande. Ðā stōd hē nacod on ðǣm strande, and
5 behēold ðā sǣ, and cwæð:

"Ēalā! ðū sǣ Neptune! manna berēafiend[3a] and unscęð-
ðigra beswīcend[3a]! ðu eart wælhrēowra ðonne Antiochus se
cyning. For mīnum ðingum ðū gehēolde ðās wælhrēow-
nesse, ðæt ic ðurh ðē gewurde[4] wǣdla[5] and ðearfa, and
10 ðæt se wælhrēowa cyning mē ðȳ īeð[6] fordōn meahte.
Hwider mæg ic nū faran? Hwæs[7] mæg ic biddan?
Oððe hwā giefð[8] ðǣm uncūðan[9] līfes fultum?"

Apollonius and the Fisherman.

Mid-ðȳ-ðe hē ðās ðing wæs sprecende tō him selfum,
ðā fǣringa gesēah hē sumne fiscere[10] gān, tō ðǣm hē
15 besēah, and ðus sārlice cwæð[11]: "Gemiltsa mē,[12] ðū ealda
mann, sīe[13] ðæt ðū sīe. Gemiltsa mē nacodum forlid-
enum. Næs[14] nā of earmlicum[15] byrdum[16] geboren; and,

---

[1] The Latin endings of proper
nouns are not always a guide to
the case (54). Here we have the
genitive.

[2] See **forweorðan.**

[3] See **79.**   [3a] See **43. 6.**

[4] MS. **gewurðe.**

[5] See **150.**

[6] MS. **eaðe.** See **178.**   ,

[7] See **156.** *b.*

[8] Zupitza's emendation for MS.
gif.

[9] See **55** and **181.**

[10] See **169.**

[11] In the original, he falls at
the fisherman's feet, and bursts
into tears. What reason may
have led to the change?

[12] See **164.** *g.*

[13] See **193.** *c.*

[14] See **189**, note.

[15] Lat. *humilibus.*

[16] Plural, where we should expect the singular.

ðæs-ðe[1] ðū geare forwite hwǣm ðū gemiltsie,[2] ic eom Apollonius, se Tyrisca[3] ealdormann.[4]

Ðā, sōna swā se fiscere[5] geseah ðæt se geonga mann æt his fōtum læg, hē mid mildheortnesse hine ūpāhōf, and lǣdde hine mid him tō his hūse, and ðā ēstas[6] him 5 beforan lęgde ðe hē him tō bēodanne hæfde. Ðā gīet hē wolde, be his mihte, māran ārfæstnesse[7] him gecȳðan; tōslāt ðā his wǣfels on twā, and sealde Apollonie ðone healfan dǣl, ðus cweðende: "Nim ðæt ic ðē tō sęllanne hæbbe, and gā intō ðǣre ceastre. Wēn[8] is[8] ðæt ðū 10 gemēte[9] sumne ðæt[9a] ðē gemiltsie.[10] Gif ðū ne finde[11] nænne ðe ðē gemiltsian wille, węnd ðonne hider ongēan, and genyhtsumien[12] unc[13] bǣm mīne lȳtlan[14] ǣhta; far ðē[15] on fiscnoð[16] mid mē. Ðēah-hwæðre ic myngie ðē, gif ðū, ful-tumiendum[17] Gode, becymst tō ðīnum ǣrran weorðmynte, 15 ðæt ðū ne forgiete[18] mīnne ðearfendlican gegierelan."

Ðā cwæð Apollonius: "Gif ic ðē[19] ne geðęnce ðonne mē bęt bið,[20] ic wȳsce[21] ðæt ic ęft forlidennesse gefare, and ðīnne[22] gelīcan[22] ęft ne gemēte."

---

[1] Here = *in order that.* See **157.** 1.

[2] See **195.**

[3] Proper adjectives in -**isc**, following the Latin, are often used where we employ the genitive. Translate, *of Tyre.*

[4] Lat. *princeps.*   [5] See **143.**
[6] Lat. *epulas.*

[7] MS. **fæstnesse.** Lat. *pietati.*

[8] Lat. *forsitan.*   [9] See **194.** *a.*

[9a] Neut. for masc.!   [10] See **195.**

[11] See **196.** *d.*

[12] See **193.** *a.*

[13] Note the rare dual (**81**).

[14] See **55.**   [15] See **184.** *a.*

[16] See **172.** 1.

[17] See **167. Gode** is supplied; the Latin has *deo favente.*

[18] See **194.** *b.*   [19] Acc.

[20] Present or future? Could Mod. Eng. *is* be used to translate it?

[21] See **30,** and **194.** *b.*

[22] Mod. Eng. still has *thy like.* See **181.**

The Incidents in the Gymnasium.

Æfter ðisum wordum hē ēode on ðone weg ðe him getǣht[1] wæs, oð-ðæt hē becōm tō ðǣre ceastre geate, and ðǣr inēode. Mid-ðȳ-ðe hē ðōhte hwone hē biddan meahte līfes fultumes,[2] ðā geseah hē ænne nacodne cnapan geond
5 ðā strǣte iernan. Sē wæs mid[3] ęle gesmierwed, and mid scīetan begyrd, and bǣr geongra[4] manna[4] plegan[4] on handa, tō ðǣm bæðstęde[5] belimpende.[6] And cleopode[7] micelre stefne,[8] and cwæð: "Gehīere,[9] gē ceasterwaran[10]! Gehīere, gē ęlðēodige,[11] frige and ðēowe, æðele and unæðele! Se
10 bæðstęde is open."

Ðā-ðā Apollonius ðæt gehīerde, hē hine unscrȳdde ðǣm[12] healfan sciccelse ðe hē on hæfde, and ēode intō ðǣm ðwēale.[13] And mid-ðȳ-ðe hē behēold hiera ānra[14] gehwilcne on hiera weorce, hē sōhte his gelīcan,[15] ac hē ne meahte hine ðǣr
15 findan on ðǣm flocce. Ðā fǣringa cōm Arcestrates, ealre ðǣre ðēode[16] cyning,[17] mid micelre męnige his manna,[18] and inēode on ðæt bæð. Ðā āgan se cyning plegian wið[19] his gefērum mid ðoðore.[20] And Apollonius hine[21] gemęngde,[21]

---

[1] See 187.

[2] MS. fultum. See 159. b.

[3] See 174.

[4] Lat. lusus juvenales.

[5] Lat. gymnasium.

[6] Modifies plegan.

[7] See 20.

[8] See 160. 1. This word is the Chaucerian steven.

[9] See 95, note.

[10] This is a compound word, formed of a Latin and an English element. Which is Latin, and what is its form in that language?

[11] Lat. peregrini. See 152.

[12] See 162.   [13] Lat. lavacrum.

[14] See 154. b.

[15] Lat. parem, Eng. peer.

[16] Lat. regionis.

[17] See 151.

[18] Lat. famularum. See 154. a.

[19] Why not mid?

[20] This curious word is very rare in Old English.

[21] Lat. miscuit se. See 184. b.

swā-swā God wolde, on ðæs cyninges plegan, and, iernende, ðone ðoðor gelǣhte,[1] and, mid swiftre hrædnesse geslægene,[2] ongēan gesęnde tō ðǣm plegiendan cyninge. Ęft hē āgēan āsęnde; hē hrædlice slōg, swā hē hine[3] nǣfre feallan ne lēt. Se cyning ðā oncnēow ðæs geongan snelnesse,[4] ðæt hē wiste[5] ðæt hē næfde his gelīcan on ðǣm plegan.[6] Ðā cwæð hē tō his gefērum: "Gāð ēow heonan; ðes cniht, ðæs-ðe mē ðyncð,[7] is mīn gelīca."

Ðā-ðā Apollonius gehīerde ðæt se cyning hine hęrede, hē arn hrædlice, and genēalǣcte tō ðǣm cyninge, and mid gelǣredre[8] handa[9] hē swang[10] ðone top mid swā micelre swiftnesse ðæt ðǣm cyninge wæs geðūht swilce hē of ielde tō geoguðe gewęnd wǣre. And, æfter ðǣm, on his cynesetle hē him[11] gecwēmlice[12] ðēnode[13]; and, ðā-ðā hē ūtēode of ðǣm bæðe, hē[14] hine[15] lǣdde be ðǣre handa, and him[16] ðā siððan ðanan gewęnde, ðæs weges[17] ðe hē ǣr cōm.

5

10

15

---

[1] See 114.

[2] Lat. *subtili velocitate percussam.* The OE. participle is a little awkward.

[3] The ball.

[4] Lat. *velocitatem.*

[5] See 126. What is the latest English quotation that you can find for this word?

[6] This clause is not very clear. The Latin has: *et quia sciebat se (i.e.* Archistrates) *in pilæ lusu neminem parem habere, ad suos ait, famuli, recedite; hic enim juvenis,* etc.

[7] Lat. *ut suspicor.* See 157. 1

and 164. *l.* What Mod. Eng. word comes from mē ðyncð?

[8] Lat. *docta.*

[9] See 51. 3.

[10] Here the English departs from the Latin: *ceroma fricavit eum tanta subtilitate, ut de sene juvenem redderet.* **Top** would seem to signify the same as ðoðor.

[11] See 164. *e.*

[12] Lat. *gratissime.*

[13] See 28.

[14] Apollonius.

[15] Archistrates.

[16] See 184. *a.*

[17] See 157.

Ðā cwæð se cyning tō his mannum,[1] siððan Apollonius āgān[2] wæs: "Ic swęrie ðurh ðā gemǣnan hǣle[3] ðæt ic mē nǣfre bęt ne baðode ðonne ic dyde[4] tō-dæg, nāt ic ðurh[5] hwilces geonges mannes ðēnunge."[6]   Ðā beseah hē

5 hine tō ānum his manna, and cwæð: "Gā, and gewite hwæt[7] se geonga mann sīe, ðe mē tō-dæg swā wel gehīersumode."

Se mann ðā ēode æfter Apollonio.   Mid-ðȳ-ðe hē geseah ðæt hē[8] wæs mid horgum[9] sciccelse bewǣfed, ðā węnde

10 hē ongēan tō ðǣm cyninge, and cwæð: "Se geonga mann ðe[10] ðū æfter āscodest is forliden[11] mann.[11]"   Ðā cwæð se cyning: "Ðurh[12] hwæt[12] wāst[13] ðū ðæt?"   Se mann him andswarode, and cwæð: "Ðēah hē hit self forswīge,[14] his gegierela hine gesweotolað."   Ðā cwæð se cyning: "Gā

15 hrædlice, and sęge him ðæt[15] 'se cyning bitt ðē ðæt ðū cume[16] tō his gereorde.'"

Apollonius at the Feast.

Ðā Apollonius ðæt gehīerde, hē ðǣm gehīersumode, and ēode forð mid ðǣm męnn, oð-ðæt hē becōm tō ðæs cyninges

---

[1] Lat. *amicos.*

[2] How is the sense of Mod. Eng. *ago* related to that of this word?

[3] This phrase shows Christian influence.

[4] Note this use of **dōn** to replace a verb of specific meaning.

[5] Governs **ðēnunge.**

[6] See **28.**

[7] How does this, as here used, differ in meaning from **hwā**?

[8] Apollonius.   [9] Lat. *sordido.*

[10] Governed by **æfter.**   See **87.** *c* and **201.** 1.

[11] Lat. *naufragus.*

[12] Lat. *unde.*

[13] See **126.**   [14] See **196.** *e.*

[15] Confusion of two constructions, the direct and the indirect.

[16] Lat. *ut venias.* Translate by the infinitive, as often in such cases.

healle.[1] Ðā ēode se mann in beforan tō ðǣm cyninge,
and cwæð: "Se forlidena[2] mann is cumen, ðe ðū æfter
sendest[3]; ac hē ne mæg for sceame ingān būtan scrūde."
Ðā hēt se cyning hine sōna gescrȳdan mid weorðfullum[4]
scrūde, and hēt hine ingān tō ðǣm gereorde.   5

Ðā ēode Apollonius in, and gesæt, ðǣr him getǣht[5]
wæs, ongēan ðone cyning.   Ðā[6] wearð ðā sēo ðēnung[7]
ingeboren, and, æfter ðǣm, cynelic[8] gebēorscipe.[8]   And
Apollonius nān ðing ne æt, ðēah-ðe ealle ōðre menn ǣton
and blīðe wǣron.   Ac hē behēold ðæt gold, and ðæt   10
seolfor, and ðā dēorwurðan[9] rēaf, and ðā bēodas, and ðā
cynelican ðēnunga.[10]   Ðā-ðā hē ðis eall mid sārnesse.[11]
behēold, ðā sæt sum eald and sum[12] æfestig ealdormann
be ðǣm cyninge.   Mid-ðȳ-ðe hē geseah ðæt Apollonius
swā sārlice sæt, and eall ðing behēold, and nān ðing ne   15
æt, ðā cwæð hē tō ðǣm cyninge: "Ðū[13] gōda cyning,
efne, ðes mann ðe[14] ðū swā wel wið gedēst, hē is swīðe
æfestfull for ðīnum gōde."   Ðā cwæð se cyning: "Ðē[15]
misðyncð; sōðlice ðes geonga mann ne æfestað on nānum
ðingum ðe hē hēr gesiehð, ac hē cȳð[16] ðæt hæfð[17] fela   20

[1] Lat. ad regem.

[2] See 55.

[3] Is this present or preterit (113)?

[4] Lat. dignis.

[5] See 187.

[6] It has been suggested that the account of this feast may have been imitated from that in Odys. 4. 71 ff.

[7] Lat. gustatio, a sort of first course.

[8] Lat. cena regalis.

[9] See 146.

[10] Lat. ministeria.

[11] Lat. dolore.

[12] Note the curious repetition of sum. The Latin has senex invidus.

[13] Lat. bone rex. See 152.

[14] Governed by wið.

[15] See 164. l.

[16] Lat. testatur.

[17] See 189, note.

forloren.[1] " Ða besealh Arcestrates se cyning blīðum[2] andwlitan[2] tō Apollonio, and cwæð: " Ðū geonga mann, bēo[3] blīðe[3] mid ūs, and gehyht[4] on God, ðæt ðū mōte self tō ðǣm sēlran becuman."

Entry of the Princess.

5   Mid-ðȳ-ðe se cyning ðās word gecwæð, ðā fǣringa ðǣr ēode in ðæs cyninges geong dohtor,[5] and cyste hiere fæder and ðā ymbsittendan.[6]   Ðā[7] hēo becōm tō Apollonio, ðā gewęnde hēo ongēan tō hiere fæder, and cwæð: " Ðū gōda cyning, and mīn se[8] lēofesta[9] fæder, hwæt[10]
10 is ðes geonga mann, ðe ongēan ðē on swā weorðlicum setle sitt, mid sārlicum[11] andwlitan; nāt[12] ic hwæt hē besorgað.[13] "   Ðā cwæð se cyning: " Lēofe[14] dohtor, ðes geonga mann is forliden; and hē gecwēmde mē manna bętst[15] on ðǣm plegan.   For-ðām ic hine gelaðode tō
15 ðisum ūrum gebēorscipe.   Nāt ic hwæt hē is, nē hwanan hē is; ac gif ðū wille witan hwæt hē sīe, āsca hine, for-ðām ðē[16] gedafenað[17] ðæt ðū wite.[18] "

Ðā ēode ðæt mǣden tō Apollonio, and mid forwandiendre[19] sprǣce cwæð: ' " Ðēah ðū stille[20] sīe and unrōt,

---

[1] See **forlēosan**, and **37**.

[2] Lat. *hilari vultu*.   See **174**.

[3] Lat. *epulare*.

[4] Lat. *spera*.   See **197**.

[5] What state and period of civilization is indicated by the presence of the girl at the banquet ?

[6] See **181**.   [7] See **202**. *d*.

[8] Redundant, according to our conceptions.   See **152**.

[9] Lat. *optime*.   [10] Lat. *quis*.

[11] Lat. *flebili*.   [12] See **126**.

[13] Lat. *dolet*.

[14] See **55**.   Lat. *dulcis*.

[15] See **66** and **154**. *d*.   Nom., belonging to **hē**.

[16] See **164**. *k*.   [17] Lat. *decet*.

[18] See **194**. *a*.

[19] Lat. *verecundo*.

[20] See **59**.

ðeah[1] ic ðīne æðelborennesse[2] on ðē gesēo. Nū[3] ðonne,[3] gif ðē[4] tō hęfig ne ðynce,[5] sęge mē ðīnne naman, and ðīn gelimp[6] āręce mē." Ðā cwæð Apollonius: "Gif ðū for nīede[7] āscast æfter mīnum naman, ic sęcge ðē, Ic hine forlēas on sæ. Gif ðū wilt mīne æðelborennesse witan, wite ðū ðæt ic hīe forlēt on Tharsum.[8]" Ðæt mǣden cwæð: "Sęge mē gewislicor,[9] ðæt ic hit mæge understandan." Apollonius ðā sōðlice hiere ārealte[10] eall[11] his gelimp, and æt ðǣre sprǣce[12] ęnde him[13] fēollon tēaras of ðǣm ēagum.

Mid-ðȳ-ðe se cyning ðæt geseah, hē bewęnde hine ðā tō ðǣre dehter,[14] and cwæð: "Lēofe dohtor, ðū gesyngodest, mid-ðȳ-ðe[15] ðū woldest witan his naman and his gelimp. Ðū hæfst nū geednīwod his eald sār,[16] ac ic bidde ðē ðæt ðū giefe him swā-hwæt-swā ðū wille. Ðā-ðā ðæt mǣden gehīerde ðæt hiere wæs ālīefed fram hiere fæder[17] ðæt[18] hēo ǣr hiere[19] self[19] gedōn wolde, ðā cwæð hēo tō Apollonio: "Apolloni, sōðlice ðū eart ūre[20];

---

[1] Second correlative = Lat. *tamen*. Translate *yet*, or omit (**201**. *e*).

[2] Lat. *nobilitatem*.

[3] Are these notes of time? The Latin has nothing similar.

[4] See **164**. *l*.   [5] See **196**. *d*.

[6] Lat. *casus tuos*. Observe the general resemblance to the story of Dido, in the *Æneid*.

[7] MS. **neode**. Lat. *necessitatis*.

[8] See p. 165, n. 1.

[9] Lat. *apertius*.

[10] See **114**.

[11] Plural.

[12]'See **153**. *i*.

[13] See **161**. 2.

[14] See **52**. 2.

[15] Lat. *dum*.

[16] Lat. *veteres ei renovasti dolores*, a reminiscence of the Virgilian (*Æn*. II. 3) *jubes renovare dolorem*.

[17] See **43**. 8.   [18] = *what*.

[19] Lat. *ipsa*.

[20] Note this predicate use of **ūre**, = Lat. *noster es* (cf. *Æn*. II. 149).

forlǣt ðīne murcnunge[1]; and, nū[2] ic mīnes fæder[3] lēafe hæbbe, ic gedō[4] ðē weligne." Apollonius hiere ðæs ðancode,[5] and se cyning blissode on his dohtor welwillendnesse,[6] and hiere tō cwæð: "Lēofe dohtor, hāt fęccean ðīne hearpan,[7] and gecīeg ðē tō ðīnum frīend,[8] and āfiersa fram ðǣm geongan his sārnesse."

A Lesson in Music.

Ðā ēode hēo ūt,[9] and hēt fęccean hiere hearpan. And sōna swā hēo hearpian ongann, hēo mid wynsumum sange gemęngde ðǣre hearpan swēg. Ðā ongunnon ealle ðā męnn hīe hęrian on hiere swēgcræfte; and Apollonius āna[10] swīgode. Ðā cwæð se cyning: "Apolloni, nū ðū dēst[11] yfele, for-ðām-ðe ealle męnn hęriað mīne dohtor on hiere swēgcræfte,[12] and ðū āna hīe, swīgende,[12a] tǣlst.[13]" Apollonius cwæð: "Ēalā, ðū gōda cyning, gif ðū mē gelīefst,[14] ic sęcge ðæt ic ongiete ðæt sōðlice ðīn dohtor gefēoll[15] on swēgcræft, ac hēo næfð hine nā wel geleornod; ac hāt mē[16] nū sęllan ðā hearpan, ðonne wāst[17] ðū nū ðæt ðū gīet nāst.[17]" Arcestrates se cyning cwæð: "Apolloni,

---

[1] Lat. mœrorem.

[2] *Now*, or *since?*

[3] See **43**. 8.

[4] Future sense, *will make*. See **173**.

[5] See **159**. *a.*

[6] Lat. *benignitate.*

[7] Lat. *lyram.*

[8] This clause is not altogether clear. It seems to stand for the Lat. *exhilara convivium*, though

of course it does not translate these words.

[9] Not in the Latin.

[10] See **79**.   [11] See **140**.

[12] Lat. *arte musica.*

[12a] For **swigiende**.

[13] Lat. *vituperas.*

[14] See **196**. *d.*

[15] Lat. *incidit*.   Translate, *has chanced.*

[16] See **164**. *a.*   [17] See **126**.

ic oncnāwe sōðlice ðæt ðū eart[1] on eallum ðingum wel gelǣred."

Ðā hēt se cyning sęllan Apollonie ðā hearpan. Apollonius ðā ūtēode, and hine scrȳdde, and sętte ænne cynehelm upon his hēafod, and nōm ðā hearpan on his hand, and inēode, and swā stōd ðæt se cyning and ealle ðā ymbsittendan wēndon ðæt hē nǣre Apollonius, ac ðæt hē wǣre Apollines,[2] ðǣra hǣðenra god. Ðā wearð stilnes and swīge[3] geworden innan ðǣre healle. And Apollonius his hearpenægl genōm, and hē ðā hearpestręngas mid cræfte āstyrian ongan, and ðǣre hearpan swēg mid wynsumum sange gemęngde.[4] And se cyning self, and ealle ðe ðǣr andwearde wǣron, micelre stefne cleopedon and hine hęredon. Æfter ðisum forlēt[5] Apollonius ðā hearpan, and[6] plegode, and fela fægerra ðinga[7] ðǣr forðtēah,[8] ðe ðǣm folce ungecnāwen wæs and ungewunelic. And him[9] eallum ðearle līcode ælc ðǣra ðinga[7] ðe hē forðtēah.

Sōðlice, mid-ðȳ-ðe ðæs cyninges dohtor geseah ðæt Apollonius on eallum gōdum cræftum swā wel wæs getogen,[10] ðā gefēoll hiere mōd on his lufe. Ðā, æfter ðæs bēorscipes geęndunge, cwæð ðæt mǣden tō ðǣm cyninge : "Lēofa[11]

---

[1] See **194**, note.   [2] Apollo.
[3] We are reminded of *Æn.* II. 1, *Conticuere omnes.*
[4] To this sentence there corresponds in the Latin : —

arripuit plectrum, animumque accommodat arti ;
cum chordis miscetur vox cantu modulata.

[5] Lat. *deponens.*

[6] The rest of this sentence paraphrases : *induit statum comicum et inauditas actiones expressit, deinde tragicum.*
[7] See **154.** *a, b.*
[8] Lat. *expressit.*
[9] See **164.** *k.*
[10] See getēon. What relation has **getogen** to Mod. Eng. *wanton?*
[11] See **55.**

fæder, ðū līefdest mē, lŷtle[1] ǣr,[1] ðæt[2] ic[2] mōste[2] giefan Apollonio swā-hwæt-swā ic wolde of ðīnum goldhorde."

Arcestrates se cyning cwæð tō hiere: "Gief him swā-hwæt-swā ðū wille.[3]"   Hēo ðā swīðe blīðe ūtēode,[4] and

5   cwæð: "Lārēow[5] Apolloni, ic giefe ðē, be mīnes fæder lēafe, twā hund punda[6] goldes,[7] and fēower hund punda[6] gewihte[8] seolfres,[7] and ðone mǣstan dǣl dēorwurðes[9] rēafes, and twēntig ðēowa[10] manna.[10]"   And hēo ðā ðus cwæð tō ðǣm ðēowum mannum: "Berað ðās ðing mid

10   ēow, ðe ic behēt Apollonio mīnum lārēowe, and lęcgeað innan būre[11] beforan mīnum frēondum."   Ðis wearð ðā ðus gedōn, æfter ðǣre cwēne hǣse[12]; and ealle ðā męnn hiere giefa hęredon ðe[13] hīe gesāwon.   Ðā sōðlice geęndode se gebēorscipe, and ðā męnn ealle ārison,[14] and

15   grētton ðone cyning and ðā cwēne, and bǣdon hīe gesunde bēon,[15] and hām gewęndon.   Ēac swilce Apollonius cwæð: "Ðū gōda cyning, and earmra[16] gemiltsiend, and ðū cwēn, lāre[16] lufiend, bēon gē gesunde.[17]"   Hē beseah ēac tō ðǣm ðēowum mannum, ðe ðæt mǣden him

20   forgiefen hæfde,[18] and him cwæð tō: "Nimað ðās ðing mid

---

[1] Lat. *paulo ante*. See **178**.

[2] Translate by the infinitive sign, *to*. The OE. follows the Latin.

[8] See **197**.

[4] Not in Latin.

[5] Lat. *magister*.

[6] See **154.** *c*.

[7] See **153.** *f*.

[8] See **174**.

[9] MS. **deorwurðan**.

[10] Lat. *servos*.

[11] Lat. *triclinio*.

[12] See the derivation of Mod. Eng. *behest*.

[13] Refers to **męnn**.

[14] So in *Bēowulf* (653–655): "Werod eall ārās; grētte þā ... guma ōðerne, ... and him hǣl ābēad."

[15] Lat. *vale dicentes*.

[16] See **153.** *d*.

[17] Lat. *valete*.

[18] See **188**.

ēow, ðe mē sēo cwēn forgeaf, and gān[1] wē sēcean ūre
giesthūs, ðæt wē mǣgen ūs[2] geręstan."

Apollonius as Teacher.

Đā ādrēd ðæt mǣden ðæt hēo nǣfre ęft Apollonium
ne gesāwe swā[3] hraðe swā hēo wolde; and ēode ðā tō
hiere fæder, and cwæð: "Đū gōda cyning, līcað ðē wel 5
ðæt Apollonius, ðe ðurh ūs tō-dæg gegōdod[4] is, ðus
heonan fare,[5] and cumen yfele męnn and berēafien
hine?" Se cyning cwæð: "Wel ðū cwǣde. Hāt hine[6]
findan hwǣr hē hine mǣge weorðlicost[7] geręstan." Đā
dyde ðæt mǣden swā hiere beboden[8] wæs; and Apol- 10
lonius onfēng ðǣre wununge ðe him betǣht wæs, and
ðǣr inēode, Gode[9] ðanciende, ðe him nė forwiernde[10]
cynelices weorðscipes and frōfre. Ac ðæt mǣden hæfde
unstille[11] niht, mid ðǣre lufe onǣled ðǣra worda[12] and
sanga ðe hēo gehīerde æt Apollonie. And nā lęng[13] hēo 15
ne gebād ðonne hit dæg wæs, ac ēode sōna swā hit
lēoht wæs, and gesæt beforan hiere fæder[14] będde. Đā
cwæð se cyning: "Lēofe dohtor, for hwȳ[15] eart[16] ðū ðus
ǣrwacol?" Đæt mǣden cwæð: "Mē āweahton ðā ge-
cneordnessa[17] ðe ic giestran-dæg[18] gehīerde. Nū bidde ic 20

[1] See 193. a.
[2] See 184. b.
[3] Swā ... wolde not in Latin.
[4] Lat. ditatus.
[5] See 194. a.
[6] MS. him.
[7] See 76.
[8] See 187.
[9] See 164. m.
[10] See 159. a.
[11] Lat. inquietam.
[12] Dependent on lufe.
[13] See 77. [14] See 43. 8.
[15] See 175. [16] See 138.
[17] Lat. studia. Translate, ac-
complishments.
[18] Lat. hesterna. Is giestran
related to the Latin word?

ðē, for-ðām,[1] ðæt ðū befæste[2] mē ūrum cuman,[3] Apollonie, tō[4] lāre.[4]" Ðā wearð se cyning ðearle geblissod, and hēt fęccean Apollonium, and him tō cwæð: "Mīn dohtor giernð ðæt hēo mōte leornian æt ðē ðā gesǣligan lāre ðe ðū canst[5]; and, gif ðu wilt ðisum ðingum[6] gehīersum bēon, ic swęrie ðē, ðurh mīnes rīces mægenu,[7] ðæt swā-hwæt-swā ðū on sǣ forlure, ic ðē ðæt on lande gestaðelie.[8]" Ðā-ðā Apollonius ðæt gehīerde, hē onfēng ðǣm[9] mǣden tō lāre, and hiere tǣhte swā wel swā hē self geleornode.[10]

The Three Suitors.

Hit gelamp ðā æfter ðisum, binnan fēawum tīdum,[11] ðæt Arcestrates se cyning hēold Apollonius hand on handa; and ēodon swā ūt on ðǣre ceastre strǣte. Ðā, æt nīehstan, cōmon ðǣr gān[12] ongēan hīe ðrīe gelǣrde[13] weras and æðelborene, ðā lange ǣr gierndon[14] ðæs cyninges dohtor. Hīe ðā ealle ðrīe tōgædere ānre stefne[15] grētton ðone cyning. Ðā smercode[16] se cyning, and him tō beseah,

---

[1] Lat. *itaque.*

[2] Lat. *tradas.*

[3] Lat. *hospiti.*

[4] Lat. *studiorum percipiendorum gratia.*

[5] Cf. Chaucer, *Miller's Tale* 18: "I *can* a noble tale." This sense occurs as late as the middle of the 17th century; Lovelace has: "Yet *can* I music too." So Jonson, *Magnetic Lady* 1.1: "She *could* the Bible in the holy tongue."

[6] Lat. *desiderio natœ meœ.* See 165.

[7] Lat. *vires.*

[8] Lat. *restituam.*

[9] See 164. *j.*

[10] Here follows, in the Latin, an account of how the girl feigned illness, on account of her love for Apollonius.

[11] Lat. *post paucos dies.*

[12] See 199. 1.

[13] Lat. *scholastici.*

[14] Lat. *in matrimonium petierunt.* Pluperfect (188).

[15] See 160. 1.

[16] Lat. *subridens.*

and ðus cwæð: "Hwæt is ðæt, ðæt gē mē ānre stefne
grētton?" Ðā andswarode hiera ān, and cwæð: "Wē
bǣdon gefyrn ðīnre dohtor; and ðū ūs oft hrǣdlice mid[1]
ęlcunge[1] geswęnctest.[1] For-ðām wē cōmon hider tō-dæg
ðus tōgædere. Wē sindon ðīne ceastergewaran, of æðelum 5
gebyrdum[2] geborene; nū bidde wē ðē ðæt ðū gecēose ðē[3]
ænne of ūs ðrīm, hwilcne ðū wille ðē[3] tō[4] āðume habban."
Ðā cwæð se cyning: "Nabbe gē nā gōdne[5] tīman ārēdod.[6]
Mīn dohtor is nū swīðe bisig ymb hiere leornunga.[7] Ac,
ðȳ-lǣs-ðe[8] ic ēow ā lęng slacie,[9] āwrītað ēowre naman on 10
gewrite, and hiere morgengiefe[10]; ðonne āsęnde ic ðā
gewritu mīnre dęhter, ðæt hēo self gecēose hwilcne
ēower[11] hēo wille." Ðā dydon ðā cnihtas swā; and se
cyning nōm[12] ðā gewritu, and geinseglode hīe mid his
hringe, and sealde Apollonio, ðus cweðende: "Nim nū, 15
lārēow Apolloni, swā hit ðē ne mislīcie,[13] and bring ðīnum
lǣringmǣdene.[14] " Ðā nōm Apollonius ðā gewritu, and
ēode tō ðǣre cynelican healle.[15]

---

[1] Lat. *differendo crucias.*

[2] Lat. *natalibus.*

[3] See **161.**

[4] Cf. Mod. Eng. 'take to wife.'

[5] Lat. *apto.*

[6] MS. **aredodne.**

[7] Lat. *studiorum.*

[8] Lat. *ne.*

[9] Lat. *videar . . . differre.*

[10] Lat. *dotis quantitatem.* The
present given on the *morning*
after marriage, according to Teutonic usage. Cf. Mod. Ger.
Morgengabe.

[11] MS. **eowerne.**

[12] See **105.**

[13] Lat. *sine contumelia tua;* an
apology for sending Apollonius on
an errand. See **196.** *c.*

[14] Lat. *discipulæ.*

[15] Lat. *domum.* The Latin adds
introivit cubiculum.

The Princess Chooses.

. Mid-ðām-ðe ðæt mǣden geseah Apollonium, ðā cwæð hēo: "Lārēow, hwȳ gǣst ðū āna[1]?" Apollonius cwæð: "Hlǣfdige[2]—næs gīet yfel wīf[3]—nim ðās gewritu, ðe ðīn fæder ðē sęnde,[4] and rǣd." Ðæt mǣden nōm, and 5 rǣdde ðǣra ðrēora cnihta naman; ac hēo ne funde[5] nā ðone naman ðǣron ðe hēo wolde. Ðā hēo ðā gewritu oferrǣd hæfde, ðā beseah hēo tō Apollonio, and cwæð: "Lārēow, ne ofðyncð[6] hit ðē gif ic ðus wer gecēose?" Apollonius cwæð: "Nā; ac ic blissie swīðor[7] ðæt ðū 10 meaht, ðurh ðā lāre ðe ðū æt mē underfēnge, ðē self on gewrite gecȳðan hwilcne hiera ðū wille.[8] Mīn willa is ðæt ðū ðē wer gecēose ðǣr ðū self wille.[9]" Ðæt mǣden cwæð: "Ēalā lārēow, gif ðū mē lufodest, ðū hit besorg-odest.[10]" Æfter ðisum wordum hēo mid mōdes[11] ānrǣd-15 nesse[11] āwrāt ōðer gewrit, and ðæt geinseglode, and sealde Apollonio. Apollonius hit ðā ūt bær on ðā strǣte,[12] and sealde ðǣm cyninge. Ðæt gewrit wæs ðus gewriten: "Ðū gōda cyning, and mīn se lēofesta fæder,

[1] The OE. is not clear. The Latin has: *Quid est quod singularis cubiculum introisti?*

[2] Lat. *domina.* How is **hlǣfdige** related in meaning to **hlāford**?

[3] Not clear either in the Latin or the English. Some MSS. have, *nondum mulier et mala;* one has, *non unquam mulier fuit mala.*

[4] Translate, *has sent.* See **188.**

[5] See **104.**   [6] Lat. *dolet.*

[7] Translate, *rather.* See **76.**

[8] She has evidently learned from him how to write, according to the English. The Latin has: *Immo gratulor quod habundantia studiorum percepta me volente nubis.*

[9] See **196.** *c.*

[10] Lat. *doleres.* Indicative, where the optative might be expected.

[11] Lat. *amoris audacia.*

[12] Lat. *forum,* as above, p. 178, l. 13.

nū ðīn mildheortnes mē lēafe sealde ðæt ic self mōste
cēosan hwilcne wer ic wolde, ic secge ðē tō sōðum, ðone
forlidenan mann ic wille; and gif ðū wundrie ðæt swā
sceamfæst[1] fǣmne[1] swā unforwandiendlice[2] ðās word
āwrāt, ðonne wite[3] ðū ðæt ic hæbbe ðurh weax āboden,[4] 5
ðe nāne sceame ne can,[5] ðæt ic self ðē for sceame secgean
ne meahte."

Ðā-ðā se cyning hæfde ðæt gewrit oferrǣd,[6] ðā nyste
hē hwilcne forlidenne hēo nemde. Beseah ðā tō ðǣm
ðrīm cnihtum, and cwæð : "Hwilc ēower is forliden?" 10
Ðā cwæð hiera ān, se hātte Ardalius : "Ic eom forliden.[7]" Se ōðer him andwyrde, and cwæð: "Swīga ðū.
Ādl ðē fornime,[8] ðæt ðū ne bēo[9] hāl nē gesund. Mid
mē ðū bōccræft[10] leornodest, and ðū nǣfre būtan ðǣre
ceastre geate fram mē ne cōme. Hwǣr gefōre[11] ðū for- 15
lidennesse?" Mid-ðȳ-ðe se cyning ne meahte findan
hwilc hiera forliden wǣre,[12] hē beseah tō Apollonio, and
cwæð: "Nim ðū, Apolloni, ðis gewrit, and rǣd hit;
ēaðe mæg geweorðan ðæt ðū wite ðæt ic nāt, ðū ðe
ðǣr andweard wǣre.[13]" Ðā nōm Apollonius ðæt gewrit, 20
and rǣdde. And sōna swā hē ongeat ðæt hē gelufod

---

[1] Lat. pudica virgo.
[2] Lat. impudenter; one MS. im-
prudenter.
[3] See 198.
[4] Lat. mandavi.
[5] See above, p. 178, n. 5.
[6] Lat. perlectis.
[7] On for- see Coleridge, Omni-
ana (Bohn ed., p. 414): "It is
grievous to think how much less

careful the English have been to
preserve than to acquire. Why
have we lost, or all but lost, the
ver or for as a prefix, — fordone,
forwearied, etc.; and the zer or
to, — zerreissen, to rend, etc.?"
[8] See 193. a.   [9] See 196. g.
[10] Lat. litteras.
[11] See 107.   [12] See 194. b.
[13] Is this optative?

wæs fram ðǣm mǣdene, his[1] andwlita[1] eall[1] āreadode.[1]
Ðā se cyning ðæt geseah, ðā nōm hē Apollonies hand,
and hine[2] hwōn fram ðǣm cnihtum gewęnde, and cwæð:
"Wāst[3] ðū ðone forlidenan mann?" Apollonius cwæð:
5 "Ðū gōda cyning, gif ðīn willa bið, ic hine wāt." Ðā
geseah se cyning ðæt Apollonius mid rōsan[4] rude[4] wæs
eall oferbrǣded.[5] Ðā ongeat hē ðone cwide, and ðus
cwæð tō him: "Blissa, blissa, Apolloni, for-ðām-ðe mīn
dohtor gewilnað ðæs[6] ðe mīn willa is. Ne mæg sōðlice
10 on ðyllicum ðingum[7] nān[8] ðing geweorðan būtan Godes[9]
willan." Arcestrates beseah tō ðǣm ðrīm cnihtum, and
cwæð: "Sōð[10] is[10] ðæt ic ēow ǣr sǣde, ðæt gē ne cōmon
on gedafenlicre[11] tīde mīnre dohtor tō biddanne, ac
ðonne[12] hēo mæg hīe fram hiere lāre geǣmetgian, ðonne
15 sęnde ic ēow word.[13]"

Ðā gewęndon hīe hām mid ðisse andsware, and Arcestrates se cyning hēold forð on Apollonius hand, and hine
lǣdde hām mid him, nā swilce hē cuma wǣre,[14] ac swilce
hē his āðum wǣre. Ðā, æt nīehstan, forlēt se cyning
20 Apollonius hand, and ēode āna intō ðǣm būre ðǣr his
dohtor inne wæs, and ðus cwæð: "Lēofe dohtor, hwone
hæfst ðū ðē gecoren tō gemæccean[15]?" Ðæt mǣden[16]
ðā fēoll tō hiere fæder fōtum, and cwæð: "Ðū ārfæsta[17]

[1] Lat. erubuit.
[2] See 184. b.
[3] See 126. Lat. invenisti.
[4] Lat. roseo rubore.
[5] Lat. perfusam.
[6] See 156. a.
[7] Lat. hujusmodi negotio.
[8] See 183.
[9] A Christian trait.
[10] Lat. certe.
[11] Lat. apto. See p. 179, l. 8.
[12] See 202. d.
[13] Note the English idiom. The Latin has, mittam ad vos.
[14] See 196. c.   [15] Lat. conjugem.
[16] See 28.   [17] Lat. piissime.

fæder, gehīer ðīnre dohtor willan.[1] Ic lufie ðone forlidenan mann, ðe wæs ðurh ungelimp[2] beswicen[2]; ac,
ðȳ-læs-ðe[3] ðē tweonie[4] ðære spræce, Apollonium ic wille,
mīnne lāreow; and gif ðū mē him ne sęlest, ðū forlætst
öīne dohtor." Se cyning ðā sōðlice ne meahte āræfnian[5]
his dohtor tēaras, ac ārærde hīe ūp, and hiere tō cwæð:
"Lēofe dohtor, ne ondræd ðū ðē æniges[6] ðinges.[6] Ðū
hæfst gecoren ðone wer ðe mē wel līcað." Ēode ðā ūt,
and beseah tō Apollonio, and cwæð: "Lāreow Apolloni,
ic smēade mīnre dohtor mōdes willan; ðā āreahte hēo
mid wōpe[7] betweox ōðre spræce, ðās ðing ðus cweðende:
'Ðū geswōre Apollonio, gif hē wolde gehīersumian mīnum
willan on lāre, ðæt ðū woldest him geinnian[8] swā-hwæt-
swā sēo sæ him ætbræd.[9] Nū, for-ðām-ðe hē gehīersum
wæs ðīnre hæse and mīnum willan, ic fōr æfter him
[mid willan and mid lāre[10]].'"

[1] Lat. *desiderium*.

[2] Lat. *fortuna deceptum*.

[3] OE. **ðȳ-læs-ðe** gives Mod.
Eng. *lest*. What phonological
rule determines the final *t* ?

[4] See **159.** *b* and **196.** *f.*

[5] Lat. *sustinens*.

[6] Lat. *de aliqua re*.

[7] Lat. *lacrimis* (cf. *Æn.* III.
348).

[8] Lat. *dares*.   [9] Lat. *abstulit*.

[10] The OE. MS. breaks off at
him. I have supplied what follows according to the Latin,
voluntate et doctrina. The story
thus continues in the Latin:
After the marriage, Apollonius
hears of the death of King Antiochus, and, with his wife, sets sail
for Antioch. There follow the
events related in the Shake-
spearean *Pericles*, in the main
as in Acts III., IV., and V.,
though with not a few differences. The infant daughter has
grown up, and, after a variety
of experiences, has been restored
to Apollonius. His queen is
priestess of Diana of Ephesus,
and thither he proceeds, being
warned by an angel in a dream
to make that, instead of Tarsus,
his next goal. At this point the
OE. fragment recommences.

Apollonius relates his Adventures.

Ðā wæs hiere[1] gecȳðed, 'ðe ðǣr ealdor[2] wæs, ðæt ðǣr
wǣre sum cyning, mid his āðume and mid his dęhter,
mid miclum giefum. Mid-ðām-ðe hēo ðæt gehīerde, hēo
hīe selfe mid cynelicum rēafe gefrætwode and mid pur-
5 pran gescrȳdde, and hiere hēafod mid golde and mid
gimmum geglęngde, and, mid miclum fǣmnena hēape
ymbtrymmed,[3] cōm tōgēanes ðǣm cyninge. Hēo wæs
sōðlice ðearle wlitig; and, for ðǣre miclan lufe ðǣre
clǣnnesse,[4] hīe sǣdon ealle ðæt ðǣr nǣŕe nān Dianan
10 swā gecwēme[5] swā hēo.

Mid-ðām-ðe Apollonius ðæt geseah, hē mid his āðume
and mid his dęhter tō hiere urnon,[6] and fēollon ealle tō
hiere fōtum, and wēndon[7] ðæt hēo Diana wǣre, sēo gyden,
for hiere miclan beorhtnesse and wlite. Ðæt hālig[8] ærn[9]
15 wearð ðā geopenod, and ðā lāc[9] wēron ingebrōhte, and
Apollonius ongan[10] ðā sprecan and cweðan: "Ic fram

---

[1] The wife of Apollonius.

[2] Chief, i.e. chief priestess.

[3] Lat. virginum constipata ca-
tervis. An epic trait. Thus in
the Æneid (4. 136), Dido goes
forth, magna stipante caterva.
Thus in the Odyssey (16. 413),
Penelope "went on her way to
the hall, with the women her hand-
maids." And thus in Beowulf
(923–925), Hrothgar

tryddode tīrfæst getrume micle
cystum gecȳðed, and his cwēn mid
    him
medostīg gemæt mægða hōse.

[4] Lat. castitatis.

[5] Lat. gratum. See 165.

[6] See 104. Does this verb agree
with its subject?

[7] Cf. Chaucer, Knight's Tale
243 ff.: —

I not whether sche be womman or
    goddesse;
But Venus is it, sothly as I gesse.

[8] Lat. sacrario. Ærn forms
part of the Mod. Eng. barn; what
does the other element of this word
stand for?

[9] Lat. muneribus.

[10] Lat. cœpit.

cildhāde wæs Apollonius genęmned, on Tyrum geboren. Mid-ðām-ðe ic becōm tō fullum andgiete,[1] ðā næs nān cræft[2] ðe wǣre[3] fram cyningum begān, oððe fram æðelum mannum, ðæt ic ne cūðe.[4] : . . Ðā wearð ic on sǣ forliden, and cōm tō Cyrenense. Ðā underfēng 5 mē Arcestrates se cyning mid swā micelre lufe ðæt ic æt nīehstan geearnode ðæt hē geaf mē his ācęnnedan[5] dohtor tō gemæccean. Sēo[6] for ðā mid mē tō onfōnne mīnum cynerīce, and ðās mīne dohtor, ðe ic beforan ðē, Diana, geandweard hæbbe, ācęnde on sǣ, and hiere gāst 10 ālēt. Ic ðā hīe mid cynelicum rēafe gescrȳdde, and mid golde and gewrite on ciste ālęgde, ðæt sē, ðe hīe funde, hīe weorðlice bebyrgde[7]; and ðās mīne dohtor befæste[8] ðǣm mānfullestum[9] mannum[9] tō fēdanne.[10] Fōr mē ðā tō Egypta lande fēowertīene gēar on hēofe. Ðā ic 15 ongēan cōm, ðā sǣdon hīe mē ðæt mīn dohtor wǣre forðfaren,[11] and mē wæs mīn sār eall geednīwod."

The Recognition.

Mid-ðām-ðe hē ðās ðing eall āreaht hæfde, Arcestrate sōðlice, his wīf, ūp ārās and hine ymbclypte. Ðā nyste nā[12] Apollonius, nē[13] ne[13] gelīefde, ðæt hēo his gemæccea 20

---

[1] Lat. scientiam.

[2] Lat. ars. [3] See 197.

[4] I have omitted the portion which relates to his adventures before his shipwreck.

[5] Translate, own.

[6] Used almost as personal pronoun. From what source is Mod. Eng. she derived?

[7] See 196. d.

[8] Lat. commendavi.

[9] MS. manfullestan mannan. Lat. nequissimis hominibus.

[10] Lat. nutriendam.

[11] Lat. defunctam.

[12] See 183.

[13] How do nē and ne differ in meaning?

wǣre,[1] ac scēaf[2] hīe fram him.   Hēo ðā micelre stefne
cleopóde, and cwæð mid wōpe : " Ic eom Arcestrate ðīn
gemǣccea, Arcestrates dohtor ðæs cyninges, and ðū eart
Apollonius mīn lārēow, ðe mē lǣrdest.   Ðū eart se for-
5 lidena mann ðe ic lufode. . . .   Hwǣr is mīn dohtor ? "
Hē bewęnde hine ðā tō Thasian,[3] and cwæð : " Ðis hēo
is."   And hīe wēopon ðā ealle, and ēac blissedon.[4]   And
ðæt word sprang geond eall ðæt land ðæt Apollonius,
se mǣra cyning, hæfde funden his wīf.   And ðǣr wearð
10 ormǣte[5] bliss, and ðā organa wǣron[6] getogene,[6] and ðā
bīeman geblāwene, and ðǣr wearð blīðe gebēorscipe
gegearwod betweox ðǣm cyning and ðǣm folce.   And
hēo gesętte hiere gingran, ðe hiere folgode, tō sācerde,
and, mid blisse and hēofe ealre ðǣre mǣgðe on Efesum,
15 hēo fōr mid hiere were, and mid hiere āðume, and mid
hiere dęhter, tō Antiochian, ðǣr Apollonio wæs ðæt
cynerīce gehealden.[7] . . .

The Fisherman's Reward.

Ðisum eallum ðus gedōnum,[8] ēode Apollonius, se mǣra
cyning, wið ðā sǣ.   Ðā geseah hē ðone ealdan fiscere,
20 ðe hine ǣr nacodne underfēng.   Ðā hēt se cyning hine

---

1 See 194. b.   2 Lat. repellit.

3 More properly, ' Tharsian ';
but cf. Shakespeare's Thaisa.

4 Cf. Macaulay's " With weeping and with laughter still is the
story told."

5 Lat. ingens.

6 Lat. disponuntur. Translate,
were played.

7 At this point there is an
account of Apollonius' travels
among his former acquaintances,
rewarding them according to
their deserts, and cheering the
last hours of Archistrates, who
divides his kingdom between his
daughter and Apollonius.

8 See 167.

fǣrlice gelæccean, and tō ðǣre cynelican¹ healle¹ gelǣdan.
Ðā-ðā se fiscere ðæt geseah, ðæt hine ðā cempan² woldon
niman, ðā wēnde hē ǣrest ðæt hine man sceolde ofslēan;
ac, mid-ðām-ðe hē cōm intō ðæs cyninges healle, ðā hēt
se cyning hine lǣdan tōforan ðǣre cwēne, and ðus cwæð: 5
"Ēalā, ðū ēadge cwēn, ðis is mīn tācenbora,³ ðe mē
nacodne underfēng, and mē getǣhte ðæt ic tō ðē becōm."
Ðā beseah Apollonius se cyning tō ðǣm fiscere, and
cwæð: "Ēalā, welwillenda⁴ ealda,⁵ ic eom Apollonius se
Tyrisca, ðǣm ðū sealdest healfne ðīnne wǣfels." Him   10
geaf ðā se cyning twā hund gyldenra⁶ peninga,⁶ and
hæfde hine tō gefēran ðā-hwīle-ðe hē lifde. . . .

The End.

Æfter eallum ðisum Apollonius se cyning . . . wel-
willendlice lifde mid his gemæccean seofon⁷ and hund-
seofontig gēara, and hēold ðæt cynerīce on Antiochia,   15
and on Tyrum, and on Cyrenense.   And hē lifde on
stilnesse and on blisse ealle ðā tīd his līfes æfter his
earfoðnesse.   And twā bēc hē self gesette be his fare⁸;
and āne āsette on ðǣm temple Diane, ōðre on bibliotheca.   20
Hēr endað ge wēa ge wela Apollonius ðæs Tyriscan.

---

¹ Lat. *palatium*.
² Lat. *militibus*.
³ Lat. *paranymphus*. The OE.
word properly translates Lat. *sig-
nifer.*   Render here by *groomsman;* the fisherman had con-

ducted him, as it were, to his
bride.
⁴ Lat. *benignissime.*
⁵ See **55** and **181**.
⁶ Lat. *sestertia auri.*
⁷ But Lat. *quatuor.*
⁸ Lat. *casus.*

Rǣde[1] se ðe wille; and gif hīe hwā[2] rǣde, ic bidde
ðæt hē ðās āwęndednesse ne tǣle, ac ðæt hē hele swā-
hwæt-swā ðǣron sīe tō tāle.[3]

[1] See 193. *a*.

[2] *Any one.* Still found in the phrase, ' as *who* should say ' (*Macb.* 3. 6. 42). In Dekker's *Satiromastix* (A.D. 1602) there oc-curs, " Suppose *who* enters now."

[3] Cf. Alfred's adjuration at p. 162, l. 12 ff.

XIII.

THE SIX DAYS' WORK OF CREATION.

(From Ælfric's Hexameron.)

[This may serve as a commentary on Selection I., which, it will be remembered, is a translation by Ælfric. Of the present work its editor, Norman, says (p. vii): "The treatise which is styled by Hickes in his 'Thesaurus' the 'Hexameron of St. Basil' is by no means a literal translation of the well known work of that father, but is partly original, and partly compiled from that work, and from the commentaries of the Venerable Bede upon Genesis. The author of it, from internal evidence, may be pronounced to be Ælfric, as frequent references are made to his homilies, and to his epistles on the Old and New Testament."

Of Basil's (d. 379) delivery of the original Hexameron, there is a brief, but spirited, account in Villemain's *Tableau de l'Éloquence Chrétienne au IVᵉ Siècle* (p. 116 ff.), from which we extract the following: "It is more interesting to survey him in the act of instructing the poor inhabitants of Cæsarea, elevating them to God by the contemplation of nature, and explaining to them the miracles of creation in discourses where the science of the orator who had been trained at Athens is concealed under a persuasive and popular simplicity. Such is the subject of the homilies which bear the name of *Hexameron*. Together with the errors in natural philosophy which are common to all antiquity, they contain many correct views, and descriptions at once felicitous and true."]

On ðǣm forman dæge ūre Dryhten gescēop seofonfeald[1] weorc: ðæt wǣron ealle englas; and ðæs lēohtes anginn; and ðæt antimber ðe[2] hē of gescēop siððan gesceafta; ðā ūplican heofonan and ðā niðerlican eorðan; ealle wæterscipas[3]; and ðā wīdgillan sǣ; and ðæt ūplice[4] lyft; eall on ānum dæge. Ðā englas hē geworhte on[5] wundorlicre   5

---

[1] See **146**.   [2] Governed by *of.*   [4] MS. **uplican.**

[3] See **143**, and p. 226, note 22.   [5] Translate, *of.*

fægernesse, and on¹ micelre stręngðe,² manige ðūsenda,
ealle līchamlēase, libbende on gāste; be ðǣm wē sǣdon
hwīlum ǣr sweotollicor on gewrite. Næs nā God būtan
lēohte ðā-ðā hē lēoht gescēop, — hē is him self lēoht ðe
5 onlīeht³ eall ðing; ac hē gescēop ðæs dæges lēoht, and
hit siððan geēacnode.mid ðǣm scīnendum tunglum, swā-
swā hēræfter sægð.⁴ Dæges lēoht hē gescēop, and tō-
drǣfde ðā ðīestru, ðæt ðā gesceafta gesewenlice wurden
ðurh ðæs dæges līehtinge on lęnctenlicre⁵ tīde; for-ðām
10 hē on lęnctentīde, swā-swā ūs lārēowas sęcgeað, gescēop
ðone forman dæg ðisse worulde — ðæt is on gerīmcræfte
xv cl. Aprilis⁶ — and siððan ðā gesceafta, swā-swā wē
sęcgeað hēr. Ðā ūplican heofonas, ðe ęnglas onwuniað,
hē geworhte ēac ðā on ðǣm ilcan dæge; be ðǣm wē
15 singað on sumum sealme⁷ ðus: *Opera manuum tua-*
rum sunt cœli — "Ðīnra handa geweorc sindon heofonas,
Dryhten." Ęft on ōðrum⁸ sealme sang se ilca wītga:
Ipse dixit, et facta sunt; ipse mandavit, et creata sunt —
"Hē self hit gecwæð, and hīe wurdon geworhte; hē self
20 hit bebēad, and hīe wurdon gesceapene." Ðæt wæter and
sēo eorðe wǣron gemęngde ōð ðone ðriddan dæg; ðā
tōdyde hīe God, swā-swā hēræfter sægð on ðisse gesęt-
nesse. Ðæt lyft hē gescēop tō ūres līfes strangunge;
ðurh ðæt wē orðiað, and ēac ðā nīetenu; and ūre fnǣst
25 ātēorað gif wē ātēon ne magon, mid ūrum orðe, intō ūs

¹ Translate, *of.*
² From what adjective? The
original ending is -iða.
³ How is this stem related to
lēoht? Cf. Jn. 1. 9.

⁴ = *it saith, is described.*
⁵ From **lęncten** is derived Mod.
Eng. *Lent.*
⁶ March 18.   ⁷ Ps. 102. 25.
⁸ Ps. 33. 9.

ðæt lyft and ęft ūtāblāwan, ðā-hwīle-ðe wē bēoð cuce.
Ðæt lyft is swā hēah swā-swā ðā heofonlican[1] wolcnu,
and ēac ealswā brād swā-swā ðǣre eorðan brādnes.   On
ðǣre[2] flēogað fuglas, ac hiera fiðru ne meahten nāhwider
hīe[3] āberan gif hīe ne ābǣre sēo lyft.   5

Secunda die fecit Deus firmamentum — "On ðǣm ōðrum
dæge ūre Dryhten geworhte firmamentum,[4]" ðe męnn
hātað rodor.   Sē[5] belȳcð[6] on his bōsme ealle eorðan[7]
brādnesse,[7] and binnan him is gelōgod eall ðes middan-
geard; and hē ǣfre gǣð ābūtan swā-swā iernende hwēol, 10
and hē nǣfre ne stęnt stille on ānum, and on ānre
węndinge.   Ðā-hwīle-ðe hē ǣne betyrnð, gǣð witodlice
forð fēower and twēntig tīda — ðæt is ðonne ealles ān
dæg and ān niht.   Ðone rodor God gehēt heofon.   Hē
is wundorlice hēalic and wīd on ymbhwyrfte; sē[5] gǣð 15
under ðās eorðan ealswā[8] dēop swā bufan, ðeah-ðe ðā
ungelǣredan męnn ðæs[9] gelīefan ne cunnon.   And God
ðā tōdǣlde ðurh his dryhtenlican miht ðā niðerlican
wæteru ðe wǣron under ðǣm rodore fram ðǣm uplicum
wæterum ðe wǣron bufan ðǣm rodore.   Be ðǣm uplicum 20
wæterum āwrāt se wītga[10] ðus: *Laudate eum cœli cœlo-*
rum, et aquœ quœ super cœlos sunt, laudent nomen Domini
— "Hęriað hine heofonas, ðāra heofona heofonas, and ēac
ðā wæteru ðe bufan heofonas sind, hęrien hīe Godes

---

[1] Translate, *of heaven.*

[2] Nearly = **hiere. Lyft** fluctu-
ates in gender, in this extract, between fem. and neut.

[3] Acc. plur.

[4] How is this word rendered in
p. 124, l. **4.**

[5] Nearly = **hē.**

[6] See **belūcan.**

[7] See **24.**

[8] What is the difference of derivation between *also* and *as ?*

[9] See **156.** *g.*

[10] Ps. 148. 4.

naman." Ðus sægð ðæt hālge gewrit. Ne heriað ðā
wæteru mid nānum wordum God, ac ðurh ðā gesceafta,
ðe hē gescēop wundorlice, his miht is gesweotolod, and
hē bið swā gehered.

5 On ðæm ðriddan dæge ūre Dryhten gegaderode ðā
sǣlican[1] ȳða fram ðǣre eorðan brādnesse. Sēo eorðe
wæs æt fruman eall ungesewenlic, for-ðām-ðe hēo eall
wæs mid ȳðum oferðeaht[2]; ac God hīe āsyndrode fram
ðǣm sǣlicum ȳðum on hiere āgenne stede, swā-swā hēo
10 stent ōð ðis.[3] Hēo ne lið[4] on nānum ðinge, ac on[5] lofte[5]
hēo stent ðurh ðæs Ānes miht ðe[6] eall ðing gescēop;
and hē eall ðing gehielt[7] būtan geswince, for-ðām-ðe his
nama is *Omnipotens Deus*, ðæt is on Englisc, "Ælmihtig
God." His willa is weorc, and hē wērig ne bið, and his
15 micle miht ne mæg nāhwǣr swincan, swā-swā se wītga[8]
āwrāt be him, cweðende, *Quia in manu ejus sunt omnes
fines terræ* — "For-ðām-ðe on his handa sindon eall ðǣre
eorðan gemǣru." Ðā sǣ hē gelōgode swā-swā hēo lið[4]
gīet wiðinnan ðā eorðan on hiere ymbhwyrfte; and ðeah-
20 ðe hēo brād sīe, and gebīeged gehū, and wundorlice dēop,
hēo wunað eall swā-ðeah on ðǣre eorðan bōsme binnan
hiere gemǣrum. God self geseah ðā ðæt hit gōd wæs
swā, and hēt ðā eorðan ārodlice spryttan grōwende gærs,
and ðā grēnan wyrta mid hiera āgnum sǣde tō manig-
25 fealdum lǣcecræfte[9]; and ðā wyrta sōna wynsumlice

---

[1] Translate, *of the sea.*
[2] See 114.
[3] *Until this, until now.*
[4] See **28**.
[5] Mod. Eng. *aloft.*

[6] Refers to **Ānes**.
[7] See **gehealdan**. Present or
preterit ?
[8] Ps. 95. 4.
[9] Cf. *Rom. and Jul.* 2. 3. 15 ff.

grēowon,[1] mid manigfealdum blōstmum, mislice geblēode. God hēt hīe ēac spryttan, ðurh his godcundan miht, manigfeald trēowcynn, mid hiera wǣstmum, mannum tō ofetum and tō ōðrum nīedum. And sēo eorðe, sōna swā-swā hiere[2] God bebēad, stōd mid holtum āgrōwen, and mid hēalicum cēderbēamum and mid manigum wudum on hiere wīdgilnesse, mid æppelbǣrum trēowum and mid ort-geardum, and mid ǣlcum trēowcynne mid hiera āgnum wǣstmum.

On ðǣm fēorðan dæge ūre Dryhten gecwæð, "Geweorðen nū lēoht" — ðæt sind, ðā lēohtan steorran on ðǣm heo-fonlican rodore — "ðæt[3] hīe tōdǣlan mægen dæg fram niht, and hīe bēon tō tācne, and tīda gewyrcen dagum and gēarum, and scīnen on ðǣm rodore, and onlīehten ðā eorðan." God geworhte ðā sōna twā scīnendu lēoht, miclu and mǣru, mōnan and sunnan — ðā sunnan on mᶒrgen tō ðæs dæges līehtinge, ðone mōnan on ǣfen mannum tō līehtinge on nihtlicre tīde mid getācnungum. And ealle steorran hē ēac ðā geworhte, and hē hīe gefæstnode on ðǣm fæstan rodore, ðæt hīe ðā eorðan onlīehten mid hiera manigfealdum lēoman, and ðæs dæges gīemden[4] and ēac ðǣre niht, and ðæt lēoht tō-dǣlden and ðā ðīestru on twā. Nǣron nāne tīda on ðǣm gēarlicum getæle ǣr-ðām-ðe se ælmihtiga Scieppend gescēop ðā tunglu tō gēarlicum tīdum, on manigum getācnungum, on lᶒnctenlicre emnihte — swā-swā lārēowas sᶒcgeað on gerīmcræfte, xii kl. Aprilis.[5] And ne bēoð

<hr />

[1] See **grōwan**. [3] Cf. p. 125, l. 9 ff.
[2] Dat. sing. [4] Cf. p. 126, l. 1 ff.
[5] March 21; cf. p. 190, l. 12.

næfre Ēastron[1] ǣr se dæg cume ðæt ðæt lēoht hæbþe ðā
ðīestru oferswīðed, ðæt is, ðæt se dæg bēo lęngra[2] ðonne
sēo niht. Be ðǣm ōðrum tīdum cwið ðēos ilce bōc swā-
swā God sǣde him self tō Noe: "Sǣdtīma and hærfest,
5 sumer and winter, ciele and hǣtu, dæg and niht, ne
geswīcað næfre." Ne standað nā ealle steorran on ðǣm
stēapan rodore, ac hīe[3] sume[3] habbað synderlicne gang
beneoðan ðǣm rodore, mislice gerędebyrde ; and ðā, ðe
on ðǣm rodore standað, tyrnað[4] ǣfre ābūtan mid ðǣm
10 brādan rodore on ymbhwyrfte ðǣre eorðan, and hiera[5]
nān ne fielð[6] of ðǣm fæstan rodore ðā-hwīle-ðe ðēos
woruld wunað swā gehāl. Eall swā gǣð sēo sunne,[7] and
sōðlice se mōna,[7] ābūtan ðās eorðan mid brādum ymbhwyrfte, eall swā feor beneoðan swā-swā hīe bufan ūs gǣð.
15 On ðǣm fīftan dæge ūre Dryhten gescēop of wætere
ānum ealle fiscas on sǣ and on ēaum, and eall ðæt on
him crīepð,[8] and ðā miclan hwalas on hiera cynrēnum,

---

[1] A plural (see the verb) used
as singular. **Ēastre** (North.
Ēostre) was, as Bede tells us,
the name of a goddess whose
festival was celebrated at the
vernal equinox; it is a derivative of **ēast** (east, cognate with
Skr. *ushās*, dawn), and this
indicates that she was originally
a goddess of the dawn. Bede
adds that the passover-tide was
so called, "Consueto antiquæ
observationis vocabulo gaudia
novæ solemnitatis vocantes."

[2] See **65.**

[3] See **151.**

[4] From the Greek word τόρνος,
one of whose senses is *lathe-
chisel*, comes the Greek, and
hence the Latin (*tornare*) verb
meaning ' to turn in a lathe,' and
hence ' to fashion,' ' smooth ';
from the Latin is derived the
English verb.

[5] Dependent on **nān.**

[6] See **feallan.**

[7] Are these genders what one
would expect ? What determines
them ?

[8] See **crēopan.**

and ˙ ēac eall fugolcynn ealswā of wætere, and forgeaf ꝺǣm fuglum flyht geond ꝺās lyft, and ꝺǣm fiscum sund on ꝺǣm flōwendum ȳꝺum. God hīe geblētsode ꝺā, ꝺus cweꝺende tō ꝺǣm fiscum, "Weaxaꝺ[1] and bēoꝺ gemanigfielde, and gefyllaꝺ ꝺā sǣ"; and ēac, "Ꝺā fuglas bēon 5 gemanigfielde bufan ꝺǣre eorꝺan"; and hit gewearꝺ ꝺā swā. Ꝺā fuglas, sōꝺlice, ꝺe on flōdum wuniaꝺ, sindon flaxfēte be Godes foresċēawunge, ꝺæt hīe swimman mǣgen and sēcean him fōdan. Sume bēoꝺ langsweorede,[2] swā-swā swanas[3] and ielfetan, ꝺæt hīe ārǣcean him 10 mǣgen mete[4] be[5] ꝺǣm grunde. And ꝺā, ꝺe be[6] flǣsce libbaꝺ, sindon cliferfēte,[7] and scearpe gebilode,[2] ꝺæt hīe bītan mǣgen on[8] sceortum sweorum, and swiftran[9] on flyhte, ꝺæt hīe gelimplice bēon tō hiera līfes[10] tilungum. Nis nā eall fugolcynn on Engla ꝺēode, nē on nānum 15 earde ne biꝺ nāht ēaꝺe eall fugolcynn, for-ꝺām-ꝺe hīe fela sindon, micle on wǣstme, and hīe mislice flēogaꝺ, swā-swā ūs bēc secgeaꝺ sweotollice be[11] ꝺǣm.

---

[1] Cf. p. 126, l. 11 ff.

[2] Not past participles, though with the same ending.

[3] **Swanas** and **ielfetan** are here virtually identical; in ON. swanr is the poetical, ālft the ordinary designation. **Swan** has been doubtfully derived from the root of Lat. sonare, and **ielfete** (cf. the ON. form) from that of Lat. albus.

[4] Object of **ārǣcean.**

[5] Here = from; cf. 'by the roots.'

[6] Cf. "Man shall not live by bread alone."

[7] **Clifer-** is apparently related to cleave = adhere.

[8] Translate, with.   [9] See **64.**

[10] An interesting word, related to Mod. Eng. leave, Germ. b(e)leiben, Gr. λιπαρεῖν = hold out, persist; originally, therefore, life = a holding out, continuance. In German, body, one of its older meanings, is the commoner one for Leib. Here = livelihood.

[11] So in Fielding's Amelia (8.2):

On ðǣm siextan dæge ūre Dryhten gecwæð: "Ācęnne[1] sēo eorðe nū cucu nīetenu on hiera cynrēne, and ðā crēopendan wyrmas, and eall dēorcynn on hiera cynrēnum." Hwæt[2]! ðā God geworhte, ðurh his wunderlican

5 miht, eall nīetencynn on hiera cynrēnum, and ðā wildan dēor ðe on wudum eardiað, and eall ðæt fīðerfēte[3] bið, of ðǣre foresǣdan eorðan, and eall wyrmcynn ðā-ðe crēopende bēoð, and ðā rēðan lēon,[4] ðe hēr on lande ne bēoð, and ðā swiftan tigres,[4] and ða sellican pardes,[4]

10 and ðā ęgeslican beran, and ðā ormǣtan elpas, ðā-ðe on Ęngla ðēode ācęnnede ne bēoð, and fela ōðru cynn ðe gē ealle ne cunnon. Ðā bēoð langsweorede ðe libbað be gærse, swā-swā olfend[5] and assa, hors and hrȳðeru, hēadēor and rāhdēor, and gehwilc ōðru; and ǣlc bið

15 gelimplic tō his līfes tilunge. Wulfas, and lēon, and witodlice beran, habbað strangne sweoran, and sciertran[6] be[7] dǣle,[7] and māran tūscas, tō hiera mętes tilunge, for-ðām-ðe hīe libbað hiera līf[8] be rēaflāce, swā-swā gehwilc ōðru dēor[9] ðe dęriað ðǣm ōðrum. Ðā elpas bēoð swā

20 micle swilce ōðre muntas,[10] and hīe magon libban ðrēo hund gēara, and man mæg hīe węnian tō wīge mid

---

"I always love to speak *by* people as I find"; Shak., *M. V.* 1. 2. 58: "How say you *by* the French lord?"

[1] Cf. p. 126, l. 15 ff.

[2] Translate, *Lo !*

[3] **Fīðer-** is akin to Lat. *quattuor.*

[4] From Latin. With **pard** cf. Shakespeare's " Bearded like the *pard.*"

[5] Not *elephant,* but *camel.* **Elp** (longer form, **elpend**) is *elephant.*

[6] See **65.**

[7] Translate, *in part.*

[8] See **168. 1.**

[9] Cf. Shakespeare's (*King Lear* 3. 4. 143): "Mice and rats and such small *deer.*" What is the German?

[10] So the ME. *Bestiary* (ca. 1220) says (l. 604): "Elpes arn

cræfte, swā ðæt menn wyrceað wīghūs him on uppan,
and of ðǣm feohtað on hiera fierdinge; ðonne flīehð ælc
hors[1] āfǣred[2] ðurh ðā elpas, and, gif him hwā wiðstent,
hē bið sōna oftreden.[3]　Ac wē nellað nā swīðor nū ymb
ðis sprecan.　　　　　　　　　　　　　　　　　　5

On ðǣm ilcan dæge ūre Dryhten wolde mannan gewyrcean of ðǣre ilcan eorðan, for-ðām-ðe on ðisum fierste
āfēoll se dēofol of ðǣre hēalican heofonan, mid his
gegadum, for his ūpāhǣfednesse, intō helle wīte.　Ūre
Dryhten cwæð be him on his hālgan godspelle,[4] *In veri-*　10
tate non stetit, quia veritas non est in eo — "Hē ne wunode
nā on sōðfæstnesse, for-ðām-ðe sēo sōðfæstnes nis nātes-
hwōn on him."　God hine geworhte wundorlicne and
fægerne.　Ðā sceolde hē, gif hē wolde, weorðian his
Scieppend mid micelre ēaðmōdnesse, ðe hine swā mǣrne　15
gescēop.　Ac hē ne dyde nā swā, ac mid dyrstigre
mōdignesse cwæð[5] ðæt hē wolde wyrcean his cynesetl
bufan Godes tunglum, ofer ðǣra wolcna hēanesse on
ðǣm norðdǣle, and bēon Gode gelīc.　Ðā forlēt hē
ðone Ælmihtigan, ðe is eall sōðfæstnes, and · nolde　20
habban his hlāfordscipe, ac wolde bēon him self on his

in Inde riche, on bodi borlic
[burly] *berges ilike.*"

[1] This seems to indicate that
Ælfric employed Ambrose's adapta-
tion of Basil's *Hexameron,* since
the original does not contain this
thought.　Ambrose has (Bk. VI.,
Chap. V.): "Quid faciat eques,
cum equus ejus perterrefactus
tantæ bestiæ immanitate diffu-

giat."　Above, where elephants
are compared to mountains, Basil
has, βουνοί τινες σάρκινοι; Ambrose, "velut quidam mobiles
montes versantur in præliis," etc.

[2] So Shak., *Macb.* 5. 1. 41:
"A soldier, and *afeard.*"

[3] See **142.**

[4] Jn. 8. 44.

[5] Isa. 14. 13.

selfes anwealde. Ðā næfde hē nāne fæstnunge, ac fēoll
sōna ādūne, mid eallum ðǣm ęnglum ðe æt his rǣde
wǣron, and hīe wurdon āwęnde tō āwiergdum dēoflum.
Be ðǣm cwæð[1] se Hǣlend hēr on ðisum līfe, "Ic geseah
5 ðone scuccan swā-swā scīnęnde līeget feallende ādūn
drēorig of heofonum," for-ðām-ðe hē āhrēas ungerydelice.

Ðā wolde God wyrcean, ðurh his wundorlican miht,
mannan of eorðan, ðe mid ēaðmōdnesse sceolde geearnian
ðone ilcan stęde·on ðǣra ęngla gefērrǣdene ðe se dēofol
10 forworhte mid his dyrstignesse; and God self cwæð ðā,
swā-swā ūs sægð ðēos bōc, *Faciamus hominem ad imaginem nostram et similitudinem nostram, et reliqua*, etc.,
ðæt is on Ęngliscre sprǣce, "Uton gewyrcean mannan
tō ūrre anlīcnesse and tō ūrre gelīcnesse, ðæt hē anweald
15 hæbbe ofer eallum fiscum, and ofer fugolcynne, and ofer
wildēorum,[2] and ofer eallum gesceafte." Hēr gē magon
gehīeran ðā hālgan ðrīnesse and sōðe ānnesse ānre god-
cundnesse. "Uton wyrcean mannan"—ðǣr is sēo hālge
ðrīnes. "Tō ūrre anlīcnesse"—ðǣr is sēo ānnes, tō
20 ānre anlīcnesse, nā tō ðrīm anlīcnessum. lOn ðæs mannes
sāwle is Godes anlīcnes, for-ðām is se mann sēlra[3] ðonne
ðā sāwullēasan nīetenu, ðe nān andgiet nabbað ymb hiera
āgenne Scieppend. ⫯ God ðā geworhte of ðǣre eorðan
lāme,[4] mid his hālgum handum, mannan tō his anlīc-
25 nesse, and āblēow on his ansīene līflicne blǣd; and hē
wearð mann geworht on libbendre sāwle. God self ðā
siððan gescēop him naman Adam, and of his ānum ribbe

---

[1] Lk. 10. 18.

[2] What is the etymology of *wilderness?* Cf. **35**.

[3] See **66**.   [4] See **24**.

worhte him gemacan.[1] Hiere nama wæs Ēva, ūre[2] ealra
mōdor. And God hīe ðā geblētsode mid ðisse blētsunge,
"Weaxað and bēoð gemęnigfielde, and gefyllað ðā eorðan,
and habbað ēow anweald ofer ðā eorðan, and ofer sǣ
fiscum, and ofer ðǣm flēogendum fuglum, and ofer eallum 5
ðǣm nīetenum ðe styriað ofer eorðan." God gescēawode
ðā eall his weorc, and hīe wǣron swīðe gōd. And se
siexta dæg wearð swā gednod.

And God ðā gefylde on ðǣm seofoðan dæge his weorc
ðe hē worhte on wundorlicum dihte, and hine[3] ðā geręste, 10
and ðone dæg geblētsode, for-ðǣm-ðe hē on ðǣm seofoðan
dæge geswāc his weorces.[4] Næs hē nā wērig, ðēah-ðe hit
swā āwriten sīe; nē hē mid ealle ne geswāc ðā gesceafta
tō ednīwianne,[5] ac hē geswāc ðæs dihtes[4] ðæs dēoplican
cræftes, swā ðæt hē seldcūðe siððan scieppan nolde, ac 15
ðā ilcan geednīwian ōð ęnde ðisse worulde, swā-swā ūre
Hǣlend on his hālgan godspelle gecwæð,[6] *Pater meus*
usque modo operatur, et ego operor, ðæt is on Ęnglisc,
"Mīn Fæder wyrcð gīet ōð ðisne andweardan dæg, and
ic ēac wyrce." Ǣlce gēare[7] bið orf ācęnned, and męnn- 20
isce[8] męnn[8] tō mannum ācęnnede, ðā-ðe God gewyrcð
swā-swā hē geworhte ðā ǣrran; and hē ne sciepð nāne
sāwle būtan ðǣm cildum ānum, and eall nīeteñu nabbað
nāne sāwle.[9]

---

[1] In Chaucer's *Sir Thopas* we
have: "For in this world no
womman is Worthy to be my
make." So in Spenser (*F. Q.* 3.
11. 2): "That was as trew in
love as turtle to her *make*."

[2] See 153. *a.*

[3] See 184. *b.*

[4] See 156. *k.*   [5] See 142.

[6] Jn. 5. 17.   [7] See 176.

[8] Translate, *human beings.*

[9] Based upon Basil 82, where
he is combating the theory of
the transmigration of souls.

XIV.

THE SONG OF THE GLEEMAN.

(Beowulf 89-100.)

[Hrothgar, King of the Danes, builds a spacious hall for the assembly of his retainers. There, from time to time, they are entertained by minstrelsy, — sometimes that of a professional gleeman, and sometimes improvised by one of the warriors, or even by the king himself (cf. *Iliad* 9. 185-189).

In reading the poetry, the paragraph of the Preface relating to the retention of MS. forms should be borne in mind.]

> Þǣr wæs hearpan swēg,
> swutol sang scopes.[1]   Sǣgde sē þe cūþe   [90]
> frumsceaft fīra   feorran reccan,
> cwæð[2] þæt se Ælmihtiga[3]   eorðan worhte,

[1] For the accord of harp and voice see p. 175, l. 11, and *Odyssey* 8. 266: "Now as the minstrel touched the lyre, he lifted up his voice in sweet song."

[2] Thorkelin, the first editor of *Beowulf*, already noticed the resemblance between this song and that of Iopas in Virgil (*Æn.* 1. 740-747), though this is Christianized in its execution. An earlier sketch of the same conception was that in the *Georgics* (2. 475-482), of which Coning-ton says: "Virgil probably had in his mind here not only Lucretius and the Greek didactic poets, such as Xenophanes, Empedocles, and Aratus, but the legendary reputation of the poetic teachers of early Greece, such as Orpheus and Musæus. His own notion of an ancient bard is that of a hierophant of nature. . . . The conception belongs not to Augustan Rome, but to primitive Greece, where science was theological and imaginative, and verse the natu-

[3] Cf. p. 124, l. 4 ff.

wlitebeorhtne wang,   swā[1] wæter bebūgeð[2];
gesętte[3] Sigelrēþig   sunnan[4] ǫnd mōnan[4]
lēoman tō lēohte   landbūendum,   [95]
and gefrætwade   foldan sceatas
5 leomum[5] ǫnd lēafum;   līf ēac gescēop
cynna[6] gehwylcum   þāra þe cwice hwyrfaþ.[7]
Swā ðā drihtguman   drēamum lifdon
ēadiglīce.   [100]

ral vehicle of all knowledge and thought. It had, however, been partially realized by Lucretius, whose example exercised a strong influence on Virgil's imagination." As to the possibility of an Old English poet's being familiar with Virgil, compare the testimony of Bede (*Eccl. Hist.* 4. 2) concerning the pupils of Theodore and Hadrian: "Usque hodie supersunt de eorum discipulis qui Latinam Græcamque linguam æque ut propriam, in qua nati sunt, norunt."

[1] Almost = *which.* In archaic German *so* is thus used: "Von allen, *so* da kamen."

[2] This phrase is found again in the *Andreas.* See p. 216, l. 18.

[3] Cf. p. 125, l. 12 ff.   [4] See **153.** *b.*

[5] See **lim,** and **174.**

[6] Dependent upon **gehwylcum** (**154.** *b*).

[7] Here ends the song. The rest refers to Hrothgar's retainers.

XV.

THE ROUT OF THE ASSYRIANS.

(From the Judith.)

[Of this extract Ten Brink has said (*Early English Literature*): " To a lucid, well-constructed narrative are joined epic profusion, vigor, and animation. In the highest degree effective is the portrayal of Judith's return to Bethulia, of the warlike advance of the Hebrews, of the surprise of the Assyrian camp, the terror of the Assyrian nobles, who dare not disturb their lord in his rest, and finally of the disbandment and flight of the heathen host."

The portion here given omits the discovery of Holofernes' dead body by the Assyrians. It is based upon the Apocryphal book of Judith, the first few verses of the fifteenth chapter, especially verses 2, 5, 7, and 11. For further particulars see my edition of the *Judith*.

Attention is called to the device employed for indicating parallel or synonymous expressions, which have constituted one of the chief difficulties of OE. poetry. The device consists in the enclosure between reference-letters of the parallel expressions, the synonyms being designated by the same letters. For an example, see p. 204, ll. 5-7.]

    Þā wurdon blīðe   burhsittende,[1]

    syððan hī gehȳrdon[2]   hū sēo hālge[3] spræc   [160]

    ofer hēanne[4] weall.   Hęre wæs on lustum,

    wið þæs fæstengeates[5]   folc ōnette,

   5 weras wīf sǫmod[6];   wornum and hēapum,

    ðrēatum[7] and ðrymmum   þrungon and urnon

    ongēan ðā þēodnes mægð   þūsendmǣlum,   [165]

[1] See **28**.   [2] See **19**.

[3] See **55**.   [4] See **58**. 1.

[5] **Wið** sometimes governs the genitive; see **158**.

[6] Here almost = **and**. Throughout the following poetry, remember **25**.

[7] See **220**.

ealde ge geonge;   æghwylcum[1] wearð

męn on ðǣre medobyrig   mōd[2] ārēted,[3]

syððan hīe ongēaton   þæt wæs[4] Iūdith cumen

ęft tō ēðle,[5]   and ðā ofostlīce

5 hīe[6] mid ēaðmēdum   in forlēton.   [170]

þā sēo glēawe[7] hēt   golde gefrætewod[8]

hyre ðīnenne[9]   þancolmōde[9]

þæs hęrewǣðan   hēafod[10] onwrīðan,

and hyt[11] tō[12] bēhðe[12]   blōdig[13] ætȳwan

10 þām burhlēodum,[14]   hū hyre   æt beaduwe[15] ge- [175]
spēow.[16]

Spræc[17] ðā sēo æðele   tō eallum þām folce:—

"Hēr gē magon sweotole,   sigerōfe hæleð,[18]

lēoda rǣswan,[18]   on ðæs lāðestan

hǣðnes heaðorinces   hēafod starian,

15 Holofernus[19]   unlyfigendes,[20]   [180]

þe ūs męnna mǣst[21]   ᵃmorðraᵃ gefręmede,

[1] Belongs to **męn**.
[2] Subject.
[3] What is the normal form of this word (**113**)?
[4] Note the auxiliary: *was come*, not *had come*.
[5] See **23**.
[6] Acc. sing.
[7] See **181**.
[8] Modifies **glēawe**.
[9] Acc. sing.
[10] Object of **onwrīðan**.
[11] For **hit**.
[12] = *as a sign*.
[13] Modifies **hyt**.

[14] Construe, **and ætȳwan hyt, blōdig, þām burhlēodum, tō bēhðe hū hyre**, etc.
[15] Unusual form for **beadwe**, from **beadu**.
[16] See **190**.
[17] For the order cf. Tennyson's line from the song in *The Princess:* "Rose a nurse of ninety years."
[18] See **152**.
[19] Genitive.
[20] **y** is sometimes found for **i**, as well as for **ie** (**19**).
[21] **Mǣst** seems to have two

sārra ᵃsorgaᵃ,   and þæt swȳðor¹ gȳt²

ȳcan² wolde;   ac him ne ūðe³ God

lęngran līfes,⁴   þæt hē mid lǣððum ūs

ęglan mōste⁵;   ic him ealdor⁶ ōðþrǫng⁷   [185]

5   þurh Godes fultum.   Nū ic ᵇgumenaᵇ gehwæne⁸

þyssa¹ ᵇburglēodaᵇ   biddan wylle,¹

ᵇrandwiggendraᵇ,   þæt gē recene ēow⁹

fȳsan¹⁰ tō gefeohte;   syððan ᶜfrymða Godᶜ,

ᶜārfæst Cyningᶜ,   ēastan sęnde   [190]

10 lēohtne lēoman,   berað ᵈlindeᵈ forð,

ᵈbordᵈ for brēostum   and byrnhǫmas,

scīre helmas   in sceaðena gemǫng,

fyllan² ᵉfolctoganᵉ   fāgum sweordum,

fǣge ᵉfrumgārasᵉ.   Fȳnd² syndon ēowere¹¹   [195]

15 gedēmed tō dēaðe   and gē ᶠdōmᶠ āgon,¹²

ᶠtīrᶠ æt tohtan,   swā ēow getācnod hafað¹³

mihtig Dryhten   þurh mīne hand.''

þā wearð ᵍsnelraᵍ werod   snūde gegearewod,

---

senses and two constructions in
this and similar passages. In one
it apparently = *chiefest*, and is
construed with the preceding genitive; in the other = *most in number*, and is construed with the following genitive. Cf. *Andr.* 1447:
"þā þe heardra mǣst hearma ge-
fręmedan"; *Bēow.* 2645: "for-
ðām hē manna mǣst mǣrða
gefręmede"; etc.

¹ See above, p. 203, n. 20.
² See 19; 199. 1.
³ See 129.

⁴ See 159. *a.*
⁵ See 137.
⁶ Neuter.
⁷ See 142.
⁸ LWS. acc. of **gehwā.** See
154. *b.*
⁹ See 184. *b.*
¹⁰ Opt. pres. 2 plur.
¹¹ Construe, **ēowere fȳnd
syndon gedēmed,** etc.
¹² See 127. What two words
in this line have the same root?
Which is the derivative?
¹³ Is this the usual form?

[g]cēnra[g] tō campe;   stōpon[1] cynerōfe   [200]
sęcgas and gesīðas,   bǣron [sige]þūfas,
fōron tō gefeohte   forð on gerihte,
hæleð[2] under helmum   of[3] ðǣre hālgan byrig
5 on[4] ðæt dægrēd sylf;   [a]dynedan[a] scildas,
hlūde [a]hlummon[a].   Þæs se hlanca gefeah[5]   [205]
   wulf in walde,[6]   and se wanna hrefn,
wælgīfre fugel: wistan[7] bēgen
þæt him[8] ðā þēodguman   þōhton[9] tilian
10 fylle[10] on fǣgum;   ac him flēah[11] on lāst
earn ǣtes[12] georn,   ūrigfeðera,[13]   [210]
salowigpāda[14]   sang hildelēoð,
hyrnednębba.   Stōpon [b]heaðorincas[b],
   [b]beornas[b] tō beadowe   [c]bordum[c][15] beðeahte,

---

[1] See **stæppan**.

[2] Nom. plur. See **43. 9.**

[3] = *from*, not *of*.

[4] = *at*.

[5] See **gefēon**.

[6] Is this the usual form? See **21.**

[7] Irregular for **wiston (126)**.

[8] Not reflexive.

[9] See **ðęncean**.

[10] = *feast*. See *Iliad* 22. 42: "Then quickly would dogs and vultures devour him on the field."

[11] See **flēogan.**

[12] See **155. c.**

[13] See Shelley's description of the rooks, in the *Lines written among the Euganean Hills* : —

Gathering round with wings all hoar,
Through the dewy mist they soar.
* * * *
So their plumes of purple grain,
Starred with drops of golden rain,
Gleam, etc.

Perhaps Milton may have borrowed the word from OE. in *Il Pens.* 146: "dewy-feathered sleep."

[14] Note the three similar epithets of the **earn.**

[15] **Bord**, *border*, like **rand**, same meaning (see above, p. 204, l. 7), is poetically used for *shield*. So Gr. ἴτυς (akin to Eng. *withe*) meant *a*) a circle or rim made of *willow; b*) the outer edge or *rim* of the shield (like ἄντυξ); *c*) the

^chwealfum lindum^c,¹   þā ðe hwīle² ǣr

· elðēodigra³   ^aedwīt^a þoledon,   [215]

hǣðenra ^ahosp^a;   ^bhim^b þæt hearde wearð

æt ðām æscplegan⁴   eallum⁵ forgolden

5 ^bAssyrium^b,   syððan Ebrēas

under gūðfanum   gegān⁶ hæfdon⁶

tō ðām fyrdwīcum.   Hīe ðā fromlīce   [220]

lēton forð flēogan   flāna scūras,

^childenǣdran^c   of hornbogan,

10 ^cstrǣlas^c stedehearde;   styrmdon hlūde

grame gūðfrecan,   gāras⁷ sendon

in heardra gemang.   ^dHæleð^d wǣron yrre,⁸ [225]

^dlandbūende^d   lāðum cynne,

stōpon ^dstyrnmōde^d,   ^dstercedferhðe^d

15 wrehton unsōfte   ealdgenīðlan⁹

round *shield* itself. A good illustration of its use is in Euripides, *Tro.* 1196–97, where Hecuba is speaking of Hector's shield. Potter translates: —

Yet how sweet to trace
The mark of his strong grasp, and on the verge
Of thy high orb (ἴτυος) the sweat.

¹ The material for the weapon, *linden* for *shield*.

² Acc. sing.: *for a time*.

³ Dependent on **edwīt**.

⁴ On *ash* as the designation of a *spear*, see Shakespeare, *Coriol.* 3. 5. 112–115: —

Let me twine
Mine arms about that body, where against

My grained *ash* an hundred times hath broke,
And scarr'd the moon with splinters.

See also *Iliad* 22. 225 (where μελίη, *ash*, is used for *spear*): "Stood leaning on his bronze-pointed (χαλκογλώχινος, like the **ǣrgescōd** of *Beowulf* 2778) *ashen-spear*." For æscplega cf. 'sword-play.'

⁵ Agrees with **him** (**164.** *h*).

⁶ Note this pluperfect, formed with an auxiliary.

⁷ What is the meaning of the *gar-* in Mod. Eng. *garlic?*

⁸ See **19.**

⁹ Acc. plur. (**168**).

medowērige[1];   mundum[2] brugdon

scealcas of scēaðum   scīrmǣled swyrd[3]   [230]

ęcgum gecoste,[4]   slōgon eornoste

Assiria[5]   ᵉōretmǣcgasᵉ,

5 ᵉnīðhycgendeᵉ,   nǣnne ne sparedon

þæs ᶠhęrefolcesᶠ   hēanne[6] ne rīcne

ᶠcwicera mannaᶠ   þe hīe ofercuman mihton.   [235]

*   *   *   *   *   *   *   *

Him[7] mǫn[8] feaht on lāst,

mægenēacen[9] folc,   ōð se mǣsta dǣl · ·

10 þæs hęriges[10] lǣg   hilde gesǣged

on ðām sigewǫnge,   sweordum[11] gehēawen,   [295]

wulfum tō willan,[12]   and ēac wælgīfrum

fuglum tō frōfre.   Flugon ðā ðe lyfdon

lāðra lindwiggendra.[13] Him on lāste fōr

15 swēot Ebrēa[14]   ᵃsigor[15] geweorðodᵃ,

ᵃdōme gedȳrsodᵃ;   him[16] fēng ᵇDryhten Godᵇ [300]

fǣgre on[17] fultum,[17]   ᵇFrēa ælmihtigᵇ.

ᶜHī ᶜ ðā frǫmlīce   fāgum swyrdum

ᶜhæleð higerōfeᶜ   hęrpað[18] worhton

---

1 Acc. plur.; agrees with **eald-geniðlan**.

2 See **174**.

8 Acc. plur.; irregular for **sweord**.

4 Agrees with **swyrd**. See **174**. *d.*

5 Gen. plur.

6 From **hēan**, not **hēah**.

7 The Assyrians.

8 See **89**. *e.*

9 See **147**.

10 See **44**. 2.

11 See **174**. *c.*

12 = (*as*) *a delight to wolves.* See **161**. 2.

13 Depends on **ðā**.

14 Gen. plur.

15 Inst. without ending.

16 The Hebrews.

17 = *to* (*their*) *help.* For the construction see **164**. *e.*

18 Irregular for **hęrepað** (for -**pæð**).

þurh lāðra gemong,   linde hēowon,

scildburh scǣron: ᵈscēotendᵈ wǣron   [305]

gūðe gegremede,   ᵈguman Ebrēisceᵈ;

, þegnas on ðā tīd   þearle gelyste¹

5 gārgewinnes.   Þǣr on grēot gefēoll

se hȳhsta² dǣl   hēafodgerīmes

ᵃAssiriaᵃ   ealdorduguðe,³   [310]

ᵃlāðan cynnesᵃ: lȳthwōn becōm

cwicera⁴ tō cȳððe. Cirdon² cynerōfe,

10 wiggend⁵ on wiðertrod,   ᵇwælscelᵇ oninnan,⁶

ᵇrēocende hrǣwᵇ;   rūm⁷ wæs tō nimanne

londbūendum   on ðām ᶜlāðestanᶜ,   [315]

hyra ᶜealdfēondum   unlyfigendumᶜ

heolfrig hererēaf, —   hyrsta⁸ scȳne,²

15 bord and brād swyrd,   brūne helmas,

dȳre² mādmas.   Hæfdon dōmlīce

on ðām folcstede   fȳnd⁹ oferwunnen   [320]

ēðelweardas,¹⁰   ealdhettende⁹

swyrdum āswefede¹¹;   hīe on swaðe reston,

20 þā ðe him tō līfe   lāðost wǣron

cwicera cynna.   Ðā sēo cnēoris eall,

---

¹ See **190**.   ² See **19**.

³ Either dependent upon, or parallel to, **hēafodgerīmes**.

⁴ Dependent on **lȳthwōn**.

⁵ For **īg** is sometimes found, as here, **igg**. What does this signify ?

⁶ Governs **wælscel** and **hrǣw**; the latter is an acc. plural.

⁷ Translate, *there was a chance* for the natives to capture from the most hated ones .(**lāðestan** for -**um**).

⁸ These nouns are all acc. plur.

⁹ Acc. plur.   ¹⁰ Nom. plur.

¹¹ Supply **hæfdon**. With **ā-swebban**, in the sense of 'slay,' cf. the similar use of the Lat. *sopire* and the Gr. εὐνδζειν (the latter in Sophocles).

mǣgða mǣrost,   ānes mōnðes fyrst,[1]   [325]
wlanc[2] wundenlocc[2]   wāgon[3] and lǣddon[3]
tō ðǣre beorhtan byrig   Bethuliam
helmas and hupseax,[4]   hāre byrnan,
5 gūðsceorp gumena   golde gefrætewod,
mǣrra[5] mādma   þonne mọn ǣnig   [330]
āsẹcgan mæge   searopọncelra[6];ʹ
eal þæt ðā ðēodguman   þrymme geēodon,
cēne[7] under cumblum   on cọmpwīge
10 þurh Iūdithe[8]   glēawe lāre
mægð[8] mōdigre.   ᵃHīᵃ tō mēde[9] hyre   [335]
of ðām sīðfate[10]   sylfre[11] brōhton
ᵃeorlas æscrōfeᵃ.   Holofernes[12]
sweord and swātigne[13] helm,   swylce ēac sīde byrnan,
15 gerēnode rēadum golde,   and eal þæt se rinca baldor
swīðmōd[14] sinces[15] āhte   oððe sundoryrfes,[15]   [340]
bēaga[15] and beorhtra māðma,[15]   hī þæt þǣre beorhtan
    idese
āgēafon gearoþọncolre.

---

[1] See 170.
[2] Agreeing with cnēoris.
[3] See wegan, and 189. 2.
[4] Acc. plur.
[5] Comp. and gen. plur.; see 60.
2. The position would seem to
require mǣrran mādmas.
[6] Depends on ǣnig.
[7] Modifies, or is parallel to,
ðēodguman.   [8] Gen. sing.

[9] See Mayhew, OE. Phonology, § 365.
[10] See 43. 2; here the a intrudes even into the sing.
[11] For selfre (166).
[12] Genitive.
[13] Lit. sweaty, but in poetry swāt usually = blōd.
[14] Agrees with baldor.
[15] Dependent on eal.

XVI.

SELECTIONS FROM THE ANDREAS.

[The *Andreas* is a poem of about 1722 lines (the numbering differs according to the edition). Jacob Grimm considered it and the *Elene* to be (Preface to his edition, p. iv) "the most ancient and instructive productions of Old English poetry, next to the *Bēowulf*." With the help of Thilo, Grimm discovered (pp. xvi ff.) its source to be the *Acts of Andrew and Matthew*, written in Greek, and now published in Tischendorf's *Acta Apostolorum Apocrypha*, pp. 132–166. Besides this poem, there is a prose version which may be profitably consulted, and which is to be found in Bright's valuable *Anglo-Saxon Reader*, pp. 113–128. It is believed by many scholars that both these versions were made from a Latin translation of the Greek original, but this cannot be said to have been demonstrated, at least for the poem. The Greek original is discussed at length by Lipsius, *Die apokryphen Apostelgeschichten und Apostellegenden*, pp. 546 ff. A portion of the Greek, corresponding to lines 235–349, is printed in Appendix III.

According to Lipsius, the scene of the poem is the northern coast of the Black Sea; though the Old English poet had Africa in mind (cf. l. 198), perhaps because the region about Colchis had by some been called the inner or second Ethiopia. The Marmedonia (l. 30) or Mermedonia of our text has been identified with Myrmecium, Gr. Μυρμήκιον, near the modern Yenikale, in the Crimea. Here are supposed to have dwelt the Cimmerians of Homer, and here, in classic times, were settled various Scythian tribes. Of the Tauri (Crimea was anciently the *Tauric* Chersonesus) Herodotus says (4. 103): "They sacrifice to the virgin all who suffer shipwreck, and any Greeks they meet with driven on their coasts, in the following manner: having performed the preparatory ceremonies, they strike the head with a club; some say they throw the body down from a precipice. . . . The Tauri themselves say that this deity to whom they sacrifice is Iphigenia, daughter of Agamemnon" (cf. Euripides' *Iphigenia in Tauris*, and Goethe's *Iphigenie*). This reputation clung to the region, for Tertullian says (*Adv. Marcionem* 1. 1): "Pontum ferocissimas gentes inhabitare, paréntum cadavera cum pecudibus cæsa convivio convorantes." Nor was the evil fame of the district diminished by the fact that Huns were settled here from the fourth to the sixth century, then Goths, and afterward Tartars.

The story of the poem, up to the beginning of our extract, is briefly this: St. Matthew was in imminent danger among the Mermedonians, a race of cannibals. In this extremity God appears to Andrew, and exhorts him to go to Matthew's assistance, which, after some reluctance, he prepares to do.

Bits of translation and interesting comments (not always correct), embracing much of our extract, are given by Brooke, *Hist. Early Eng. Lit.* pp. 169 ff., 413 ff.]

Conversation between Andrew and the Sea-Captain.

Gewāt[1] him þā ᵃon ūhtan ᵃ   ᵃmid ǣrdæge ᵃ   [235]

ofer sandhleoðu   tō sǣs faruðe

þrīste on geþance,   ǫnd his þegnas mid,

gangan[2] on grēote;   gārsecg[3] hlynede,[4]

5   bēoton brimstrēamas.   Se beorn wæs on[5] hyhte,[5]

syððan hē on waruðe   wīdfæðme[6] scip   [240]

mōdig gemētte.   þā cōm ᵇmorgen torht ᵇ,

ᵇbēacna beorhtost ᵇ,   ofer breomo snēowan,

hālig of heolstre;   heofoncandel[7] blāc[8]

---

[1] See **184.** *a.*   [2] See **199.** 1.

[3] Sweet (*Engl. Stud.* 2. 314–316) explains this word as being, not a compound of **gār** and **sęcg** (= *spear + man*, according to Bosworth, as if a personification like Neptune with his trident; or = *spear + sedge*, with Leo, the tips of the waves being likened to spears), but as arising by metathesis from the Runic word **gāsric** (cf. the name of the Vandal king, Gaisaricus), as if **gās** + **ric**. The **gās-** would correspond to Old Norse **geisa**, *to*

chafe, rage; the -**ric** as in Ger. *wüterich;* so that **gāsric** would = *the rager.*

[4] Brooke translates this line: "Trampled o'er the shingle. Thundered loud the ocean."

[5] Nearly = *joyful, rejoiced.* Gr. 'rejoiced with very great joy.'

[6] Poetic license; Gr. 'a little ship.' Cf. the Homeric κοίλη νηῦς.

[7] = *the sun.* Of 'candle' the *New Eng. Dict.* says: "One of the Latin words introduced at the English Conversion, and long associated chiefly with religious

[8] See **blīcan.**

ofer lagoflōdas.   Hē ðǣr ^clidweardas^c

þrymlīce þrȳ   ^cþegnas^c gemētte,[1]   [245]

^cmōdiglīce mẹnn^c,   on mẹrebāte

sittan sīðfrọme,   swylce hīe ofer sǣ cōmon.[2]

5 Þæt[3] wæs Drihten sylf,   dugeða[4] Wealdend,[4]

ēce, ælmihtig,   mid his ẹnglum twām.

Wǣron ^dhīe^d on gescirplan   ^escipfērendum^e, [250]

^deorlas^d onlīce   ^cēalīðendum^c,

þonne hīe on flōdes fæðm[5]   ofer feorne weg

10 on cald wæter   cēolum[6] lācað.[7]

Hīe ðā gegrētte   sē ðe on grēote stōd,

fūs[8] on[8] faroðe   fægn[9] reordade : —   [255]

"Hwanon cōmon gē   cēolum līðan,

mācræftige mẹnn,   on mẹreþissan

15 āne[10] ǣgflotan?   hwanon ēagorstrēam

ofer ȳða gewealc   ēowic[11] brōhte?"

Him þā ọndswarode   ælmihti[12] God,   [260]

swā[13] þæt ne wiste   sē ðe þæs wordes bād,[14]

observances. . . . This sacred character of the word bears on the OE. poetic compounds." Cf. *Rom. and Jul.* 3. 5. 9.: "Night's candles are burnt out." See also Shakespeare's metaphorical sense of *lamp*, and cf. the Gr. λαμπάς, Lat. *lampas*, in poetical use.

[1] So Sievers ; not in MS.

[2] = *had come.*

[3] What is the antecedent of þæt?

[4] = *Lord of hosts.*

[5] = *expanse,* originally *embracing arms, embrace.*

[6] Not *keel,* but *ship.*

[7] The radical meaning is, *to move in any swift or impetuous manner.*

[8] = *ready, eager for.* One would expect the acc. faroð.

[9] MS. frægn.   [10] Inst. sing.

[11] See 81. 1.   [12] See 28.

[13] = *in such a manner.* One is inclined to substitute ðēah, as making better sense.

[14] See bīdan, and 156. l.

hwæt sē manna wæs   meðelhēgendra,[1]
þe hē þǣr on waroðe   wiðþingode: —
" Wē of Marmedónia   mǣgðe syndon
feorran gefęrede;   ūs mid flōde bǣr   [265]
5 on hranrāde[2]   ᵃhēahstefn[3] naca ᵃ,
ᵃsnellīc sǣmearh ᵃ⁴   snūde[5] bewunden,[5]
ōð-þæt wē þissa lēoda   land gesōhton
wǣre[6] bewrecene,   swā ūs wind fordrǣf."
Him þā Andreas   ēaðmōd oncwæð: —   [270]
10 "Wolde ic þē biddan,   þēh[7] ic þē ᵇbēaga ᵇ lȳt,
ᵇsincweorðunga ᵇ,   syllan meahte,
þæt þū ūs gebrōhte   ᶜbrante[8] cēole ᶜ,
ᶜhēa hornscipe ᶜ,   ofer hwæles ēðel
on þǣre mǣgðe;   bið[9] ðē meorð[10] wið God,   [275]
15 þæt[11] þū ūs on lāde   līðe weorðe."
Ęft him ǫndswarode   æðelinga Helm[12]
of[13] ȳðlide,   ęngla Scippend: —
"Ne magon þǣr gewunian   wīdfērende,

---

[1] Cf. the Homeric μέροψ as an epithet, and in later use as an equivalent, of *men, mortals* (so *Il.* 2. 285), and see p. 222, l. 9.

[2] With this sense of **rād**, *road*, may be compared the Gr. κέλευθος, πόρος, as in the Homeric ἰχθυόεντα κέλευθα (*Od.* 3. 177), *fishy roads;* see also Æschylus' πόρον οἰωνῶν (*Prom.* 281), *track of birds.*

[3] Cf. the Gr. ὑψίπρῳρος.

[4] Cf. *Od.* 4. 708: "Swift ships, that serve men for horses on the sea " (ἁλὸς ἵπποι). See p. 226, l. 2.

[5] = *encompassed with speed, swift.*

[6] An unusual word for *ocean.*

[7] In this poem, ea (ēa) not seldom becomes e (ē), especially before palatal consonants (10).

[8] See **174. a.**

[9] Future sense, as frequently with **bið.**

[10] Anglian form for WS. **mēd**, related to Gr. μισθός (Mayhew, *OE. Phon.* § 365).   [11] **þær** = *if?*

[12] Not *helmet*, but *protector.*

[13] = *from*, as often.

nē þǣr ęlþēodige   eardes[1] brūcaðˀ,   [280]
ah in þǣre ceastre   cwealm[2] þrōwiaðˀ
þā ðˀe feorran þyder   feorh[3] gelǣdaþ[3];
ǫnd þū wilnast[4] nū   ofer wīdne męre,
5 þæt ðˀū on þā fǣgðˀe   þīne fēore spilde ? "
Him þā Andreas   āgef ǫndsware : —   [285]
" Ūsic lust hwęteðˀ[5]   on þā lēodmearce,
mycel mōdes hiht[6]   tō þǣre mǣran byrig,
þēoden[7] lēofesta,   gif þū ūs þīne[8] wilt
10 on męrefaroðˀe   miltse gecȳðˀan."
Him ǫndswarode   ęngla þēoden,   [290]
Nęregend[9] fīra,   of nacan[10] stefne : —
" Wē ðˀē ēstlīce   mid ūs willaðˀ
fęrigan[9] frēolīce   ofer fisces[11] bæðˀ[11]
15 efne tō þām lande,   þǣr[12] þē lust myneðˀ
tō gesēcanne,   syðˀðˀan[13] gē ēowre   [295]
ᵃgafulrǣdenneᵃ   āgifen habbaðˀ,
ᵃsceattas gescrifeneᵃ;   swā ēow scipweardas
āra[14] ofer ȳðˀbord   unnan willaðˀ."
20 Him[15] þā ofstlīce   Andreas wiðˀ,
wineþearfende,   wordum mǣlde : —   [300]

---

[1] See **156.** *e.*
[2] Acc.
[3] Periphrastic for 'go.'
[4] Elliptic, like Shakespeare's (*M. W.* 3. 2. 88) " I *will* to my honest knight."
[5] A following verb of motion understood.
[6] Here = *bent.*
[7] Formed from **ðˀēod**, as **dryht**-

en from **dryht**; cf. **cyning**, with a different ending, from **cyn**.
[8] Agrees with **miltse.**
[9] See **18.**   [10] Gen. sing.
[11] Kenning (**215**) for ' ocean.'
[12] Almost = *that.* Cf. *there* in Mod. Eng. *thereto.*
[13] = *as soon as.*
[14] MS. **aras.** See **156.** *i.*
[15] Governed by **wiðˀ.**

"Næbbe ic fǣted gold   nē feohgestrēon,
welan nē wiste,[1]   nē wīra gespann,
landes[2] nē locenra bēaga,[3]   þæt ic þē mæge *lust*
    āhwęttan,
willan in worulde,   swā ðū worde becwist.[4] "

5 Him þā beorna Breogo,   þǣr[5] hē on bolcan sæt,   [305]
ofer waroða[6] geweorp[6]   wiðþingode : —
"Hū gewearð þē þæs,[7]   wine lēofesta,
ðæt ðū sǣbeorgas   sēcan woldes,[8]
męrestrēama gemet,   māðmum bedǣled
10 ofer cald cleofu[9]   cēoles[10] nēosan ?   [310]
Nafast þē tō frōfre   on faroðstrǣte
hlāfes wiste   nē hlutterne[11]
drync tō dugoðe[12]?   Is se drohtað strang
þām þe lagolāde   lange[13] cunnaþ."

15 Ðā him Andreas   ðurh ǫndsware,   [315]

[1] Not the verb.

[2] The construction suddenly changes to the genitive, as if some word like āht, *aught*, had been introduced. The poet is apparently trying to adapt to this place the **landes and locenra bēaga** of *Bēowulf* 2296, there a partitive genitive.

[3] Now only existing as *bee*, a nautical term for a ring or hoop of metal. See *New Eng. Dict.* s.v. *Bee*[2].

[4] See **becweðan.**

[5] Nearly = *from where.*

[6] Kemble translates, *the dashing of the waves;* but **waroð**

does not mean *wave.* I would suggest *the smiting of the shores,* perhaps meaning the plunging of the breakers.

[7] Anticipatory of the relative sentence, **þæt þū,** etc.

[8] On the omission of final **t,** see 95.

[9] See **clif,** and 20.

[10] See 156. *m.*

[11] An instance of an originally long vowel rendered short by the gemination of the following consonant.

[12] The Greek has διατροφήν, *sustenance* (p. 240).

[13] Adj.

wīs on gewitte,   wordhord[1] onlēac[1]: —

"Ne gedafenað[2] þē,   nū þē Dryhten geaf[3]

welan ǫnd wiste   ǫnd woruldspēde,

ðæt ðū ǫndsware[4]   mid oferhygdum,

5 sęcge[4*] sārcwide[5];   sēlre bið æghwām   [320]

þæt hē ēaðmēdum[6]   ęllorfūsne

oncnāwe cūðlīce,   swā þæt Crīst bebēad,

þēoden þrymfæst.   Wē his þegnas[7] synd,

gecoren tō cęmpum.   Hē is Cyning on[8] riht,[8]

10 Wealdend ǫnd Wyrhta   wuldorþrymmes,   [325]

ān ēce God   eallra gesceafta,

swā hē ealle befēhð   ānes[9] *cræfte*

hefon[10] ǫnd eorðan   *hālgum mihtum*,

sigora sēlost.[11]   Hē ðæt sylfa cwæð,

15 Fæder folca[12] gehwæs,   ǫnd ūs fēran hēt   [330]

geond ginne grund   gāsta[13] strēonan: —

'Farað[14] nū geond ealle   eorðan scēatas[15]

emne swā wīde   swā wæter bebūgeð,[16]

[1] That is, *spoke.*   [2] See **190.**

[3] Translate, *hath given.*

[4] Acc. sing.   [4*] MS. sece.

[5] Inst. sing., parallel with **mid oferhygdum** (174).

[6] Perhaps adv. (72).

[7] When did the word *thane* cease to be employed in literature?

[8] Either=*rightfully, by rights,* or perhaps an adj. **onriht**=*legitimate, rightful.*

[9] = *sole,* lit. *of one (alone).*

[10] Unusual for **heofon.**

[11] One is inclined to substitute **sęllend,** *bestower,* which occurs three times with **sigora** in the poetry, whereas **sigora sēlost** is otherwise unknown.

[12] Dependent on **gehwæs.**

[13] See **156.** *n*; **199.** 1.

[14] An interesting parallel to this paraphrase (a free one even in the Greek original) of Matt. 10. 1 ff. is found in the poem of *Christ,* 480–489.

[15] MS. **sceattas.**

[16] Cf. p. 201, l. 1.

oððe stędewangas   strǣte[1] gelicgaþ[2];

bodiað æfter burgum   beorhtne gelēafan   [335]

ofer foldan fæðm;   ic ēow freoðo healde.[3]

Ne ðurfan[4] gē on þā fōre   frætwe lǣdan,[5]

5 gold ne seolfor;   ic ēow gōda gehwæs[6]

on ēowerne āgenne dōm   ēst āhwętte.[7]’

Nū ðū seolfa[8] miht   sīð ūserne[9]   [340]

gehȳran hygeþancol[10];   ic sceal hraðe cunnan

hwæt ðū ūs tō[11] duguðum[11]   gedōn wille.”

10 Him þā ǫndswarode   ēce[12] Dryhten:—

“Gif gē syndon þegnas   þæs[13] þe þrym āhōf

ofer middangeard,   swā gē mē sęcgaþ,   [345]

ǫnd gē gehēoldon[14]   þæt ēow se Hālga bēad,

þonne ic ēow mid gefēan   fęrian wille

15 ofer brimstrēamas,   swā gē bēnan[15] sint.”

þā in cēol stigon[16]   collenfyrhðe,[17]

ęllenrōfe;   æghwylcum wearð   [350]

on męrefaroðe   mōd geblissod.

Ðā ofer ȳða geswing   Andreas ongann

20 męrelīðendum[18]   miltsa[19] biddan[20]

---

[1] Acc. sing.   [2] = border.

[3] Future sense.

[4] For ðurfon (131).

[5] Not lead, but carry (Gr. βαστάζετε).

[6] Dependent on ēst.

[7] = supply; not the normal sense of the word.

[8] See self, and 21.

[9] See 81. 1.

[10] Agrees with ðū.

[11] = for (our) benefit, lit. bene-

fits; Gr. τὴν φιλανθρωπίαν, (as a) kindness.   [12] MS. ęce.

[13] = of that one, of him.

[14] Translate, have kept, observed.

[15] = petitioners.

[16] So in Latin: ascendere navem.

[17] -fyrhðe irregular for -ferhðe.

[18] = for the seafarers.

[19] See 156. b.

[20] Biddan here takes three cases after it. Explain.

wuldres Aldor,   ǫnd þus wordum cwæð:—
"Forgife þē ᵃDryhtenᵃ   dōmweorðunga—   [355]
willan in worulde,   ǫnd in wuldre blǣd—
ᵃMeotud manncynnesᵃ,   swā ðū mē hafast[1]
5 on þyssum sīðfæte   sybbe gecȳðed!"

The Voyage.— Storm at Sea.

Gesæt him þā se hālga   Holmwearde[2] nēah,
æðele be Æðelum.   Ǣfre ic ne hȳrde   [360]
þon[3] cymlīcor   cēol gehladenne[4]
hēahgestrēonum.   ᵇHæleðᵇ insǣton,
10 ᵇþēodnasᵇ þrymfulle,   ᵇþegnasᵇ wlitige.
Ðā reordode   rīce þēoden,
ēce, ælmihtig,   heht[5] his ᵃ ǫngelᵃ gān,   [365]
ᵃmǣrne maguþegnᵃ,   ǫnd mete syllan,[6]
frēfran fēasceaftne[7]   ofer flōdes wylm,
15 þæt hīe þē[8] ēað[9] mihton   ofer ȳða geþring
drohtað ādrēogan.   Þā ᵇgedrēfedᵇ wearð,
ᵇonhrēredᵇ hwælmere;   hornfisc plegode,   [370]
glād[10] geond gārsecg,   ǫnd se grǣga mǣw

---

[1] Is this the normal form?

[2] Probably **Helmwearde** = *guardian of the tiller or helm;* but see Vocabulary.

[3] = *than that,* inst. of ð**æt**.

[4] This sentence seems to be imitated from *Bēow.* 38–39:—
Ne hȳrde ic cymlīcor cēol gegyrwan hildewǣpnum and heaðowǣdum.
Note that the past participle is substituted in the passage from

Andreas for the infinitive of *Bēo-wulf.* The former construction is unusual.

[5] Anglian (probably identical with the original) form for **hēt** (110).

[6] For s**ẹllan**.

[7] Meaning Andrew, though the next line has **hīe**.

[8] For ðȳ (84).   [9] For *ieð*.

[10] See **glīdan**.

wælgīfre[1] wand; wedercandel swearc,[2]
windas wĕoxon,[3] wǣgas grundon,
strēamas styredon, strẹngas gurron,[4]
wǣdo gewǣtte[5]; wæterẹgsa stōd[6]   [375]
5 þrēata þrȳðum. Þegnas wurdon

[1] Agrees with mǣw.

[2] See sweorcan.

[3] There is no hint of any extraordinary commotion, much less of a storm, in the original. Of all this long description there is nothing except, "They were troubled because of the sea." Brooke says (p. 416): "The storm is now described in words that come, one after another, short, heavy, and springing, like the blows of the waves, and the gusts of wind. We know as we read that the writer had seen the thing."

[4] See georran.

[5] Part of Baskervill's note, in his edition, is: "wǣdo gewǣtte, *the wet weeds (sails); wet with waters*, Kemble; *waves swelled*, Grein; *replebatur aquis, vadum madefiebat*, Grimm; wǣdo gewǣtte is in apposition with strengas." Wǣdo (with short æ) might be nom. (acc.) plur. of wǣd, *sea*. But the phrase is obscure.

[6] A peculiar use of standan, to indicate motion rather than rest. In Mod. Eng. this general sense is represented by phrases like 'stand back,' 'stand off from shore,' 'stand up,' 'stand out,' etc. In OE. poetry, standan is frequently used with ẹge or ẹgesa (similarly in ON.); thus in Ps. 104. 33 (105. 38), *cecidit timor eorum super eos:* him þǣr ẹgesa . . . stōd, where the King James version has, *the fear of them fell upon them.* The transformation of this idiom into *stand in awe of* is interesting. Note that the dative is still retained in this quotation, of about A.D. 1380 (*Sir Ferumbras* 408): "Of whame *men* stondeð aye" [*i.e.* awe]. However, *men* being eventually understood as nom. in such a sentence as the last (cf. *Towneley Mysteries*, 305 [ab. 1460]: "*I* stand great aghe''), *in* was supplied before *awe*, as in this from Lydgate (ab. 1413): "Of theyre lord and god to stande *in* awen." See *New Eng. Dict.* s.v. *awe.* The Scandinavian influence in Middle English confirmed the idiom, and assisted in its development.

äcolmōde;   ǣnig[1] ne[1] wēnde[2]

þæt hē lifgende   land begēte,

þāra[3] þe mid Andreas   on ēagorstrēam

cēol gesōhte.   Næs[4] him cūð þā gȳt   [380]

5 hwā þām sǣflotan   sund[5] wīsode.

Him þā ᵃse hālgaᵃ   on holmwege

ofer ārgeblǫnd   ᵃAndreasᵃ þā gīt,

ᵃþegn þēodenhold,ᵃ   þanc gesægde

rīcum Rǣsboran,   þā hē gereordod wæs:— [385]

10 " Ðē þissa swǣsenda[6]   ᵇsōðfæst Meotud,ᵇ

ᵇlīfes Lēohtfruma,ᵇ   lēan forgilde,

ᵇweoruda Waldend,ᵇ   ǫnd þē wist[7] gife,

heofonlīcne hlāf,   swā ðū ᶜhyldoᶜ wið mē

ofer firigendstrēam[8]   ᶜfrēodeᶜ gecȳðdest!   [390]

15 Nū synt geþrēade   ᵈþegnas mīneᵈ,

ᵈgeonge gūðrincasᵈ;   ᵉgārsecgᵉ hlymmeð,

ᵉgeofon[9] gēotendeᵉ;   grund[10] is onhrēred,[11]

dēope[12] gedrēfed;   ᶠduguðᶠ[13] is geswǫnced,

---

[1] Translate, *no one.*   [2] See 4.

[3] Dependent on **ǣnig.**

[4] For lines 4–14 the Greek has: "Andrew answered and said unto Jesus, not knowing that it was Jesus, The Lord give thee heavenly bread from his kingdom."

[5] = either *ocean* or *course,* probably the latter; cf. p. 226, l. 2.

[6] See 153. *e.*

[7] = *as food.*

[8] For **firgenstrēam.**

[9] MS. **heofon**; but this seems like an echo of *Bēow.* 1690–91:—

syððan flōd ofslōh,
gifen gēotende

(= *streaming sea; rushing sea,* Garnett; *gurgling currents,* Hall; *rushing ocean,* Earle).

[10] Probably = *sea;* an unusual sense. Cf. p. 223, l. 1.

[11] See p. 218, ll. 16, 17.

[12] Adv.

[13] Related to Ger. *tugend* (cf. 30), OE. **dugan** (128), and Mod. Eng. *doughty.* There is an interesting OE. phrase, **duguð and geoguð** (cf. *Bēow.* 160, etc.),

ᶠmōdigra mægenᶠ   myclum¹ gebysgod."   [395]

Him of holme² oncwæð   hæleða Scyppend: —

"Læt nū gefęrian   ᵃflotanᵃ ūserne,

ᵃlidᵃ tō lande   ofer lagufæsten,

5 ǫnd þonne gebīdan³   beornas þīne,

āras on earde,   hwænne⁴ þū ęft cyme."   [400]

Ēdre⁵ him þā ᵇeorlasᵇ   āgēfan⁶ ǫndsware,

ᵇþegnas þrohthearde ᵇ—þafigan⁷ ne woldon

ðæt hīe forlēton   æt lides stefnan⁸

10 lēofne lārēow,   ǫnd him⁹ land curon —

"Hwider hweorfað wē   hlāfordlēase,   [405]

gēomormōde,   gōde¹⁰ orfeorme,

synnum¹¹ wunde,   gif wē swīcað þē¹²?

Wē¹³ bīoð ᶜlāðeᶜ   on landa gehwām,

15 folcum ᶜfracoðeᶜ,   þonne fīra bearn,

ęllenrōfe,   æht¹⁴ besittaþ,   [410]

which almost = *knights and squires*. The word is worth a little study.

¹ See 72.

² Perhaps mistaken for **helman**, the *helm* of the ship.

³ Construe, **læt þine beornas gebīdan**.

⁴ Here = *until*.

⁵ For **ǣdre**.

⁶ For **āgēafon**.   ⁷ See 18.

⁸ See **stefna**, a collateral form of **stefn**.

⁹ See 184. *a*.   ¹⁰ See 165. 1.

¹¹ See 174. *d*.   ¹² See 164. *o*.

¹³ This reply is largely original, and exhibits a characteristic trait of our ancestors — loyalty to a rightful lord. See Gummere, *Germanic Origins*, pp. 261-269; to the citations given there might be added the account of Cynewulf and Cyneheard, from the Saxon Chronicle for 755. One sentence from it will illustrate: "Ǫnd þā cuǣdon hīe þæt him nænig mǣg lēofra nǣre þonne hiera hlāford, ǫnd hīe nǣfre his banan folgian noldon."

¹⁴ Æht (sometimes **eaht**) is not to be confounded with **ǣht** (4); **æht besittan** = *sit in council;* here almost = *consult, discuss, debate.*

hwylc hira sēlost[1]   symle gelǣste
hlāforde[2] æt hilde,   þonne hand ǫnd rǫnd
on beaduwange   billum forgrunden[3]
æt nīðplegan   nearu þrōwedon."

Andrew relates Christ's Stilling of the Tempest.

5   Þā reordade . [a]rīce þēoden[a],   [415]
    [a]wǣrfæst Cining[a]   word stunde[4] āhōf: —
    "Gif ðū þegn sīe   þrymsittenðes
    Wuldorcyninges, . swā ðū worde becwist,
    rǫce þā gerȳnu,   hū hē reordberend[5]
10   lǣrde under lyfte.   Lang is þes sīðfæt   [420]
    ofer fealuwne flōd ;   frēfra þīne
    mǣcgas on mōde.   Mycel is nū gēna
    lād ofer lagustrēam,   land swīðe feorr
    tō gesēcanne[6];   sund is geblǫnden,[7]

[1] Adv. (76).

[2] In Carlyle's *Past and Present* (Bk. 3, Chap. 10) occurs this piece of etymologizing: " Ironcutter, at the end of the campaign, did not turn off his thousand fighters, but said to them: ' Noble fighters, this is the land we have gained ; be I Lord in it, — what we will call *Law-ward*, maintainer and *keeper* of Heaven's *Laws:* be I *Law-ward*, or in brief orthoepy *Lord* in it, and be ye Loyal Men around me in it.' " Again (Chap. 13): "If no pious *Law-ward* would remember it, always some pious Lady (' *Hlaf-dig*,' Benefactress, ' *Loaf-giveress*,' they say she is, — blessings on her beautiful heart !) was there." So Ruskin, in *Sesame and Lilies* (Of Queens' Gardens): " Lady means ' bread-giver ' or ' loaf-giver,' and Lord means ' maintainer of laws.' "
Are these etymologies correct ?

[3] MS. **foregrunden.**

[4] = *at this time, now.*

[5] Acc. plur. (43. 6). See p. 213, note 1.

[6] Cf. our modern ' far to seek.'

[7] Cf. *Æn.* 1. 107: " furit æstus harenis.'' MS. reads **sand.**

grund[1] wið grēote.   God ēaðe mæg   [425]
hēaðolīðendum[2]   helpe[3] gefremman.[4]”
Ongan þā glēawlīce   ᵃgingran sīneᵃ
ᵃwuldorspēdige werasᵃ   wordum trymman: —
5 “Gē þæt gehogodon,   þā gē on holm stigon,
þæt gē on fāra[5] folc   feorh[6] gelǣddon,[6]   [430]
ǫnd for Dryhtnes lufan[7]   dēað prōwodon[8]
on Ælmyrcna[9]   ēðelrīce,
sāwle[10] gesealdon.[8]   Ic þæt sylfa wāt,
10 þæt ūs gescyldeð   Scyppend ęngla,
weoruda Dryhten.   Wæterȩgesa sceal,   [435]
geðȳd[11] ǫnd geðrēatod   þurh þrȳðcining,
lagu lācende,   līðra wyrðan.[12]
Swā[13] gesǣlde[14] īu   þæt wē on sǣbāte
15 ofer waruðgewinn   wǣda[15] cunnedan
faroðrīdende.   Frēcne pūhton   [440]
egle ēalāda;   ēagorstrēamas
bēoton bordstæðu;   brim oft oncwæð,
ȳð ōðerre.[16]   Hwīlum uppāstōd

---

[1] Probably = sea. Cf. p. 220, note 10.

[2] Perhaps for hēahð̄o-, in the sense of the high sea; cf. Lat. altum.   [3] Acc. sing.

[4] It is not till this point is reached, in the Greek original, that the journey is begun !

[5] From fāh (43. 3).

[6] Periphrastic, something like our ‘ directed your steps.’

[7] From the weak lufe.

[8] Optative.

[9] Allmurk(y) = Ethiopians; but the poet is here mistaken. See the prefatory remarks, p. 210.

[10] Here = life.   [11] Cf. p. 227, l. 19.

[12] For weorðan.

[13] Brooke remarks (p. 417): “ It is a happy situation which the poet conceives, for Andrew, not knowing that Christ himself is seated beside him in the stern, tells Christ a story of Christ.” Cf. Mk. 4. 36 ff.

[14] See 190.   [15] See 156. d.

[16] Dat. sing. Cf. Ps. 42. 7.

of brimes bōsme   on bātes fæðm

ẹgesa ofer ȳðlid.   Ælmihtig þǣr,   [445]

Meotud mancynnes,   on merẹþyssan

beorht bāsnode.   Beornas wurdon

5 forhte on mōde;   friðes[1] wilnedon,

miltsa[1] tō[2] Mǣrum.[3]   Þā sēo menigo ongan

clypian on cēole;   Cyning sōna ārās,   [450]

ẹngla Ēadgifa   ȳðum[4] stilde,

wæteres wælmum;   windas þrēade;

10 sǣ sessade,[5]   smylte wurdon

merestrēama gemeotu.[6]   Ðā ūre mōd āhlōh,[7]

syððan wē gesēgon[8]   under swegles gang   [455]

windas ọnd wǣgas   ọnd wæterbrōgan

forhte gewordne   for Frēan[9] ẹgesan.

15 For-þan ic ēow tō sōðe   secgan wille

þæt næfre[10] forlǣteð   lifgende God

eorl on eorðan,   gif his ẹllen dēah.[11] ”   [460]

Swā hlēoðrode   hālig cempa

ðēawum[12] geþancul;   þegnas lǣrde

20 ēadig ōreta,[13]   eorlas trymede,

ōð-ðæt hīe semninga   slǣp oferēode

---

[1] See 156. a.

[2] Here = from.

[3] Meaning Christ.

[4] See 164. i.

[5] This word does not otherwise occur, but the meaning is obvious. There is a noun sess, meaning seat.

[6] See gemet, and 20.

[7] See 107.

[8] Anglian form of gesāwon (106).

[9] See 153. d.

[10] This gnomic sentence resembles that in Bēow. 572–573. Perhaps it is imitated from the Latin proverb, “Fortune favors the brave.”

[11] See 128.   [12] See 174. d.

[13] Usually ōretta.

mēðe[1] be mæste. Męre sweoðerade, [465]
ªȳða ongin ª ęft oncyrde,
ªhrēoh holmþracuª. þā þām hālgan wearð
æfter gryrehwīle gāst geblissod.

Andrew desires Instruction in Seamanship.

5 Ongan þā reordigan rǣdum snottor,
   wīs on gewitte wordlocan onspēonn[2]: — [470]
   "Nǣfre ic sǣlidan[3] sēlran mētte,
   mācræftigran, þæs-ðe[4] mē þynceð,
   rōwend rōfran, rǣdsnotterran,
10 wordes wīsran. Ic wille þē,
   eorl unforcūð, āhre[5] nū gēna [475]
   bēne biddan: þēah ic þē ªbēagaª[6] lȳt,
   ªsincweorðungaª, syllan mihte,[7]
   ªfǣtedsincesª, wolde ic frēondscipe,[8]
15 þēoden þrymfæst, þīnne, gif ic mehte,[7]
   begitan gōdne. Þæs[9] ðū gife hlēotest,[10] [480]
   hāligne hyht on heofonþrymme,
   gif ðū lidwērigum lārna þīnra
   ēste[11] wyrðest. Wolde ic ānes[12] tō ðē,
20 cynerōf hæleð, cræftes nēosan —
   ðæt ðū mē getǣhte, nū þē tīr[13] Cyning [485]
   ǫnd miht forgef,[14] manna Scyppend,

---

[1] Agrees with **hīe**.
[2] See **onspannan**.
[3] Acc. sing.
[4] Here = *so far as, as* (157. 1).
[5] See **156.** *b.*   [6] See **154.** *a.*
[7] Variants of **meahte**.
[8] Object of **begitan**.
[9] = *for that.*
[10] Future sense.
[11] See **165.**   [12] See **156.** *m.*
[13] Acc. sing.
[14] Variant of **forgeaf.**

hū ðū ᵃwǣgflotanᵃ   wǣre bestēmdon,¹

ᵃsǣhẹngeste,ᵃ   sund² wīsige.

Ic wæs on³ gifeðe³   īu ọnd nū

syxtȳne sīðum⁴   on sǣbāte,   [490]

5 ᵇmẹreᵇ hrērendum⁵   mundum⁶ frēorig,⁷

ᵇēagorstrēamasᵇ—   is ðys⁸ āne⁹ mā—,

swā¹⁰ ic ǣfre ne geseah   ǣnigne mann,

þrȳðbearn hæleð,¹¹   þē gelīcne

stēoran ofer stæfnan.   Strēamwelm hwileð,¹² [495]

10 bēatað¹³ brimstæðo;   is þes bāt ful scrid,

fǣreð fāmigheals   fugole¹⁴ gelīcost,

glīdeð on geofone.   Ic georne wāt

þæt ic ǣfre ne geseah   ofer ȳðlāde,¹⁵

on sǣleodan¹⁶   syllīcran¹⁷ cræft.   [500]

15 Is þon¹⁸ geliccost¹⁹   swā²⁰ hē²¹ on landsceare²²

¹ For **bestēmdan**, the (weak) past part., according to Wülker. It would then agree with **wǣgflotan** (dat. sing.).

² See p. 213, note 4, and p. 220, l. 5.   ³ = *by chance.*

⁴ See **176. 1.**

⁵ Governs **mẹre** (and **ēagorstrēamas**), and agrees with **mundum.**   ⁶ = *in hands?*

⁷ Agrees with **ic.**

⁸ For **ðis**, neut. nom. sing.

⁹ Inst. adv. = *once. This makes another journey*, added to the sixteen. The Greek has, "Behold, this is the seventeenth." Brooke (p. 414) attributes this to the OE. poet.   ¹⁰ Almost = *yet.*

¹¹ It is unusual to have two synonymous nouns thus joined.

¹² See **hwelan.**

¹³ Unusual ending of 3 sing.

¹⁴ Cf. *Odyssey* 7. 36: "Their ships are swift as the flight of a bird." See also *Od.* 13. 86–87; 11. 125.

¹⁵ MS. **ȳðlāfe**, which would mean *sand*, that which is *left* by the *waves.*   ¹⁶ See **sǣlīda.**

¹⁷ For **sel-**, contracted from **seld-**, the root of *seldom.*

¹⁸ = *to that.*

¹⁹ For **gelīcost**; see l. 11.

²⁰ = *as if.*   ²¹ = *the boat* (**bāt**).

²² = simply *land;* the Greek has: ἐπὶ τῆς γῆς.

stille stande,   þǣr hine *storm* ne mæg,
wind āwęcgan,   nē wæterflōdas
brecan brǫndstæfne;   hwæðere on brim snēoweð[1]
snel under[2] segle.[2]   Ðū eart seolfa geong,   [505]
5 wīgendra hlēo,   nālas wintrum frōd:
hafast þēh[2*] on fyrhðe,   faroðlācende,[3]
eorles ǫndsware,   ǣghwylces[4] canst
worda[5] for[6] worulde   wīslīc andgit.[7] "

The Pilot recognizes God's Presence with Andrew.

Him ǫndswarode   ēce Dryhten: —   [510]
10 "Oft þæt gesǣleð   þæt wē on sǣlāde,
scipum under[8] scealcum,   þonne scēor[9] cymeð,
brecað[10] ofer bæðweg   *brimhęngestum*.
Hwīlum ūs on ȳðum   earfoðlīce
gesǣleð on sǣwe,[11]   þēh[12] wē sīðnesan   [515]
15 frēcne gefēran. ᐧ Flōdwylm ne mæg
manna ǣnīgne   ofer[13] Meotudes ēst
lungre gelęttan[14];   āh[15] him līfes geweald
sē ðe brimu bindeð,   brūne ȳða
ðȳð and þrēatað.[16]   Hē þēodum sceal   [520]
20 racian mid rihte,   sē ðe rodor āhōf

[1] MS. snoweð.
[2] So yet, *under sail.*   [2*] MS. þe.
[3] See 152.
[4] Dependent on andgit.
[5] Dependent on ǣghwylces.
[6] Almost = *in.*
[7] Object of canst (130).
[8] = *among;* but this half-line
is a little obscure.

[9] See 18.
[10] Almost = *break away.*
[11] Irreg. dat.; usually sǣ.
[12] For ðēah.   [13] = *against.*
[14] Cf. *Hamlet* 1. 4. 85: "I'll
make a ghost of him that *lets*
me."
[15] See 127; here reflexive.
[16] See note 13, p. 226.

ǫnd gefæstnode   folmum[1] sīnum,
worhte and wrę̆ðede,   wuldras[2] fylde
beorhtne boldwelan;   swā geblēdsod wearð
engla ēðel   þurh his ānes miht.   [525]
5 For-þan is ªgesȳneª,   sōð[3] ªorgeteª,
cūð ªoncnāwenª,   þæt ðū Cyninges eart
þegen geþungen   þrymsittendes[4];
for-þan þē sōna   ᵇsǣholmᵇ oncnēow,
ᵇgārsecges begangᵇ,   þæt ðū gife hæfdes[5]   [530]
10 Hāliges Gāstes.   ᶜHærnᶜ ęft onwand,
ᶜārȳða geblǫndᶜ;   ęgesa gestilde,
wīdfæðme wǣg;   wǣdu swæðorodon
seoðþan hīe ongēton   þæt ðē God hæfde
wǣre[6] bewunden,[7]   sē ðe wuldres blǣd   [535]
15 gestaðolade   strangum mihtum."

*   *   *   *   *   *   *   *

Andrew is carried to the City.[8]

Þus Andreas   ǫndlangne dæg[9]
hęrede[10] hlēoðorcwidum   Hāliges lāre,
ōð-ðæt hine sęmninga   slǣp oferēode[11]   [820]
on hrǫnrāde   Heofoncyninge nēh.[12]
20 þā ªgelǣdanª hēt[13]   līfes Brytta

---

[1] See **174**.
[2] Perhaps Anglian genitive; used for the inst. after **fylde**, as in the poem of *Christ*, ll. 408–409.
[3] Here a noun.
[4] Agrees with **Cyninges**.
[5] Original form (**95**).
[6] = *with his covenant.*
[7] MS. **bewunde.**
[8] Note the break here (ll. 537–817). The interval is occupied by discourses.
[9] See **170**.   [10] MS. **berede.**
[11] See p. 224, l. 21.
[12] For **nēah.**
[13] Construe, **hēt** . . . **sīne ęn-**

ofer ȳða geþræc   ᵹnglas sīne,
fæðmum *fᵹrigean*   on Fæder[1] wǣre
lēofne mid lissum   ofer lagufæsten.[2]   [825]

*   *   *   *   *   *   *   *

Lēton þone hālgan   be hᵹrestrǣte
5 swefan on sybbe   under swegles hlēo,
blīðne[3] bīdan   burhwealle nēh,[4]
his nīðhᵹtum,   nihtlangne fyrst,
ōð-þæt Dryhten forlēt   dægcandelle   [835]
scīre scīnan.   Sceadu sweðerodon
10 wᵹnn under wolcnum.   Þā cōm wederes blæst,[5]
hādor heofonlēoma,   ofer hofu blīcan.
Onwōc þā wīges[6] heard,   wang scēawode;
fore burggeatum   *beorgas* stēape,   [840]
hleoðu[7] hlifodon;   ymbe hārne stān
15 tigelfāgan trafu,[8]   torras stōdon,
windige weallas.   Þā se wīsa[9] oncnēow
þæt hē Marmedonia   mǣgðe hæfde
sīðe[10] gesōhte,   swā him sylf bebēad,   [845]
þā[11] hē him foregescrāf,   Fæder mancynnes.

glas . . . gelǣdan lēofne . . .
ofer lagufæsten . . . on Fæder
wǣre.
    [1] Genitive.
    [2] Here follow four lines which
are probably corrupt, and are
therefore omitted.
    [3] = kindly, amiable.

    [4] Is construed both with burh-
wealle and nīðhᵹtum.
    [5] Not blast.   [6] See 155.
    [7] See hlīð, and 20.
    [8] See 47. 4.
    [9] MS. wīs.
    [10] See 174. a.
    [11] MS. þam. Translate, when.

Andrew's Disciples relate their Adventure.

Geseh[1] hē þā on grēote[2]   gingran[3] sīne,
beornas beadurōfe,   bīryhte[4] him
swefan on slǣpe.   Hē sōna ongann
wīgend weccean,   ǫnd worde cwæð: —   [850]
5 "Ic ēow secgan mæg   sōð[5] orgete,[6]
þæt ūs gystrandæge[7]   on geofones strēam[8]
ofer ārwelan   æðeling ferede.
In þām cēole wæs   cyninga Wuldor,[9]
Waldend werðēode[10];   ic his word oncnēow,   [855]
10 þeh hē his mægwlite   bemiðen hæfde."
Him þā æðelingas   ǫndsweorodon
geonge ªgēncwidumª,   ªgāstgerȳnumª: —
"Wē þē, Andreas,   ēaðe gecȳðað
sīð ūserne,   þæt ðū sylfa miht   [860]

[1] For **geseah**.

[2] Gr. 'on the earth' (ἐπὶ τὴν γῆν).   [3] See **169**.

[4] The only occurrence of this word; **ætrihte**, similarly formed, is found three times in poetry.

[5] Noun in acc.

[6] Agrees with **sōð**.

[7] See **176**.

[8] Cf. the 'stream of Oceanus,' *Od.* 11. 21, and often in Homer.

[9] To this kenning there are several analogies in Greek and Latin. Thus Ulysses is referred to as 'great glory of the Achaians,' *Il.* 9. 673, and elsewhere; the bull is called the 'glory of the herd' by Ovid (*A. A.* 1. 290); and *decus* is used by Virgil(?) almost exactly as here, — *decus Asteriæ* (*Cul.* 15) for *decens* or *pulchra Asteria*, like **cyninga wuldor** for **wuldorlīc cyning**. An interesting mediæval parallel is the line by Hilary, a disciple of Abelard, and probably an Englishman, cited by Lenient, *La Satire en France au Moyen Age*, p. 20, note: "Papa summus, paparum gloria." So he apostrophizes a girl with "Ave, splendor puellarum" (Wright, *Biog. Brit. Lit.*, Anglo-Norman Period, p. 93).

[10] MS. **weorðode**.

ongitan glēawlīce   gāstgehygdum.

Ūs sǣwērige   slǣp oferēode;

þā cōmon earnas[1]   ofer ȳða wylm

faran[2] on flyhte   feðerum hrēmige,[3]

5 ūs of slǣpendum   sāwle ābrugdon,   [865]

mid gefēan fᶒredon   flyhte[4] on lyfte

brehtmum blīðe,[5]   beorhte[6] ᶒnd līðe[6];

lissum[7] lufodon   ᶒnd in lofe wunedon

þǣr wǣs singāl sang   ᶒnd[8] swegles gᶒng,

10 wlitig weoroda hēap[9]   ᶒnd wuldres þrēat.[10]   [870]

Ūtan ymbe Æðelne[11]   ᶒnglas stōdon,

þegnas ymb Þēoden   þūsendmǣlum;

hᶒredon on hēhðo   hālgan stefne

dryhtna Dryhten.[12] "

---

[1] Related to Gr. ὄρνις, *a bird.*

[2] Not in MS., but supplied for the verse-structure.

[3] See **174.** *d.* Like Gr. γαῦρος; Archilochus has, *exulting in his curls.*   [4] Inst. (**174.** *a*).

[5] = *blithe, joyful.* Note the rime and assonance in these lines.

[6] Nom. plur.; or possibly adverbs. Will the last consonants permit of associating **līðe** with Germ. *gelind?*

[7] How may this contain the stem (**līð-**) of the last word (**34**)?

[8] Possibly miswritten for **geond,** or perhaps the rare preposition **and** (= *in, in presence of*); this is on the supposition that **swegles gᶒng** means *revolution*

of the sky, cf. p. 224, l. 12. The music of the spheres is even suggested, though hardly in the poet's mind. **Swegel** *may* sometimes mean *music,* and possibly so here, but then one hardly knows how to translate **gᶒng.**

[9] So in Shakespeare: *Rich. III.* 2. 1. 53, "Amongst this princely *heap*"; *Jul. Cæs.* 1. 3. 23, "There were drawn Upon a *heap* a hundred ghastly women."

[10] A Hebraism; *multitude of glory,* nearly = *glorious multitude.*

[11] Jesus, according to the original.

[12] Biblical expression; see Rev. 17. 14; 19. 16.

APPENDIXES.

APPENDIX I

SOME USEFUL BOOKS FOR THE STUDY OF OLD ENGLISH.

I. A SELECTION FOR THE BEGINNER.

Political and Social History.

GREEN, *Short History of the English People.* (Various editions.)

FREEMAN, *Old English History.* New York, 1876.

TRAILL, *Social England*, Vol. I., Chap. II. London and New York, 1894.

Religious and Cultural History.

LINGARD, *The Anglo-Saxon Church.* London, 1858, 2 vols.

BRIGHT, *Early English Church History.* 3d ed. New York, 1897.

TURNER, *History of the Anglo-Saxons.* London, 1852, 3 vols.

GILES, Translation of *Bede's Ecclesiastical History of England, and the Anglo-Saxon Chronicle.* (Temple Classics.)

Literary History.

TEN BRINK, *Early English Literature.* New York, 1883. (The best.)

BROOKE, *History of Early English Literature.* New York, 1892.

——, *English Literature from the Beginning to the Norman Conquest.* New York, 1898.

MORLEY, *English Writers*, Vols. I. and II. New York, 1888.

Biography.

ASSER, *Life of King Alfred.* Boston, 1905.

PLUMMER, *Life and Times of Alfred the Great.* Oxford, 1902.

WHITE, *Ælfric: A New Study of his Life and Writings.* (*Yale Studies in English* II.) New York, 1898.

Biography. (*Continued.*)

PLUMMER, *Life of Bede.* (As below, under **Religious and Cultural History.**)

BEDE, *Account of Cædmon.* (In *Select Translations from Old English Poetry*, Appendix III.) (See **Translations.**)

MULLINGER, *Schools of Charles the Great.* London, 1877.

WEST, *Alcuin and the Rise of the Christian Schools.* New York, 1892.

For reference :

Dictionary of Christian Biography. London, 1877–87, 4 vols.

Dictionary of National Biography. London, 1885–1901, 63 vols., and Supplement, 3 vols.

Translations.

COOK AND TINKER, *Select Translations from Old English Poetry.* Boston, 1902. (Contains *Judith, The Phœnix, Widsith, The Battle of Maldon, The Battle of Brunanburh, The Dream of the Rood, The Seafarer, The Wanderer*, etc. ; selections from *Beowulf, Genesis*, and other poems.)

TINKER, *Beowulf.* New York, 1902.

HALL (J. R. C.), *Beowulf, and the Fight at Finnsburg.* London, 1901.

SEDGEFIELD, *King Alfred's Version of the Consolations* (sic) *of Boethius.* Oxford, 1900.

ROOT, *Andreas: The Legend of St. Andrew.* (*Yale Studies in English* VII.) New York, 1899.

WHITMAN, *Cynewulf's Christ.* Boston, 1900.

HOLT, *The Elene of Cynewulf.* (*Yale Studies in English* XXI.) New York, 1904.

HARGROVE, *King Alfred's Old English Version of St. Augustine's Soliloquies.* (*Yale Studies in English* XXII.) New York, 1904.

(See also under **Literary History.**)

Readers.

SWEET, *Anglo-Saxon Reader.* 7th ed. Oxford and New York, 1894.

BRIGHT, *Anglo-Saxon Reader.* 3d ed. New York, 1894.

Readers. (*Continued.*)

ZUPITZA-MACLEAN, *Old and Middle English Reader.* New York, 1893.

BASKERVILL AND HARRISON, *Anglo-Saxon Prose Reader.* New York, 1898.

Poetical Texts.

WYATT, *Beowulf.* Cambridge and New York, 1894.

COOK, *Judith.* Boston, 1889; also in *Belles Lettres Series.* Boston and London, 1904.

——, *The Christ of Cynewulf.* Boston and London, 1899.

——, *Dream of the Rood.* Oxford and New York, 1905.

——, *Elene.* Boston and London, 1905. (Forthcoming.)

——, *Phœnix.* Boston and London, 1905. (Forthcoming.)

STRUNK, *Juliana.* Boston and London, 1904.

SEDGEFIELD, *Battle of Maldon, and Short Poems from the Saxon Chronicle.* Boston and London, 1904.

Prose Texts.

BRIGHT, *Gospel of St. Matthew.* Boston and London, 1904.

——, *Gospel of St. Luke.* Oxford and New York, 1893.

——, *Gospel of St. John.* Boston and London, 1904.

SWEET, *Selected Homilies of Ælfric.* Oxford and New York, 1885.

——, *Extracts from Alfred's Orosius.* Oxford and New York, 1886.

BOSWORTH AND WARING, *Gothic and Anglo-Saxon Gospels, with the Versions of Wycliffe and Tyndale.* London, 1888.

COOK, *Biblical Quotations in Old English Prose Writers,* Vol. I., New York and London, 1898. Vol. II., New York, 1903.

History of the English Language.

EMERSON, *History of the English Language.* New York, 1894.

——, *Brief History of the English Language.* New York and London, 1896.

LOUNSBURY, *History of the English Language.* Revised ed. New York, 1894.

History of the English Language. (*Continued.*)

NESFIELD, *Historical English.* New York, 1899.

CHAMPNEYS, *History of English.* New York, 1893.

COOK, *English Language.* (In the *Universal Cyclopœdia.* New York, 1903.)

Etymology.

SKEAT, *Principles of English Etymology: Series I., The Native Element.* New York, 1887.

(See also **Dictionaries.**)

Grammar.

SIEVERS-COOK, *Old English Grammar.* 3d ed. Boston, 1903.

WYATT, *Elementary Old English Grammar.* Cambridge, 1897.

HENRY, *Short Comparative Grammar of English and German.* New York, 1894.

Phonetics.

SWEET, *Primer of Phonetics.* Oxford and New York, 1890.

BELL, *English Visible Speech for the Million.* London and New York.

——, *Manual of Vocal Physiology and Visible Speech.* New York.

Dictionaries.

HALL, *Concise Anglo-Saxon Dictionary.* New York, 1894.

SWEET, *Student's Dictionary of Anglo-Saxon.* New York and London, 1897.

MURRAY, BRADLEY, AND CRAIGIE, *New English Dictionary:* A–Mandragon, O–Pennached, Q–Reign. Oxford and New York, 1884-1905. (Cited as *New Eng. Dict.*)

II.   A SELECTION FOR THE ADVANCED STUDENT.

Bibliography.

WÜLKER, *Grundriss zur Geschichte der Angelsächsischen Litteratur.* Leipzig, 1885.

KÖRTING, *Grundriss der Geschichte der Englischen Litteratur.* 3d ed. Münster i. W., 1899.

Bibliography. (*Continued.*)

GROSS, *The Sources and Literature of English History.* London and New York, 1900.

TINKER, *The Translations of Beowulf: a Critical Bibliography.* (*Yale Studies in English* XVI.) New York, 1902.

Jahresbericht . . . der Germanischen Philologie. Berlin (later Leipzig), 1879–. (Section XV is devoted to English.)

Political and Social History.

KEMBLE, *The Saxons in England.* London, 1876, 2 vols.

LAPPENBERG, *History of England under the Anglo-Saxon Kings.* 2 vols. (Bohn Library.)

GREEN, *The Conquest of England.* New York, 1884.

——, *The Making of England.* New York, 1883.

FREEMAN, *History of the Norman Conquest,* Vol. I., Chaps. I.-III. Oxford and New York, 1873.

PALGRAVE, *Rise and Progress of the English Commonwealth,* Vol. I. London, 1831.

STUBBS, *Constitutional History of England,* Vol. I., Chaps. I.-VIII. Oxford and New York, 1875.

ADAMS (and others), *Essays on Anglo-Saxon Law.* New York, 1876.

ANDREWS, *The Old English Manor.* Baltimore, 1892.

CHADWICK, *Studies on Anglo-Saxon Institutions.* Cambridge, 1905.

Religious and Cultural History.

PLUMMER, *Venerabilis Bædæ Opera Historica.* Oxford and New York, 1896, 2 vols.

STEVENSON, *Asser's Life of King Alfred.* Oxford and New York, 1904.

GRIMM, *Teutonic Mythology.* London, 1879–89, 4 vols.

HADDAN AND STUBBS, *Councils and Ecclesiastical Documents.* London, 1869–78, 3 vols.

PADELFORD, *Old English Musical Terms.* (*Bonner Beiträge zur Anglistik* IV.) Bonn, 1899.

STEVENS, *The Cross in the Life and Literature of the Anglo-Saxons.* (*Yale Studies in English* XXIII.) New York, 1904.

Religious and Cultural History. (*Continued.*)

Roeder, *Die Familie bei den Angelsachsen*, I. Teil. Halle, 1899.

Keary and Grueber, *A Catalogue of English Coins in the British Museum: Anglo-Saxon Series.* London, 1887–93, 2 vols.

Akerman, *Remains of Pagan Saxondom.* London, [1852]–55.

Wright, *The Celt, the Roman, and the Saxon.* London, 1861.

Literary History.

Ebert, *Allgemeine Geschichte der Litteratur des Mittelalters im Abendlande.* Leipzig, 1874–87, 3 vols. (Especially Vols. I. and III.)

Cook, *Biblical Quotations in Old English Prose Writers*, Vol. I. London and New York, 1898. (Introduction contains a sketch of Old English Biblical translations, prose and poetical, with bibliography.)

Biography.

Wright, *Biographia Britannica Literaria*, Vol. I. London, 1842.

Montalembert, *Monks of the West.* Edinburgh, 1861–79, 7 vols.; also London, 1895, 6 vols. (A fascinating work.)

Translations.

Grein, *Dichtungen der Angelsachsen, stabreimend übersetzt.* Göttingen, 1857–59, 2 vols.

Readers.

Sweet, *Second Anglo-Saxon Reader.* Oxford and New York, 1887. (Archaic and dialectal; consists largely of glosses.)

Kluge, *Angelsächsisches Lesebuch.* 2d ed. Halle, 1897.

Körner, *Angelsächsische Texte, mit Uebersetzung, Anmerkungen, und Glossar.* Heilbronn, 1880.

Rieger, *Alt- und Angelsächsisches Lesebuch.* Giessen, 1861.

Poetical Texts. (See also **Prose Texts.**)

Grein-Wülker, *Bibliothek der Angelsächsischen Poesie.* Kassel, 1887–98.

Gollancz, *The Exeter Book*, Part I. London (Early English Text Society), 1895.

Thorpe, *Codex Exoniensis.* London, 1842.

Prose Texts.

SWEET, *Oldest English Texts.* London (E. E. T. S.), 1885.

——, *King Alfred's West Saxon Version of Gregory's Pastoral Care.* London (E. E. T. S.), 1871–72.

——, *King Alfred's Orosius.* London (E. E. T. S.), 1883.

MILLER, *Old English Version of Bede's Ecclesiastical History of the English People.* London (E. E. T. S.), 1890–98.

SEDGEFIELD, *King Alfred's Old English Version of Boethius de Consolatione Philosophiæ.* Oxford, 1899.

HARGROVE, *King Alfred's Old English Version of St. Augustine's Soliloquies.* (*Yale Studies in English* XIII.) New York, 1902.

GREIN, *Bibliothek der Angelsächsischen Prosa,* Vol. I. Kassel, 1872. (Mostly translations from the Old Testament.)

THORPE, *Homilies of Ælfric.* London (Ælfric Society), 1844–46, 2 vols.

MORRIS, *Blickling Homilies.* London (E. E. T. S.), 1874–80, 3 vols. in 1.

SKEAT, *Ælfric's Metrical Lives of Saints.* London (E. E. T. S.), 1881–90, 2 vols.

——, *The Gospels in Anglo-Saxon and Northumbrian Versions.* Cambridge, 1871–87.

ASSMANN, *Angelsächsische Homilien und Heiligenleben.* (*Bibliothek der Angelsächsischen Prosa* III.) Kassel, 1889.

EARLE, *Handbook to the Land-Charters and other Saxonic Documents.* Oxford and New York, 1888.

EARLE AND PLUMMER, *Two of the Saxon Chronicles Parallel.* Oxford and New York, 1892–99, 2 vols.

SCHMID, *Die Gesetze der Angelsachsen.* 2d ed. Leipzig, 1858. (This has a much completer apparatus than the following.)

THORPE, *Ancient Laws and Institutes of England.* London, 1840, 2 vols.

LIEBERMANN, *Die Gesetze der Angelsachsen,* Vol. I. (Text and Translation.) Halle, 1903.

HECHT, *Bischofs Wærferth von Worcester Uebersetzung der Dialoge Gregors des Grossen.* (*Bibliothek der Angelsächsischen Prosa* V.) Leipzig, 1900.

HERZFELD, *Old English Martyrology.* London (E. E. T. S.), 1900.

Prose Texts. (*Continued.*)

SCHRÖER, *Die Angelsächsischen Prosabearbeitungen der Benediktin-
erregel.* (*Bibliothek der Angelsächsischen Prosa* II.) Kassel,
1885, 1888.

NAPIER, *Wulfstan.* Berlin, 1883.

COCKAYNE, *Leechdoms, Wortcunning, and Starcraft, of Early England.* London, 1864–66, 3 vols.

Facsimiles of Manuscripts.

SKEAT, *Twelve Facsimiles of Old English* [*i.e.* Old and Middle
English] *Manuscripts, with Transcriptions and Introduction.*
Oxford and New York, 1892. (From Alfred's translation of
the *Pastoral Care,* the poetical *Exodus,* and the *Chronicle.*)

ZUPITZA, *Beowulf: Autotypes of the Unique Cotton MS., with a
Transliteration and Notes.* London (E. E. T. S.), 1882.

WÜLKER, *Codex Vercellensis: Die Angelsächsische Handschrift
zu Vercelli in Getreuer Nachbildung.* Leipzig, 1894.

WESTWOOD, *Facsimiles of the Miniatures and Ornaments of Anglo-
Saxon and Irish Manuscripts.* London, 1868.

——, *Palæographia Sacra Pictoria.* London, 1843–45.

(See also Cook's edition of *Judith,* under **Poetical Texts,** p. 237.)

History of the English Language.

KLUGE, BEHRENS, AND EINENKEL, *Geschichte der Englischen
Sprache.* (In Paul's *Grundriss der Germanischen Philologie,*
2d ed., I. 926–1151.) Strassburg, 1899–.

Grammar.

MÄTZNER, *Englische Grammatik.* 3d ed. Berlin, 1885–89, 3 vols.
(English Translation by C. J. Grece, London, 1874.)

KOCH, *Historische Grammatik der Englischen Sprache.* Kassel,
1863–78, 3 vols.

COSIJN, *Altwestsächsische Grammatik.* The Hague, 1883–88.

——, *Kurzgefasste Altwestsächsische Grammatik.* 2d ed. Lei-
den, 1893.

SWEET, *New English Grammar,* Parts I. and II. Oxford and
New York, 1892–1898.

BÜLBRING, *Altenglisches Elementarbuch,* I. Teil: Lautlehre.
Heidelberg, 1902.

Phonology.

SWEET, *History of English Sounds.* Oxford and New York, 1888.

MAYHEW, *Synopsis of Old English Phonology.* Oxford and New York, 1891.

COOK, *Phonological Investigation of Old English.* Boston, 1888.

Syntax.

CHASE, *Bibliographical Guide to Old English Syntax.* Leipzig, 1896.

WÜLFING, *Die Syntax in den Werken Alfreds des Grossen,* I.–II. Teil. Bonn, 1894–1901. (Contains a useful bibliography.)

SHEARIN, *The Expression of Purpose in Old English Prose. (Yale Studies in English* XVIII.) New York, 1903.

CALLAWAY, *The Absolute Participle in Anglo-Saxon.* Baltimore, 1888.

——, *The Appositive Participle in Anglo-Saxon. (Pub. Mod. Lang. Assoc.* XVI.) Baltimore, 1901.

Prosody.

SIEVERS, *Altgermanische Metrik,* pp. 120–149. Halle, 1893.

——, *Angelsächsische Metrik.* (In Paul's *Grundriss der Germanischen Philologie,* 1st ed., II. 1. 888–893; a very brief, but clear, sketch.) Strassburg, 1891.

Dictionaries.

BOSWORTH-TOLLER, *Anglo-Saxon Dictionary.* New York, 1882–98.

GREIN, *Sprachschatz der Angelsächsischen Dichter.* Göttingen, 1861–4.

COOK, *Glossary of the Old Northumbrian Gospels.* Halle, 1894.

LINDELÖF, *Glossar zur Altnorthumbrischen Evangelienübersetzung in der Rushworth Handschrift.* Helsingfors, 1897.

——, *Wörterbuch zur Interlinearglosse des Rituale Ecclesiæ Dunelmensis. (Bonner Beiträge zur Anglistik* IX.) Bonn, 1901.

HARRIS, *Glossary of the West Saxon Gospels. (Yale Studies in English* VI.) New York, 1899.

KLUGE, *Etymologisches Wörterbuch der Deutschen Sprache* (with Janssen's Index). 6th ed., Strassburg, 1899; 4th ed. translated, New York, 1891. (For comparison of Old English with German words.)

Periodicals.

Anglia.   Halle, 1878–.

Englische Studien.   Heilbronn, 1878–.

Archiv für das Studium der Neueren Sprachen.   Berlin, 1846–.
(Especially the recent volumes.)

Beiträge zur Geschichte der Deutschen Sprache und Litteratur (ed.
by Paul and Braune).   Halle, 1874–.

Publications of the Modern Language Association of America.
Baltimore, 1886–.

Modern Language Notes.   Baltimore, 1886–.

The Journal of (English and) Germanic Philology.   Boston,
London, and Leipzig, 1897–.

APPENDIX II.

CORRESPONDENCES OF OLD ENGLISH AND MODERN
GERMAN VOWELS.

Only a selection of the more regular correspondences
is here given. The student must not be surprised at
the occurrence of correspondences which he cannot
reconcile with these; profounder study will usually
show the reason for the discrepancy. The great
majority of instances, however, will be found to fall
under the following heads. The graphic representa-
tions of the vowels, not their sounds, is all that is
here considered, but this will be found of much
assistance in tracing and fixing cognates.

OLD ENGLISH SHORT VOWELS AND DIPHTHONGS.

OE. a : Ger. a . . . . **baðian** : *baden.*

OE. æ : Ger. a . . . . **cræft** : *Kraft.*

    Sometimes OE. æ : Ger. e . . . **hærfest** : *Herbst.*

OE. e : Ger. e . . . . **brecan** : *brechen.*

OE. ę : Ger. e (*ee*) . . . . **będd** : *Bett;* **hęre** : *Heer.*

OE. i : Ger. i . . . . **fisc** : *Fisch.*

OE. o : Ger. o . . . . **lof** : *Lob.*

OE. u : Ger. u . . . . **burg** : *Burg.*

OE. y : Ger. ü . . . . **fyllan** : *füllen.*

    Sometimes OE. y : Ger. u . . . **hyldu** : *Huld.*

OE. ea (**20, 21**) : Ger. a . . . . . **hearpe** : *Harfe.*

OE. eo (**20, 21**) : Ger. e . . . . . **eorðe** : *Erde.*

OLD ENGLISH LONG VOWELS AND DIPHTHONGS.

OE. ā : Ger. *ei* . . . . **brād** : *breit.*

    Sometimes OE. ā : Ger. *e* (*ee*) . . . **ār** : *Ehre ;* **sāwol** : *Seele.*

OE. ǣ : Ger. *ei.* . . . . **hǣl** : *Heil.*

    Sometimes OE. ǣ : Ger. *a* or Ger. *e .* $\begin{cases} \textbf{lǣtan} : lassen ; \\ \textbf{ǣrest} : erst. \end{cases}$

OE. ē : Ger. *ü* . . . . **grēne** : *grün.*

OE. ī : Ger. *ei* . . . . **īdel** : *eitel.*

OE. ō : Ger. *u* . . . . **fōt** : *Fuss.*

OE. ū : Ger. *au* . . . . **hūs** : *Haus.*

OE. ēa : Ger. *au.* . . . . **hēafod** : *Haupt.*

    Before **h**, and dental consonants

      (6), OE. ēa : Ger. *o* . . . . **dēað** : *Tod.*

OE. ēo : Ger. *ie* . . . . **dēor** : *Tier.*

In tracing back the history of these vowels, many correspondences become clearer. Thus, take OE. ō : Ger. *u.* The Old High German correlative of ō is *uo*, that is, the one long vowel is diphthongized into two short ones. Of these it is the *u* which has survived. If now we consider that the **i**-umlaut of ō is ē, and of Ger. *u* is *ü*, we shall better understand such a pair as **grēne** : *grün.*

It should be observed that Ger. *ei* corresponds to OE. ā, ǣ, and ī, and Ger. *au* to OE. ū and ēa ; similarly Ger. *o* to OE. **o** and ēa, Ger. *u* to OE. **u** and ō, etc. Note, too, that the *sound* of the vowel in Ger. *eitel, Haus*, corresponds precisely to the Mod. Eng. sound into which the OE. vowels of **īdel, hūs**, have respectively developed.

See Kluge, under **Dictionaries**, p. 241.

APPENDIX III.

ANDREW'S NEGOTIATIONS WITH THE STEERSMAN.

[This extract from the Greek is found on pp. 136–138 of Tischendorf's *Acta Apostolorum Apocrypha*, and corresponds to lines 235–349 of the Old English *Andreas*.]

Ἀναστὰς δὲ Ἀνδρέας τῷ πρωὶ ἐπορεύετο ἐπὶ τὴν θάλασσαν ἅμα τοῖς μαθηταῖς αὐτοῦ, καὶ κατελθὼν ἐπὶ τὸν αἰγιαλὸν ἴδεν πλοιάριον μικρὸν καὶ ἐπὶ τό πλοιάριον τρεῖς ἄνδρας καθεζο- μένους· ὁ γὰρ κύριος τῇ ἑαυτοῦ δυνάμει κατεσκεύασεν πλοῖον, καὶ αὐτὸς ἦν ὥσπερ ἄνθρωπος πρωρεὺς ἐν τῷ πλοίῳ· καὶ εἰσή- νεγκεν δύο ἀγγέλους οὓς ἐποίησεν ὡς ἀνθρώπους φανῆναι, καὶ ἦσαν ἐν τῷ πλοίῳ καθεζόμενοι. ὁ οὖν Ἀνδρέας θεασάμενος τὸ πλοῖον καὶ τοὺς τρεῖς ὄντας ἐν αὐτῷ ἐχάρη χαρὰν μεγάλην σφόδρα, καὶ πορευθεὶς πρὸς αὐτοὺς εἶπεν Ποῦ πορεύεσθε, ἀδελφοί, μετὰ τοῦ πλοίου τοῦ μικροῦ τούτου; καὶ ἀποκριθεὶς ὁ κύριος εἶπεν αὐτῷ Πορευόμεθα ἐν τῇ χώρᾳ τῶν ἀνθρωποφά-

Then Andrew arose early, and went to the sea with his dis- ciples, and, when he had gone down to the sea-shore, he saw a little boat, and in the boat three men sitting. For the Lord had prepared a ship by his own power, and he himself was as it were a steersman in the ship; and he brought two angels whom he made to seem as men, and they were seated in the ship. Andrew, therefore, when he saw the ship and the three men in it, rejoiced with very great joy, and, coming to them, said, Whither go ye, brethren, with this little ship? And the Lord answered and said unto him, We are journeying into the country of the man-eaters. Now Andrew, when he saw Jesus,

γων. ὁ δὲ Ἀνδρέας θεασάμενος τὸν Ἰησοῦν οὐκ ἐπέγνω αὐτόν·
ἦν γὰρ ὁ Ἰησοῦς κρύψας τὴν ἑαυτοῦ θεότητα, καὶ ἦν φαινόμενος
τῷ Ἀνδρέᾳ ὡς ἄνθρωπος πρωρεύς· ὁ δὲ Ἰησοῦς ἀκούσας τοῦ
Ἀνδρέου λέγοντος ὅτι κἀγὼ εἰς τὴν χώραν τῶν ἀνθρωποφάγων
πορεύομαι, λέγει αὐτῷ Πᾶς ἄνθρωπος φεύγει τὴν πόλιν ἐκείνην,
καὶ πῶς ὑμεῖς πορεύεσθε ἐκεῖ; καὶ ἀποκριθεὶς Ἀνδρέας εἶπεν
Πρᾶγμά τι μικρὸν ἔχομεν ἐκεῖ διαπράξασθαι, καὶ δεῖ ἡμᾶς
ἐκτελέσαι αὐτό· ἀλλ᾽ εἰ δύνασαι, ποίησον μεθ᾽ ἡμῶν τὴν φιλανθρωπίαν ταύτην τοῦ ἀπάξαι ἡμᾶς ἐν τῇ χώρᾳ τῶν ἀνθρωποφάγων,
ἐν ᾗ καὶ ὑμεῖς μέλλετε πορεύεσθαι. ἀποκριθεὶς δὲ ὁ Ἰησοῦς εἶπεν
αὐτοῖς Ἀνέλθατε.

Καὶ εἶπεν Ἀνδρέας Θέλω σοί τι φανερὸν ποιῆσαι, νεανίσκε,
πρὸ τοῦ ἡμᾶς ἀνελθεῖν ἐν τῷ πλοίῳ σου. ὁ δὲ Ἰησοῦς εἶπεν
Λέγε ὃ βούλῃ. ὁ δὲ Ἀνδρέας εἶπεν αὐτῷ Ναῦλον οὐκ ἔχομέν σοι
παρασχεῖν, ἀλλ᾽ οὔτε ἄρτον ἔχομεν εἰς διατροφήν. καὶ ἀποκριθεὶς
ὁ Ἰησοῦς εἶπεν αὐτῷ Πῶς οὖν ἀπέρχεσθε μὴ παρέχοντες ἡμῖν
τὸν ναῦλον μήτε ἄρτον ἔχοντες εἰς διατροφήν; εἶπεν δὲ Ἀνδρέας
τῷ Ἰησοῦ Ἄκουσον, ἀδελφέ· μὴ νομίσῃς ὅτι κατὰ τυραννίαν οὐ

knew him not, for Jesus was hiding his godhead, and appearing
to Andrew as a steersman. Jesus hearing Andrew say, I also
am going to the country of the man-eaters, saith unto him,
Every one fleeth from that city, and why go ye thither? Andrew
answered and said, We have a certain little business to perform
there, and must needs finish it; if thou canst, do us this kindness
to carry us to the country of the man-eaters, to which ye also are
bound. Jesus answered and said unto them, Come.

And Andrew said, I will make known to thee somewhat, young
man, before we enter into thy ship. Jesus said, Say what thou
wilt. Then Andrew said unto him, We have no passage-money to
give thee, neither have we bread for food. Jesus answered and said
unto him, Why then do ye depart, seeing that ye neither give us
passage-money nor have bread for food? Andrew said unto Jesus,

διδομέν σοι τὸν ναῦλον ἡμῶν, ἀλλ᾽ ἡμεῖς μαθηταί ἐσμεν τοῦ
κυρίου ἡμῶν Ἰησοῦ Χριστοῦ τοῦ ἀγαθοῦ θεοῦ. ἐξελέξατο γὰρ
ἡμᾶς τοὺς δώδεκα, καὶ παρέδωκεν ἡμῖν ἐντολὴν τοιαύτην λέγων
ὅτι πορευόμενοι κηρύσσειν μὴ βαστάζετε ἀργύριον ἐν τῇ ὁδῷ
μήτε ἄρτον μήτε πήραν μήτε ὑποδήματα μήτε ῥάβδον μήτε δύο
χιτῶνας. εἰ οὖν ποιεῖς τὴν φιλανθρωπίαν μεθ᾽ ἡμῶν, ἀδελφέ,
εἰπὲ ἡμῖν συντόμως· εἰ οὐ ποιεῖς, φανέρωσον ἡμῖν, καὶ πορευ-
θέντες ζητήσομεν ἑαυτοῖς ἕτερον πλοῖον. ἀποκριθεὶς δὲ ὁ Ἰησοῦς
εἶπεν τῷ Ἀνδρέᾳ Εἰ αὕτη ἐστὶν ἡ ἐντολὴ ἣν ἐλάβετε καὶ τηρεῖτε
αὐτήν, ἀνέλθατε μετὰ πάσης χαρᾶς ἐν τῷ πλοίῳ μου. ἀληθῶς
γὰρ βούλομαι ὑμᾶς τοὺς μαθητὰς τοῦ λεγομένου Ἰησοῦ ἀνελθεῖν ἐν τῷ πλοίῳ μου ἢ τοὺς παρέχοντάς μοι χρυσίου καὶ ἀργυ-
ρίου· πάντως γὰρ ἄξιός εἰμι ἵνα ὁ ἀπόστολος τοῦ κυρίου ἀνέλθῃ
ἐν τῷ πλοίῳ μου. ἀποκριθεὶς δὲ ὁ Ἀνδρέας εἶπεν Συγχώρησόν
μοι, ἀδελφέ, ὁ κύριος παράσχῃ σοι τὴν δόξαν καὶ τὴν τιμήν.
καὶ ἀνῆλθεν Ἀνδρέας μετὰ τῶν αὐτοῦ μαθητῶν εἰς τὸ πλοῖον.

Hearken, brother; think not that because of arrogance we give
thee not our passage-money, since we are disciples of the good
God, our Lord Jesus Christ. For he chose us, the twelve, and
gave us this commandment, saying, As ye go to preach, carry
neither money on the way, neither bread, nor scrip, nor shoes,
nor staff, nor two coats. If, therefore, thou wilt do us this kindness, brother, tell us plainly; if thou wilt not, declare it unto
us, and we will go and seek for ourselves another ship. Jesus
answered and said unto Andrew, If this is the commandment
which ye have received and do keep, enter with all joy into my
ship; for verily I had rather that ye, the disciples of him who
is called Jesus, should enter into my ship, than those who give
me gold and silver; for I am certainly worthy that the apostle
of the Lord should enter into my ship. Then Andrew answered
and said, Agree with me, brother, and the Lord give thee glory
and honor. And Andrew entered into the ship with his disciples.

APPENDIX IV.

The three best sources of information on the OE. dialects are Sievers' *OE. Grammar*, Bülbring's *Altenglisches Elementarbuch*, and Professor E. M. Brown's work on Mercian. The last is in two parts — (Part I.) *Die Sprache der Rushworth Glossen* (Göttingen, 1891), comprising the vowels, and (Part II.) *The Language of the Rushworth Gloss* (Göttingen, 1892), comprising a continuation of the vowels, the consonants, and inflection.

In some respects the non-West Saxon dialects agree. These common features, so far as they relate to the vowels, have been signalized by Sievers, and are here extracted from § 150 of my edition of his Grammar: —

1. In place of the West Saxon $\bar{æ}$ = Germ. $\bar{e}$, West Germ. $\bar{a}$, stands the vowel $\bar{e}$.

2. The WS. **ie, īe** is wanting, and hence the same is true of the unstable **y, ȳ** (**i, ī**) (**19**).

3. The sounds **ea, eo** (**io**), as well as their corresponding long diphthongs, are not so accurately discriminated as in WS. In Northumbrian especially there is great confusion between **ea** and **eo**. Kentish has a preference for **ia** and **io**, the former standing as well for WS. **ea** as for **eo**.

4. The sound **œ** is of more extensive occurrence.

I. Northumbrian.

1. Cædmon's Hymn.

According to Sweet (*Oldest English Texts*, p. 148), "The hymn of Cædmon is written at the top of the page [*i.e.* in the famous Moore MS. of Bede] in a smaller hand than that of the List of Kings which follows it. It is not impossible that the hymn may have been written later than the List [which, according to Sweet, was written 'most probably in 737'], to fill the blank space. But the hand is evidently contemporary."

The **ae** is not always joined into a digraph, and the signs of length and of i-umlaut (ę) are wanting. These have been supplied, together with the punctuation and the division into lines; in other respects the manuscript has been followed.

The translation of the Hymn, as given by Bede (*Hist. Eccl.* IV. 24), is as follows, though it should be observed that Bede adds, "Hic est sensus, non autem ordo ipse verborum quæ dormiens ille canebat": —

"Nunc laudare debemus auctorem regni cælestis, potentiam creatoris et consilium illius, facta patris gloriæ, quomodo ille, cum sit æternus deus, omnium miraculorum auctor extitit; qui primo filiis hominum cælum pro culmine tecti, dehinc terram custos humani generis omnipotens creavit."

With reference to the words, "**heben til hrōfe**," it is interesting that Alcuin (*Anglia* VII. 7) has, "ut primum Creator mundum *quasi domum* præpararet, et post introduceret habitatorem, id est, dominum domus";

cf. " lacunar, hūsbefen, oððe heofenhrōf " (Wülker-Wright, *Vocabularies*, 432. 8).

Variations from the EWS. norm are : —

1. Final -æs instead of -es : -rīcæs, metudæs, -cynnæs.
2. Final -i for -e : mæcti, ēci.
3. Final -æ for -e : āstęlidæ, tīadæ.
4. Final -æn, -en for -on : hefæn-, heben.
5. Final -un for -on : scylun.
6. Final -un for -an : middun-.
7. Final -ur for -er : fadur.
8. Final -ur for -or : wuldur-.
9. Final -ud for -od : metud-.
10. Final -in for -en : dryctin.
11. Final -ist for -est : ǣrist.
12. Final -u for -an : foldu.
13. Final -eg for -ig : hāleg.
14. Final -en for -end : scępen.
15. ā for ea (æ) : āll-, uārd, bārnum.
16. e for eo : uerc, heben, hefæn-, metud-.
17. y for u : scylun.
18. ę for a, ǫ : ęnd.
19. ęli for eal : āstęlidæ.
20. ǣ for ie : ǣlda.
21. æ, e, ę for i, ie : mæcti, -mectig, scępen.
22. īa for ēo : tīadæ.
23. a for æ : -fadur.
24. ē for ā : suē.
25. ō for ēo (ō) : scōp.
26. gi- for ge- : gihuæs.
27. d for ð (þ) : -gidanc.
28. th for ð (þ) : thā.
29. ct for ht : dryctin, mæcti, -mectig.
30. b for f : heben.
31. til for tō.

Most of the foregoing variations are due either to the age of the document, or are common to at least two of the non-West Saxon dialects. The only ones that seem peculiarly Northumbrian are 17, 31, and possibly 12. Of the rest, 16 and 25 do not agree with later Northumbrian (Lind.), and 22 looks not unlike Kentish. But 17 has that palatalization of u by preceding sc which we find in scyūr, -scȳade, scyldor, scyniga, scuia (ui as in druige for drȳge), and even shȳa (WS. scūa), of the Lind. Gospels. Til, which in Old Norse replaces OE. tō, is found here and in Lind. Matt. 26. 31, besides being read in the Runic inscription on the Ruthwell Cross. Foldu resembles the eorðu, -o of Lind. Matt. 15. 35, 27. 45, etc., which is the regular form in these Glosses.

The Hymn is as follows: —

> Nū scylun hergan   hefænrīcæs uārd,
> metudæs mæcti   end his mōdgidanc,
> uerc uuldurfadur;   suē hē uundra gihuæs,
> ēci dryctin,   ōr āstelidæ.
> 5   Hē ǣrist scōp   ǣlda bārnum
> heben til hrōfe,   hāleg scepen.
> Thā middungeard   moncynnæs uārd,
> ēci dryctin,   æfter tīadæ,
> fīrum foldu,   frēa āllmectig.

2. Bede's Death Song.

Of this Sweet says: "Preserved in the St. Gall MS. 254, of the ninth century, in the usual continental minuscule hand, evidently an accurate copy of an Old Northumbrian original."

As translated by Cuthbert, his pupil, it runs: —

"Ante necessarium exitum prudentior quam opus fuerit nemo existit, ad cogitandum videlicet, antequam hinc profiscatur anima, quid boni vel mali egerit, qualiter post exitum judicanda fuerit."

Its variations from EWS. are: —

1. It has some of the peculiarities of I. 1, such as (1) gōdæs, yflæs, (2) ni, (3) -færæ, -hycggannæ, -iǫngæ, gāstæ, uueorthæ, (8) -snottur-, (15) thārf, (28) there, uuiurthit, thǫnc-, than, thārf, æththa, dēoth-, uueorthæ.
2. Final -a for -e: æþþa.
3. Final -it for -eð (cf. 35): uuiurthit.
4. Final -id for -ed: dœ̄mid.
5. ēi for īe: nēid-.
6. ē for ǣ: thēre.
7. iu for eo (ie): uuiurthit.
8. ēo for ēa: dēoth-.
9. æ for o: æththa.
10. ō̄ for ē: dœ̄mid.
11. hin- (otherwise almost always poetical).
12. cgg for cg: -hycggannæ.
13. i for g (ge): -iǫngæ.

Of the foregoing only 8 and 13 are unmistakably Northumbrian. With dēoth- may be compared ēoro, Lind. Lk., p. 8, l. 15 (cf. Jn. 18. 26); ēostro, Lk. 22. 1, etc. (15); ēoðe, Matt. 27. 64, Lk. 14. 8 (cf. Matt. 10. 15); ēoung, Matt., p. 22, l. 15. The iǫng (for gǫng < gang) is simply an attempt to express the palatal g (ge); geong occurs frequently in the Lindisfarne Gospels, eight times uncompounded. Rushworth has iarw-, but not iǫng (p. 253, note 10). At least Anglian (North. Merc.) is (9) æþþa; as eðða (eþþa) it occurs in Rush. Matt. 5. 18, and in the Riddles ascribed to Cynewulf (44. 17).

The text is: —

> Fore thēre nēidfæræ   nǣnig ni uuiurthit
> thǫncsnotturra   than him thārf sīe,
> tō ymbhycggannæ   ǣr his hiniǫngæ
> huæt his gāstæ   gōdæs æththa yflæs
> 5 æfter dēothdæge   dœmid uueorthæ.

3. The Day of Judgment.

The text is taken from Skeat's edition of Matthew. As far as practicable the readings have been conformed to the norms of the Lindisfarne Gospels (ca. 950). But as there is often great variation in the spelling and endings of the same word, normalizing has not been attempted in all cases. Where changes have been made, the MS. reading is given in a note. The equivalent for Lat. *et* is nearly always represented by a contraction, as is frequently that for *vel*, *aut;* these have been rendered by the usual words, **and, oððe.** The second of two alternative glosses has been enclosed in square brackets, and so has occasionally a superfluous word.

Variations from EWS: are (only the more important are registered): —

1. Of I. 1: (5, but not regularly, see foot-notes), (15) **ālle, -sāldes, -sāldon,** (21) **mæht,** (23) **fadores** (cf. 24, **suǣ**); of I. 2: (10) **geblœdsad.**
2. Loss of final -n : **eatta, drinca, befora, ðęnde.**
3. Uncontracted ind. pres. 3 sing. (cf. I. 2. 3): **sittes, scēades, sętteð,** etc.
4. Plurals in **-as** (**s**), as well as **-að** : **bȳas, āgnigas, gaas.**
5. Change of gender: **-mæhtes.**
6. Plural of long neuters in **-o : cynno.**

7. Plural of adjectives and past participles in -o: sōðfæsto, āwœrgedo.
8. Weak plurals in -o: ilco.
9. Shortened plurals of verbs in -o, instead of -e: sōhto.
10. ea (representing eo) for o: eatta.
11. œ for e after w (denoted by u): cuœðas.
12. ē for ēa before palatals: ēc.
13. ēg for āw: sēgon.
14. ē for y: dēdon.
15. i for y before palatals: drihten.
16. Irregular umlaut: cymmeð.
17. Irregular gemination: eatta, cymmeð, untrymmig.
18. cg for cc: ticgen-.
19. cg for g: hyncg-.
20. d for t (d original): geblœdsad.
21. ð for t: seðel.
22. ð for d: mið.
23. -ig for -ing: cynig.
24. Inorganic initial h: hriordadon.
25. Loss of final -e: rīc.
26. The form bið on.
27. The form hīa.

Under the Northumbrian is printed the corresponding passage from the Vulgate, with collations of the Latin versions on which the Lindisfarne and Rushworth glosses are respectively based. The text is:—

Miððy uut'[1] cymes Sunu Mǫnnes in mæht his, and ālle ęnglas[2] mið him, ða hē sittes ofer seðel godcundmæhtes[3] his. And gesǫmnad bið on befora hine ālle cynno,[4] and tōscēades hīa betuīh, suā[5] hiorde tōscēades[6] scīp[7] frǫm ticgenum. And hē sętteð ða scīp ēc sōð [uut'] tō suīð-

[1] Abbreviation of uutedlice (-tet-), WS. witodlice.
[2] MS. engles.
[3] MS. -mæht.
[4] cynne.
[5] MS. sua.
[6] MS. -as.
[7] MS. scipo; this neuter is exceptional in its preponderance of plur. nom. acc. without ending.

rum his, ðā ticgeno sōðlice of winstrum. Ðonne [hē] cueðes ðe[1] cynig ðǣm ðā-ðe tō suīðrum his biðon [hīa], "Cymmeð gīe, geblǣdsad fadores mīnes, bȳas[2] [āgnigas[3]] gegearwad[4] īuh rīc frǫm frymðo middangeardes. Ic gehyncgerde [ic wæs hyncgrig[5]] for-ðon, and ðū gesāldes mē eatta; ic wæs ðyrstig, and gesāldon mē drinca[6]; gęst ic wæs, and gīe sǫmnadon mec[7]; nacod, and gīe clǣðdon [gīe wrigon] mec[7]; untrymig,[8] and gīe sōhton mec[7]; in carcern,[9] and gīe cuōmon[10] tō mē. Ðā ǫndueardas [ǫndsuerigað] him sōðfæsto, cuœðas, Drihten, huœnne ðec wē sēgon hungrig [hyngrende], and wē hriordadon[10] ðec? ðyrstende [ðyrstig], and wē sāldon[11] ðē drinca[12]? huœnne[13] uutetli' ðec wē sēgon gęstig, and wē sǫmnadon ðec, oððe nacod, and wē āwrigon ðec? huœnne ðec wē gesēgon untrymig and in carcern, and wē cuōmon[10] tō ðē?" And geǫndweardeð ðe cynig, cuœðes ðǣm, "Sōðlice ic cuœðo īuh, ðęnde gīe dydon[14] ānum of ðisum brōðrum mīnum lȳtlum, mē gīe dydon." Ðā cuœðes[15] and ðǣm ðā-ðe tō winstrum biðon, "Ofstīgað[16] gīe frǫm mē, āwœrgedo, in fȳr ēce,[17] se-ðe foregegearuuad is dīwle and ęnglum [ðegnum] his. Mec gehyncgerde, and ne sāldo[18] gīe mē eatta; mec ðyrste, and ne sāldo gīe mē drinca; gęst ic wæs, and ne gesǫmnade gīe mec; nacod, and ne āwrigon gīe mec; untrymig[8] and in carcern, and ne sōhto gīe mec." Ðā ǫndueardas and ðā ilco [hīa], cuœðendo, "Drihten, huœnne ðec wē sēgon hyncgrende,[19] oððe ðyrstende,[20] oððe gęst, oððe nacod, oððe untrymig, oððe in

---

[1] Se is about one-half ⸱re numerous than ð'e.	[5] MS. hincgrig.	[13] MS. huonne.
[2] MS. byes.	[6] MS. dringe.	[14] MS. dyde.
[3] MS. agneges ; for ⸱gas, etc., -as and -að ⸱r3 frequently found in ⸱hese verbs.	[7] MS. meh.	[15] MS. coeðes.
	[8] MS. untrymmig.	[16] MS. -es.
	[9] MS. carchern.	[17] MS. écce.
[4] MS. gegearwað.	[10] MS. -un.	[18] MS. sealdo.
	[11] MS. sealdon.	[19] MS. hyncgerende.
	[12] MS. ðringe.	[20] MS. -a.

carcern, and ne ẹmbehtadon[1] wē ðē?" Ðā hē ọnduearðeð
ðǣm, cweðende, "Sōðlice ic cueðo īuh, ða hwīle ne dyde
gīe ānum of lȳtlum ðissum [suā lọng gīe ne dēdon[2] ānum
ðisra[3] metdmaasta], ne mē gīe dydon.[4]" And gaas[5] ðās
5 in tintergo ēce, sōðfæsto[6] uut' in līf ēce.

Cum autem venerit Filius hominis in majestate sua, et
omnes angeli cum eo, tunc sedebit super sedem majestatis
suæ. Et congregabuntur ante eum omnes gentes, et sepa-
rabit eos ab invicem, sicut pastor segregat oves ab hædis.
Et statuet oves quidem a dextris suis, hædos autem a
sinistris. Tunc dicet rex his, qui a dextris ejus erunt:
"Venite, benedicti Patris mei, possidete paratum[7] vobis
regnum a constitutione mundi. Esurivi enim, et dedistis
mihi manducare; sitivi, et dedistis[8] mihi bibere; hospes
eram, et collegistis[9] me; nudus,[10] et cooperuistis[11] me;
infirmus, et visitastis me; in carcere eram,[12] et venistis
ad me." Tunc respondebunt ei justi, dicentes: "Domine,
quando te vidimus esurientem, et pavimus te? sitientem,[13]
et dedimus tibi potum? quando autem te vidimus hospitem, et collegimus[14] te, aut nudum et cooperuimus te[15]?
aut quando te vidimus infirmum, aut[16] in carcere, et veni-
mus ad te?" Et respondens rex, dicet illis: "Amen dico
vobis, quamdiu fecistis uni[17] ex[18] his fratribus meis minimis, mihi fecistis." Tunc dicet et[19] his, qui a[20] sinistris[21]

[1] MS. embigto.

[2] Less common form for dydon.

[3] MS. ðassa.   [5] MS. gaes.

[4] MS. dyde.   [6] MS. -fæste.

[7] R. regnum quod vobis para-tum est ab origine mundi.

[8] L. dedisti.

[9] L. collexistis.

[10] R. nudus eram.

[11] L. operuistis.

[12] L. om.; R. fui.

[13] R. aut sitientem.

[14] L. colleximus.

[15] L. om.   [16] L. et.

[17] R. uni ex minimis his fra-tribus meis.

[18] L. de.   [19] R. rex.

[20] L. ad.

[21] R. sinistris ejus.

erunt : "Discedite[1] a me, maledicti, in ignem æternum, qui paratus[2] est diabolo et angelis ejus. Esurivi enim, et non dedistis mihi manducare; sitivi, et non dedistis mihi potum[3]; hospes eram, et non collegistis[4] me; nudus, et non cooperuistis[5] me; infirmus et in carcere, et non visitastis me." Tunc respondebunt ei[6] et ipsi, dicentes : "Domine, quando te vidimus esurientem, aut sitientem, aut hospitem, aut[7] nudum,[7] aut infirmum, aut[8] in carcere, et non ministravimus tibi ? " Tunc respondebit illis, dicens : "Amen dico vobis, quamdiu non fecistis uni de minoribus his, nec mihi fecistis." Et ibunt hi in supplicium æternum, justi autem in vitam æternam.

[1] L. *discendite.*
[2] L. *præparatus;* R. *quem præparavit pater meus diabolo.*
[3] R. *bibere.*
[4] L. *collexistis.*
[5] L. *operuistis.*
[6] L. om.
[7] R. om.
[8] L. *vel.*

II. MERCIAN.

Mercian has been thus characterized by Brown (*ut supra*, Part I., p. 81, with which should be compared his Part II., p. 91) : —

"There is naturally much general agreement with Northumbrian, since both are Anglian. Variations from North. are in some cases approximations to WS., but not in all. In certain respects Mercian stands quite by itself; in particular —

"1. OE. stable e [*i.e.* not ę] is usually retained in Mercian, yet is more or less frequently changed to æ.

"2. The o-umlaut of a scarcely occurs in WS., and not at all in either Kentish or Northumbrian, but is well developed in Mercian.

" 3. The **u-**, **o**-umlaut of **e** to **eo**, and of **i** to **io, eo,** occurs at least more regularly in Mercian than in WS. and the other dialects.

" It is true that these peculiarities give no sharp outlines to Mercian, yet they sufficiently characterize it as a dialect, and not merely as Northumbrian modified by West Saxon scribes, or the reverse."

1. The Day of Judgment.

The text is from Skeat's edition of Matthew, normalized like the last. There is a difference of opinion about the date of the Gloss. Skeat says (ed. of Mark, p. xii) that it may be referred to the latter half of the tenth century, Brown (Part I., p..83) would date it just before the decay of Latin studies to which Alfred testifies; the latter also infers that its origin was not near the Kentish border. The phonological and inflectional points of difference from both West Saxon and Northumbrian should be noted.

The passage is as follows : —

And[1] miÐ-þy[2] cymeþ þonne Sunu[3] Monnes in Ðrymme his, and ælle[4] englas miÐ hine, þonne[5] gesiteþ[6] on sedle[7] his þrymmes. And gesomnade[8] beoÐ beforan him ælle[4]

---

[1] Represented in MS. only by the abbreviation ; and occurs but once in the Gospel, and is accordingly restored here; a, too, is more likely to occur in proclitics.

[2] Both **miÐ** and **mid** are found; here the following **þ** may have influenced.

[3] MS. **sune**.

[4] MS. **ealle**; a is more common before **l** + cons., though **eall** and **healf** are somewhat exceptional.

[5] **þonne** is much commoner, and so o before nasals in general.

[6] MS. **gesiteþ**.

[7] This word has **þ** and **t** (**tt**), as well as **d**.

[8] MS. **gesomnede**.

þēode, and gescēadeþ[1] hīæ in twā,[2] swā hiorde[3] āscēadeþ[4]
scēp from ticnum. And sęteþ þā scēp[5] on þā[6] swīðran
hālfe,[7] his ticcen þonne on þā winstran hālfe.[7] Þonne
cwæþ[8] se Cyning þǣm þe on þā swīþran hālfe his bēon,
"Cumaþ,[9] geblētsade mīnes Fæder, gesittað rīce þte ēow
geiarwad[10] wæs from sętnisse middangeardes. For-þon-ðe
mec[11] yngrade,[12] and ge sāldun mē etan; mec þyrste, and
gē sāldun[13] mē drincan; cuma ic wæs, and gē feormadun
mec[11]; nacud ic wæs, and gē wrigun[14] mec; untrum,[15] and
gē nēosadun mīn; in carcerne[16] ic wæs, and ge cwōmun[17]
tō mē." Þonne andswarigaþ[18] him[19] [þǣm] sōþfæste,[20]
cwæþende,[21] "Dryhten, hwonne[22] gesēgun[23] wē ðē hyng-
rende, and wē fǣddun[24] þē? oþþe þyrstigne, and wē þē
drincan sāldun? hwanne[22] þonne gesēgun[23] wē þē[11] cuman,
and gefeormadun ðē[11]? oþþe nacudne, and wē þec[11]
wrigun[14]? oþðe hwonne[22] wē þē[11] sēgun untrymne[15] oþðe
in cwarterne,[25] and wē cwōmun[17] tō þē?" And and-
swarade se Cyning, cwæþ tō heom,[19] "Sōþ ic sæcge ēow,
swā longe swā gē dydun ānum þe[26] lǣsesta[26] þāra brōþre[26]

[1] MS. gesceadiþ.
[2] MS. tu, but less common.
[3] heorde also occurs.
[4] MS. ascadeþ.
[5] MS. scæp.
[6] Lat. omits suis.
[7] MS. healfe.
[8] Usual form for pres., as well as pret.; pres. also cweþ.
[9] MS. cymeþ.
[10] Less common than gegear-wad.
[11] mec, ðec rather commoner in acc.
[12] Loss of initial h exceptional.
[13] MS. salden.
[14] MS. forms are wriogan, wreogan, but this verb is ex-ceptional.
[15] With i-umlaut, and without.
[16] MS. carkærn.
[17] MS. coman.
[18] MS. andswærigaþ.
[19] Sing. him, plur. heom.
[20] -fæste rather more common.
[21] cwæþende nearly as com-mon as cweþende.
[22] hwanne and hwonne about equal.
[23] MS. gesagun.
[24] MS. fœddan.
[25] MS. quartern.
[26] Here nom.; þe occasional for se.

mīne,[1] gē mē dydun.[2]" Þonne cwæÞ se Cyning ēc tō Þǣm
Þā-Þe on Þǣm winstran hālfe bēoÞan, "GewitaÞ frǫm mē,
āwærgde,[3] in ēce[4] fȳr, ꝥte wæs geiarwad[5] Fæder[6] mīn[6]
dēofle and his ꬲnglum.[7] For-Þon-Þe mec[8] hyngrede, and
5 gē ne sāldun mē etan; mec[8] ðyrste, and gē ne sāldun mē
drincan; cuma[9] ic wæs, and gē ne feormadun mec[8]; nacud,
and gē ne wrigun[10] mec[8]; untrum[11] and in carcerne,[12] and
gē ne nēosadun mīn." Þonne andswarigað hīæ swǣlce,[13]
cwæÞende,[14] "Dryhten, hwanne[15] gesēgun[16] wē ðē[8] hyng-
10 rende, oÞÞe Þyrstigne, oÞÞe cuman, oÞðe untrum,[11] oÞÞe
in carcerne,[17] and wē ne Þegnadun[18] Þē?" Þonne and-
swaraÞ[19] heom,[20] cweÞende,[14] "Sōþ ic sæcge ēow, swā lǫnge
swā gē ne dydun ānum meodumra[21] Þissa, ne mē gē ne
dydun." And gǣÞ[22] hīæ in ēce[4] tintergu,[23] Þā sōÞfeste[24]
15 Þonne in ēce[4] līf.

[1] See p. 253, note 26.
[2] MS. **dydon.**
[3] MS. **awærgede.**
[4] **æce** rather more common.
[5] MS. **geiarward.**
[6] Cf. the Latin of this text.
[7] MS. **englas.**
[8] See p. 253, note 11.
[9] MS. **cuman.**
[10] See p. 253, note 14.
[11] See p. 253, note 15.
[12] MS. **carkern.**
[13] MS. **swilce**; the only other instance in the Gospel is **swælce.**

[14] See p. 253, note 21.
[15] See p. 253, note 22.
[16] See p. 253, note 23.
[17] MS. **carcrænnæ.**
[18] MS. **Þegnedun.**
[19] MS. **andswareÞ.**
[20] See p. 253, note 18.
[21] MS. **meoduma.**
[22] More common than **gāð**; influence of the sing.?
[23] Only instance of **u** in plur. of disyllabic neuters; cf. **ticcen,** above.
[24] See p. 253, note 20.

2. Psalm XX. (XXI.)

The Psalm is taken from the Vespasian Psalter as
printed in Sweet's *Oldest English Texts*. This was
formerly regarded as Kentish, and even yet Brown

(Part I., p. 82) is inclined to think that its Mercian is that of the region adjoining Kent. Sweet (p. 184) refers the gloss to the first half of the ninth century. The forms are less varied than in the last. The Latin is the Vulgate version, collated with that on which the gloss is based. The text is:—

Dryhten, in megne ðīnum bið geblissad cyning; ǫnd ofer hǣlu ðīne gefīð[1] swīðlice! Lust sāwle his ðū sāldes him, ǫnd willan weolera his ðū ne biscęredes hine. For-ðon ðū forecwōme hine in blēdsunge[2] swœ̄tnisse[3]; ðū sęttes hēafde his bēg of stāne dēorwyrðum.[4] Līf bed, 5 ǫnd ðū sāldes him lęngu dæga[5] in weoruld weorulde. Micel is wuldur his in hǣlu ðīnre; wuldur ǫnd micelne wlite ðū onsętes ofer hine. For-ðon ðū sęlest hine in blēdsunge in weoruld weorulde; ðū geblissas hine in gefīan mid ǫndwleotan[6] ðīnum. For-ðon cyning gehyhteð 10 in Dryhtne, and in mildheortnisse ðes hēstan ne bið onstyred. Sīe [bið] gimœ̄ted hǫnd ðīn āllum fēondum ðīnum; sīe swīðre ðīn gemœ̄teð ālle ðā-ðe ðec[7] fīgað. Ðū sętes hīe swē-swē ofen fȳres in tīd ǫndwleotan[8] ðīnes; Dryhten in eorre his gedrœ̄feð hīe, ǫnd forswilgeð 15 hīe fȳr. Wēstem heara of eorðan ðū forspildes, and sēd heara frǫm bearnum mǫnna. For-ðon hīe onhǣldun[9] in ðē yfel; ðōhtun geðæht ðæt hīe ne mæhtun gesteaðulfestian. For-ðon ðū sętes hīe bec, in lāfum ðīnum ðu gearwas ǫndwleotan heara. Hęfe ūp, Dryhten, in megne 20 ðīnum; we singað aḥd singað megen ðīn.

<hr>

¹ MS. gefihð.
² We should expect blōēdsunge.
³ MS. swētnisse.
⁴ MS. deorwyrðem.
⁵ MS. dęga.

⁶ In this word io is commoner; but the rule is eo.
⁷ MS. ðe.
⁸ MS. ǫndwliotan; see note 5.
⁹ MS. onhældon.

Domine, in virtute tua lætabitur rex; et super salutare tuum exultabit vehementer. Desiderium cordis[1] ejus tribuisti ei, et voluntate labiorum ejus non fraudasti eum. Quoniam prævenisti eum in benedictionibus dulcedinis; posuisti in capite ejus coronam de lapide pretioso. Vitam petiit[2] a[2] te,[2] et tribuisti ei longitudinem dierum in sæculum, et in sæculum sæculi. Magna est gloria ejus in salutari tuo; gloriam et magnum decorem impones super eum. Quoniam dabis eum in benedictionem in sæculum sæculi; lætificabis eum in gaudio cum vultu tuo. Quoniam rex sperat[3] in Domino, et in misericordia Altissimi non commovebitur. Inveniatur manus tua omnibus inimicis tuis; dextera tua inveniat[4] omnes qui te oderunt. Pones eos ut clibanum ignis in tempore vultus tui; Dominus in ira sua conturbabit eos, et devorabit eos ignis. Fructum eorum de terra perdes; et semen eorum a filiis hominum. Quoniam declinaverunt in te mala; cogitaverunt consilia,[5] quæ[6] non potuerunt stabilire. Quoniam pones eos dorsum[7]; in reliquis tuis præparabis vultum eorum. Exaltare, Domine, in virtute tua; cantabimus et psallemus virtutes tuas.

[1] MS. *animæ.*	[3] MS. *sperabit.*	[6] MS. *quod.*
[2] MS. *petit.*	[4] MS. *inveniit.*	[7] MS. *deorsum.*
	[5] MS. *consilium.*	

III. KENTISH.

The preference for the **e**-sound (both long and short) is, according to Zupitza (*Haupt's Zeitschrift*, XXI. 4), characteristic of the Kentish dialect. Sievers remarks (§ 154) that a distinctive characteristic of Kentish is the substitution of **e**, **ē**, for **y**, **ȳ**, and to some extent the converse.

In our reproduction of the following pieces, ę is employed only where it is found in the MSS., in order to avoid confusion between the theoretical and the MS. ę.

1. Lufa's Confirmation of her Bequest.

The will of which this is the concluding portion dates from 832. It is printed by Sweet in his *Oldest English Texts*, pp. 446–447, and by Earle, *Land Charters*, pp. 165–166. Earle adds: " This piece is given in Thorpe's Analecta as a specimen of East Anglian; but Kemble remarked that Mundlingham is in Kent." Note the e (ē) for æ (ǣ), ia (īa) for eo (ēo); b for f is of course not peculiar to Kentish (I. 1. 30). The text is as follows: —

✠ Ic Luba, ēaðmōd Godes ðīwen, ðās forecwedenan gōd, and ðās elmessan, gesette and gefestnie, ob mīnem erfelande et Mundlinghām, ðēm hiium tō Crīstes ciriean; and ic bidde, and an Godes libgendes naman bebīade, ðēm men ðe ðis land and ðis erbe hebbe et Mundlingham, ðet 5 hē ðās gōd forðlēste ōð wiaralde ende. Se man, se ðis healdan wille, and lēstan ðet ic beboden hebbe an ðisem gewrite, sē him seald and gehealden sīa hiabenlice blēdsung; se his ferwerne, oððe hit āgēle, sē him seald and gehealden helle wīte, būte hē tō fulre bōte gecerran 10 wille, Gode and mannum. *Uene ualete.*

✠ Lufe þincggewrit.

2. The Kentish Hymn.

The Hymn is No. 8 of Grein's *Bibliothek* (II. 290–291). The text is conformed to that of Kluge in his *Lesebuch*, pp. 111–112.

To be noted are the **io**, **ia** for **eo** (**hiofen, hiafen**), **īo** for **ēo**, **e** for **æ** (**fegere, Feder, heleða, -fest**), **ǣ** for **ē**, *i.e.* **œ** (**blǣtsiað, hrǣmig**) and for **īe** (**geflǣmdest**), and especially the **e** for **y** (**senna, gefelled**), and **ē** for **ȳ** (**ālēs, gerēna**). Standard West Saxon vowels are also found, and perhaps indicate a West Saxon scribe.

With respect to consonants, the omission of the middle one of three is noted by Zupitza as characteristic (**ænlum**). The loss of final **d** (**walden**) is found elsewhere in Kentish (Zupitza, p. 11); but see also I. 1. 14. **Nc** (**ngc, ncg**) for **ng** (**cyninc, cyningc**; cf. **þincg-**, p. 257, l. 12) is another mark (Zupitza, p. 13).

The Hymn is as follows:—

Wuton wuldrian   weorada Dryhten,
hālgan hlīoðorcwidum   hiofenrīces Weard,
lufian līofwendum   līfęs Āgend,
and him simle sīo   sigefęst wuldor
5 uppe mid ænlum   and on eorðan sibb   [5]
gumena gehwilcum   goodes willan!
Wē ðē heriað   hālgum stefnum,
and þē blǣtsiað   bilewitne Fęder,
and ðē þanciað,   þīoda Wālden,
10 ðīnes weorðlīcan   wuldordrēames   [10]
and ðāre miclan   mægena gerēna,
ðe ðū God Dryhten   gāstes mæhtum
hafest on ǧewealdum   hiofen and eorðan,
ān ēce Fęder,   ælmehtig God!
15 Ðū eart cyninga Cyningc   cwicera gehwilces;   [15]
ðū eart sigefest Sunu   and sōð Hęlend
ofer ealle gescęft   angla and manna!
Ðū Dryhten God   on drēamum wunast
on ðǣre upplīcan   æðelan ceastre,
20 Frēa folca gehwæs,   swā ðū æt fruman wǣre   [20]

efenēadig Bearn   āgenum Fæder!
Đū eart heofenlic līoht   and ðæt hālige lamb,
ðe ðū[1] mānscilde   middangeardes
for þīnre ārfęstnesse   ealle tōwurpe,

5 fīond geflǽmdest,   follc generedes,   [25]
blōde gebōhtest   bearn Israēla
ðā ðū āhōfe   ðurh ðæt hālige trīow
ðīnre ðrōwunga   ðrīostre senna,
þæt ðū on hǽahsetle   heafena rīces

10 sitest sigehrǽmig   on ðā swīðran hand   [30]
ðīnum God-Fæder   gāsta gemyndig.
Mildsa nū meahtig   manna cynne,
and of leahtrum ālēs   ðīne ðā līofan gescęft,
and ūs hāle gedō,   heleða Sceppend,

15 niða Nergend,   for ðīnes naman āre!   [35]
Đū eart sōðlīce   simle hālig,
and ðū eart āna   ǽce Dryhten,
and ðū āna bist   eallra Dēma
cwucra ge dēadra,   Crīst Nergend,

20 for-ðan ðū on ðrymme rīcsast   and on ðrīnesse [40]
and on ānnesse,   ealles Wāldend,
hiofena hēahcyninc,   Hāliges Gāstes
fegere gefelled   in Fæder wuldre!

[1] MS. ðy.

APPENDIX V.

The earliest Germanic language represented by existing specimens is the Gothic. Much the most considerable part of these specimens consists of fragments of a translation of the Bible, or rather of the Bible with the exception of the Books of Kings, made by Wulfila (less correctly, Ulphilas), a Goth of the fourth century. While it would be a serious error to regard Gothic as the parent of the other Germanic tongues, it is undoubtedly true that in many respects it most nearly represents what we may conceive to have been the character of the Primitive Germanic language. In particular, the original vowels of stem-endings and inflectional terminations are often extant in Gothic, while by the time of Old English they are either lost, or exist in a modified form.

From what has been said, it is manifest that a comparison of Gothic forms with those of Old English is often very instructive. The phenomenon known as i-umlaut, for example, becomes much more intelligible through such a comparison, as a few illustrations will render evident.

In the revised version of 2 Cor. 10. 12, the marginal reading is, "For we are not bold to judge ourselves among . . . certain of them that commend themselves." The Gothic has, " Unte ni gadaursum *dōmjan* unsis silbans," etc. Here the English word *judge* is represented by the Gothic *dōmjan* (pronounced *dōmyan*), to which corresponds the OE. **dēman**. Again, for OE. **sēc(e)an** (114), **nęrian** (116), the Gothic has *sōkjan*, *nasjan* (*s* changing to **r**), as in Lk. 19. 10: "Qam auk sunus mans *sōkjan* jah *nasjan* pans fralusanans."

According to **103**, the ind. pres. 3 sing. of **forbēodan** is **forbīet** or **forbīett**. The corresponding Gothic form occurs in Lk. 8. 25: "Hwas siai sa, ei jah windam *faurbiudip* jah watnam?" (Who then is this, that he commandeth even the winds and the water(s)?) The stem of the Gothic verb *faurbiudip* is *biud-*, which in OE. is represented by **bēod-**. Umlaut is caused by the -*i*- of the ending -*ip*, which is sometimes retained in OE. as -(e)ð, but frequently disappears, according to **23** and **34**. Similarly Gothic *fraliusip* is represented in OE. by **forlīest**, as in Lk. 15. 8, where, for the "if she lose one piece" of the English, the Gothic has, "jabai *fraliusip* drakmin ainamma." Again, take the OE. **hātan**, of which the ind. pres. 3 sing. is **hǣt(t)**. Here the Gothic infinitive is *haitan*, and the ind. pres. 3 sing. *haitip*. Thus, in Lk. 15. 9, "*gahaitip* frijondjos" (calleth together her friends).

In Mk. 1. 16, where our version has *net*, the OE. has **nętt**, and the Gothic *nati:* "wairpandans *nati* in marein." The doubling of **t** is to be accounted for according to **36**, as the Gothic stem-ending was -*ja*. For OE. **cynn** the Gothic has *kuni*, as in Mk. 8. 12: "Hwa pata *kuni* taikn sōkeip?" (What would be the OE. representatives of *taikn* and *sōkeip?*) In Mk. 7. 35, where the OE. has "**tungan bęnd**," the Gothic has "*bandi* tuggons."

Many more illustrations might be given, but these will no doubt suffice to render the principle clear.

APPENDIX VI.

The chief Germanic dialects cognate with the Old English are Gothic, Old High German, Old Saxon, Old Norse, and Old Frisian (cf. Sievers' *Gram. of OE.* 1, and my *Phonological Investigation of OE.*). Of these, Gothic is the oldest, and Old Norse and Old Frisian, in their present forms, the latest; the others are fairly contemporary with Old English. By a comparison of these tongues, the basic, unitary Germanic language is reconstructed. Thus, to take a few of the words introduced below, we gain the Germanic stems **ain-**, *one;* **gast-**, *guest* or *stranger;* **sīuk-**, *sick;* **kweþan**, *say;* others will readily be discovered by a little attention. In general, the Gothic forms stand nearest to the Primitive Germanic, but some Gothic words have died out, or are replaced by others in the remaining tongues. The Germanic forms of many English words are given in the *New English Dictionary*, with those of the cognate dialects, and in some cases the remoter Indo-European form.

As far as possible, the texts below repose upon the same original, Matt. 25. 38–46. This affords an opportunity for comparison with Selection III, pp. 134–136, and with the dialectic texts on pp. 256–262. There being no corresponding prose text of Old Saxon, the poetic paraphrase, from the *Heliand*, is thrown to the end. The Old Frisian stands by itself, its documents being chiefly legal.

As the Gothic text of this chapter covers only verses 38 to 46, the corresponding selections have been limited to these verses.

GOTHIC.

[From the version by Wulfila (ca. 311–383); see the article on Wulfila by Sievers, in Paul's *Grundriss der Germanischen Philologie*, Vol. 2. w has been substituted for the v used by the Germans in their editions, and the quantity of the vowels has been marked more regularly than usual; ai is generally long, but is short in **aiþþau** (cf. ON. *eða*), **fairra, garaihtans**; ei is always long (like Eng. *ee*).]

"Hwanuh þan þuk sēhwum gast, jah galaþōdēdum?[1] aiþþau naqadana, jah wasidēdum? hwanuh þan þuk sēhwum sīukana aiþþau in karkarai,[2] jah atiddjēdum[3] du þus?" Jah andhafjands sa þiudans[4] qiþiþ du im, "Amen qiþa izvis, jah þanei tawidēduþ ainamma þizē 5 minnistanē brōþrē meinaizē, mis tawidēduþ." Þanuh qiþiþ jah þaim af hleidumein fērai, "Gaggiþ fairra mis, jus fraqiþanans,[5] in fōn þata aiweino,[6] þata manwidō unhulþin[7] jah aggilum is. Unte grēdags[8] was, jan ni gēbuþ mis matjan[9]; afþaursiþs was, jan ni dragkidēduþ[10] 10 mik; gasts, jan ni galaþōdēduþ mik; naqaþs, jan ni wasidē- duþ mik; sīuks jah in karkarai, jan ni gaweisōdēduþ meina." Þanuh andhafjand jah þai qiþandans, "Frauja,[11] hwan þuk sēhwum grēdagana, aiþþau afþaursidana, aiþþau gast, aiþ- þau naqadana, aiþþau sīukana, aiþþau in karkarai, jan ni 15

---

[1] See Glossary, gelaðian.
[2] From Latin.
[3] As if OE. *ætēodon (from *ætgangan).
[4] See Gl. ðēoden.
[5] Like OE. forcweden.

[6] From same Indo-European root as Gr. *αἰών*, Lat. *ævum*.
[7] Cf. OE. unhold(a).
[8] Cf. Eng. *greedy*.
[9] Verb; cf. Gl. mete.
[10] gk for nk.   [11] See Gl. frēa.

andbahtidēdeima¹ þus ? " Þanuh andhafjiþ im qiþands, "Amen qiþa izwis, jah þanei ni tawidēduþ ainamma þizē leitilanē, mis ni tawidēduþ." Jah galeiþand ² þai in bal- wein ³ aiweinon, iþ þai garaihtans ⁴.in libain aiweinon.

¹ Cf. OE. **ambiht**, German   ³ Cf. OE. **bealu**.
Amt.   ² See Gl. **līðan**.   ⁴ Cf. German *gerecht*.

OLD HIGH GERMAN.

[The longer extract is from Sievers' edition of Tatian. The Latin ver- sion of the Gospel harmony by the Assyrian Tatian (second century) was translated by a monk of Fulda, A.D. 830-835. The dialect is East Frank- ish. The translation is, in general, much more literal than that of the Rhine Frankish version, a specimen of which, from the beginning of the ninth century, is given in a note (from Hench's edition of the Monsee Fragments).

uu is of course used for **w.**]

" Uuanne gisāhun uuir thih gast uuesentan, inti gihalō- tunnmēs¹ thih ?   oda nacotan, inti bithactumēs²?   oda uuanne gisāhumēs thih unmahtigan oda in carkere, inti quāmunmēs zi thir ? "   Inti antlingenti ther cunig³ quidit 5 in, " Uuār quidih īu, sō lango sō ir tātut einemo fon thesēn mīnēn bruoderon minnistōn, thanne tātut ir iz mir."   Thanne quidit her thēn thīe zi sīneru uuinistrūn sint, " Eruuīzzet fon mir, ir foruuergiton, in ēuuīn fiur, thaz dār garo ist themo dīufale inti sīnēn ęngilon.   Mih hungrita, inti 10 ir ni gābut mir ezzan ; mih thursta, inti ir ni gābut mir trincan ; ih uuas gast, inti ir ni gihalōtut mih ; nacot, inti ir ni bithactut mih ; unmahtic inti in carkere, inti ir ni uuīsōtut mīn."   Thanne antlingent sīe inti quedent, " Trohtin,⁴

¹ Cf. German *holen*.   ² German *bedecken*.   ³ German *König*.
⁴ The Monsee Matthew has here :
"Truhtin, huuanne kasāhun uuir dih hungragan, odo durstagan, odo gast, odo nahhatan, odo sīuhhan, sō in carcere, enti ni ambahti- tum dir ? "   Danne antuurtit im quidit, " Uuār īu sagem, sō lange·sō ir iz nī tātut einhuuelihhemo dero minnistōno, noh mir iz nī tātut."

uuanne gisāhun uuir thih hungrentan, oda thurstentan, oda
gast, oda nacotan, oda unmahtigan, oda in carkere, inti ni
ambahtitumēs thir?" Thanne antlingit her in quedenti,
"Uuār quidih īu, sō lango sō ir ni tātut einemo fon thēn
minnirōn, noh mir ni tātut." Inti farent thiē in ēuuīnaz ₅
uuīzzi, thiē rehton in ēuuīn līb.

Old (?) Norse.

[The Norse extract is from the version of Odd the Wise, which appeared
in 1540, and is here reproduced from the text in Vigfusson and Powell's *Ice-
landic Prose Reader*, w being substituted for v. The editors say of Odd's
work (p. 438): "It is well worthy to stand by the side of that of Tyndal or
Luther, and higher praise could hardly be given to it. Like our own Version, it was made just at the right time, when the spoken language was
in the main still pure and classical, but yet rich and flexible enough to be
easily adapted to the idioms and vocabulary of the Greek and Hebrew."]

"Hwenar sāu wǣr þig hungraðan, og söddum þig? eðr
þyrstan, swo wǣr gǣfum þēr drekka? eðr hwenar sāum
wǣr þig gęstkominn, og hȳstum[1] þig? eða nakinn, og
klǣddum þig? eða hwenar sāu wǣr þig sjūkan, eða ī myrkwastofu,[2] og kōmum til þīn?" Og konungrinn[3] mun[4] ₅
swara, og sęgja til þeirra, "Sannliga sęgi eg yðr, hwat þēr
gjörðut[4] einum af þessum mīnum minztum brǣðrum, þat
gjörðu þēr mēr." Þā mun hann og sęgja til þeirra sem til
winstri handar eru, "Farit burt frā mēr, þēr bölwaðir,[5] ī
eilīfan eld, þann sem fyri būinn er fjandanum og hans ārum. ₁₀
Þwīat hungraðr war eg, og þēr gāfut mēr eigi at[6] eta;
þyrstr war eg, og þēr gāfut mēr eigi at drekka; gęstr war

---

[1] The verb **hȳsa**, from **hūs**, house.

[2] '*Mirkcloset*' (**stofa** = German *Stube*, Eng. *stove*).

[3] **-inn** is the postpositive article.

[4] Still used dialectally in Eng-land for *shall* or *will*; cf. the *Eng. Dial. Dict.*

[4] *Gar* is still used in Burns; cf. *New Eng. Dict.*

[5] See Gothic, p. 272, note 3.

[6] So in Eng. *ado*, from *at do*.

eg, og þēr hȳstuð mig eigi ; nakinn war eg, og þēr klǣddut
mig eigi ; sjūkr og ī myrkwastofu war eg, og þēr witjuðut
mīn eigi."   Þā munu þeir swara og sęgja, " Herra, hwenar
sāu wǣr þig hungraðan eða þyrstan, gęst eða nakinn,
5 sjūkan eða ī myrkwastofu, og höfum þēr eigi þjōnat?"
Þā mun hann swara þeim og sęgja, " Sannliga sęgi eg yðr,
hwat þēr gjörðut eigi einum af þessum enum minztum, þat
gjörðut þēr mēr eigi."   Og munu þeir þā ganga ī eilīfar
pīslir, en rēttlātir ī eilīfit līf.

Old Frisian.

[Though the texts of Old Frisian are of a comparatively late period,
its grammatical condition fairly entitles it to rank with Old High German
and Old Saxon. The extract which follows is from a paraphrase of the
Ten Commandments which serves as a preface to a certain code of laws
(Richthofen, *Friesische Rechtsquellen*, pp. 131–132). Frisian is next of kin
to Old English among the Germanic dialects (Sievers, *Gram*. 1 ; Siebs,
Zur Geschichte der Englisch-Friesischen Sprache, Halle, 1889.]

Thīn God thet is thi ēna, ther skippere is himulrīkes
and irthrīkes, tham skaltu thīania.   Thu ne skalt thīnes
Godis nǫma nāwet[1] īdle untfā, thermithi send ti urbēden[2]
alle mēnētha.[3]   Thu skalt firia[4] thene hēlega Sunnandi,
5 hwante God hini ręste thā hi eskipin[5] hede himulrīke
and irthrīke; thērumbe[6] skaltu ierne[7] firia thene hēlega
Sunnandi.   Thu skalt ēria[8] thīnne feder and thīnne mōder,
thet tu theste[9] langor libbe.   Thu ne skalt nenne mǫn-
slaga dūa.

[1] OE. **nāwiht** ; see Gl. **nāht.**
[2] Eng. *forbid.*
[3] German *Meineid.*
[4] German *feiern.*
[5] With the prefix *e-* compare
Eng. *y-* in *yclept.*

[6] German *darum.*
[7] OE. *georne.*
[8] German *ehren.*
[9] German *desto*, OE. ðæs-ðe.

OLD SAXON.

[Next to Old Frisian, Old Saxon is most nearly related to Old English. It is interesting, too, because a considerable part of an OE. poem, the *Genesis*, has been adapted from an Old Saxon original (see Cook and Tinker, *Select Translations from Old English Poetry*, pp. 104–105, 184–185). The most important text is the *Heliand*, written between 822 and 840, a versified harmony of the Gospels. Our extract consists of vv. 4405–4451 of the Munich MS.]

Huan gisah thi man ēnig
bethuungen an sulīcun tharabun?   Huat, thu habes allarō
    thīodō giuuald,
iac sō samo therō mēdmō   therō the īo mannō barn
geuunnun an thesaro uueroldi."   Than sprikid im eft
    Uualdand God:
"Sō huat sō gi dādun," quidit he,   "an īuuues Drohtines   5
    namon,
gōdes fargābun   an Godes ēra
thēm mannum the hēr minnistōn sindun   therō nu undar
    thesaru męnegi stand[a]d,
ęndi þurh ōdmōdi   arme uuārun
uueros, huand sie mīnan uuilleon fręmidun, —   sō huat sō
    gi im īuuuaro uuelono fargābun,
gidādun thurh dīurida mīna,   that antfeng īuuua Drohtin   10
    selbo,
thīu helpe quam te Hebencuninge.   Bethīu uuili īu the
    hēlago Drohtin
lōnōn īuuu[an] gilōbon;   gibid īuu līf ēuuig."
Uuęndid ina than Uualdand   an thea uuinistron hand,
the Drohtin te thēm farduanun mannun,   sagad im that sie
    sculin thea dād antgelden,
thea man iro mēngiuuerk: "Nu gi fan mi sculun,"   15
    quidit he,
"farun sō farflocane   an that fīur ēuuig
that thār gigareuuid uuard   Godes andsācun,
fīundō folke   be firinuuerkun,
huand gi mi ni hulpun   than mi hunger ęndi þurst

uuēgde te uundrun,   eftha ik geuuādies lōs
geng iāmermōd —   uuas mi grōtun tharf;
than ni habde ik thār ēnige helpe   than ik geheftid uuas,
an lithokospun bilokan,   eftha mi legar bifeng,
5 suāra suhti;   than ni uueldun gi mīn sīokes thār
uuīsōn mid uuihti.   Ni uuas īu uuerd ēouuiht
that gi mīn gehugdin;   bethīu gi an hẹllie sculun
tholon an thīustre."   Than sprikid imu ẹft thīu thīod
        angegin :
"Uuola, Uualdand God," quedad sie,   "huī uuilt thu sō
        uuit thit uuerod sprekan,
10 mahlien uuid these mẹnegi ?   Huan uuas thi īo mannō
        tharf,
gumonō gōdes ?   Huat, sie it al be thīnun gēbun ē[g]un,
uuelon an the[sa]ro uueroldi."   Than sprikid ẹft Uualdand
        God :
"Than gi thea armostun," quidid he,   "ẹldibarno,
mannō thea minnistōn   an īuuuomu mōdsebon,
15 helidos farhugdun,   lētun sea īu an īuuuomu hugi lēthe,
bedēldun sie īuuuaro dīurda,   than dādun gi īuuomu Droht-
        ine sō sama,
giuuẹrnidun imu īuuuaro uuelonō;   bethīu ni uuili īu
        Uualdand God
antfāhen Fader īuuua,   ac gi an that fīur sculun
an thene dīopun dōd   dīublun thīonon,
20 uurēdun uuidersakun,   huand gi sō uuarhtun biuoran."
        Than aftar thēm uuordun   skēdit that uuerod an tuē,
thea gōdun ẹndi thea ubilon.   Farad thea fargriponon man
an thea hētun hẹl   hrīuuigmōde,
thea faruuarhton uueros,   uuīti antfāhat,
25 ubil ẹndilōs.   Lēdid ūp thanen
hēr Hebencuning   thea hlūttaron thēoda
an that langsame līoht ;   thār is līf ēuuig,
gigareuuid Godes rīki   gōdarō thīadō.

VOCABULARY

VOCABULARY.

[The vowel æ follows **ad**, and ð follows **t**. The main or typical forms of words are those of Early West Saxon, the dialectic or late forms of the poetry and of Appendix IV being referred to that as the standard. Actual forms, when different from the type, are enclosed in parenthesis. Figures in parenthesis refer to the sections (and subdivisions) of the. Grammar. Semicolons are employed to separate different *groups* of meanings; definitions separated by commas are more nearly synonymous. The sign < indicates derivation from. Modern English words cited in brackets, and not preceded by *cf.*, are direct derivatives; cognates thus cited are directly derived from the common ancestral form; where the relationship is more remote, or only a part of the word corresponds, *cf.* precedes. Old English words preceded by *cf.* or *see* are parallel or related forms. Direct derivatives included among the definitions are not repeated in brackets. The asterisk before a word indicates a theoretical form; for the manner in which such are framed see my *Phonological Investigation of Old English* (Ginn & Co.). The ending -līc(e) is assigned to adjectives and adverbs employed in the poetry; -lic(e) to those in prose.]

A.

ā, *always;* repeated for emphasis, ā ā ā, *for ever and ever.* [Cf. Mod. Eng. *ay*, from an allied root; in ME. our word appears as *o, oo*, — so in Chaucer, *Tr. and Cress.* 2. 1034: 'for ay and *oo*.']

ā- (142).

ā-belgan (III. **104**), *anger, incense.*

ā-bēodan (II. **103**), *announce, communicate.*

ā-beran (IV. **105**), *carry, convey; sustain.*

ā-blāwan (R. **109**), *blow.*

ā-bregdan (III. **104, 28**), *liberate, disengage.* [Cf. Spenser's *abrade, abrayd, abraid*, e.g. *F. Q.* 3. 11. 8.]

ā-būtan, *about. around.*

ac (ah) (**4**), *but.*

ā-cęnnan (**113**), *produce, beget, bring forth.*

ācol-mōd (**58, 146**), *frightened, terrified.*

adesa (**53**), *adze, hatchet.*

ādl (**51.** *b*), *disease.*

ā-drǣdan (R. **110**), *fear.*

ā-drēogan (II. **103**), *endure.*

ā-drīfan (I. **102**), *expel.*

ā-dūn(e), *down.* [< **of dūne**; see **dūn**.]

ǣce, see ēce.

279

æcer (43), *field.* [Cf. Mod. Eng.
  broad *acres, God's Acre,* the
  latter as in Longfellow's poem;
  Ger. *Acker.* Cognate with Lat.
  ager, Gr. ἀγρός.]
ædre (ēdre), *straightway, immediately, at once.*
æfen (47. 7), *evening* (but *evening*
  itself is from the derivative **æfn-
  ung**). [Ger. *Abend.*]
æfen-glōmung (51. 3), *evening
  twilight.* [Cf. Mod. Eng. *gloam-
  ing.*]
æfestfull (146), *envious.* [**æfest**
  is compounded of **æf-**, a parallel
  form of **of**, and **ēst**, q.v.]
æfestian (118), *envy, be envious
  at.*
æfestig (146), *envious.*
æfre, *ever, always;* **æfre ne,**
  never.   [*afterward.*
æfter, *after; according to; about;*
æfter-ꝥon-ꝥe, *after.*
æg- (142).
æg-flota (53), *sea-floater, ship.*
æg-hwā (88), *every one;* neut.
  every thing.
æg-hwanan (75), *from all sides,
  on all sides.*
æg-hwilc (-hwylc) (89), *every
  (one), any (one).*
ægꝥer ge . . . ge (202), *both . . .
  and.*
æht (51. *b*), *council.*
æht (51. 1), *possession;* plur.
  goods. [Cf. **āgan.**]
æl (51. *b*), *awl.* [Ger. *Ahle.*]
ælc (89. *a*), *each, every, all.*
  [Mod. Eng. *each.*]
ælde, see **ielde.**
ælmesse (el-) (53. 1), *alms.*
  [See *New Eng. Dict.* s.v. *alms.*]
æl-mihtig (-mihti) (57. 3), *al-
  mighty.* [Ger. *allmächtig.*]

Æl-myrcan (53), plur. *Ethiopians.*
æmetta (53), *leisure.* [Cf.
  æmtig.]
æmtig (57. 3; 146), *empty, void.*
  [Cf. **æmetta.**]
æne, *once.*
ænig (89. *a*; 154. *a*; 146), *any
  (one).* [<**ān**; Ger. *einig.*]
æppel-bære (59, 146), *fruit-bear-
  ing.*
ær (47), *copper.* [See **ār**, *copper;*
  cf. the Ger. adj. *ehern.*]
ær, adv., *before, formerly, afore-
  time, ago;* frequently to be
  regarded as a mere sign of the
  pluperfect tense.
ær, prep., *before.* [Mod. Eng. *ere.*]
ær-dæg (43. 2), *dawn, break of
  day.*
ærend-wreca (53), *ambassador,
  envoy.* [Cf. Mod. Eng. *errand;*
  OE. **wrecan** has a sense = *relate.*]
ærest, *first, at first, in the first
  place.* (Mod. Eng. *erst;* Ger.
  erst.]
ær-ge-dōn (62), *previously done,
  former.* [**ær** + **dōn.**]
ærn (47), *edifice.*
ærra (67, 60), *former.*
ær-ꝥām-ꝥe, *before.*
ær-wacol (57, 146), *wakeful,
  sleepless.*
æsc-plega (53, 147), *ash-play,
  spear-play.*
æsc-rōf (58, 147), *spear-valiant,
  valiant with the spear.*
æt (47), *food.* [Cf. **etan.**]
æt (4), *at; from; to* (*New Eng.
  Dict.* s.v. *at,* I. 11, 12).
æt- (142).
æt-berstan (III. 104), *escape.*
æt-bregdan (III. 104, 162, 28),
  withdraw, take away.

æt-ēowian (118), *appear.* [Cf. ætīewan.]

æt-foran, *before.*

æt-gædere, *together;* strengthening samod, — samod ætgædere = Lat. *simul.*

æt-īewan (113), *reveal, display.* [Cf. ætēowian.]

æt niehstan, see niehstan.

ætȳwan, see ætīewan.

æðel-boren (62; 57.3; 147), *highborn, patrician.*

æðel-borennes (51.5; 147), *noble birth, rank, station.*

æðele (59), *noble, gentle, illustrious.* [Cf. *Ethel, Athel-,* and Ger. *edel.*]

æðeling (43, 143), *noble one, hero, man.*

æðða, see oððe.

æx (51. *b*), *ax.* [Cf. Gr. ἀξίνη, Lat. *ascia* (?), Ger. *Axt* (the *t* a late addition).]

ā-fǣran (113), *frighten, terrify.*

ā-feallan (R. 109), *fall.*

ā-fēdan (113), *nourish, support.*

ā-fierran (113), *remove, banish, put away.* [< feorr, by 16.]

ā-fiersian (118), *drive away, banish.*

ā-flīeman (113), *put to flight, expel.*

ā-gǣlan (-gēlan) (113), *neglect.*

āgan (127), *own, possess, have.* [Cf. Mod. Eng. *ought,* and see Schmidt's *Shakespeare Lexicon,* s.v. *owe,* 2.]

ā-gān (141), *depart.*

ā-gēan, *back.* [< ongēan. Distinguish the meaning of this word from that of bæcling.]

āgen (57. 3), *own.* [Past part. of āgan; Ger. *eigen.*]

āgend (43. 6), *owner, possessor.*

ā-gēotan (II. 103), *pour out, dissipate, destroy.*

ā-giefan (V. 106), *give, pay.*

ā-ginnan (III. 104), *begin.* [Cf. Ger. *-ginnen.*]

āgnian (118), *appropriate.* [Cf. āgan; Ger. *eignen.*]

ā-grōwan (R. 109), *grow up, grow over.*

ah, see ac.

ā-hebban (VI. 107), *raise* (i.e. *utter); exalt; endure, suffer, undergo.* [Ger. *erheben.*]

ā-hierdan (113), *harden (embolden?).* [Ger. *erhärten.*]

ā-hliehhan (VI. 107), *rejoice.* [Cf. Mod. Eng. *laugh,* Ger. *lachen.*]

āhōf, see āhebban.

ā-hrēosan (II. 103), *fall.*

āht (ōht) (47; 89. *b*), *something.*

ā-hwettan (113), *excite, whet; supply, fulfil.* [Cf. Mod. Eng. *whet,* Ger. *wetzen.*]

ā-lǣtan (R. 110), *give up.* [Ger. *erlassen.*]

aldor, see ealdor.

ā-lecgean (115, note), *deposit.*

ā-līefan (113), *permit, allow.* [< lēaf, *leave;* Ger. *erlauben.*]

ā-līehtan (113), *illuminate, give light to.* [< lēoht; Ger. *erleuchten.*]

ā-līesan (-lēsan) (113), *deliver.* [Ger. *erlösen.*]

ā-līesend (43. 6), *redeemer.*

ān (79), *one, a, a single, alone; admirable;* wk. āna, *alone;* on ān, *anon, at once;* ānra gehwilc, *every one.* [Ger. *ein.*]

and (ǫnd), *and.*

and- (142).

and-giet (-git) (47), *sense, meaning, understanding.* [Cf. gietan.]

and-gietfullice (76), *clearly, in-telligibly.*

and-lang (ọndlang) (58), *live-long, whole, all . . . long.* [Cf. Ger. *entlang* and the Chaucerian *endelong (Knight's Tale* 1820).]

an(d)-lícnes (51. 5), *image.* [Cf. Mod. Eng. *likeness,* Ger. *Gleich-niss,* for (*ge*)*leichniss.*]

and-lifan (51. *b*), *sustenance.*

and-swarian (ọndswarian, ọnd-sweorian) (118), *answer.*

and-swaru (ọndswaru) (51. *a*), *answer.*

and-weard (58, 146), *present.*

and-weardan (ọnd-) (113), *answer.*

and-wlita (53), *countenance, face;* also in the sense of 'angry coun-tenance,' 'anger,' Lat. *vultus.* [Cf. Ger. *Antlitz.*]

and-wyrdan (113), *answer.* [Cf. Ger. *antworten.*]

ān-feald (58), *plain, simple.* [Cf. Ger. *Einfalt, einfältig.*]

angel (43. 4), *hook.* [Mod. Eng. *angle,* Ger. *Angel.*]

an-ginn (ongin) (47), *beginning; vehemence, impetuosity, violence.*

an-gríslic (58), *fierce, raging.* [Cf. Mod. Eng. *grisly.*]

an-líc (on-) (58), *like, similar.*

anlícnes, see andlícnes.

ān-nes (51. 5), *oneness, unity.*

ān-rǽdnes (51. 5), *boldness, con-fidence, assurance.*

an-síen (51. *b*), *countenance.*

an-timber (47), *material, sub-stance.*

an-weald (43), *power, rule, juris-diction.* [Ger. *Anwalt.*]

ār (43), *messenger.*

ār (51. *b*), *honor; dignity, station.* [Ger. *Ehre.*]

ār (47), *copper.* [See ǽr, *copper;* Mod. Eng. *ore.*]

ā-rǽcean (114), *reach.* [Ger. *erreichen.*]

ā-rǽfnian (118), *endure, stand.*

ā-rǽran (113), *lift.* [Cf. Mod. Eng. *rear.*]

ā-rēadian (118), *redden, blush.* [Cf. Ger. *erröthen.*]

ā-rẹccean (114; 164. *b*), *relate, narrate, say.*

ā-rēdian (118), *find, choose.*

ā-rētan (113), *gladden.*

ār-fæst (58, 146), *gracious, lov-ing; glorious;* often translates Lat. *pius.* [See ār, *honor.*]

ār-fæstnes (51. 5), *kindness; com-passion.*

ār-gẹ-bland (-blọnd) (47), *com-motion of the sea, mingling of the waves.* The word = ēar(h)-geblọnd, *El.* 239; *Met.* 8 [30]; *Brun.* 26 ; see ēargrund, *depth of ocean;* ēar, *ocean.*

ā-rísan (I. 102), *arise.*

ārodlice, *immediately, forthwith.*

ār-wela (53), *oar-riches,* i.e. *sea.*

ār-wierðe (59, 146), *venerable.* [Cf. Ger. *ehrwürdig.*]

ār-wierðnes (51. 5), *reverence.*

ār-ȳð (51. *b*), *oar-billow, wave.*

ā-scēadan (R. 110), *divide.*

āscian (āxian) (118; 159. *b*; 32), *ask.* [Ger. *heischen,* properly *eischen.*]

ā-sẹcgean (123), *say, relate.*

ā-sẹndan (113), *send.*

ā-sẹttan (113), *place, deposit.*

assa (53), *ass.*

ā-stǽnan (113), *adorn, set.* [<stān, by 16.]

ā-stẹllan (114), *establish.*

ā-stigan (I.102), *ascend, go aboard; descend.* [Ger. *ersteigen.*]

ā-streccean (114), *prostrate.* [Cf. Mod. Eng. *stretch.*]

ā-styrian (118), *touch.* [Cf. Mod. Eng. *stir.*]

ā-swebban (115. *a*), *put to sleep*, i.e. *slay.*

ā-syndrian (118), *separate, sever, divide.* [Cf. Mod. Eng. *sunder.*]

ā-tēon (II. 103), *draw; inhale.*

ā-tēorian (118), *fail, give out.*

ā-ðennan (115. *a*), *apply, direct.* [Cf. Ger. *dehnen.*]

ā-ðindan (III. 104, 62, 60), *swell.*

āðum (43), *son-in-law.* [Ger. *Eidam.*]

āðundnan, see āðindan.

ā-weccean (114), *awaken, arouse.* [Ger. *erwecken.*]

ā-wecgean (115. *a*), *move.*

ā-wendan (113), *change, shift, transform.*

ā-wendednes (51. 5), *translation, version.*

ā-wiergan (113), *curse;* past part., *accursed.*

ā-wiht (89.*b*), *aught, a bit;* almost as an adv., *at all.* [Mod. Eng. *aught.*]

ā-wrēon (I. 102), *clothe.*

ā-wrītan (I. 102), *write.* [Cf. Ger. *reissen, ritzen.*]

ā-wyrcean (114), *perform, do.* [Ger. *erwirken.*]

āxian (32), see āscian. [Mod. Eng. dial. *axe.*]

B.

bæc, *back.*

bæcling, *back;* on bæcling, *back.*

bæð (47. 4), *bath.* [Ger. *Bad.*]

bæð-stede (44, 147), *gymnasium.*

bæð-weg (43, 215), *bath-way, bath-road.*

baldor, see bealdor.

bān (47, 24), *bone.* [Ger. *Bein,* (*Elfen*)*bein.*]

bana (53), *slayer, murderer.* [Mod. Eng. *bane.*]

bāsnian (118), *wait, bide one's time.*

bāt (43), *boat.*

baðian (118), *bathe.* [Ger. *baden.*]

be, *near; concerning; according to; on.* [See *New Eng. Dict.* s.v. *by.*]

be- (142).

bēacen (47, 24), *portent? standard?* [Mod. Eng. *beacon.*]

beadu (51. *a*), *battle, war.*

beadu-rōf (58), *valiant in war.*

beadu-wang (43), *battle-plain, field of battle.*

bēag (43), *torque, armilla, bracelet, collar, crown.* [Cf. būgan, 103.]

beald (24), *bold.* [Ger. *bald.*]

bealdor (baldor) (43), *ruler, king.* [See beald.]

bearn (47, 38), *son, child.* [Scotch *bairn;* cf. beran.]

bēatan (R. 109), *beat, smite, strike.*

be-bēodan (II. 103), *command, bid; commend.*

be-būgan (II. 103), *encircle, encompass, surround; extend.*

be-byrgan (113), *bury, inter.*

be-clȳsan (113), *enclose, shut up.* [< Lat. *clūsus*, by 16.]

bēc-rǣding (51. 3), *reading.*

be-cuman (IV. 105), *come, befall, arrive, attain, fall.* [Ger. *bekommen.*]

be-cweðan (V. 106), *say, declare.* [Mod. Eng. *bequeathe.*]

be-dælan (113, 177), *deprive*.

bedd (47), *bed, couch*. [Ger. *Bett*.]

beēodon, see **begān**.

be-fæstan (113), *commit, give over*.

be-fōn (R. 110), *embrace, grasp, comprehend*.

be-foran, *before*.

be-gān (141), *practise, pursue, ply*.

be-gang (43), *circuit, compass*.

be-gangan (R. 109), *practise; ply*.

bēgen (79), *both*.

√ **be-gietan** (-gitan) (V. 106), *acquire, obtain, reach*.

be-gyrdan (113), *begird*. [Ger. *-gürten*.]

be-hātan (R. 110; 164. *a*), *promise*.

be-healdan (R. 109), *behold*.

be-hēfe (59, 165), *useful*.

bēhð (51. *b*), *sign, proof*.

be-hygdig (57), *shrewd, sagacious*.

belg (43), *bellows*.

be-limpan (III. 104), *belong, pertain*.

be-lūcan (II. 103), *belock* [Shak.], *enclose*.

be-mīðan (I. 102), *conceal, disguise*. [Ger. *-meiden*.]

bēn (51. *b*), *prayer, petition, entreaty, supplication*. [See **bēna**, and cf. Mod. Eng. *boon*.]

bēna (53), *petitioner, suppliant*. [See **bēn**.]

be-nǣman (113,177), *deprive, strip*.

be-neoðan, *beneath*.

bēod (43), *table*.

bēodan (II. 103), *offer; command*. [Ger. *bieten*.]

bēon, see **wesan**.

beorg (21, 24), *hill, mountain*.

[Ger. *berg*, and Mod. Eng. (*ice*)-*berg*.]

beorht (58, 64, 21), *bright, fair, brilliant, radiant, glorious*. [Mod. Eng. *bright* is due to metathesis (31).]

beorhte, *brightly*.

beorhtnes (51. 5), *brightness*.

beorn (43, 21), *warrior, hero, man*.

bēor-scipe (44. 1; 143), *banquet, feast*.

bera (53), *bear*.

beran (IV. 105; 184. *a*),*bear, carry; berende, productive* (155. *b*).

be-rēafian (118), *despoil*. [Mod. Eng. *bereave*, Ger. *berauben*.]

be-scierian (bi-scerian) (116), *withhold*.

be-sēon (V. 106, 101), *look* (often almost *turn*). [Ger. *besehen*.]

be-sittan (V. 106), *sit in, hold*. [Ger. *besitzen*.]

be-sorgian (118, 142), *grieve for, be concerned about*; translates Lat. *dolere*. [Ger. *besorgen*.]

be-stīeman (-stēman) (113), *wet, moisten*.

be-swīcan (I. 102), *deceive*.

be-swīcian (118), *escape*.

bet, adj., *better*.

bet, adv. (77), *better*.

be-tǣcean (114), *assign*.

betst (66), *best*.

be-tweoh, *among*.

be-twēon, *toward*.

be-twēonan, *among*; **betwēonan him**, *towards one another*.

be-tweox, *among, between*.

be-tyrnan (113), *revolve*.

be-ðeccean (114), *cover, protect*. [Ger. *bedecken*.]

be-wǣfan (113), *clothe*. [See **wǣfels**.]

be-wendan (113 ; 184. *b*), *turn.*
[Ger. *bewenden.*]

be-windan (III. 104), *encompass.*
[Ger. *bewinden.*]

be-wrecan (V. 106), *surround*
(lit. *beat around*).

bibliotheca (Lat.), *library.*

bīdan (I. 102; 156. *l*), *await,*
wait.

biddan (V. 106 ; 156. *b*; 159. *b*),
ask, request, implore, beseech;
bid; seek. [Ger. *bitten.*]

bīegan (113), *bow, bend.* [Caus-
ative of būgan (103), from
bēag, pret. sing., by 16; cf.
Ger. *beugen.*]

bīema (53), *trumpet, clarion.*
[Cf. Chaucer, *Nun's Priest's*
Tale 578.]

big-leofa (53, 20), *food, suste-*
nance. [Cf. libban.]

bile-wit (57), *merciful.* [See *New*
Eng. Dict. s.v. *bilewhit.*]

√ bill (47), *broadsword, falchion.*
[Ger. *bille.*]

bindan (III. 104), *bind.* [Ger.
binden.]

binnan, *within.* [Ger. *binnen.*]

bīoð, see wesan.

bī-rihte (-ryhte), *beside.*

bisceop (43), *bishop.* [< Lat.
episcopus, Gr. ἐπίσκοπος, from
ἐπί, *upon*, and σκέπτομαι, *look;*
cf. Ger. *Bischof.* A Continental
borrowing, ca. A.D. 400.]

biscerian, see bescierian.

bisgian (118), *occupy, engross.*
[See bisig.]

bisgu (51. *a*), *concern, trouble.*
[See bisig.]

bisig (57), *busy.*

bītan (I.102), *bite.* [Ger. *beissen.*]

biter (57), *bitter, baneful, griev-*
ous. [Ger. *bitter;* cf. bītan.]

bīð, see wesan.

blæc (57. 2), *black.*

blæcan (113), *bleach, fade.* [Mod.
Eng. *bleach.*]

blǣd (43), *breath; abundance,*
blessedness. [Cf. blāwan.]

blǣst (43), *flame.* [Cf. blāwan.]

blāwan (R. 109), *blow.* [Cf.
Ger. *blähen,* Lat. *flare.*]

blētsian (118, 33), *bless.* [<
blōd.]

blētsung (51. 3; 144; 33), *bless-*
ing, benediction.

blēwð, see blōwan.

blīcan (I. 102), *shine.* [Ger.
-bleichen.]

blinnan (III. 104), *cease.* [See
Spenser, *F. Q.* 3. 5. 22.]

bliss (51. *b* ; 34), *joy.* [< blīðe.]

blisse-sang (43, 147), *song of*
gladness.

blissian (118, 34), *rejoice.*
[< bliss.]

blīðe (59, 24), *blithe, merry, jo-*
vial, joyous, gladsome.

blīðe (70), *joyously.*

blōd (47, 24), *blood.* [Ger.
Blut.]

blōdig (57.3 ; 146), *bloody.* [Ger.
blutig.]

blōstma (53), *blossom.* [Cf.
blōwan, and Lat. *flos.*]

blōwan (R. 109, 24), *blossom,*
bloom. [Mod. Eng. *blow;* cf.
Ger. *blühen,* Lat. *florere.*]

bōc (52, 24), *book.* [Ger. *Buch.*]

bōc-cræft (43, 147), *literature.*

Bōc-lǣden (47), *Latin.* [< OE.
bōc + Lat. *Latinus.*]

bōc-land (47, 147), *freehold es-*
tate.

bodian (118), *proclaim, preach.*
[Mod. Eng. *bode.*]

bolca (53), *gangway.*

bold-wela (53, 215), *Eden, Paradise* (lit. *house-wealth*).

bord (47), *shield*.

bord-stæð (47. 4), *shore, strand*. [Cf. Ger. *Gestade*.]

bōsm (43, 24), *bosom, surface* (cf. Shakespeare, *Tr. and Cress.* 1. 3. 112). [Ger. *Busen*.]

bōt (51. *b*), *repentance, amendment*.

brād (58, 24), *broad, spacious*. [Ger. *breit*.] [*face*.

brādnes (51.5), *breadth, face, sur-*

brǣdan (113; 184. *b*), *spread, dilate, expand*. [< brād, by 16; Ger. *breiten*.]

brand-stefn (brǫnd-stæfn) (43), *lofty-prowed* (reading brant-stefn; cf. hēahstefn naca, *Andr.* 265, brante cēole, *Andr.* 273).

brant (58), *high, lofty*.

breahtm (brehtm) (43; 21. *a*), *beat, pulsation, stroke* (of wings).

brecan (IV. 105), *break; break away, burst away, hurry, speed*. [Ger. *brechen*.]

bregdan (III. 104), *draw*. [Mod. Eng. *braid*.]

breogo (brego) (45, 20), *leader, king*.

brehtm, see breahtm.

breomo, see brim.

brēost (47, 24), *breast*.

Breoton (54, 20), *Britain; Briton*.

brim (47, 20), *billow, ocean, deep*.

brim-hęngest (43), *wave-steed, sea-horse*, i.e. *ship*. [Cf. Ger. *Hengst*, and the OE. proper name *Hęngist*, associated with *Horsa*.]

brim-stæð (47. 4; 147), *shore of the sea*. [Cf. Ger. *Gestade*.]

brim-strēam (43, 147), *ocean-stream, current*.

bringan (114), *bring, carry, take*. [Ger. *bringen*.]

brǫndstæfn, see brandstefn.

brōðor (46. 1; 24), *brother*. [Ger. *Bruder*.]

brūcan (II. 103; 156. *e*; 17), *hold, possess, enjoy, make use of*. [Mod. Eng. *brook*, Ger. *brauchen*.]

brūn (58, 24), *burnished, glistening; dusky*. [Ger. *braun*; see *New Eng. Dict.* s.v. *brown*.]

brycg (51. *b*; 24), *bridge*. [Ger. *Brücke*.]

brytta (53), *dispenser*.

Bryttas (43), plur., *Britons*.

bufan, *above*. [< be + ufan.]

būr (43, 24), *dining-room; private apartment, boudoir, bower*. [Mod. Eng. *bower*.]

burg (52. 1; 24), *city*. [Mod. Eng. *borough*, Ger. *Burg*.]

burg-geat (47, 147), *city-gate*.

burg-lēode (44. 4; 147), *city-people, citizens*.

burh-sittende (61, 28), *city-dwellers, citizens*.

burh-weall (43, 28), *city-wall*.

būtan, prep. (24), *without, outside of, except, besides*. [< be + ūtan; cf. the Scotch 'but and ben.']

būtan, conj., *except*.

bycgean (114), *buy*.

byrd (51. *b*), *birth, extraction*.

byrig, see burg.

byrne (53), *hauberk, corslet, mail-coat*.

byrn-hama (-hǫma) (53), *hauberk, corslet*.

bȳsen (51. *b*), *example, illustration; suggestion*.

C.

cald, see ceald.

camp (43), *fight, battle.* [Ger. *Kampf.*]

campian (118), *strive, struggle, fight.* [< camp.]

camp-wīg (cǫmp-) (47), *combat.*

carcern (47), *prison.* [< Lat. *carcer,* under influence of ærn.]

cāsere (44. 1), *emperor, Cæsar.* [Lat. *Cæsar.*]

ceald (cald) (58; 21. *a*), *cold.* [Ger. *kalt.*]

ceaster (51. 4), *city.* [Lat. *castra;* Mod. Eng. *Chester, -caster, -cester.*]

ceaster-(ge)-waran (53), plur., *citizens.*

cēder-bēam (43), *cedar-tree, cedar.* [< Lat. *cedrus* + bēam.]

cǫmpa (53), *soldier.* [< camp.]

cēne (59), *valiant.* [Ger. *kühn,* Mod. Eng. *keen.*]

√ cēol (43), *ship.*

ceorl (43, 24), *layman.* [Mod. Eng. *churl,* Ger. *Kerl;* cf. Chaucer, *Knight's Tale* 1601.]

cēosan (II. 103; 184. *a;* 37), *choose, seek.* [Archaic Ger. *kiesen;* cf. Chaucer, *Knight's Tale* 737.]

cīegan (113), *call.*

ciele (44, 18), *cold.* [Mod. Eng. *chill;* cf. Ger. *Kühle.*]

cīepan (113), *sell.* [Cf. Ger. *-kaufen.*]

cierran (cirran) (113; 184. *a;* 18), *turn; turn back.*

cild (50, 38, 24), *child.*

cild-hād (43, 143), *childhood.*

cining, see cyning.

cirice (53. 1), *church.* [Ger. *Kirche;* see *Phil. Soc. Dict.* s.v. *church.*]

cirran, see cierran.

cist (51. *b*), *chest.* [< Lat. *cista,* OE. orig. cest, then ciest (18), cist.]

clǣne (57, 24), *pure.* [Mod. Eng. *clean,* Ger. *klein.* The Ger. word has come to its present meaning through the series 'pure,' 'clean,' 'neat,' 'delicate,' 'fine,' 'tiny,' 'small.']

clǣnnes (51. 5), *chastity.*

cleofu (20), see clif.

cleopian (clypian) (118, 20), *call.* [Cf. our poetical *clepe, yclept,* and *Haml.* 1. 4. 19.]

clif (47, 20), *cliff.* [Cf. Ger. *Klippe.*]

clifer-fēte (59), *claw-footed.*

clypian, see cleopian.

cnapa (53), *boy, lad.* [Cf. Ger. *Knabe.*]

cnēo (47. 3; 27), *knee.* [Ger. *Knie;* cf. Lat. *genu.*]

cnēoris (like 51. 5), *tribe, nation.*

cniht (43), *young man, youth.* [Ger. *Knecht,* Mod. Eng. *knight.*]

cnyssan (115. *a*), *smite.*

collen-ferhð (-fyrhð) (58), *inspirited, elated.*

cōm, see cuman.

cǫmpwīg, see campwīg.

costnung (51. 3; 144), *temptation.*

cræft (43), *power; skill, cleverness; art, trade, occupation.* [Mod. Eng. *craft,* Ger. *Kraft.*]

crēopan (II. 103), *creep, crawl.*

Crīst (43), *Christ.* [< Lat. *Christus.*]

cucu (27; in this form irregular, according to the declensions of this book; see also cwic), *liv-ing, live, alive.*

culter (43 ?), *coulter.* [< Lat. *culter.*]

cuma (53), *stranger, visitant, guest.*

cuman (IV. 105), *come.* [Cf. Ger. *kommen.*]

cumbol (47), *banner, standard.*

cunnan (130), *know, know how, can.* [Ger. *können.*]

cunnian (118; 156. *d*), *make trial of.*

cūð (58), *known, manifest;* the combination of cūð and on-cnāwen, *Andr.* 527, presents a difficulty — perhaps for cūðe, adv. [Cf. 130.]

cūðlīce (70), *certainly; kindly.*

cwæð (pret.), see cweðan.

cwealm (43), *death.* [Mod. Eng. *qualm;* cf. cwellan.]

cweart-ern (47), *prison.* [Perhaps modified from Lat. *carcer,* under the influence of ærn.]

cwellan (114), *kill.*

cwēn (51. 1; 24), *queen, princess.*

cweðan (V. 106, 37), *say, speak.* [Cf. Mod. Eng. *quoth.*]

cwic (57, 27), *alive, living.* [See cucu. Cf. Mod. Eng. 'quick and dead,' 'cut to the *quick.*']

cwic-sūsl (51. *b*), *hell-torment* (lit. *living torment*).

cwīde (44), *remark.*

cwuc, see cwic.

√ cymlīce (70), *finely, beautifully.*

cyne-helm (43), *crown.*

cynelic (57, 146), *royal.*

cyne-rīce (48, 145), *kingdom.*

cyne-rōf (58), *royally brave.*

cyne-setl (47), *throne.*

cyning (cining) (43, 143, 24), *king.* [Ger. *König.*]

cynn (47), *kind; tribe, nation, people.*

cyn-rēn (47), *generation.*

Cyrenisc (57), *of Cyrene.*

Cyrenense, *Cyrene.*

cyssan (113), *kiss.* [Ger. *küssen.*]

cȳðan (113, 30), *announce, make known, show.* [< cūð, by 16; Ger. *-künden.*]

cȳððu (51. *a*; 144), *native land.*

D.

dǣd (51. 1), *deed, act;* mid dǣde, *indeed, in fact.*

dæg (43. 2; 24), *day.* [Ger. *Tag.*]

dæg-candel (51. *b*; 215), *candle of day.*

dæges (74), *by day.*

dæg-hwǣmlīce (70), *daily, day by day.*

dæg-rēd (47), *dawn.*

dǣl (43; 78. 4; 24), *part; amount, quantity, number.* [Ger. *Teil.*]

dǣlan (113; 164. *a*), *distribute, dispense, bestow.* [Ger. *teilen,* Mod. Eng. *deal.*]

dǣl-lēas (56; 155. *a*; 146), *destitute, devoid.*

dagung (51. 3), *dawn.*

dēad (58, 24), *dead.* [Ger. *tot.*]

dēað (43), *death.* [Ger. *Tod.*]

dēað-dæg (dēoth-) (43. 2), *death-day.*

dēma (53), *judge.*

dēman (113, 90, 17), *doom, condemn.* [Cf. Chaucer, *Knight's Tale* 1023.]

dēofol (43, 24), *devil, demon.* [< Lat. *diabolos;* so Ger. *Teufel.*]

dēop (58, 24), *deep.* [Ger. *tief.*]

dēope (70), *deeply.* [Cf. Chaucer, *K. T.* 1782.

dēoplic (57), *profound.*

dēor (47), *beast, animal.* [Ger.
Tier.]

dēor-cynn (47), *kind (race) of
animals.*

dēor-wierðe (59, 146), *precious.*

dēor-wurð (58, 146), *precious.*

dĕrian (116), *harm, injure.* [Cf.
Chaucer, *K. T.* 964.]

dīc (43), *dike.*

dīcian (118, 90), *ditch, dike.*

dīegelnes (51. 5), *retreat.*

dīere (dȳre) (59), *precious, valuable.* [Ger. *teuer.*]

diht (47), *plan, design.* [< Lat.
dictum.]

dohtor (52. 2), *daughter.* [Ger.
Tochter.]

dōm (43, 17), *judgment; reputation, glory; choice, decision.*

dōmlīce (70), *gloriously.*

dōm-weorðung (51. 3), *honor.*

dōn (140), *do; make; put.* [Ger.
thun.]

drēam (43), *joy, bliss.* [Ger.
Traum, Mod. Eng. *dream, but
in different sense.*]

drĕnc (43), *drink.*

drēorig (57), *headlong? melan-
choly?*

drihten, see dryhten.

drihtguma, see dryhtguma.

drinc (drync) (43), *drink.*

drincan (III. 104), *drink.* [Ger.
trinken.]

drohtað (43), *(mode, way of)
life.*

drȳgnes (51.5), *dryness, dry land.*

dryhten (43. 4. c; 154. d), *lord.*

dryhtenlic (57), *lordly, of the
lord.*

dryht-guma (driht-) (53), *retainer, vassal.*

drync, see drinc.

dugan (128), *avail.* [Ger.*taugen.*]

duguð (dugoð) (51. b), *host,
band; sustenance; benefit.* [Ger.
Tugend.]

dūn (51. b), *mountain, hill.*

dūst (47), *dust.* [Ger. *Dunst.*]

dynnan (115. a), *clash.*

dȳre, see dīere.

dyrstig (57), *rash, headstrong.*
[Cf. durran, 132.]

dyrstignes (51. 5), *presumption,
temerity.*

E.

ēa (52), *river.*

ēac, *also, likewise;* ēac swilce,
also; swilce ēac, *also, more-
over, as also, likewise;* swā ēac,
also. [Ger.*auch.* Mod. Eng.*eke.*]

ēad-gicfa (-gifa) (53), *bliss-giver,
happiness-giver.*

ēadig (57. 3; 146), *happy, blessed.*

ēadiglīce (70), *blissfully, in bliss.*

ēadignes (51. 5), *bliss.*

ēage (53. 2), *eye.* [Ger. *Auge.*]

ēagor-strēam (43), *ocean-stream.*

ēag-ðȳrel (47), *window.* [ðȳr-
< ðurh, by 16 and 29.]

eahta (78; 154. c; 21), *eight.* [Ger.
acht.]

ēalā, *O.*

ēa-lād (51. b), *ocean-way.*

eald (65, 58, 21, 19, 17), *old.*

eald-fēond (46. 3), *ancient foe.*

eald-genīðla (53), *ancient, invet-
erate enemy.*

eald-hĕttend (43. 6), *ancient enemy.*

ealdor (aldor) (43. 4), *chief; king.*

ealdor (47), *life.*

ealdor-dōm (43), *primacy, supremacy, chief place.*

ealdor-duguð (51. b), *nobility,
leaders.*

ealdor-mann (46), *leader, head, prince, noble.*

ealdor-scipe (44. 1; 143), *primacy, supremacy, chief place.*

ēa-līðende (61 ; or 43. 6 ?), *ocean-traversing.*

eall (58, 35, 24), *all, every;* eall swā, *just as, also;* ealne weg, *always;* mid ealle (175), *completely;* ðurh ealle, *entirely.*

ealles (71), *in all.*

eal-swā, *also, as.* [Ger. *also.*]

eard (43), *country.*

eardian (118), *dwell.*

earfoðlice (70), *distressfully, hard.* [Cf. Ger. *Arbeit.*]

earfoðnes (51. 5), *hardship.*

earfoð-rīme (59), *difficult to number.*

earg (58), *cowardly.* [Ger. *arg.*]

earm (58, 21), *poor, wretched.* [Ger. *arm.*]

earmlic (57), *humble, lowly.* [Cf. Ger. *ärmlich.*]

earmlice (70), *miserably.*

earn (43), *eagle.*

earnung (51. 3), *merit, desert.*

ēastan (75), *from the east.*

East-engle (44. 4), plur., *East Angles,* i.e. *East Anglia.*

ēast-norðerne (59), *northeasterly.*

Ēastron (53, irregular), *Easter.* [Ger. *Ostern.*]

ēast-sǣ (43; 51. *b*), *sea on the east.*

ēast-sūð-dǣl (43), *southeast quarter.*

ēaðe (77), *easily, unhesitatingly;* comp. **ieð,** irreg. **ēað.**

ēað-mēdu (51. *a*), *reverence; humility, kindness.*

ēað-mōd (58, 146), *humble, lowly.*

ēað-mōdlice (70), *humbly.*

ēað-mōdnes (51. 5), *humility, reverence.*

Ēbrēas (54), plur., *Hebrews.* [<Lat. *Hebræus.*]

Ēbrēisc (57, 146), *Hebrew.*

ēce (59), *everlasting, eternal.*

ecg (51. *b*), *edge.*

ed- (142).

ed-nīwian (118), *renew.*

ēdre, see **ǣdre.**

ed-wit (47), *abuse, insolence.* [Cf. **wīte,** and Mod. Eng. *twit.*]

efen-ēadig (57), *co-blessed, equally blessed.* [Among moderns, Bishop Ken seems most to have employed such compounds as these.]

efne (emne), *behold; just.*

eft, *again, once more; afterward; back.*

eft-hweorfan (III. 104), *return.*

egesa (53), *dread, fear, terror; peril.* [Related to ON. *agi,* from which Mod. Eng. *awe.*]

egeslic (57), *dreadful, terrible.* [See **egesa.**]

eglan (113), *plague, harass, afflict.* [Mod. Eng. *ail.*]

egle (59), *grievous, hateful.* [See **eglan.**]

Egypta (54), plur., *Egyptians.*

ēhtan (113), *pursue.*

elcung (51. 3), *delay, postponement.*

ele (44), *oil.* [<Lat. *oleum.*]

ellen (47), *courage.*

ellen-rōf (58), *strenuous in courage, of undaunted courage.*

elles (71), *else.* [el- = *other.*]

ellor-fūs (58, 30), *bound elsewhither.* [el- = *other.*]

elmesse, see **ælmesse.**

elp (43), *elephant.* [<Lat. *elephas.*]

el-ꝺeodig (57. 3), *foreign*. [From el- = *other*, and ꝺeod, q. v.]

emne, see efne.

emniht (52, but no *visible* umlaut), *equinox*. [< efen-niht; cf. emne for efne.]

ende (44), *end*. [Ger. *Ende*.]

endian (118, 90), *end*.

engel (43. 4; 23; 10), *angel*. [< Lat. *angelus*, Gr. ἄγγελος.]

Engle (44. 4), *the Angles, English*. [Of the invaders of Britain Bede says (*Hist. Eccl.* I. 15): "Advenerant autem de tribus Germaniæ populis fortioribus, id est, Saxonibus, Anglis, Jutis. . . . Porro de Anglis, hoc est, de illa patria quæ Angulus dicitur, et ab eo tempore usque hodie manere desertus inter provincias Jutarum et Saxonum perhibetur, Orientales Angli, Mediterranei Angli, Merci, tota Nordanhymbrorum progenies, id est, illarum gentium quæ ad Boream Humbri fluminis inhabitant cæterique Anglorum populi sunt orti." Cf. also the pun of Pope Gregory the Great (*Hist. Eccl.* II. 1): "Rursus ergo interrogavit, quod esset vocabulum gentis illius. Responsum est, quod Angli vocarentur. At ille, 'Bene,' inquit; 'nam et angelicam habent faciem, et tales angelorum in cælis decet esse coheredes.' "]

Englisc (57), *English*. [Note that any term corresponding to 'Anglo-Saxon,' as the designation of a language, does not exist in Old English. See the *Phil. Soc. Dict.* s. vv. *Anglo-Saxon* and *English;* Bailey's Dictionary (1783) is the first authority given for the English term 'Anglo-Saxon' in its application to the tongue.]

eode, see gān.

eorl (43), *hero, man*. [Not to be translated 'earl' in these texts.]

cornoste (70), *sharply, vehemently*. [Cf. Mod. Eng. *earnest*, Ger. *Ernst*.]

eornostlice (70), *then, accordingly, thus*.

eorre, see ierre.

eorꝺe (53. 1), *earth; ground; land*. [Ger. *Erde*.]

eorꝺlic (57, 146), *earthly*.

eorꝺ-tilꝺ (51. *b*; 147), *agriculture*. [Cf. Mod. Eng. *tilth*.]

eorꝺ-waran (53), plur., *dwellers on earth*.

eorꝺ-weall (43), *rampart of earth, earthwork*. [weall = Lat. *vallum;* one of the oldest Germanic words borrowed from Latin.]

eower (81, 83), *your, of you*.

erbe(-), erfe(-), see ierfe(-).

est (51. 1; 165; 43; 30), *provision; consent, will*. [Cf. unnan, æfestfull, and Ger. *Gunst*.]

este (59, 165), *bountiful*. [Cf. est.]

estlice (70), *willingly*. [Cf. est.]

etan (V. 106), *eat*. [Ger. *essen*.]

eꝺel (43. 4. *a*), *country, native land, home*.

eꝺel-rice (48), *fatherland*.

eꝺel-weard (43), *guardian of his country*.

F.

fæc (47), *time, period, interval, space*. [Ger. *Fach*.]

fæder (43. 8; 24), *father*. [Ger. *Vater*.]

fǣge (59), *fated, death-doomed.* [Scotch *fey,* Ger. *feige.*]

fæger (57), *fair, beautiful, agreeable, lovely.*

fægernes (51. 5), *beauty.*

fægn (58), *glad, joyous.*

fǣgre (70 ; vowel long in poetry), *fairly.*

fǣgð (51. *b*), *certain death(?)*

fǣmne (53), *virgin, maiden, damsel.*

fǣringa (70), *suddenly, on a sudden.*

fǣrlice (70), *suddenly.* [Cf. āfǣred, and Mod. Eng. *fear.*]

fæst (58), *fixed, stable.* [Ger. *fest,* properly *fast.*]

fæsten (47), *fortification.* [Cf. Mod. Eng. *fastness.*]

fæsten-geat (47), *fortress-gate.*

fæst-hafol (57 ; 155. *d*), *tenacious.* [hafol from the root of habban.]

fæstnes (51. 5), *firmament.*

fæstnung (51. 3), *hold, stay, support.*

fæt (47. 4), *utensil, implement.*

fǣted (57), *beaten? ;* fǣted gold, *gold leaf?*

fǣted-sinc (47), *treasure of plated articles?*

fæðm (43), *embracing arms; body; expanse, surface.* [Mod. Eng. *fathom.*]

fāg (58), *gleaming, glittering.*

fāh (58; but used as noun), *foe, enemy.* [Mod. Eng. *foe.*]

fāmig-heals (58), *foamy-necked, foamy-throated.* [Cf. Ger. *Hals.*]

faran (VI. 107 ; 184. *a*), *go.*

faroð (faruð) (43), *shore;* more generally, as in the next three words, it appears to mean *surge* (and so, possibly, p. 212, l. 12).

faroð-lācende (61, 215), *surge-swimming.* [See lācan.]

faroð-rīdende (61, 215), *surge-riding.*

faroð-strǣt (51. *b* ; 215), *surge-street, street over the billows.* [strǣt < Lat. *strāta.*]

faru (51. *a*), *adventure.*

feallan (R. 109), *fall.* [Ger. *fallen.*]

fealu (57. 5), *dusky* (as often translated; but perhaps rather its literal signification), *yellow* (as Tennyson applies it, *Geraint and Enid* 829, 'And white sails flying on the *yellow* sea'; but Tennyson, in *The Battle of Brunanburh,* translates fealone flōd by '*fallow* flood'). [Cf. Ger. *fahl, falb,* and our '*fallow* deer.']

fēa-sceaft (58), *destitute.*

fēawe (58), plur., *few.*

fęccean (119, irreg.), *fetch.*

fēdan (113), *feed, nourish, support.* [< fōd-, by 16.]

fela (indecl. adj.; 154. *a*), *much; numerous, many (things).*

feoh-ge-strēon (47), *riches.* [See gestrēon, and Mod. Eng. *fee.*]

feohtan (III. 104, 21), *fight.* [Ger. *fechten.*]

fēon (113), *hate.*

fēond (143 ; 46. 3 ; 24), *foe, enemy.* [Mod. Eng. *fiend,* Ger. *Feind;* see fēon.]

fēore, see feorh.

feorh (43, 47, 29), *life, soul.*

feorh-nęru (51. *a*), *sustenance.* [Cf. nęrian.]

feormian (118), *take in, entertain.*

feor(r) (67; 35. *a*), *far, distant.* [Mod. Eng. *far.*]

feorr, *far, from (to) a distance.*

feorran (75), *from afar, from of old.* [Cf. Ger. *fern.*]

fēorða (78), *fourth.* [Ger. *vierte.*]

fēower (78), *four.* [Ger. *vier.*]

fēower-tīene (78), *fourteen.* [Ger. *vierzehn.*]

fer-, see for-.

fēran (113), *go, journey.* [Cf. Ger. *führen.*]

ferhð (fyrhð) (43, 47), *mind.*

fęrian (-ig(e)an) (116), *ferry, carry.*

fēða (53), *troop.*

feðer (51. *b*; 24), *wing, pinion.* [Ger. *Feder*, Mod. Eng. *feather.*]

fiellan (fyllan) (113), *fell, slay.* [Ger. *fällen*, Mod. Eng. *fell.*]

fierd (51. 1), *expedition, campaign.* [Ger. *Fahrt;* cf. faran.]

fierding (51. *b*), *warfare.*

fierd-wīc (fyrd-) (47), plur., *camp.*

fierst (fyrst) (43), *period, space, interval.* [Ger. *Frist.*]

fīfta (78, 30), *fifth.* [Ger. *fünfte*, Gr. πέμπτος.]

fīgað, see fēon.

findan (III. 104), *find, devise; encounter.* [Ger. *finden.*]

fīras (43, 29), plur., *men.*

firgen-strēam (firigend-) (43), *mountain-stream*, i.e. *ocean-stream.*

firmamentum (Lat.), *firmament.*

fisc (43, 24), *fish.* [Ger. *Fisch*, Lat. *piscis.*]

fisc-cynn (47), *sort of fish.*

fiscere (44, 143), *fisher(man).* [Ger. *Fischer.*]

fiscnoð (43), *fishing.*

fiðer-fēte (59), *four-footed.*

fiðru (47), plur., *wings.* [Cf. feðer, and Ger. *Gefieder.*]

flǣsc (47, 24), *flesh.* [Ger. *Fleisch.*]

flān (43), *arrow.*

flax-fēte (59), *web-footed.*

flēogan (II. 103), *fly.* [Ger. *fliegen.*]

flēon (II. 103), *flee.* [Ger. *fliehen.*]

flocc (43), *company.*

flōd (43), *flood.* [Ger. *Flut.*]

flōd-wielm (-wylm) (43), *seething of the flood.*

flota (53), *vessel* (lit. *float*).

flōwan (R. 109), *flow.*

flyht (43), *flight.*

fnǣst (43), *breath.*

fōda (53), *food.*

fōdor (47), *fodder.* [Ger. *Futter.*]

folc (47), *folk, people, nation.* [Ger. *Volk.*]

folc-stęde (44), *folkstead, battle-ground.*

folc-toga (53), *leader of the people, commander.* [toga < same root as tēon; cf. Ger. *Herzog*, OE. hęretoga, and the meaning of Lat. *dux.*]

folde (53), *earth.*

folgian (118; 164. *f*), *attend, serve.* [Ger. *folgen;* cf. fylgan.]

folm (51. *b*), *hand.* [Cognate with Lat. *palma.*]

fōn (R. 110), *catch; reach forth.*

fōr (51. *b*), *journey.*

fōr, see faran.

for (166, 175, 4), *for; before; of; on; in* (Fr. *selon*).

for- (142).

for-bærnan (113), *scorch, parch.*

for-dīlgian (118), *destroy.* [Ger. *vertilgen.*]

for-dōn (142), *destroy.* [Shak.]

for-drīfan (I. 102), *drive, impel.* [Ger. *vertreiben.*]

fore, *before*.

fore- (142).

fore-cuman (IV. 105), *anticipate, forestall, prevent*.

fore-cweden (62), *aforesaid*.

fore-ge-gearwian (118), *prepare*.

fore-ge-scrifan (I. 102), *prescribe*. [Ger. *vorschreiben;* Lat. *scribo* underlies both.]

fore-sǣd (62), *aforesaid*. [Past part. of **foresęcgean**.]

fore-scēawung (51. 3), *providence*. [Cf. Ger. *Vorsehung.*]

fore-sęttan (113), *close in*. [Ger. *vorsetzen.*]

fore-sprecen (62), *aforesaid*. [Past part. of **foresprecan**.]

fore-tȳnan (113), *cut off*. [Cf. **tūn**, and 16.]

for-giefan (V. 106, 18), *give, grant*. [See **giefan** ; Ger. *vergeben.*]

√ **for-gieldan** (-gildan) (III. 104; 24; 18; 164. *h*), *requite, recompense; pay, give*. [Ger. *vergelten.*]

for-gietan (V. 106, 18), *forget*. [Ger. *vergessen.*]

√ **for-grindan** (III. 104), *wear out* (like Lat. *conterere*).

forht (58), *afraid, terrified*.

forhtian (118), *tremble*.

for hwon, *why*.

for hwȳ, *why*.

for-ierman (113), *ruin, reduce to poverty*. [< **earm**, by 16 ; cf. Ger. *verarmen.*]

for-lǣtan (R. 110), *let, allow; let go; lay down; leave, leave off; abandon, forsake; lose*. [Ger. *verlassen.*]

for-lēosan (II. 103), *lose*. [Cf. Mod. Eng. *forlorn*, and Ger. *verlieren.*]

for-liden (62), *shipwrecked*. [Past part. of **forliðan**.]

for-lidennes (51. 5), *shipwreck*.

forma (60, 68, 78), *first*.

for-niman (IV. 105), *waste, desolate, consume ;* **fornumen bēon**, *perish, decay*.

for-spildan (113), *destroy*.

for-swelgan (III. 104), *devour*.

for-swīgian (118), *keep secret, conceal*. [Ger. *verschweigen.*]

for-tredan (V. 106), *tread down, tread under foot*. [Ger. *vertreten.*]

forð, *forth*.

for-ðām, *because, for this reason, therefore*.

for-ðām-ðe, *because*.

for-ðan, *wherefore*.

forð-ā-tēon (II. 103), *bring forth*.

forð-bringan (114), *bring forth*.

forð-faran (VI. 107), *pass away, depart ;* **forðfaren**, *deceased, dead*. [Ger. *fortfahren.*]

forð-fōr (51. *b*), *departure*.

forð-ge-lēoran (113), *pass away, die*.

forð-lǣstan (-lēstan) (113), *continue, supply*.

for-ðon (-ðe), *for, because ; therefore ; wherefore*.

forð-tēon (II. 103), *perform, represent, exhibit ; bring forth*.

forð-weard, *advanced*.

for-wandian (118), *reverence ; hesitate ;* **forwandiende**, *deferential, diffident*.

for-weorðan (III. 104), *perish*.

for-wiernan (113 ; 156. *j*), *refuse, deny*.

for-witan (126), *know in advance*.

for-wyrcean (114), *forfeit*. [Ger. *verwirken.*]

fōt (46), *foot*. [Ger: *Fuss*.]

fracoð (57, 165), *odious, abominable.* [< *fra-cūð, cf. Mayhew, *OE. Phon.* § 160.]

frægn, see **frignan**.

frætwa (-we) (51. *a*), plur., *ornaments.*

frætwian (118), *adorn, bedeck.*

frætwung (51. 3), *array.*

fram, *from ; by ; of ; from among.*

fram-gān (141), *make headway.*

framlīce (fram-) (70), *promptly, bravely.*

frēa (53), *lord.*

frēcne (59), *perilous, fearful, direful, terrible.*

frēcne (70), *fearlessly, dauntlessly, valiantly.*

frēcnes (51. 5 ; 144), *danger, peril.*

℣/frēfran (115. *b*), *comfort, cheer.*

fremde (59), *foreign, alien.* [Ger. *fremd.*]

fremman (115. *a*; 117; 164. *e*), *benefit, profit.* [Cf. the **fram-** (16) in **framgān**.]

frēo (irreg. plur. **frige**), *free.*

℣ frēod (51. *b*), *good-will, kindness.*

frēolīce (70), *freely.* [Ger. *freilich.*]

frēond (46. 3), *friend.* [Ger. *Freund*, Goth. *frijōnds*, pres. part. of *frijōn*, to love; cf. **fēond.**]

frēond-scipe (44. 1 ; 143), *friendship.* [Cf. Ger. *Freundschaft*, with a different ending.]

frēorig (57 ; 174. *d*), *cold, benumbed.*

freoðu (freoðo) (51. *a*), *defense.* [Ger. *Friede.*]

frige, see **frēo**.

frignan (III. 104), *ask, inquire.*

frið (47), *countenance, support, aid, protection.* [Cf. **freoðu**, and Mod. Eng. *Frede(rick)*.]

frōd (58), *old.*

frōfor (51. *b*), *comfort, consolation; sustenance.*

frǫmlīce, see **framlīce**.

fruma (53), *beginning, first.*

frum-gār (43), *principile, captain, chief.* [Cf. **fruma.**]

frum-sceaft (51. *b*), *creation.* [Cf. **fruma.**]

frymð(u) (51, 144), *creation.* [Cf. **fruma**, and **16.**]

fugol (43. 4), *bird.* [Ger. *Vogel*, Mod. Eng. *fowl.*]

fugol-cynn (47), *kind of birds.*

fūl (58), *vile, foul.* [Ger. *faul ;* more remotely related are Lat. *pus, puteo.*]

full (58), *full.* [Ger. *voll.*]

ful(l), adv., *full.*

full-fremman (115. *a* ; 117), *finish.*

fultum (43), *help, aid, assistance, support.*

fultumian (118, 90), *assist.*

furðra (67), *first* (lit. *former*).

furðum, *even; whatever.*

fūs (58, 30), *ready.*

fylgan (113), *follow.* [Cf. **folgian**, and Ger. *folgen.*]

fyllan (113), *fill.* [< **full**, by 16; Ger. *füllen.*]

fyllan, see **fiellan**.

fyllu (51. *a*), *fill, feast.*

fȳr (47), *fire.* [Ger. *Feuer.*]

fyrdwīc, see **fierdwīc**.

fyrhð, see **ferhð**.

fyrmest (78. 1 ; 69), *first.*

fȳr-spearca (53), *spark.*

fyrst, see **fierst**.

fȳsan (113 ; 184. *b*), *hasten.* [< **fūs.**]

G.

gād (51. *b*), *goad.*

gærs (47, 31), *herb, grass.* [Ger. *Gras.*]

gaful-ræden (51. 5; 144), *fare.*

gagates (Lat.), *jet.*

gālnes (51. 5), *lust, lewdness.* [Cf. Ger. *Geil(heit).*]

gān (141), *go.* [Ger. *gehen.*]

gang (gong) (43), *course; circuit, revolution.*

gangan (R. 109), *go.*

gār (43), *spear, javelin.* [Cf. Mod. Eng. *garlic.*]

gār-ge-winn (47), *battle of spears.* [See gewinn.]

√ gārsecg (43), *ocean.* [See p. 211, note 3.]

gāst (43), *spirit, ghost.* [Ger. *Geist.*]

gāst-ge-hygd (47), *thought of the mind.*

gāst-ge-rȳne (48, 215), *secret of the soul, thought of the heart*(?). [See gerȳne.]

gāt (52), *goat.* [Ger. *Geiss.*]

gē (18).

ge . . . and, ge . . . ge (202), *both . . . and.*

ge- (142).

ge-æmetgian (118), *release, disengage.* [Cf. æmetta, æmtig.]

ge-āgnian (118), *inherit, occupy, take possession of.* [See āgnian.]

ge-and-weard (58), *present.* [See andweard.]

ge-and-weardan (-ond-) (113), *answer.* [See andweardan.]

gēar (47, 18), *year.* [Ger. *Jahr.*]

gēara, *formerly, of yore.*

geare (70), *well.* [See yare(*ly*)

in Shakespeare, *Temp.* 1. 1, and elsewhere.]

gēarlic (57), *yearly, annual.* [Ger. *jährlich.*]

gearu-ðancol (gearoðoncol) (57), *ready-witted.* [See geare, geðancol, ðancolmōd.]

gearwian (118), *prepare.* [See geare.]

geat (47; 18), *gate.*

ge-āxian (118), *learn, discover.* [See āscian.]

ge-bed (47, 142), *prayer.* [Ger. *Gebet;* cf. biddan.]

ge-beorg (47), *defense, protection; outlook* (*on*).

ge-bēorscipe (44. 1), *banquet, feast.* [See bēorscipe.]

ge-beran (IV. 105), *bear.* [See beran.]

√ ge-bīdan (I. 102), *await, wait.* [See bīdan.]

ge-biddan (V. 106), *pray.* [See biddan.]

ge-bīegan (113), *bend, curve.* [See bīegan.]

ge-bierhtan (113), *grow bright, shine.* [< beorht, by 16.]

ge-bilod (57), *billed.*

√ ge-bisgian (-bysgian) (118), *fatigue, weary, exhaust.* [See bisig.]

ge-bland (-blond) (47), *mingling, mixture, confusion.*

ge-blandan (-blondan) (R. 110), *mingle.*

ge-blēdsian, see gebletsian.

ge-blēod (58), *hued, colored.*

ge-blētsian (-blēdsian) (118), *bless.* [See *New Eng. Dict.* s.v. .*bless.*]

ge-blissian (118), *rejoice, make joyful;* geblissod wesan, *joy.* [See blissian.]

geblǫnd(an), see gebland(an).

ge-blōwan (R. 109), *blow*. [See blōwan.]

ge-brec (47), *uproar, din*. [Cf. brecan.]

ge-bringan (114), *waft, carry, convey*. [See bringan.]

ge-bycgean (114), *buy; redeem*. [See bycgean.]

ge-byrd (51. *b*), *birth, extraction, lineage*. [Ger. *Geburt;* see byrd.]

✓ gebysgian, see gebisgian.

ge-cēosan (II. 103), *choose, select*.

ge-cīegan (113), *call*. [See cīegan.]

ge-cierran (113, 18), *turn; return*. [See cierran.]

ge-cneordnes (51. 5), *accomplishment*.

ge-cost (58 ; 174. *d*), *tried, trusty*.

ge-cwēman (113), *please*.

ge-cwēme (59), *pleasing, acceptable*.

ge-cwēmlice (70), *acceptably, agreeably*.

ge-cweðan (V. 106), *say, speak*. [See cweðan.]

✓ ge-cȳðan (113 ; 164. *b*), *announce; prove, evince, show, exhibit, display; designate*. [See cȳðan.]

ge-dǣlan (113), *divide, separate*. [See dǣlan.]

ge-dafenian (118 ; 164. *k*), *befit*.

ge-dafenlic (57), *fitting, suitable*.

ge-deorf (47), *labor, toil*.

ge-dīcian(118),*construct*. [<dīc; see dīcian.]

ge-diersian (-dȳrsian) (118, 90), *exalt, magnify, celebrate*. [<dīere.]

ge-dōn (140), *do, perform; make*. [See dōn.]

✓ ge-drēfan (113), *disturb, agitate, trouble*. [Cf. Ger. *trüben*.]

gedȳrsian, see gedīersian.

ge-ēacnian (118), *increase, augment*. [<ēac.]

ge-earnian (118), *merit*. [See earnung.]

ge-ed-nīwian (118), *renew*. [See ednīwian.]

ge-ęnde-byrdan (113), *order, arrange*.

ge-ęndian (118), *end, come to an end*. [<ęnde; see ęndian.]

ge-ęndung (51. 3), *end, close*.

ge-fæstnian (118), *fasten, confirm, establish*.

ge-faran (VI. 107), *experience, suffer*. [See faran, and 142, ge-(2).]

ge-fēa (53), *pleasure, joy, delight, gladness*.

ge-feallan (R. 109), *fall, chance*. [See feallan.]

ge-feoht (47), *battle*.

ge-feohtan (III. 104), *fight*. [See feohtan.]

ge-fēon (V. 106 ; 156. *c*; 29), *rejoice*.

ge-feormian (118), *take in, entertain*. [See feormian.]

ge-fēra (53, 142), *companion, fellow*.

gefēran (113), *undertake, experience*. [See fēran.]

✓ ge-ferian (116), *ferry, carry, bear*. [See ferian.]

ge-fēr-rǣden (51. 5; 144), *company, fellowship, society*.

ge-fēr-scipe (44. 1; 143), *attendance, companionship ; retinue*.

geflīeman (-flǣman) (113), *put to flight*.

ge-flit (47), *strife, dispute*. [Cf. Ger. *Fleiss*.]

ge-frætwian (118), *adorn*. [See frætwian.]

ge-frēfran (115. *b*), *console, cheer.*
[See frēfran.]

ge-fremman (115. *a*), *effect, perform, work, perpetrate.* [See fremman.]

ge-fultumian (118), *assist, help.* [See fultumian.]

ge-fyllan (113, 156), *fill; end, finish, accomplish.* [See fyllan.]

ge-fyrn, adv., *a long time ago.*

ge-gada (53), *associate, companion.*

ge-gaderian (118), *gather.*

ge-gaderung (51. 3), *gathering together, assembly, congregation.*

ge-gān (141), *go; win, obtain.* [See gān.]

ge-gearcian (118), *prepare.* [Cf. geare.]

ge-gearwian (118), *prepare.* [See gearwian, and cf. gegierwan.]

ge-gierela (53), *garment; raiment, apparel.*

ge-gierwan (-gyrwan) (113), *prepare.* [Cf. gegearwian.]

ge-glengan (113), *adorn.* [< gleng.]

ge-gōdian (118), *enrich.* [< gōd.]

ge-gremman (115. *a*), *irritate, enrage.* [See gremian.]

ge-grētan (113), *greet, salute.*

ge-gyrwan, see gegierwan.

ge-hāl (58), *whole, intact.* [See hāl.]

ge-hālgian (118), *hallow.* [< hālig.]

ge-hātan (R. 110), *promise, pledge; call.* [See hātan.]

ge-healdan (R. 109), *observe, keep; reserve; maintain, sustain.* [See healdan.]

ge-hēawan (R. 109), *cut down, slay.* [See hēawan.]

ge-herian (116), *glorify.* [See herian.]

ge-hīeran (113), *hear.* [See hīeran.]

ge-hīersum (57, 146), *obedient.*

ge-hīersumian (118; 164. *f*), *obey.*

ge-hīersumnes (51. 5), *obedience.*

ge-hladan (VI. 107), *lade, load, freight.*

ge-hogian (118), *consider, have in mind.*

ge-hrīnan (I. 102), *attack.*

ge-hū, *in every direction.* [See hū.]

ge-hwā (89. *c*; 154. *b*), *each (one).* [See hwā.]

ge-hwilc (-hwylc) (89. *a*; 154. *b*), *each (one), every (one); ānra gehwilc, every (one).* [See hwilc.]

ge-hyhtan (113), *hope, trust.* [< hyht.]

ge-hȳran, see gehīeran.

ge-innian (118), *give, bestow (on).*

ge-in-seglian (118), *seal.* [< Lat. sigillum.]

ge-læccean (114), *catch, seize.* [Cf. Shak., *Macb.* 4. 3. 195.]

ge-lǣdan (113), *bring, carry.* [See lǣdan.]

ge-lǣred (62), *taught, educated, trained, skilled, skilful.* [Past part. of lǣran.]

ge-lǣstan (113), *stand by, assist.* [See lǣstan.]

ge-laðian (118), *invite.* [See laðian.]

ge-lēafa (53), *faith.* [Ger. *G(e)-laube.*]

ge-leornian (118), *learn.* [See leornian.]

ge-lettan (113), *hinder.* [Ger.

-*letzen;* cf. Shak., *Haml.* 1. 4. 85, and (Auth. Vers.) Rom. 1. 13.]

ge-lic (58, 163), *like.* [< lic *body;* cf. Ger. *gleich.*]

ge-lica (53), *like, equal.*

ge-lice (70), *similarly, likewise.*

ge-licgan (V. 106), *border.* [See licgan.]

ge-licnes (51. 5), *likeness.* [Ger. *Gleichniss.*]

ge-liefan (113; 156. *g*), *believe.* [Ger. *g(e)lauben.*]

ge-lif-fæstan (113), *make alive, endow with life.* [See lif.]

ge-limp (47), *adventure, misfortune.*

ge-limpan (III. 104), *happen, befall.*

ge-limplic (57), *adapted.*

ge-logian (118), *place, set.*

ge-lomlice (70), *frequently.*

ge-lufian (118), *love.* [See lufian.]

ge-lystan (113, 190), *desire.* [See lystan, and Ger. *gelüsten.*]

ge-maca (53), *mate, companion.*

ge-mæccea (53), *mate, consort, spouse.*

ge-mæne (59), *common, universal.*

gemænelice (70), *in common.*

ge-mære (48), *boundary, end.*

ge-mang (-mong) (47), *troop, phalanx.*

ge-manig-fieldan (113), *multiply.*

ge-mengan (113; 184. *b*), *mingle, associate.*

ge-meotu, see gemet.

ge-met (47, 20), *boundary; sort; effect; law.*

ge-metan (113), *find, encounter.* [See metan.]

ge-miltsian (118; 164. *g*; 33), *pity, have compassion on.* [< milts.]

ge-miltsiend (43. 6), *pitier.*

gemong, see gemang.

ge-munan (134), *remember, be mindful.*

ge-myndig (57), *mindful.*

ge-myngian (118), *recount, relate.*

gena, see giena.

ge-nacodian (118, 162), *strip.* [< nacod.]

gen-cwide (44, 28), *reply.* [See cwide.]

ge-neahhe (70), *often, frequently.*

ge-nea-læcan (113), *approach, draw nigh.* [See nealæcan.]

ge-nemnan (115. *b*), *name.* [See nemnan.]

ge-neosian (118), *visit.* [See neosian.]

ge-nerian (116), *save.*

ge-niman (IV. 105), *take, seize.* [See niman.]

ge-nyhtsum (57, 146), *abundant.* [Cf. nugan (136), Ger. *genügen,* and Mod. Eng. *enough.*]

ge-nyhtsumian (118; 164. *e*), *avail, suffice, be sufficient for, be of use.*

geofon (47), *ocean.*

geoguð (51. *b*; 18), *youth.* [Ger. *Jugend.*]

geomor-mod (58, 18), *sorrowful-minded.* [Cf. Ger. *Jammer.*]

geond (18), *along, through, throughout, over.* [Cf. Mod. Eng. *beyond.*]

geong (58, 65, 18), *young.* [Ger. *jung.*]

ge-openian (118), *open.* [< open; cf. Ger. *öffnen.*]

georn (58; 155. *e*; 21. *b*), *eager.* [See giernan.]

georne (70), *surely, certainly.* [Ger. *gern.*]

georn-full (58), *busied, occupied.*
georn-fulnes (51. 5), *piety, zeal.*
geornlice (70), *assiduously, zealously.*
√ **georran (IH. 104)**, *rattle.*
√ **gēotan (II. 103)**, *stream.* [Ger. *giessen.*]
ge-rǣdan (113), *read;* **gerǣd is**, *reads.* [Cf. Ger. *rathen;* see **rǣdan.**]
ge-reccean (114), *interpret, expound.* [See **reccean.**]
ge-rēnian (118, 28), *adorn.*
ge-reord (47), *repast.*
√ **ge-reordian (118, 90)**, *feed, refresh.*
ge-restan (113; 184. b), *rest, repose.* [< **rest.**]
ge-rētan (113), *refresh, invigorate, cheer.* [< **rōt**, *glad.*]
ge-riht (47), *direct way.* [See **riht.**]
ge-rīm-cræft (43), *arithmetic, chronology.*
ge-rȳne (48), *mystery.* [< **rūn**, by 16.]
ge-sǣgan (113), *lay low.*
ge-sǣlan (113, 190), *happen, befall, chance.*
ge-sǣlig (57. 3), *delightful.* [Cf. Ger. *selig.*]
ge-samnian (-somnian) **(118)**, *gather.*
ge-scēadan (R. 110), *separate.*
ge-sceaft (51. b), *creature, creation.*
ge-scēawian (118), *behold.* [See **scēawian.**]
ge-scieldan (-scyldan) **(113)**, *defend, protect.* [Cf. **scield.**]
ge-scieldnes (51. 5), *defense, protection.*
ge-scieppan (VI. 107), *create.* [See **scieppan.**]

ge-scierpan (113), *clothe, apparel.*
ge-scierpla (-scirpla) **(53)**, *raiment, apparel.*
ge-scrēpe (59), *suitable, adapted.*
ge-scrifen (62), *prescribed, fixed, regular, customary.* [Past part. of **gescrīfan** < Lat. *scribo.*]
ge-scrȳdan (113, 16), *clothe.* [See **scrȳdan.**]
ge-scyldan, see **gescieldan.**
ge-sēcean (114), *visit, gain, touch, attain.* [See **sēcean.**]
ge-secgean (123), *say; give (thanks).* [See **secgean.**]
ge-sellan (114), *give.* [See **sellan.**]
ge-sendan (113), *send, throw.* [See **sendan.**]
ge-sēon (V. 106), *see;* **gesegen is**, *seems,* Lat. *videtur.*
ge-setennes (51. 5), *institute, ordinance.*
ge-setnes (51. 5), *narrative.*
ge-settan (113), *set, place; occupy; appoint, settle; compose.* [See **settan.**]
ge-sewenlic (57), *visible.*
ge-sīene (-sȳne) **(59)**, *visible.*
ge-sihð (51. 1), *countenance.*
ge-sittan (V. 106), *sit; possess, inherit.* [See **sittan.**]
ge-sīð (43), *companion.* [Cf. **sīð**, and Ger. *Gesinde.*]
ge-slēan (VI. 107), *smite, strike.* [See **slēan.**]
ge-smierwan (113), *anoint.*
ge-smyltan (113, 17), *calm.* [< **smolt**, *serene;* cf. **smylte.**]
gesomnian, see **gesamnian.**
ge-spann (47), *clasp, network.*
ge-spōwan (R. 109, 190), *succeed.*
ge-sprec (47), *conversation.* [Ger. *Gespräch;* cf. **sprecan.**]

ge-standan (VI. 107), *assail.*
[See standan.]

ge-staðelian (-staðolian) (118), *establish, render steadfast; restore.*

ge-staðolfæstian (-steaðulfestian) (118), *establish, perform.*

ge-stigan (I. 102), *ascend to.*
[See stigan.]

ge-stillan (113), *still, pacify, quiet; subside.* [See stillan.]

ge-strangian (118), *strengthen.*
[< strang.]

ge-stregdan (III. 104), *sprinkle.*

ge-strēon (47), *profit, gain.* [Cf. strēonan.]

ge-strēowian (118), *strew.*

ge-sund (58), *well.* [Ger. *gesund.*]

ge-swęncan (113), *torment, vex, wear out.* [See swęncan.]

ge-swęngan (113), *swinge, toss.*

ge-sweotolian (118), *manifest; bewray, expose, discover.* [< sweotol.]

ge-swęrian (VI. 107), *swear.*
[See swęrian.]

ge-swīcan (I. 102 ; 156. *k*), *cease; fail.* [See swīcan.]

ge-swinc (47), *toil, effort.* [Cf. swincan.]

ge-swing (47), *rolling, undulation.* [Cf. swingan.]

ge-syndig (57. 3), *fair, favoring, propitious.* [< gesund, by 16.]

gesȳne, see gesīene.

ge-syngian (118), *sin.* [Cf. synfull.]

getācnian (118), *signify, indicate.*
[See tācnian.]

ge-tācnung (51. 3), *sign.* [< tācen.]

ge-tǣcean (114), *point out, direct; appoint; teach.* [See tǣcean.]

ge-tæl (47), *reckoning.*

ge-tēon (II. 103), *bring up; play.*
[See tēon.]

ge-timbran (115. *b*), *furnish, supply* (lit. *construct*).

ge-trymman (115. *a*), *fortify.*
[See trymman.]

ge-ðanc (47), *thought, mind.*

ge-ðancol (-ðancul) (57), *considerate.* [See ðancolmōd, gearoðancol.]

ge-ðeaht (47), *counsel, advice.*

ge-ðeahtend (43. 6), *counsellor.*

ge-ðęncean (114), *remember.* [See ðęncean.]

ge-ðræc (47), *commingling, turbulence, tumult.*

ge-ðrǣstan (113), *afflict.*

ge-ðrēan (113), *dismay.* [See ðrēan.]

ge-ðrēatian (118), *rebuke.* [See ðrēatian.]

ge-ðring (47), *throng, rush.*

ge-ðungen (62), *excellent.* [< ðeon, thrive.]

ge-ðwǣrian (118), *agree.*

ge-ðwǣrnes (51. 5), *concord, agreement.*

ge-ðȳn (113), *restrain.*

ge-ðyncean (114), *seem, appear; geðūht is, seems.* [See ðyncean.]

ge-un-trumian (118), *enfeeble, debilitate, prostrate;* geuntrumod, *sick,* Lat. *infirmus.* [< untrum.]

ge-wǣgan (113), *plague, molest.*

ge-wǣtan (113), *wet, moisten.*

ge-wealc (47), *welter.*

ge-weald (47), *control, rule, dominion.* [Ger. *Gewalt;* see wealdend.]

ge-węndan (113), *turn; return, depart, go; translate.* [See węndan.]

ge-weorc (47), *work*. [See weorc.]

ge-weorp (47), *smiting*.

ge-weorðan (III. 104), *become, be; make; happen; convert*. [See weorðan.]

ge-weorðian (118), *distinguish*. [See weorðian.]

ge-wieldan (113), *rule, have dominion over*. [< geweald, by 16; see Mod. Eng. wield.]

ge-wiht (47), *weight*. [Ger. *Gewicht*.]

ge-wilnian (118; 156. *a*), *desire*. [See wilnian.]

ge-winn (47), *labor, toil; hardship, distress*. [See winnan.]

ge-winna (53), *enemy*. [See winnan.]

ge-winnfullic (57), *laborious, toilsome, fatiguing*.

ge-wislice (70, 76), *openly, plainly*.

ge-wissian (118), *guide, direct*.

ge-witan (126), *find out, learn*. [See witan.]

ge-wītan (I. 102; 184. *a*), *depart, go*.

ge-witt (47), *understanding*.

ge-writ (47), *writing, writ; letter; document, instrument, will*.

ge-wrītan (I. 102), *write*.

ge-wuna (53), *custom, wont*.

ge-wunian (118), *be wont, use; dwell*. [See wunian.]

ge-wyrcean (114), *make, build*. [See wyrcean.]

giefan (gifan) (V. 106, 18), *give*. [Ger. *geben*.]

giefeðe (gifeðe) (48), *chance*.

giefu (gifu) (51. *a*), *gift; boon*.

gieman (113; 156. *f*), *rule over*.

gīena (gēna), *yet*.

giernan (113), *desire; solicit (the hand of), woo*. [< georn, by 16.]

giest-hūs (47), *inn*. [Cf. Mod. Eng. *guest-chamber*.]

giestran-dæg (gystran-) (43), *yesterday*.

gīet (gīt, gȳt), *yet; still; as yet, hitherto*.

gif, *if*. [Not related to giefan.]

gifeðe, see giefeðe.

gifu, see giefu.

gim-cynn (47), *gems of every kind*.

gimm (43), *gem, precious stone*. [Borrowed from Lat. *gemma* before ca. 650.]

ginn (58), *spacious, ample*.

gingra (65, 53), *disciple*.

gīo, *formerly, long ago, once upon a time*. [See īu.]

gīt, see gīet.

glæs (47), *glass*.

glēaw (58), *prudent, wise*.

glēawlīce (70), *shrewdly, judiciously, wisely*. [*lishment*.

gleng (51. *b*), *adornment, embel-

glīdan (I. 102), *glide*. [Ger. *gleiten*.]

gōd (58, 5, 4), *good*. [Ger. *gut*.]

gōd (47), *prosperity;* plur., *goods, good things, property; benefactions*.

God (43, 5, 4), *God*. [Ger. *Gott;* according to Kluge, the 'Being invoked.']

god-cund (58), *divine*. [*godhead*.

god-cundnes (51. 5), *divinity,

godcundmiht (-mæht) (51. 1), *majesty*. [*Divine Father*.

God-Fæder (43. 8), *God-Father;*

god-spell (47), *gospel*.

gōd-webb (47), *purple*.

gold (47), *gold*.

gold-frætwa (51. *a*), plur., *golden ornaments.*

gold-hord (47), *treasure.*

gold-lēaf (47), *gold leaf.*

gǫng, see gang.

grǣg (58), *gray.* [Ger. *grau.*]

gram (57), *fierce, raging.*

gremman (115. *a*), *enrage.* [< gram, by 16.]

grēne (59), *green.* [Ger. *grün.*]

grēot (47), *dust; shingle.* [Ger. *Griess.*]

grētan (113), *greet, salute; take leave of.* [Ger. *grüssen.*]

grēwð, see grōwan.

grindan (III. 104), *whirl.* [Mod. Eng. *grind.*]

grōwan (R. 109), *grow.*

grund (43), *earth; bottom; sea* (perhaps orig. *shallow, shoal*). [Ger. *Grund,* Mod. Eng. *ground.*]

gryre-hwīl (51. *b*), *period of terror.*

gurron, see georran.

guma (53), *man, hero.* [Mod. Eng. *(bride)groom.*]

gūð (51. *b*; 30), *war.* [Ger. *-gund,* in *Hildegund,* e.g.; cf. *Gondibert.*]

gūð-fana (53), *gonfalon, standard.* [See Mod. Eng. *gonfalon;* cf. Ger. *Fahne,* Mod. Eng. *vane.*]

gūð-freca (53), *warrior.*

gūð-rinc (43), *warrior.*

gūð-sceorp (47), *war-trappings.*

gyden (51. *b*; 17), *goddess.*

gylden (146, 17), *golden.*

gystran-dæg, see giestran-dæg.

gȳt, see gīet.

H.

habban (121, 188), *have; possess; accept, keep; receive.* [Ger. *haben;* cf. Lat. *habere.*]

hād (43), *sex.*

hādor (57), *bright, serene.* [Ger. *heiter.*]

hǣl (47), *salvation; rescue, escape.* [Ger. *Heil.*]

Hǣlend (43. 6), *Saviour, Jesus.* [Ger. *Heiland.*]

hæleð (43. 9), *hero, man.* [Ger. *Held.*]

hǣlu (51. *a*), *salvation; rescue.*

hærfest (43), *harvest.* [Ger. *Herbst;* cf. Lat. *carpere,* Gr. καρπός.]

hærn (51. *b*), *ocean.*

hǣs (51. *b*), *order, direction, command.* [Cf. Mod. Eng. *behest,* Ger. *Geheiss.*]

hǣtu (51. *a*), *heat.* [hāt, by 16.]

hǣðen (57. 3), *heathen.* [Cf. Ger. *Heide,* and Mod. Eng. *heath;* so Lat. *paganus < pagus.*]

hāl (58), *whole, hale;* hāl gedōn, *save.* [Ger. *heil.*]

hālig (57. 3; 146), *holy.* [< hāl; Ger. *heilig.*]

hālsian (118), *conjure, implore, entreat.* [< hāl.]

hām (74, 24), *home.* [Ger. *heim.*]

hand (51. 1. 3), *hand.* [Ger. *Hand.*]

hār (58), *hoar(y), gray.*

hāt (58), *hot, fervent.* [Ger. *heiss.*]

hātan (R. 110), *call; command;* hātte, *is, was called.* [Ger. *heissen;* cf. archaic Eng. *hight.*]

hē (81).

hēa, see hēah.

hēa-clif (47), *lofty cliff.*

hēa-dēor (47), *high-deer.* [Cf. Ger. *Hochwild;* without a prefix, OE. *dēor* rarely, if ever, means 'deer.']

hēafod (47. 1, 6; 23), *head.* [Ger. *Haupt,* Lat. *caput,* for *cauput.*]

hēafod-ge-rīm (47), *number by heads, poll.*

hēah (hēa) (65 ; 58. 1 ; 17), *high ; great.* [Ger. *hoch.*]

hēah-cyning (43), *high king.*

hēah-ge-strēon (47), *sumptuous, superb treasure.* [See gestrēon.]

hēah-setl (hēah-) (47), *throne.*

hēah-stefn (58), *lofty-prowed.*

healdan (R. 109), *hold; observe, maintain; keep, reserve.* [Ger. *halten.*]

healf (51. *b*), *hand,* i.e. *side.*

healf (58), *half.* [Ger. *halb.*]

hēalic (57, 146), *lofty.*

heall (51. *b*), *hall.* [Ger. *Halle.*]

hēan (58), *lowly, servile, of low degree; poor.*

hēanes (51. 5), *height, highest point.*

hēanne, see hēah.

hēap (43), *crowd, swarm, throng, assemblage.* [Ger. *Haufe.*]

heard (58; 21. *a* ; 24), *brave, intrepid.* [Ger. *hart.*]

hearde (70), *painfully, grievously.*

hearm (43 ; 21. *a*), *injury.* [Ger. *Harm.*]

hearpe (53. 1 ; 21. *a*), *harp, lyre.* [Ger. *Harfe.*]

hearpe-nægl (43), *plectrum.*

hearpe-streng (43), *harpstring.*

hearpian (118, 90), *harp, play the harp.* [Ger. *harfen.*]

hēaðu-līðend (hēaðo-) (43. 6), *seafarer.*

hēaðu-rinc (hēaðo-) (43, 21), *warrior.*

hēaðu-wǣd (51. *b*), *warlike garment, martial weed.*

hēawan (R. 109), *hew, cleave.*

hebban (VI. 107), *elevate, lift; hebban ūp, be exalted.*

hefon, see heofon.

hefig (57), *grievous, irksome.*

hefigian (118), *become worse.*

hefignes (51. 5), *burden.*

hehðo, see hiehðu.

helan (IV. 105), *conceal.* [Cf. Chaucer, *Nun's Priest's Tale* 235; Ger. *hehlen.*]

hell (51. *b*), *hell.* [Ger. *Hölle.*]

helm (43), *helmet; protector.* [Ger. *Helm.*]

help (51. 5 ; 5), *help.* [Cf. Ger. *Hilfe.*]

hēo (81).

hēof (43), *mourning, weeping.*

heofon (43. 4. *d* ; 20), *heaven.*

heofon-candel (51. *b* ; 215), *candle of heaven.*

heofon-cyning (43), *king of heaven.*

heofone (53. 3), *heaven.*

heofon-fȳr (47), *celestial fire, fire from heaven.*

heofon-lēoma (53), *radiance of heaven.*

heofonlic (57), *heavenly, celestial, of heaven.*

heofonlice (70), *from heaven.*

heofon-rīce (48), *kingdom of heaven, heavenly kingdom.*

heofon-ðrymm (43), *glory of heaven.*

heolfrig (57), *gory.*

heolstor (47), *darkness.*

heonan (75), *hence.*

heorte (53. 1 ; 24 ; 21. *b*), *heart.* [Ger. *Herz.*]

hēr (75, 24), *here.* [Ger. *her.*]

hēr-æfter, *hereafter.*

here (44. 2 ; 18), *army, host.* [Ger. *Heer;* cf. Mod. Eng. *harbor, heriot.*]

here-folc (47), *army.*

here-pæð (herpað) (43), *highway.* [Cf. Ger. *Heerstrasse.*]

hęre-rēaf (47), *plunder. spoil.*

hęre-strǣt (51. *b*), *highway*, lit. *military road.* [Ger. *Heer-strasse.*]

hęre-wǣða (53), *warrior.*

hęrgian (118), *harry, ravage, lay waste.* [Ger. (*ver*)*heeren.*]

hęrian (116), *praise.*

hęriges, see hęre.

hęrpað, see hęrepæð.

hēt, see hātan.

hī (81).

hider (75), *hither.*

hiehsta, see hēah.

hiehðu (hēhðo) (51. *a*), *height, high.*

hīenan (113), *insult, oppress.* [<hēan, by 16.]

hīenð (51. *b*), *injury, harm.* [<hēan, by 16.]

hīeran (hȳran) (113, 117), *hear.*

hiera, hiere (81, 83).

hīernes (51. 5), *obedience.*

higerōf, see hygerōf.

hiht, see hyht.

hiium, see hīwan.

√ hild (51.5), *conflict, battle.* [Orig. Hild, goddess of war.]

hilde-lēoð (47), *battle-lay.*

hilde-nǣdre (53. 1; 215), *battle-adder, arrow.* [See *New Eng. Dict.* s.v. *adder.*]

hilde-wǣpen (47. 1), *battle-weapon.*

him, hine, his, hit (81, 83).

hin-gang (-iong) (43), *departure.* [Ger. *Hingang.*]

hīw (47), *kind; color.* [Cf. Spenser, *F. Q.* 3. 6. 33, 35.]

hīwan (53), plur. *brethren, brotherhood, conventual household, chapter.*

hlǣfdige (53. 1), *lady.* [Cf. p. 222, note 2.]

hlæst (47), plur., *wares, merchandise, cargo.* [Ger. *Last*; cf. hladan.]

hlāf (43), *bread; food.* [Archaic Ger. *Laib*; Mod. Eng. *loaf.*]

hlāford (43), *lord.* [< hlāf + weard.]

hlāford-lēas (58), *lordless, without a leader.*

hlāford-scipe (44. 1), *lordship, rule.*

hlanc (58), *lank, gaunt.*

hlēo (47. 3), *shelter; protector.* [Mod. Eng. *lee.*]

hlēotan (II. 103), *obtain, gain.* [Cf. Ger. *Loos*, Mod. Eng. *lot.*]

hlēoðor-cwide (44), *narrative, story; hymn.*

hlēoðrian (118), *speak; proclaim.*

hleoðu, see hlið.

hlifian (118), *tower.*

√ hlimman (hlymman) (III. 104), *resound.*

hlið (47, 20), *hill.*

hlōðian (118), *pillage, plunder.*

hlūde (70), *loudly.*

√ hlūtor (hlutter) (57), *pure, clear.*

√ hlymman, see hlimman.

hlynnan (115. *a*), *roar, boom.*

hōc (43), *hook.*

hof (47), *building, dwelling, abode.*

holm (43), *ocean, sea.*

holm-ðracu (51. *a*), *tossing of the sea, boisterous sea.*

holm-weard (43), *warden of the sea.*

√ holm-weg (43), *path of the ocean.*

holt (47), *grove, forest.* [Ger. *Holz*; cf. Chaucer, *Prol.* 6.]

hōlunga (70), *in vain.*

horig (57), *squalid.*

horn-boga (53), *bow of horn.*

horn-fisc (43), *sword-fish ?*

horn-scip (47), *beaked ship.*

hors (47, 31), *horse.* [Ger. *Ross.*]

hosp (43 ?), *reproach, abuse.*

hrædlice (70), *with speed ; immediately.*

hrædnes (51. 5), *celerity.*

hræfn (hrefn) (43), *raven.* [Ger. *Rabe.*]

hrǽw (47), *corpse.*

hran (43), *whale.*

hran-rād (hrǫn-) (51. *b*), *path of the whale.*

hraðe (70), *quickly.*

hrefn, see hræfn.

hrēmig (57 ; 174. *d*), *exulting.*

hrēoh (58), *rough, fierce, rude.*

hrēohnes (51. 5), *tempest.*

hrēosan (II. 103), *fall.*

hrēran (113), *agitate, toss.* [Ger. *rühren.*]

hring (43), *ring.* [Ger. *Ring.*]

hrōf (43, 24), *roof.*

hrǫnrād, see hranrād.

hrȳðer (47), plur., *cattle.*

hū, *how.*

hund (78, 79), *hundred.*

hund-seofontig (78), *seventy.*

hund-tēontig (78), *a hundred-(fold).*

hunger (43), *famine, starvation.* [Ger. *Hunger.*]

hungrig (57), *hungry, an hungered.* [Ger. *hungrig.*]

hup-seax (47), *hip-dagger.*

hūs (47), *house.* [Ger. *Haus.*]

hwā (88 ; 89. *c*), *who ; any one.*

hwæl (43. 2), *whale.* [Cf. Ger. *Wall(fisch).*]

√ hwæl-mẹre (44), *whale-mere, whale-sea.*

hwænne, see hwonne.

hwǽr (75), *where.*

hwæt, *what.*

hwæt-hwega (-hwugu) (89. *b* ; 154. *b*), *something.*

hwætlice (70, 76), *quickly.*

hwæðer, *whether.*

hwæðre (-ere), *yet, still, nevertheless.*

hwanan (hwanon) (75), *whence.*

hwaðerian (118), *rage.*

hwealf (58), *vaulted, hollow.*

hwelan (IV. 105), *roar, thunder.*

hwēol (47), *wheel.* [Cognate with Gr. κύκλος, Mod. Eng. *cycle,* (*bi*)*cycle.*]

√ hweorfan (hwyrfan) (III. 104), *return ; turn ; move.*

hwẹttan (113), *incite.*

hwider (75), *whither.*

hwīl (51. *b*), *while, time;* ðā hwile ðe, *the while that, while.*

hwilc (hwylc) (88 ; 89. *a*), *which, what ; any.*

hwīlum (72), *sometimes ; a while.* [Mod. Eng. *whilom ;* cf. Chaucer, *Knight's Tale* 1.]

hwōn, *somewhat, a little.*

hwone, see hwā.

hwonne (hwænne, hwænne), *when ; until.*

hwylc, see hwilc.

hwyrfan, see hweorfan.

hyge-rōf (hige-) (58), *valiant-souled.*

hyge-ðancol (57), *thoughtful-minded.*

hȳhsta, see hiehsta.

hyht (hiht) (43) *hope ; joy, gladness, bliss ; bent.*

√ hyldu (hyldo) (51. *a*), *kindness.* [Cf. Ger. *Huld.*]

hyngran (115. *b* ; 190), *hunger.*

hȳran, see hieran.

hyre, see hiere.

hyrned-nẹbb (58, 17), *horny-beaked.*

hyrst (51. *b*), *ornament.*

I.

ic (81).

īdel (57), *empty, void,* Lat. *inanis* (Auth. Vers. ' without form '). [Ger. *eitel;* cf. Shak., *Oth.* 1. 3. 140, ' deserts idle.']

īdelnes (51. 5), *idleness, indolence.*

ides (51. *b*), *maid, nymph, woman.* [From the Norse mythology we learn that this Germanic word signified 'demi-goddess,' or perhaps ' female guardian-angel,' as well as ' maid '; it was applied to giantesses and Norns, to heroic women, resembling the Valkyries, such as Brunhild and Gudrun, and to goddesses, such as Freyja. Cf. the remarks of Tacitus, *Germania* 8: "They even believe that the sex has a certain sanctity and prescience, and they do not despise their counsels, or make light of their answers. In Vespasian's days we saw Veleda, long regarded by many as a divinity."]

īe, see **ēa.**

īecan (ȳcan) (113, 33), *augment, aggravate.* [< **ēac.**]

ielde (ælde) (44. 4), plur. *men.*

ieldra, see **eald.**

ieldu (51. *a*; 19; 17), *age.* [Mod. Eng. *eld;* see Chaucer, *K.T.* 1589.]

ielfete (53. 1), *swan.*

ierfe (48), *inheritance.*

ierfe-land (47), *heritable land, inheritance.*

ierman (113), *afflict.* [< **earm,** by 16.]

iermðu (51. *a*), *poverty.* [< **earm;** see 144.]

iernan (III. 104, 31), *run; revolve.*

ierre (eorre) (48), *wrath.*

ierre (59), *wrathful.*

ierð (51. *b*), *field of corn, crop.*

ierðling (43, 143), *plowman, husbandman, farmer.*

īcð, see **ēaðe.**

īg-land (47), *island.*

ilca (86), *same.* [Cf. Chaucer, *Prol.* 64.]

in, prep., *in; into; by; through.*

in, adv., *in.*

in-beran (IV. 105), *carry in.*

in-gān (141), *enter.*

in-gangan (R. 109), *enter.*

in-ge-bringan (114), *bring in.*

innan, *within.*

inne (69), *within, inside.*

in-segel (47), *seal.* [Borrowed from Lat. *sigillum,* ca. A.D. 500; the form *sigil* is earlier, ca. 400.]

in-sittan (V. 106), *sit within.*

intinga (53), *cause; account.*

in-tō, *into.*

in-weardlice (70), *fervently, ardently.*

īsern (47), *iron.* [Ger. *Eisen.*]

īsern (57), *iron.*

īu (see gīo), *of old, formerly.*

L.

lā, *indeed, O.*

lāc (47), *present, gift.*

lācan (R. 110), *bound, leap, toss; sail.*

lād (51. *b*), *way, journey.*

lǣce-cræft (43), *remedy.* [Mod. Eng. *leechcraft;* cf. Spenser, *F. Q.* 3. 3. 18.]

lǣdan (113), *lead, bring, take; carry; produce.* [Ger. *leiten.*]

Lǣden (47), *Latin.*

lǣran (113, 17), *teach, direct.*

lǣring-mǣden (47), *pupil.*

lǣs (51. *b*, but irregular; the termination -**we** as in **beadu**, 51. *a*), *pasture.* [Archaic Mod. Eng. *leasow.*]

lǣs, lǣs(es)t, see **lȳtel**, and **ðȳ-lǣs-ðe.**

lǣstan (113), *carry out, perform, do.* [Ger. *leisten*, Mod. Eng. *last.*]

Lǣstinga ēa, *Lastingham* (near Whitby).

lǣtan (R. 110), *let, allow.* [Ger. *lassen.*]

lǣðð'u (51. *a*), *affliction.* [<**lāð**, by 16.]

lāf (51. *b*), *remnant;* **tō lāfe**, *left.*

lago-, see **lagu-**.

lagu (45), *ocean, sea.*

√ **lagu-fæsten** (47), *ocean, deep.*

lagu-flōd (lago-) (43), *sea-flood.*

lagu-lād (lago-) (51. *b*), *ocean-journey.*

lagu-strēam (43), *ocean-stream.*

lām (43), *dust* (lit. *loam*). [Ger. *Lehm;* more remotely cognate (ablaut relation) with Lat. *limus.*]

lamb (50), *lamb.*

land (47, 24), *land, country;* **hēr on lande**, *in this country.* [Ger. *Land*, and cf. *hier zu Lande.*]

land-būend (lond-) (43. 6), *dweller in the land.*

land-ge-mǣre (48), *border.*

land-scearu (51. *a*), *land.*

lang (58, 65), *long.* [Ger. *lang.*]

lange (70, 77), *long* (of time).

lang-sweored (57), *long-necked.* [Cf. Koch, *Gram.* III. 71; Mätzner, I. 470.]

lār (51. *b*), *study; instruction, teaching; counsel, guidance.* [Ger. *Lehre*, Mod. Eng. *lore.*]

lārēow (43), *teacher, master; learned man.* [<**lār** + **ðeow**.]

lāst (43), *track, footprint.* [Mod. Eng. *last* (for shoes), Ger. *Leiste(n).*]

lāttēowdōm (43, 14), *guidance.* [Cf. the etymology of **lārēow**.]

lāð (58), *hostile; hateful.*

laðian (118), *summon.* [Ger. (*ein*)*laden.*]

lēad (47), *lead.* [Ger. *Lot.*]

lēaf (51. *b*), *leave, permission.* [Ger. (*Ur*)*laub*, (*Er*)*laub*(*niss*).]

lēaf (47), *leaf.* [Ger. *Laub.*]

leahtor (43), *sin, iniquity.*

lēan (43), *reward, recompense.* [Ger. *Lohn.*]

lęcgean (115, note), *place, put, set.* [From the second stem (92) of **licgan**, by 16; Ger. *legen*, Mod. Eng. *lay.*]

lęnctenlic (57), *vernal.*

lęncten-tid (51. 1), *spring.* [Cf. Ger. *Lenz*, Mod. Eng. *Lent.*]

lęng, see **lange**.

lęngra, see **lang**.

lęngu (51. *a*), *length.*

lēo (Lat.), *lion.*

lēoda (lēode) (44. 4), plur., *people.* [Ger. *Leute.*]

lēod-mearc (51. *b*), *region.* [Cf Mod. Eng. *margrave, Marcl, marquis.*]

lēof (58, 64, 165), *dear, beloved;* sb. *sir, master;* com dearer, preferable. [Ger. *liet* Mod. Eng. *lief, lieve;* cf. Spense F. Q. 3. 2. 33.]

leofa, see **libban**.

lēofwęnde (59), *friendly;* **lēofwęndum**, *ardently, fervently.*

lēoht (47), *light.* [Ger. *Licht.*]

lēoht (58), *bright, radiant.* [Ger. *licht.*]

lēoht-fruma (53), *author of light ;* for līfes lēohtfruma cf. Jn. 8. 12, Acts 3. 15. [Cf. fruma.]

lēoma (53), *light, radiance, brightness.*

leomu, see lim.

leornian (118), *learn.* [Ger. *lernen.*]

leornung (51. 3), *study.* [Mod. Eng. *learning.*]

lēoð (47), *poetry, verse.* [Ger. *Lied.*]

lēt, see lǣtan.

✓ libban (122), *live.* [Ger. *leben.*]

✓ licgan (V. 106), *lie ; rest.* [Ger. *liegen.*]

līc-hama (53), *body.* [hama = *shape, cover ;* cf. Ger. *Leichnam.*].

līc-ham-lēas (58, 146), *bodiless, incorporeal.*

līc-hamlic (57), *bodily.*

līcian (118 ; 164. *k*), *please.* [Mod. Eng. *like ;* cf. Spenser, *F. Q.* 2. 7. 27.]

✓ lid (47), *vessel, craft, bark.* [Cf. līðan.]

lid-weard (43), *shipmaster.*

lid-wērig (57), *weary with voyaging.*

līefan (113), *allow, permit.* [< af ; Ger. (*er*)*lauben.*]

... 3), *thunderbolt, levin.*

..egᴜᴜ (47. 7), *lightning.*

.lehting (51. 3), *lighting, illumination.* [< lēoht, by 16.]

.lf (47), *life.* [Ger. *Leib.*]

lifde, lifgende, see libban.

līflic (57), *of life.* [Ger. *leiblich ;* cf. Spenser, *F. Q.* 2. 7. 20.]

lim (47, 20), *limb, bough, branch.*

lind (51. *b*), *linden shield, shield.*

lind-wīgend (-wiggend) (43. 6), *shield-warrior.*

liss (51. *b*), *gentleness, tenderness ;* (mid) lissum, *gently, tenderly.*

līðan (I.102), *set out ; sail, cruise.*

līðe (59, 30), *good, obliging, friendly ; gentle, mild.* [Ger. (*ge*)*lind ;* cf. Spenser, *Virgil's Gnat* 221.]

līðe (70), *gently.*

loc (47), *lock.*

locen, see lūcan.

lōcian (118), *look.*

lof (43), *honor, praise ;* in lofe, *praising.* [Ger. *Lob.*]

loft (47), *air, sky.*

lond-, see land-.

lor (47), *destruction ;* tō lore weorðan, *perish.*

lūcan (II. 103), *link ? weave ? close ?*

lufe (53. 1), *love.* [adore.]

lufian (118, 119), *love ; worship,*

lufiend (43. 6), *lover.*

lufiendlic (57), *loving.*

luflice (70), *dear.*

lufu (51. *a*; 53. 3; 24), *love.*

lungre, *speedily.*

lust (43), *joy, desire, longing.* [Ger. *Lust ;* cf. Spenser, *F. Q.* 4. 4. 44.]

lyfdon, see libban.

lyft (47 ; 51. *b*), *air ;* under lyfte, cf. our 'under the sun.' [Cf. Ger. *Luft.*]

lyre (44), *loss.* [Stem formed from that of the third stem of lēosan, *lose*, by 16.]

lystan (113), *list, like, cause enjoyment.* [< lust, by 16 ; cf. Spenser, *F. Q.* 2. 7. 18, 19.]

lȳt (3 (*but*) *few*.

lȳt, : .., (*but*) *little.*

lȳtel (57, 66), *little ;* comp. *less*(*er*) *smaller ;* superl. *least.*

lȳt-hwōn (58), (*but*) *few.*

M.

mā (77), *more, further; rather.*

mā-cræftig (57), *very expert? expert in seamanship?* [In favor of the latter may be quoted Grimm's note in his edition of *Andreas und Elene*, p. 103: "257. mācräftig, und nochmals A. 472 der comparativ mācräftigra. daher es selbst unpassend aus dem comparativ mā, magis gedeutet würde, der sonst nirgends und in keinem andern dialect bei zusammensetzungen verstärkt. Auch scheint der sinn etwas bestimmteres zu fordern, ein des meeres, der schiffahrt kundig; ich vermute ein altes subst. mā, synonym und wurzel von mere, mācräftig = merecräftig."]

mādm, see **māðm.**

mæcg, see **męcg.**

mǣden (47, 38, 28), *girl, maiden, damsel.*

mæg, see **mugan.**

✓**mægen** (47. 1), *power, strength; virtue; force, band.* [Eng. *main.*]

mægen-ēacen (57), *abundant in might, powerful.*

mægen-ðrymm (43), *glory, majesty.*

mægen-ðrymnes (51. 5), *glory, majesty.*

mǣgð (51. b), *tribe, nation, province.*

mægð (52), *maid, maiden.* [Ger. *Magd.*]

mægð-hād (43, 143), *virginity.*

mǣg-wlite (44), *appearance, aspect.* [Cf. **andwlita.**]

mǣlan (113), *speak.*

mǣre (59), *renowned; splendid; great.*

mǣrðu (51. a), *achievement, famous exploit.* [Cf. **mǣre.**]

mæsling (47), *brass.*

mæsse-prēost (43), *priest.* [**mæsse** < Lat. *missa, mass;* **prēost** < *presbyter,* from what Greek word?]

mæst (43), *mast.*

mǣst, see **micel.**

mæð (51. b), *ability, capacity.*

mæðel-hēgende (meðel-) (61), *speech-uttering, council-attending.*

mǣw (43), *gull, sea-mew.* [Ger. *Möwe.*]

magan, see **mugan.**

magu-ðegn (43), *vassal, retainer.*

man (89. e), *one.*

mān-full (58. 2), *wicked, evil.*

mangere (44, 143), *merchant.* [Mod. Eng. *-monger.*]

manian (118), *admonish.*

manig (57), *many.*

manig-feald (58, 146), *manifold.*

mann (mǫnn) (46, 35, 17), *man.* [Ger. *Mann;* cf. Tacitus, *Germania,* Ch. II., and the proper name Manu.]

manna (53; cf. 53. 3), *man.*

mann-cynn (man-) (47), *mankind.*

mān-scyld (-scild) (51. b), *sin, iniquity.*

māra, see **micel.**

marman-stān (43), *marble.*

māðm (43), *treasure, jewel.*

meahte, see **mugan.**

meahtig, see **mihtig.**

męcg (mæcg) (43), *disciple* (lit. *man*).

mēd (51. b), *meed, reward.* [Cf. **meorð.**]

med-micel (57), *short.*

medome (meodume) (59), *little,
least.*

medu-burg (medo-) (52), *mead-
city.* [Cf. Ger. *Met.*]

medu-wērig (medo-) (57), *mead-
weary, drunken with mead.*

menigu (51. *a*), *company, number.* [Ger. *Menge;* cf. Spenser,
F. Q. 1. 12. 9.]

mennisc (57, 146), *human.*
[< mann, by 16; cf. Ger.
Mensch.]

meodume, see medome.

meorð (51. *b*), *reward.* [Cf.
mēd.]

meotud (43), *creator.* [As it
were, the 'Meter,' 'Appor-
tioner,' 'Fixer of Bounds.']

mere (44), *mere, sea.* [Ger. *Meer;*
cf. Mod. Eng. *mermaid.*]

mere-bāt (43), *sea-boat, vessel.*

mere-faroð (43), *sea-waves (sea-
voyage?).*

meregreote (53), *pearl.*

mere-liðend (43. 6) *seafarer.*

mere-strēam (43), *ocean-stream.*

mere-swīn (47), *dolphin.*

mere-ðissa (-ðyssa) (53), *ocean-
scourer, rusher through the deep.*

mergen (43), *morning.*

mētan (113), *meet; find; find
out.*

mete (44), *food.* [Mod. Eng.
meat.]

mēðe (59), *fatigued, weary.* [Ger.
müde.]

meðel-, see mæðel-.

micel (mycel) (57), *much, great,
large; long; loud.* [Cf. Scotch
mickle, Eng. *much,* and Spenser,
Shep. Cal., Feb. 109.]

miclum (myclum) (72), *greatly.*

mid (57; 166. 1), *middle.*

mid (168; 172. 1; 177), *with;*
mid ealle (175), *completely.*

middan-geard (43), *world.* [Cf.
Cleasby and Vigfusson's *Ice-
landic-English Dictionary,* s.v.
mið-garðr: "The earth (Miðgarð), the abode of men, is
seated in the middle of the uni-
verse, bordered by mountains
and surrounded by the great sea
(úthaf); on the other side of
this sea is the Út-garð (*out-
yard*), the abode of giants; the
Miðgarð is defended by the
'yard' or 'burgh' As-garð (*the
burgh of the gods*), lying in the
middle (the heaven being conceived as rising above the earth).
Thus the earth and mankind are
represented as a stronghold be-
sieged by the powers of evil from
without, defended by the gods
from above and from within."]

mid-ðām-ðe, *when.*

mid-ðȳ, *when, while.*

mid-ðȳ ðe, *when, while.*

miht (51. 1), *power, might.* [Ger.
Macht.]

miht, see mugan.

mihtig (57), *mighty.* [Ger. *mächt-
ig.*]

mild-heortnes (51. 5), *mercy,
compassion, loving-kindness.*

milts (51. 5), plur. as sing., *mercy,
loving-kindness.* [< mild, *mild,*
by 33.]

miltsian (mildsian) (118), *have
mercy upon.*

min (83, 81), *my.*

mis- (142).

mislic (57), *various.*

mislice (70), *variously, in different ways;* mislice geblēod,
variegated.

mis-līcian (118), *displease.*

missenlic (57), *various (kinds of).*

mis-ꝺyncean (114; 164. *l*), *misjudge;* ꝺē misꝺyncꝺ, Lat. *male suspicaris.* [Cf. Milton, *P. L.* 9. 289, Shak., *3 Hen. VI.* 2. 5. 108, *Ant. and Cleop.* 5. 2. 176.]

mōd (47, 146), *heart, soul, mind; courage.* [Ger. *Mut.*]

mōd-ge-ꝺanc (43), *thought of the heart, counsel.* [Cf. Ger. *Gedanke.*]

√mōdig (57), *noble-minded, magnanimous, courageous.* [Ger. *mutig.*]

mōdiglīc (57), *high-souled.*

mōdlignes (51. 5), *pride, arrogance.*

mōdor (52. 2), *mother.* [Ger. *Mutter,* Lat. *mater.*]

mōna (53), *moon.* [Cf. Ger. *Mond,* where *d* is a late addition.]

mōnaꝺ (43. 4. *a*), *month.* [Ger. *Monat.*]

mǫn(n), see man(n).

morgen (43), *morning.* [Ger. *Morgen,* Mod. Eng. *morn.*]

morgen-giefu (51. *a*), *dowry, marriage portion.*

morꝺor (47), *deadly injury.* [Mod. Eng. *murder.*]

mōtan (137), *may.* [Cf. Spenser, *F. Q:* 1. 9. 27.]

mugan (135), *can, be able.*

mund (51. 5), *hand.*

munt (43), *mountain.* [Lat. *mont(em).*]

munuc (43), *monk.* [Ger. *Mönch.*]

murcnung (51. *b*; 144), *sorrow, unhappiness, lamentation.*

muscule (Lat.), *mussel.*

mycel, see micel.

myclum, see miclum.

myngian (118), *admonish, ad jure.*

mynian (118), *direct, inspire.*

mynster (47), *monastery.*

N.

nā (nō), *not even, by no means, not at all; no.*

nabban (121, 29), *have not.*

naca (53), *bark.* [Ger. *Nachen.*]

nacod (57), *naked; clothed in a tunic only* (p. 168).

nǣdl (51. *b*), *needle.* [Ger. *Nadel.*]

nǣdre, nǣddre (53. 1), *serpent.*

nǣfre, *never.*

nǣnig (89. *a*), *no one.*

nǣre, nǣron, nǣs, see 138.

nāht (nōht) (47; 89. *b*; 27), *naught, nothing; not.*

nā-hwǣr, *nowhere.*

nā-hwider, *nowhither.*

nālæs (nālas), *not at all.*

nama (53, 24), *name.* [Ger. *Namen.*]

nān (89. *a*; 154. *b*), *no (one).*

nāt, see 126.

nātes-hwōn, *not at all.*

ne (ni), *not.*

nē, *nor;* nō ... nē (202), *neither ... nor.*

nēah (58, 67, 60), *nigh, near;* æt niehstan, *at length, finally.*

nēah, adv., *near, nigh at hand;* superl. *nearly.*

nēah (nēh), prep., *near.*

nēa-lǣcan (113), *approach.*

nearunes (nearo-) (51. 5), *anguish, agony.*

nearu (51. *a*), *difficulty;* nearu ꝺrōwian, *be in straits.* [Cf. Mod. Eng. *narrow.*]

nēat (47), *cattle.* [Cf. Mod. Eng. ·neatherd,' 'neat's-foot oil,' 'neat cattle.' Shakespeare has (*Wint. T.* 1. 2. 124) : 'The steer, the heifer, and the calf Are all called *neat; Cymb.* 1. 1. 148: 'Would I were A *neatherd's* daughter.']

nefne, *except.*

nēh, see nēah, prep.

nellan (139), *will not.* [See Chaucer, *Prol.* 550, Spenser, *F. Q.* 1. 6. 17 ; 1. 9. 15, Shak., *Haml.* 5. 1. 19.]

nemnan (115. *b*), *mean* (lit. *name*).

nēosian (nēosan) (118 ; 156. *m*), *seek, look for.*

nēowolnes (51. 5), *abyss, deep.* [Orig. from nihol-, *nihold-, *nihald-, *sloping.*]

neriend (neregend) (43. 6), *Savior.*

nīed (51. *b*), *need, necessity; use.*

nīed-faru (nēid-) (51. *a*), *needful journey.*

nīed-ðearflic (57), *needful, necessary.*

nīehst, see nēah, adv.

nīehsta, see nēah, adj.

nīeten (47. 1), *creature, beast, cattle.* [<nēat, by 16.]

nīeten-cynn (47), *kind of cattle.*

niht (52), *night.*

nihtes (74), *by night.*

niht-lang (58), *night-long, of a night, one night.*

nihtlic (57), *night.*

niman (IV. 105), *take; seize; capture, catch; pluck up.* [Ger. *nehmen;* cf. a character in .ak., *M. W.*]

nis, see 138.

nið (43), *man.*

niðerlic (57), *low-lying.* [Cf. Ger. *nieder.*]

nīð-hete (44), *malignant foe.*

nīð-hycgende (61), *evil-scheming.*

nīð-plega (53), *hostile play, martial game.*

nō, see nā.

nōht, see nāht.

noldon, see nellan.

norð (69), *northward.*

norðan, *from the north.*

norð-dæl (43), *northern part, north.*

notian (118; 164. *o*), *use.*

nū, *now; yet.*

nyste, see nytan.

nytan (126), *know not.* [See Chaucer, *Prol.* 284.]

O.

of- (142).

of, *of; from; out of; by.*

ofen (43), *oven.*

ofer, *over; across; upon; in.*

ofer- (142). [Ger. *über-.*]

ofer-brædan (113), *suffuse.*

ofer-cuman (IV. 105), *overcome, overthrow.*

ofer-gān (141), *overcome, come upon.*

ofer-hygd (51. *b*), *pride, arrogance;* mid oferhygdum, *arrogantly, haughtily, superciliously.*

ofer-rædan (113), *read through.*

ofer-swiðan (113), *overcome, conquer.*

ofer-ðeccean (114), *cover over.*

ofer-winnan (III. 104), *conquer, subdue, overthrow.*

ofer-wrēon (I. 102), *cover over.*

ofestlice (ofost-, ofst-) (70), *quickly, forthwith.*

ofet (47), *fruit.* (Ger. *Obst,* properly *Obs.*]

ofostlice, see ofestlice.

of-slēan (VI. 107), *slay, kill.*

of-stīgan (I. 102), *descend.*

ofstlice, see ofestlice.

oft, *often, frequently.*

of-tredan (V. 106), *tread down, trample upon.* [Ger. *abtreten.*]

of-ðyncean (114), *offend, grieve, vex.*

ōht, see āht.

olfend (43), *camel.* [<Lat. *elephantem ?*]

on, *on, upon ; in ; into ; with ;* on ān, see ān.

on- (142).

on-ǣlan (113), *inflame.*

on-cierran (-cyrran) (113), *turn.*

on-cnāwan (R. 109), *know ; perceive ; recognize ; acknowledge.*

on-cweðan (V. 106), *address, call unto.*

ond(-), see and(-).

on-drǣdan (R. 110 ; 159. *a*), *fear.*

ōnettan (113), *hasten, hurry.*

on-fangennes (51. 5), *reception.*

on-fōn (R. 110 ; 164. *j*), *receive, accept.*

on-gēan, adv., *again, back.*

on-gēan, prep., *against ; toward ; opposite.* [Cf. Ger. *entgegen,* for *engegen.*]

on-ge-slēan (VI. 107), *slay.*

on-gierwan (113), *divest, strip.* [Cf. geare.]

on-gietan (-gitan) (V. 106, 18), *perceive, learn, understand.* [Cf. andgiet.]

ongin, see anginn.

on-ginnan (III. 104), *begin.*

ongitan, see ongietan.

on-hieldan (-hǣldan) (113), *intend.*

on-hrēosan (II. 103), *fall upon.*

on-hrēran (113), *stir up, agitate.*

on-innan, *into, among.*

onlīc, see anlīc.

on-liehtan (113), *light, illuminate.* [<lēoht, by 16.]

on-līesan (113), *release.*

on-lūcan (II. 103), *unlock.*

on-sendan (113), *send.*

on-settan (113), *lay.*

on-spannan (R. 109), *open.*

on-styrian (116), *move.*

on-tȳnan (113), *open.* [<tūn, by 16.]

on-wacan (VI. 107), *awake.*

on-weg, *away.*

on-windan (III. 104), *retreat.* [Cf. Ger. *entwinden.*]

on-winnan (III. 104), *assail.*

on-wrīðan (I. 102), *uncover, disclose.*

on-wunian (118), *inhabit.*

open (57), *open.* [Ger. *offen.*]

ōr (47), *beginning.*

or- (142).

ōra (53), *vein ? ore ?*

ōreta, see ōretta.

ōret-mecg (-mæcg) (43), *warrior.*

ōretta (53), *combatant.*

orf (47), *cattle.*

or-feorme (59), *deprived, abandoned, forsaken.*

organa (Lat.), plur., *organs.*

or-giete (-gete) (59), *manifest.*

or-mǣte (59), *boundless ; enormous.*

or-mōdnes (51. 5), *despair, desperation.*

oroð (47. 6), *breath.*

ort-geard (43), *garden (orchard ?).*

orðian (118), *breathe.* [<oroð.]

ōð, *until.*

ōð- (142).

ōðer (80; 89. a; 24), other; second; rest of.

ōð-ðæt, until.

oððe (æðða), or.

ōð-ðringan (III. 104), wrest away.

P.

pæll (43), purple garment.

pard (Lat.), panther.

pening (43), penny (but this does not represent the Latin, which has sestertia, not sestertios; the latter would represent four cents each, the former about forty-three dollars each). [Cf. Ger. Pfand.]

Piht (43), Pict.

plega (53), game, play.

√plegian (118), play; act.

pliht (43), peril, risk. [Ger. Pflicht, Mod. Eng. plight.]

pund (47), pound, Lat. talentum, pondus. [< Lat. pondus.]

purpre (53. 1), purple garment. [< Lat. purpura.]

R.

racian (118; 164. i), rule, govern, sway.

rǣd (43), counsel, advice; order(s); benefit. [Ger. Rat; archaic Mod. Eng. rede; cf. Shak., Haml. 1. 3. 51.]

rǣdan (113), read. [Cf. Ger. (er)raten.]

rǣd-snottor (57), discreet in counsel.

√rǣs-bora (53), counselor.

rǣswa (53), chief, leader.

rāh-dēor (47), roebuck.

√raud (rǫnd) (43), shield.

rand-wīgend (-wiggend) (43. 6), shield-warrior.

rēad (58), red. [Ger. rot.]

rēaf (47), raiment, apparel. [Ger. Raub, Mod. Eng. robe, through Fr. robe; cf. Ital. roba.]

rēaf-lāc (47), rapine, plunder.

reccean (114), relate, narrate; expound.

rēce-lēasian (118, 156), despise.

recene, straightway.

regn (rēn) (43), rain; shower. [Ger. Regen.]

regollic (57), regular. [< Lat. regula; cf. Ger. regel(recht).]

rēn, see regn.

rēocan (II. 103), reek. [Ger. riechen.]

reord-berend (43. 6), man gifted with speech (lit. speech-bearer).

reordian (-igan) (118), speak. √

rest (51. b), couch, bed. [Cf. Ger. Rast.]

restan (113), rest.

rēðe (59), fierce, violent.

rēðnes (51. 5), violence.

ribb (47), rib.

rice (48.1), kingdom. [Ger. Reich, Mod. Eng. (Frede)rick, (Hen)ry, (bishop)ric; cf. Lat. rex.]

rīce (59), powerful, noble. [Ger. reich, Mod. Eng. rich.]

rīcsian (118), bear rule, have dominion. [< rīce.]

riht (47), right. [Ger. Recht.]

riht (58), right; direct. [Ger. recht.]

rihtlice (70), accurately, correctly.

riht-wīs (58, 146), righteous.

riht-wīsnes (51. 5), righteousness.

rīnan (113, 161), rain.

rinc (43), warrior, man.

rīpe (59), ripe. [Ger. reif.]

rōd (51. *b*), *cross*. [Ger. *Rute*, Mod. Eng. *rod*, *rood;* cf. *rood-loft, Holyrood, Haml.* 3. 4. 14.]

rodor (43), *firmament, heaven.*

rōf (59), *stout.*

Romanisc (57, 146), *Roman.*

Romane (Lat.), plur., *Romans.*

√rǫnd, see rand.

rōse (53. 1), *rose.* [Lat. *rosa.*]

rōwan (R. 109), *row.*

rōwend (43. 6), *rower.*

rōwnes (51. 5), *rowing.*

rudu (51. *a*), *redness.*

rūm (43), *room, opportunity.* [Ger. *Raum.*]

rūwe (53. 1), *tapestry ?*

S.

sācerd (51. *b*), *priestess.* [< Lat. *sacerdos.*]

sǣ (43; 51. *b*), *sea.* [Ger. *See;* cf. note, p. 324.]

sǣ-bāt (43), *sea-boat, vessel.*

sǣ-beorg (43), *sea-cliff.*

sǣd (47), *seed.* [Ger. *Saat.*]

sǣd-tīma (53), *seedtime.*

√sǣ-flota (53), *sea-floater.*

sǣ-hengest (43), *sea-steed.* [Cf. Ger. *Hengst,* Eng. *Hengist.*]

sǣ-holm (43), *sea* (*swelling sea?*).

sǣ-lād (51. *b*), *sea-voyage.*

sǣleoda, see sǣlida.

sǣlic (57), *marine, of the sea.*

sǣ-lida (-leoda) (53), *seaman, sailor, mariner.* [Cf. līðan.]

sǣ-mearh (43), *sea-steed.* [Cf. Jebb, *Classical Greek Poetry,* pp. 91–92: "Homer speaks of 'swift ships, which are the horses of the sea for men'; Hesiod would not have scrupled to use the phrase 'horses of the sea' as a substitute for the word 'ships,' leaving his meaning to be guessed."]

sǣ-werig (57), *sea-weary.*

sǣ-wiht (51. *b*), *sea-animal.*

salowig-pād (58), *dark-coated.*

samninga (70), *all at once, suddenly.* [Cf. semninga.]

samod (somod), *together.*

sand (47), *sand.* [Ger. *Sand.*]

sand-hlið (47, 20), *sand-hill.*

sang (43), *song.* [Ger. (*Ge*)*sang.*]

sār (47), *sorrow.*

sār (58), *grievous, sore.* [Cf. Ger. *sehr,* (*ver*)*sehren.*]

sār-cwide (44), *taunt, gibe, raillery, sarcasm.*

sārlic (57), *doleful.*

sārlice (70), *lamentably, mournfully.*

sārnes (51. *b*), *grief, unhappiness.*

sāw(o)l (51. 4), *soul; life.* [Ger. *Seele.*]

sāwol-lēas (58, 146), *soulless.*

sceadu (51. *a*; 18), *shadow.* [Cf. Ger. *Schatten.*]

sceal, see sculan.

scealc (43, 18), *man.*

sceam-fæst (58, 18), *modest.* [Mod. Eng. *shamefast;* see Spenser, *F. Q.* 5. 5. 25.]

sceamu (51. *a*; 18), *shame.* [Ger. *Scham.*]

scēap (47, 18), *sheep.* [Ger. *Schaf.*]

scēap-hierde (44), *shepherd.* [Ger. *Schafhirt.*]

scearpe (70, 18), *sharp.* [Ger. *scharf.*]

scēat (43), *corner, region, quarter.* [Ger. *Schooss;* in the sense of Lat. *angulus, plaga,* as Isa. 11. 12, Rev. 7. 1.]

sceatt (43, 18), *coin.* [Ger. *Schatz.*]

scēað (51. *b*; 18), *sheath*. [Ger. *Scheide*.]

sceaða (53, 18), *enemy*. [Cf. Ger. *Schade*, *Schädiger*, Mod. Eng. *scathe*.]

scēawian (118), *watch; behold, see*. [Ger. schauen, Mod. Eng. *show* (with changed meaning).]

scęncan (113), *pour out, give to drink*. [Ger. (*ein*)*schenken*, archaic Mod. Eng. *skink;* cf. Shak., *1 Hen. IV.* 2. 4. 26.]

sceolde, see sculan.

scēor (18), see scūr.

sceort (58, 65, 18), *short*.

scēotend (43. 6), *shooter, marksman*.

scēo-wyrhta (53, 18), *shoemaker*.

sciccels (43), *cloak, mantle*.

scield (scild) (43, 18), *shield*.

scield-burh (scild-) (52, 28), *testudo, roof of shields, shield-roofed phalanx*.

sciene (scȳne) (59, 18), *beautiful*. [Ger. *schön;* cf. Chaucer, *K. T.* 210, Spenser, *F. Q.* 2. 1. 10.]

scieppan (VI. 107, 18), *create*. [Ger. *schöpfen*.]

scieppend (scippend, scyppend) (43. 6; 18), *creator*.

scieran (IV. 105, 18), *cut, cleave*. [Ger. *scheren*, Mod. Eng. *shear*.]

sciertra, see sceort.

scīete (53. 1), *sheet, linen cloth*. [< scēat.]

scild, see scield.

scīnan (I. 102), *shine*. [Ger. *scheinen*.]

scip (47), *ship*. [Ger. *Schiff*.]

scip-fērend (43. 6; 147), *sailor*.

scip-here (44. 2; 147), *naval force, fleet*.

scippend, see scieppend.

scip-weard (43), *shipmaster*.

scīr (58), *bright, gleaming*. [Cf. Spenser, *F. Q.* 3. 2. 44, Shak., *Rich. II.* 5. 3. 61.]

scīre (70), *dazzlingly, radiantly*.

scīr-mǣled (57), *splendidly marked, splendidly decorated*.

scop (43), *minstrel*.

Scottas (43), plur., *Scots*.

scrid (57), *fleet?* (Grimm, *rigged*).

scrūd (47), *clothing, raiment, attire*. [Mod. Eng. *shroud*.]

scrȳdan (113), *clothe, array*.

scucca (53), *the devil, Satan*.

scūfan (II. 103), *thrust*.

sculan (133, 188), *ought, must; shall*. [Cf. Ger. *sollen*.]

scūr (scēor) (43, 18), *storm; shower*. [Ger. *Schauer*.]

scȳne, see sciene.

scyppend, see scieppend.

se (84; 87; 154. *b*).

sealm (43), *psalm*. [< Lat. *psalmus*.]

sealt-sēað (43), *salt-spring*.

sēamere (44. 1; 143), *tailor*. [Cf. Ger. *Saum*, Mod. Eng. *seam*.]

searu (49), *device, contrivance*.

searu-ðancol (searo-ðǫncol) (57), *discerning, sagacious*.

sēcean (sēcan) (114), *seek; seek out; visit*. [Ger. *suchen*.]

sęcg (43), *man, hero*.

sęcgean (sęcgan) (123, 36), *say; speak; tell*.

sedl, see setl.

segl (47?), *sail*. [Ger. *Segel*.]

seld-cūð (58), *strange, novel, out of the way*. [Cf. *F. Q.* 4. 8. 14.]

sęlen (51. *b*), *bounty, bestowal*.

self (seolf, sylf) (86), (*my, him*) *self; own; same; very*. [Ger. *selb*(*er*).]

sęllan (syllan) (114, 36), *give; give to be; sell*.

sēlest (sēlost) (66), *best.*

sellic (syllīc) (57), *strange, queer, remarkable.* [< seldīc.]

sēlost (76), *best.*

sēlra (53, 66), *better.*

sęmninga (70), *suddenly.* [See samninga.]

sęndan (113), *send; hurl.*

sēo, see se.

seofon (78, 20), *seven.* [Ger. *sieben.*]

seofon-feald (58, 146), *seven-fold.*

seofoᵭa (78, 80), *seventh.*

sēol, see seolh.

seolh (43. 3; 21), *seal.*

seolf, see self.

seolfor (47, 20), *silver.* [Ger. *Silber*, Goth. *silubr.*]

seolfren (57), *silver.* [Ger. *silbern.*]

seoᵭᵭan, see siᵭᵭan.

sessian (118), *subside.*

setl (sedl) (47), *seat; throne.* [Ger. *Sessel;* Mod. Eng. *settle.*]

sętnes (51. 5), *foundation.*

sęttan (113), *set, set down; place; make; make to turn.* [Formed, by 16, from the second stem of sittan (cf. lęcgan); Ger. *setzen.*]

sibb (51. *b*), *peace; love.* [Cf. Mod. Eng. *gossip.*]

sīd (58), *roomy, ample.*

sīde (53.1), *silk.* [< Lat. *sēta;* cf. Ger. *Seide.*]

sīe(n), see wesan.

siexta (78, 80), *sixth.*

siextīene (syxtȳne) (78), *sixteen.* [Ger. *sechszehn.*]

sige (44), *victory.* [Ger. *Sieg.*]

sige-fæst (58, 146), *victorious, triumphant.* [*ulting in victory.*

sige-hrēmig (-hrǣmig) (57), *ex-*

sige-hrēᵭig (57), *exultant with victory.*

sige-rōf (58), *of victorious energy.*

sige-ᵭūf (43), *triumphal banner.* [ᵭūf < Lat. *tufa.*]

sige-wang (-wǫng) (43), *field of victory.*

sigor (43), *victory, triumph.*

simle, *always.*

sīn (83), *his.*

sinc (47), *treasure, riches.*

sinc-weorᵭung (51. 3), *gift of treasure, costly gift.*

sind, see wesan.

sin-gāl (58), *constant, never-ceasing.*

singan (III.104, 22), *sing; praise.* [Ger. *singen.*]

sittan (V. 106), *sit.* [Ger. *sitzen.*]

sīᵭ (43, 30), *journey; adventure; plan, errand; time.* [Cf. Ger. *Gesinde*, Chaucer, *Prol.* 485, Spenser, *F. Q.* 3. 10. 33.]

sīᵭ-fæt (43. 2), *journey; passage.*

sīᵭ-fram (-frǫm) (57), *ready for (their) journey.*

sīᵭ-nese (53. 1), *prosperous voyage.*

sīᵭᵭan (seoᵭᵭan, syᵭᵭan) (84.3), *when; after; as soon as; afterward.* [Ger. *seitdem;* cf. Chaucer, *Knight's Tale* 1244, Shak., *Cor.* 3. 1. 47.]

slacian (118), *defer, delay.* [Mod. Eng. *slack(en).*]

slǣp (43), *sleep.* [Ger. *Schlaf.*]

slǣpan (R. 110), *sleep.* [Ger. *schlafen.*]

slēan (VI. 107, 37), *smite, strike; strike down, slay.* [Ger. *schlagen;* cf. Chaucer, *Prol.* 661.]

slęcg (51. *b*), *hammer, sledge.* [Cf. slēan.]

smēan (113), *consider, inquire into.*

smēaung (51. 3), *meditation; investigation.*

smercian (118), *smile.* [Mod. Eng. *smirk.*]

smiꝺ (43), *blacksmith.* [Ger. *Schmied.*]

smiꝺꝺe (53. 1), *smithy.*

smylte (59), *calm, smooth, unruffled.*

smyltnes (51. 5), *serenity, calm.*

snel(l) (58; 35. *a*), *active, swift, fleet.* [Ger. *schnell,* Scotch *snell.*]

snellīc (57), *swift.*

snelnes (51. 5), *agility, celerity.*

snēowan (II. 103), *hasten, speed.*

snottor (57), *wise.*

snūd (43?), *speed.*

snūde (70), *quickly.*

somod, see samod.

sōna, *soon; immediately; at once; as soon; when.*

sorg (51. *b*), *distress; anxiety, trouble.* [Mod. Eng. *sorrow.*]

sorgian (118), *be anxious.* [Mod. Eng. *sorrow,* Ger. *sorgen.*]

sōꝺ (47), *truth.* [Mod. Eng. *sooth;* cf. *forsooth, soothsayer.*]

sōꝺ (58), *true.*

sōꝺ, adv., *verily.* [Cf. Spenser, *F. Q.* 3. 3. 13.]

sōꝺ-fæst (58), *just and true; righteous.* [Mod. Eng. *soothfast.*]

sōꝺ-fæstnes (51. 5), *truth.* [Cf. Chaucer, *Nun's Priest's Tale* 508.]

sōꝺlice (70), *indeed, truly.* [Cf. *soothly,* Spenser, *F. Q.* 5. 10. 8.]

sparian (118), *spare.* [Ger. *sparen.*]

spell (47), *account.*

spildan (113), *fling away.* [Cf. Shak., *Haml.* 4. 5. 20.]

sprǣc (51. *b*), *speech; language; tale.* [Ger. *Sprache.*] [*sprechen.*

sprecan (V. 106), *speak.* [Ger.

springan (III. 104), *spread.* [Ger. *springen,* Mod. Eng. *spring.*]

spryttan (113), *bring forth.* [Cf. Ger. *spriessen,* Eng. *sprout.*]

stæfna, see stefna.

stǣnen (57), *stone.* [< stān, by 16; Ger. *steinen.*]

stæppan (VI. 107), *step, march.*

stān (43), *stone.* [Ger. *Stein.*]

standan (VI. 107), *stand; stand still; fall upon.*

starian (118), *gaze.* [Mod. Eng. *stare.*]

stēap (58), *lofty.* [Mod. Eng. *steep.*]

stede (44), *place, position.* [Mod. Eng. *stead;* cf. Ger. *Statt, Stätte.*]

stede-heard (58), *firm, strong.*

stede-wang (43), *plain.*

stefn (51.*b*), *voice.* [Ger. *Stimme;* cf. Chaucer, *Knight's Tale* 1704, Spenser, *Shep. Cal., Sept.* 224.]

stefn (43), *prow.* [Cf. 'from stem to stern.']

stefna (stæfna) (53), *prow.*

stēoran, see stīeran.

steorra (53), *star.* [Cf. Ger. *Stern,* Lat. *stella,* Gr. ἀστήρ.]

sterced-ferhꝺ (58), *resolute-souled, stout-hearted.*

stīeran (stēoran) (113), *steer.* [Cf. Ger. *steuern;* and cf. Gr. σταυρός?]

stiern-mōd (styrn-) (58), *stern of mood.*

stīg (51. *b*), *road, course, line.* [Cf. Mod. Eng. *stile, stirrup, stair.*]

stīgan (I. 102, 28), *ascend, enter, go aboard; go down (cf. Ps. 107.*

23). [Ger. *steigen*, Gr. στείχειν ; cf. Spenser, *F. Q.* 4. 9. 33.]

stillan (113 ; 164. *i*), *calm, appease, hush.* [Ger. *stillen*.]

stille (59), *still; quiet, silent.* [Ger. *stille.*]

stilnes (51. 5), *calm, quietness.*

storm (43), *storm.* [Cf. Ger. *Sturm.*]

stōw (51. *b*), *place.* [Cf. Mod. Eng. *stow.*]

strǣl (43), *arrow.* [Ger. *Strahl.*]

strǣt (51. *b*), *street; public place.* [< Lat. *strāta ;* Ger. *Strasse.*]

strand (43), *strand, sea-shore.* [Ger. *Strand.*]

strang (58, 65), *strong; power-*'*ful; violent; hard, severe, arduous.* [Cf. Ger. *streng.*]

strangung (51. 3), *invigoration, quickening.*

√ **strēam** (43), *stream, current.* [Ger. *Strom.*]

strēam-wielm (-welm) (43), *whirlpool, maelstrom.*

√ **stręng** (43), *rope ;* plur. *cordage, rigging, tackle.* [Cf. Mod. Eng. *string.*]

stręngre, see **strang.**

stręngð̄u (51. *a* ; 144), *strength.*

strēonan, see **strīenan.**

strīenan (strēonan) (113), *win over, gain over, convert.* [See **gestrēon.**]

stund (51. *b*), *while ;* **stunde** (176), *now.* [Ger. *Stunde,* archaic Mod. Eng. *stound,* as in Chaucer, *Knight's Tale* 354, Spenser, *F. Q.* 1. 8. 25, 38.]

stycce-mǣlum (72), *gradually, little by little.* [Cf. Ger. *stückweise.*]

√ **styrian** (118), *move ; flow, roll.* [Mod. Eng. *stir.*]

styriendlic (57), *moving, that moves.*

styrman (113), *storm.* [< **storm,** 17 ; Ger. *stürmen.*]

styrnmōd, see **stiernmōd.**

sulh-scear (43 ?), *plowshare.* [Cf. Lat. *sulcus.*]

sum (89. *a* ; 151), *some* (*one*) *; (a) certain; one.* [Cf. Chaucer, *Knight's Tale* 397, 399.]

sumer (43. 5), *summer.* [Ger. *Sommer.*]

sund (47), *swimming; course; sea.*

sundor-ierfe (-yrfe) (44), *private property.*

sunne (53. 1), *sun.* [Ger. *Sonne.*]

sunu (45), *son.* [Ger. *Sohn.*]

sūð-dǣl (43), *southern part; south.*

sūð-westerne (59), *southwestern.* [Cf. Ger. *südwest.*]

swā, *so ; as ; yet ; since ; such ; which ;* **call swā,** see **eall ; swā** (swā) . . . **swā** (202), *so . . . as, as . . . as ; the . . . the ; inasmuch as ; whether . . . or.*

swǣsendu (47), plur., *viands, food.* [For the plural, cf. Lat. *epulæ.*]

swæð̄orian, see **swe(o)ð̄erian.**

swā-hwæð̄er (89. *a*), *whichever.*

swā-hwæt-swā (89. *d*), *what* (*so*)*- ever.*

swan (43), *swan.* [Ger. *Schwan.*]

swā-swā, *like ; as ; just as ; as if.*

swātig (47), *bloody.* [Ger. *schweissig.*]

swā-ð̄ēah, *nevertheless.*

swað̄u (51. *a*), *track, footprint.*

swefan (V. 106), *sleep.*

swefel (43), *sulphur.* [Ger. *Schwefel.*]

swēg (43), *music.*

swēg-cræft (43), *music.*

swegel (47), *sky, heaven.*

swēging (51. 3), *noise.*

swęncan (113), *weary, fatigue, wear out.* [Formed from the second stem of swincan, by 16.]

sweora (53), *neck.*

sweorcan (III. 104), *grow dark, become overcast.*

sweord (swyrd) (47), *sword.*

swēot (47), *troop, army.*

sweotol (swutol) (57), *clear.*

sweotole (70), *clearly, plainly.*

sweotollice (70), *plainly, clearly.*

swęrian (VI. 107), *swear.* [Ger. *schwören.*]

swēte (59), *sweet.* [Ger. *süss;* cf. Lat. *suavis,* Gr. ἡδύς.]

swētnes (51. 5; 144), *sweetness; goodness.*

swe(o)ðerian (118), *depart, melt away, vanish; subside.*

swīcan (I. 102; 164. *n*), *desert.*

swift (58), *swift, fleet.*

swiftnes (51. 5; 144), *swiftness, celerity.*

swige (53. 1), *silence.*

swigian (118), *be silent, keep silence.*

swilc (89. *a*), *such, this sort.* [< *swalic < swā + līc;* cf. *swich,* Chaucer, *Prol.* 3.]

swilce, adv., *likewise.*

swilce (swylce), conj., *as if;* ēac swilce, swilce ēac, see ēac.

swimman (III. 104), *swim.* [Ger. *schwimmen.*]

swincan (III. 104), *work with effort.* [Cf. swęncan, and archaic Mod. Eng. *swink,* as in Chaucer, *Prol.*186, Milton, *Com.* 293.]

swingan (III. 104), *whip? throw?*

swīð (58, 64, 30), *strong;* comp. *right.* [Cf. Ger. *geschwind.*]

swīðe (swȳðe) (70), *much. greatly, very;* comp. *rather. more.*

swīðlice (70), *exceedingly, greatly*

swīð-mōd (58), *vehement-souled.*

swutol, see sweotol.

swylce, see swilce.

swyrd, see sweord.

swȳðe, see swīðe.

sybb, see sibb.

sylf, see self.

syllan, see sęllan.

syllīc, see sellic.

syn(n) (51. *b*), *sin.* [Cf. Ger. *Sünde.*]

synderlic (57, 146), *separate, individual.* [Cf. Ger. *sonderlich.*]

syndon, see wesan.

syn-full (58), *sinful.*

syððan, see siððan.

syxtȳne, see siextiene.

T.

tācen (47), *sign, signal.* [Ger. *Zeichen,* Mod. Eng. *token.*]

tācen-bora (53), *groomsman* (lit. *standard-bearer*).

tācnian (118), *signify, betoken, indicate.*

tǣcean (114), *teach.*

tǣlan (113), *blame, censure.*

tāl (51. *b*), *censure;* tō tāle, *censurable, blameworthy.*

tēar (43), *tear.* [Cf. Ger. *Zähre* and Gr. δάκρυ.]

tęlg (43), *dye.*

tempel (47), *temple.* [< Lat. *templum.*]

tēon (II. 103), *pull, bring.* [Ger *ziehen.*]

tēon (tīan) (113), *arrange, or dain.*

ticcen (47), *goat.* [Ger. *Zicke.*]

tīd (**51**. 1), *time, season; while; day; hour.* [Ger. *Zeit,* Mod. Eng. *tide* in *Christmastide, Whitsuntide.*]

tigel-fāg (**58**), *variegated with tiles.* [tigel < Lat. *tegula.*]

tigris (Lat.), *tiger.*

til, *to.* [Mod. Eng. *till;* cf. Ger. *Ziel.*]

tilian (**118**), *gain, obtain, provide.* [Ger. *zielen,* Mod. Eng. *till.*]

tilung (**51**. 3), *acquisition, procuring.*

tīma (**53**), *time.*

timbran (**115**. *b*), *build, construct.* [Ger. *zimmern.*]

tin (**47**), *tin.* [Ger. *Zinn.*]

tinterg (**47**), *punishment.*

tīr (**43**), *glory, fame.* [Ger. *Zier.*]

tið (**51**. *b ;* **28**), *boon.*

tiðian (**118**; **159**. *a ;* **28**), *grant, bestow.* [Cf. tið.]

tō, prep., *to ; for ; according to ;* the sign of the gerund, and governing the following infinitive as a noun in the dative. [Ger. *zu.*]

tō, adv., *too.* [Ger. *zu.*]

tō- (**142**). [Cf. Spenser, *F. Q.* 4. 7. 8 ; 5. 9. 10.]

tō-berstan (III. **104**), *break up, go to pieces.* [Cf. Chaucer, *Knight's Tale* 1753, 1833, 1899.]

tō-brecan (IV. **105**), *break in pieces, shatter.* [Ger. *zerbrechen.*]

tō-dæg, *to-day.* [Cf. Ger. *heut zu Tage.*]

tō-dǣlan (**113**), *divide, part asunder, separate, disperse.* [Ger. *zertheilen.*]

tō-dōn (**140**), *separate.*

tō-drǣfan (**113**), *drive away.*

[drǣfan < second stem of drīfan (**102**), by **16**.]

tō-foran, *before.*

tō-gædere, *together.*

tō-gēanes, *towards, to meet.*

tō-ge-īecan (**113**), *add.*

tō-ge-lǣdan (**113**), *bring.*

tō-glīdan (I. **102**), *glide away, slip away.*

tō-hopa (**53**), *hope.* [Cf. Ger. *hoffen.*]

tō-hrēosan (II. **103**), *fall away.*

tohte (**53**. 1), *conflict.*

tō hwon, *why.*

tō-middes, *amidst, in the midst of.*

top (**43**), *top? ball?* [Ger. *Zopf.*]

torht (**58**), *resplendent.*

torr (**43**), *tower; watch-tower; crag.* [< Lat. *turris.*]

tō-sceacan (VI. **107**), *depart, pass away.*

tō-scēadan (R. **110**), *separate, divide.*

tō-slītan (I. **102**), *rend, tear, destroy.* [*rupt.*

tō-twǣman (**113**), *divide; inter-*

tō-weorpan (III. **104**), *blot out, forgive* (lit. *break in pieces*)*; quell, compose,* Lat. *dissolvere.*

træf (**47**. 4), *building.*

trēo (**47**. 3), *tree.*

trēow-cy .. (**47**), *sort of tree.*

trēownes (**51**. 5 ; **144**), *trust.*

trēow-wyrhta (**53**, **147**), *carpenter.* [Cf. wyrhta.]

trum (**57**), *secure, strong.*

trymman (**115**. *a*), *confirm, establish, strengthen.* [< trum, by **16**.]

tungol (**47**. 6), *'ar, heavenly body.*

tūsc (**43**), *tusk.*

twā, see twēgen.

twēgen (78, 79), *two*. [Mod. Eng. twain, Chaucerian *tweye* (*Prol.* 704), archaic Ger. *zween*.]

twelf (78, 24), *twelve*. [Ger. *zwölf*.]

twēntig (78), *twenty*. [Ger. *zwanzig*.]

twēonian (118; 159. b), *doubt*.

Tyrisc (57), *Tyrian*.

tyrnan (113), *revolve*. [Mod. Eng. *turn*.]

Ð.

ð̄a, pron.; see 84, 87. [Cf. Chaucer, *Prol.* 498.]

ð̄a (84. 1), *then, when; there, where*. [Ger. *da;* archaic Mod. Eng. *tho*, as in Chaucer, *Knight's Tale* 135, Spenser, *F. Q.* 1. 1. 18.]

ð̄æce (53. 1), *roof*. [Ger. *Dach*, Mod. Eng. *thatch*.]

ð̄æm, see 84.

ð̄ær (75), *there, where*. [Cf. Chaucer, *Prol.* 34, 172, 547.]

ð̄æra, ð̄ære, see 84.

ð̄ær-on, *therein*.

ð̄ær-tō-ēacan, *besides, in addition to that*.

ð̄æs, see 84.

ð̄æs-ð̄e, see 157. 1.

ð̄æt, see 84; 189. 3.

ð̄æt, conj., *that*.

ð̄ætte (34), *that;* tō ð̄on ð̄ætte, *so that*. [< ð̄æt-ð̄e.]

ð̄afian (-igan) (118), *permit, allow*.

ð̄ā-hwæð̄re, *yet*.

ð̄ā-hwīle-ð̄e, *while, so long as*. [Cf. Ger. *dieweil*.]

ð̄ām, see 84.

ð̄anan (ð̄e) (75), *thence, from there; whence; from which; of which; by which*. [Ger. *dannen;* cf. Mod. Eng. *thence*.]

ð̄anc (43), *thank(s)*. [Ger. *Dank*.]

ð̄ancian (118; 159. a), *thank*. [Ger. *danken*.]

ð̄ancol-mōd (58), *discreet, heedful, attentive*.

ð̄anc-snottor (ð̄onc-snottur) (57), *wise of thought*.

ð̄āra, see 84.

ð̄ās, see 85.

ð̄ā-ð̄ā, *when;* ð̄ā-ð̄ā ... ð̄ā (202), *when ... (then)*.

ð̄ā-ð̄e, ð̄e, see 87.

ð̄e ... ð̄e (202), *whether ... or*.

ð̄ēah (ð̄ēh), *though, although; yet;* ð̄ēah ... ð̄ēah (202), *though ... yet*. [Ger. *doch*.]

ð̄ēah-hwæð̄re, *nevertheless*.

ð̄ēah-ð̄e, *though, although;* ð̄ēah-ð̄e ... hwæð̄re, ð̄ēah-ð̄e ... swā-ð̄ēah (202), *though ... yet*.

ð̄earf (51. b; 21. a), *need; profit, benefit*. [Cf. ð̄urfan.]

ð̄earfa (53; 21. a), *needy (one), poor*. [Cf. ð̄urfan.]

ð̄earfendlic (57), *poor*.

ð̄earle (70), *greatly, very, very much, exceedingly*.

ð̄earlice (70), *violently*.

ð̄ēaw (43), *conduct;* plur. *morals, virtues*. [Cf. Spenser, *F. Q.* 1. 1. 33.]

ð̄egn (43, 28, 24), *vassal, retainer, thane*. [Archaic Ger. *Degen;* cf. Gr. τέκνον.]

ð̄ēh, see ð̄ēah.

ð̄encean (114), *think, consider, reflect; devise*. [Ger. *denken*.]

ð̄enden (ð̄ende), *inasmuch as*.

ð̄ēnian (118; 164. e; 28), *serve, minister to*.

ðenung (51. 3; 28), *ministration, service; first course.*

ðeod (51. *b*), *people, nation; region, country, province.* [Cf. Ger. *Deutsch.*]

ðeoden (43), *lord.* [< ðeod; cf. dryhten < dryht, cyning < cynn.]

V ðeoden-hold (58), *faithful to his lord.*

ðeod-guma (53), *man of the people.*

ðeod-scipe (44. 1; 144), *discipline.*

ðeos, see 85.

ðeow (58), *bond, unfree, serving.*

ðeow-dōm (43), *service.*

ðes, see 85.

ðider (ðyder) (75), *thither, wherever.*

ðiestru (ðriostru) (47), plur., *darkness.* [Cf. Ger. *düster,* and, for the plural, Lat. *tenebræ.*]

ðin (83, 81), *thy, thine.* [Ger. *dein.*]

ðinen (51. 5), *handmaid.* [Cf. ðegn.]

ðing (47), *thing; sake;* ænige ðinga, *in any way, by any means.*

ðing-gewrit (47), *document.*

ðis, ðisne, ðissa, ðisse, ðisses, ðissum, see 85.

ðīwen (51. 5), *handmaid.*

ðolian (118), *endure, experience.* [Scotch *thole;* cf. Ger. *dulden.*]

ðon, see 84, 175 ff.; sometimes for ðǣm, ðām, through the shortened ðam, ðan.

ðone, see 84.

ðonne, *then; when; since; than* (with comparatives); ðonne ... ðonne (202), *when ... (then).*

ðoðor (43), *ball.*

ðrēan (113), *rebuke.*

ðrēat (43), *band, crowd, multitude.*

ðrēatian (118), *reprove, chide.* [Cf. Mod. Eng. *threaten.*]

ðridda (78), *third.* [Ger. *dritte.*]

ðrīe (ðrȳ) (78, 79), *three.* [Ger. *drei.*]

ðrines (51. 5; 144), *trinity.*

ðringan (III. 104), *press forward.* [Ger. *dringen;* cf. Mod. Eng. *throng.*]

ðriostru, see ðiestru. [*dreist.*]

ðrīste (59), *bold, confident.* [Ger.

ðritig (78), *thirty.*

ðriðcyning, see ðrȳðcyning.

ðroht-heard (58), *patient, much-enduring.*

ðrōwian (118), *suffer, endure.*

ðrōwung (51. 3), *passion.*

ðrȳ, see ðrīe.

ðrym(m) (43), *force; troop; glory.*

ðrym-fæst (58, 146), *glorious.*

ðrym-full (58, 146), *glorious.*

ðrymlīc (57), *glorious.*

ðrym-sittende (61), *sitting in glory.*

ðrȳð (51. *b*), *might;* the translation of þrēata þrȳðum, p. 219, l. 5, is doubtful.

ðrȳð-bearn (47, 38), *mighty son,* i.e. *mighty youth.*

ðrȳð-cyning (ðrīð-) (43), *king of might.*

ðū, see 81.

ðūhton, see ðyncean.

ðurfan (131), *need.* [Ger. (*be*)-*dürfen.*]

ðurh, *through; throughout; in; by; by means of;* ðurh eall, see eall. [Mod. Eng. *th(o)rough;* Chaucer has *thurgh, Knight's Tale* 362.]

ðurstig (57), *thirsty.* [Ger. *durstig.*]

ðus, *thus* (always with a verb of utterance in these texts).

ðūsend (78, 79), *thousand.*

ðūsend-mǣlum (72), *by thousands.*

ðwēal (47), *bath.*

ðwīeres (ðwēores) (71), *transversely.*

ðȳ, see 84, 175 ff.

ðȳs, see 85.

ðyder, see ðider.

ðȳ-lǣs-ðe, *lest.* [Cf. Lat. *quominus.*]

ðyllic (89. *a*), *such like, this kind.*

ðȳn (113), *coerce, restrain.*

ðyncean (114; 164. *l*), *seem.* [Ger. *dünken,* Mod. Eng. *(me)-thinks.*]

ðȳrel (47), *hole.* [< *ðurhil (16). Cf. Chaucer, *Knight's Tale* 1852; Spenser, *F. Q.* 1. 11. 20, 22.]

ðyrstan (113, 190), *thirst.* [Ger. *dursten,* Mod. Eng. *thirst.*]

ðyssum, see 85.

U.

ufan-weard (58; 166. 1), *upper, above.*

ūhte (53. 1), *dawn, daybreak.*

un-æðele (59), *plebeian, simple.*

un-ā-sęcgende (61), *unspeakable, ineffable.*

un-ā-swundenlice (70), *forthwith, without delay.*

un-cūð (58, 30), *unknown.* [Mod. Eng. *uncouth;* see Chaucer, *Knight's Tale* 1639, Spenser, *F. Q.* 1. 11. 20, Shak., *Tit. And.* 2. 3. 211.]

un-cystig (57, 146), *wicked.*

under, *under; among.* [Ger. *unter.*]

under-fōn (R. 110), *assume; receive, take in, entertain.*

under-standan (VI. 107), *understand.*

under-ðeodnes (51. 5; 144), *submission.* [See underðiedan.]

under-ðiedan (113), *subjoin, add.* [< ðeod, by 16.]

un-ēaðe, *with difficulty, hardly.* [Cf. unieðe, and *F. Q.* 2. 1. 27.]

un-for-cūð (58), *excellent.* [Cf. fracoð.]

un-for-wandiendlice (70), *boldly, saucily, forwardly.*

un-ge-cnāwen (62, 109), *unknown.*

un-ge-lǣred (62), *untaught, unlearned, uneducated.* [See lǣran.]

un-ge-limp (47), *mishap, ill-luck.*

un-ge-rydelice (70), *suddenly, on a sudden.*

un-ge-sewenlic (57), *invisible.*

un-ge-ðanc-full (58, 146), *unthankful, ungrateful.*

un-ge-ðwǣrnes (51. 5; 144), *wickedness, depravity.*

un-ge-wēned (63), *unexpected.* [See wēnan.]

un-ge-wērged (62), *unwearied.* [See wērig.]

un-ge-wunelic (57, 146), *unusual.* [See wunian].

un-īeðe (59), *difficult.* [See unēaðe.]

un-lifiende (-lyfigende) (61), *unliving, dead.* [Cf. libban.]

unnan (129; 159. *a*), *grant, allow.* [See ēst.]

un-nyt (57, 155), *devoid, destitute.*

un-riht-wīs (58, 146), *unright-eous.*

un-riht-wisnes (51. 5 ; 144), *un-righteousness.*

un-rim (47 ; 154. *a* ; 142), *multi-tude.*

un-rōt (58), *sorrowful, dejected.*

un-sceðð̄ig (57, 146), *innocent.*

un-scrȳdan (113, 162), *divest.* [See scrȳdan.]

un-sōfte (70), *harshly, cruelly.* [Cf. Ger. *unsanft.*]

un-stille (59), *unquiet, restless.*

un-stilnes (51. 5 ; 144), *disorder, confusion.*

un-trum (57), *sick.*

un-trymnes (51. 5 ; 144), *illness, disease, infirmity.* [< untrum.]

ūp, *up.*

ūp-ā-hæfednes (51. 5 ; 144), *pride, arrogance.* [Cf. ūpāhᵉbban.]

ūp-ā-hᵉbban (VI. 107), *lift up.* [Cf. Chaucer, *Knight's Tale* 1570.]

ūp-ā-standan (upp-) (VI. 107), *rise up.* [Cf. Ger. *auferstehen.*]

ūp-ā-stīgan (I. 102), *rise, as-cend.*

ūp-gān (141), *go up.* [Ger. *auf-gehen.*]

ūp-gang (43), *rising.*

ūplic (57, 146), *upper, above.*

uppan, *upon, on top of.*

uppe, *up.*

✓ ūre (ūser) (83), *our, ours.* [Ger. *unser.*]

ūrig-feð̄ere (59), *dewy-feathered.*

urnon, see iernan.

✓ ūser, see ūre.

ūt, *out.*

ūt-ā-blāwan (R. 109), *blow out, breathe out; exhale.*

ūtan, *about, externally, on the out-side.* [Ger. *aussen.*]

ūte (69), *outside.*

ūt-gān (141), *go out.*

ūt-gangan (R. 109), *go out.*

uton (wuton), *let us.*

W.

wæccen (51. *b*), *vigil.*

wæd (47), *water, billow, flood.*

wǣd (51. *b*), *garment; rope.* [Cf. Chaucer, *Knight's Tale* 148, Spenser, *F. Q.* 2. 3. 21, Shak., *Sonn.* 76. 6, and our 'widow's weeds.']

wǣdla (53), *poor man, destitute one.*

wǣfels (43), *cloak, mantle.*

wǣg (43), *billow, flood.* [Cf. Chaucer, *K. T.* 1100, Spenser, *F. Q.* 2. 12. 4.]

wǣg-flota (53), *water-floater, ship.*

wæl (47), *slaughter.* [Cf. *Wal-halla, Walkyrie.*]

wæl-gīfre (59), *greedy for slaugh-ter.*

wæl-grim (57), *fierce, cruel, san-guinary.*

wæl-hrēow (58), *cruel.*

wæl-hrēownes (51. 5 ; 144), *cru-elty.*

wælm, see wielm.

wæl-scel (47?), *carnage.*

wǣpen (47. 1), *weapon;* plur. *arms.*

wær (47), *ocean.*

wǣr (51. *b*), *covenant; protection, care, safe-keeping.*

wǣr-fæst (58, 146), *covenant-keeping, faithful.*

wǣstm (43), *growth, size ; fruit.* [Cf. weaxan, and Ger. *Wachs-tum;* Mod. Eng. *waist.*]

wæter (47. 1, 6), *water.* [Ger. *Wasser.*]

wæter-brōga (53), *water terror, terrible waters.*

wæter-egesa (-egsa) (53), *dread of the waters, dreadful waters.*

wæter-flōd (43), *water-flood.*

wæter-scipe (44. 1), *body of water.*

wafian (118), *waver.*

wald, see weald.

waldend, see wealdend.

wana (158), *wanting, lacking.*

wang (43), *field, mead.*

wann (wonn) (58), *dark, black.* [Mod. Eng. *wan.*]

waroð, waruð, see wearoð.

wāt, see witan.

wēa (53), *woe.* [Cf. Ger. *Weh.*]

weald (wald) (43), *weald, forest.*

wealdend (waldend) (43. 6), *ruler, lord.*

wealh-stōd (43), *interpreter, translator.*

weall (43), *wall, rampart.* [< Lat. *vallum.*]

weallan (R. 109), *seethe, foam.* [See wielm.]

weard (43), *guardian, warden.* [Ger. *-wart.*]

wearoð (waroð, waruð) (43), *strand, shore, beach.*

wearoð-gewinn (waruð-) (47), *strife of the shore, i.e. surf, breakers.*

wearð, see weorðan.

weax (47), *wax.* [Ger. *Wachs.*]

weaxan (R. 109, 24), *grow, be fruitful, increase.* [Ger. *wachsen;* cf. Shak., *M. N. D.* 2. 1. 56, *Haml.* 1. 3. 12.]

weccean (114), *wake.*

wecg (43), *metal.* [Mod. Eng. *wedge;* cf. Shak., *Rich. III.* 1. 4. 26.]

weder (47), *weather.* [Ger. *Wetter.*]

weder-candel (51. 5), *weathercandle,* i.e. *the sun.*

weg (43, 24), *way.* [Ger. *Weg.*]

wegan (V. 106), *carry.*

wel, *well.*

wela (53), *wealth, riches, weal.* [Cf. Chaucer, *Knight's Tale* 37.]

welig (57, 146), *rich, wealthy, abounding.* [Cf. our ' well off,' ' well to do.']

wel-willende (61), *benevolent, kind-hearted, generous.*

wel-willendlice (70), *lovingly.*

wel-willendnes (51. 5; 144), *generosity, liberality.*

wēn (51. 1), *expectation, prospect, chance;* wēn is ðæt, *perhaps, perchance.* [Ger. *Wahn.*]

wēnan (113; 156. g), *expect, look for; think, suppose, imagine.* [Ger. *wähnen,* Mod. Eng. *ween;* cf. Shak., *1 Hen. VI.* 2. 5. 88.]

wendan (113), *turn; return; translate.* [Ger. *wenden;* cf. Mod. Eng. *wend, went.*]

wending (51. 3), *rotation.*

wenian (116), *accustom, train.*

weoloc (43, 20), *cockle, whelk.*

weoloc-rēad (58), *scarlet.*

weoloc-sciell (51. b), *cockle-shell.*

weolor (-ur) (51. b; 20), *lip.*

weorc (47; 21. b), *work; exercise; deed; energy.* [Ger. *Werk.*]

weorod (weorud, werod) (47, 20), *host.* [< wer.]

weorðan (wyrðan) (104; 187; 21. b), *become; be;* weorðan tō sometimes nearly = weorðan. [Ger. *werden;* cf. our ' woe worth the day.']

weorðian (118; 21. b), *honor, exalt.* [Cf. Shak., *Lear* 2. 2. 128.]

weorð-full (58, 146), *honorable.*

weorðlic (-līc) (57, 146), *honorable; exalted.*

weorðlice (70), *worthily, honorably.*

weorð-mynt (43 — orig. 51. *b* — 144; 34), *dignity.* [<*weorð-mundiþa.]

weorð-scipe (44. 1; 143), *honor, dignity.* [Mod. Eng. *worship;* cf. Shak., *W. T.* 1. 2. 314, *Lear* 1. 4. 288.]

weoruld, see **woruld.**

wēpan (R. 109), *weep.* [< **wōp,** by 16.]

wer (43), *man, husband.* [Cf. Lat. *vir.*]

wer-hād (43), *male sex.* [Cf. **hād.**]

wērig (57, 146), *weary.*

werod, see **weorod.**

wer-ðēod (51. *b*), *nation.*

wesan (138, 187), *be.*

westan, *from the west.*

west-sǣ (43; 51. *b*), *sea on the west.*

wīc (47), *dwelling.* [Cf. Mod. Eng. *bailiwick;* cognate with Lat. *vicus,* Gr. οἶκος.]

wīcian (118), *visit, lodge, sojourn.* [< **wīc.**]

wid (58), *wide.* [Ger. *weit.*]

wīde (70), *widely, far.*

wīd-fērende (61), *traveling (traveler) from a distance.*

wīd-fæðme (59), *capacious, extensive.* [See **fæðm.**]

wīd-gill (58), *extensive; spacious.*

wīd-gilnes (51. 5; 144), *extent, compass.*

wielm (wylm, wælm) (43), *boiling, swelling, surging.* [See **weallan,** and Mod. Eng. *whelm.*]

wierdan (113), *mar, injure.*

wif (47, 38), *wife; woman.* [Ger. *Weib;* cf. Chaucer, *Prol.* 445, Shak., *T. N.* 5. 139.]

wif-hād (43), *female sex.*

wig (47), *war.*

wīgend (wiggend) (43. 6), *warrior.*

wig-hūs (47), *war-house, tower.*

wiht (47; cf. 89. *b*), *whit.*

wild (58), *wild.* [Ger. *wild.*]

wildēor (47, 38), *wild animal, wild beast.*

willa (53), *will; request; desire; delight.* [Ger. *Wille.*]

willan (wyllan) (139, 188), *will, wish, desire.* [Cf. Ger. *wollen,* Lat. *velle.*]

wilnian (118), *desire.* [See Chaucer, *Knight's Tale* 751.]

wīn (47), *wine.* [<Lat. *vinum;* Ger. *Wein.*]

wind (43), *wind.* [Ger. *Wind.*]

windan (III. 104), *fly about.* [Ger. *winden,* Mod. Eng. *wind.*]

windig (57, 146), *windy.* [Ger. *windig.*]

wine (44. 2, 4), *friend.*

wine-ðearfende (61), *needing a friend.* [Cf. **ðearf.**]

wīn-geard (43), *vineyard.*

winnan (III. 104), *struggle, toil.*

winstre (60), *left.*

winter (43. 5), *winter (year); storm.* [Ger. *Winter.*]

winterlic (57, 146), *winter, wintry.* [Ger. *winterlich.*]

wīr (43), *wire.*

wīs (58; 155. *e*), *wise.* [Ger. *weise.*]

wīsian (118), *point out.* [Ger. *weisen.*]

wīslīc (57, 146), *wise, true.*

wist (51. *b*), *provisions, food.* [Cf. **wesan.**]

witan (126), *know.* [Mod. Eng. *to wit*, Ger. *wissen*; cf. Chaucer, *K. T.* 402, Spenser, *F. Q.* 1. 3. 6.]

wītan (I. 102), *blame, censure.* [Cf. Spenser, *F. Q.* 2. 12. 16.]

wīte (48), *punishment, penalty, torture.* [Cf. wītan.]

wītga (53), *prophet (psalmist?).*

witodlice (untedlice) (70), *indeed, truly.*

wið, *with* (hostility); *against; toward; in return for.* [Not to be confounded with mid; cf. *withstand.*]

wiðer- (142).

wiðer-trod (47), *retreat.*

wiðer-winna (53), *adversary.*

wið-innan, *within.*

wið-sacan (VI. 107; 164. *m*), *renounce.*

wið-standan (VI. 107), *withstand.*

wið-ðingian (118), *talk with, speak to.* [Cf. Mod. Eng. *hustings.*]

wlanc (58), *proud, lordly.*

wlęncu (51. *a*), *pomp, splendor.* [< wlanc, by 16.]

wlite (44), *beauty.* [Cf. andwlita.]

wlite-beorht (58), *beautiful.*

✓ wlitig (57, 146), *beautiful, comely.*

wolcen (47), *cloud.* [Cf. Ger. *Wolke*, Mod. Eng. *welkin.*]

wolde, see willan.

wǫnn, see wann.

wōp (43), *weeping (tears).*

word (47), *word.* [Ger. *Wort.*]

word-hord (47, 147), *treasury of words.* [Cf. Ger. *Hort.*]

word-loca (53, 147), *coffer of words.*

worhte, see wyrcean.

worn (43), *multitude.*

woruld (51. 1, 3; 26 ; 20), *world; in woruld worulde, for ever and ever.*

woruld-bisgu (51. *a*), *worldly occupation.*

woruld-cræft (43), *secular art, secular occupation.*

woruld-ge-ðyngð (51. *b*), *worldly honor, worldly dignity.*

woruld-līf (47), *worldly life.*

woruld-spēd (51. *b*), *worldly success.*

wręccean (114), *awake, arouse.*

wrēon (I. 102), *clothe.*

wręðian (118), *support, uphold.*

wrigon, see wrēon.

wudu (45), *forest, wood.*

wudu-bearu (-bearo) (43. 7), *forest, grove.*

wuldor (47), *glory, splendor.*

wuldor-cyning (43), *king of glory, king of majesty.* [Cf. Ps. 24. 7.]

wuldor-drēam (43), *heavenly joy, heavenly rapture* (lit. *glory-joy*).

wuldor-fæder (43. 8), *father of glory.*

wuldor-spēdig (57, 146), *glorious.*

wuldor-ðrym(m) (43), *glorious majesty.*

wuldrian (118), *glorify, magnify, celebrate.*

wulf (43, 24), *wolf.* [Ger. *Wolf.*]

✓ wund (58), *wounded, sore.* [Ger. *wund.*]

wundenlocc (58), *curly-haired.*

wundor (47. 1), *wonder.* [Ger. *Wunder.*]

wundorlic (57, 146), *wonderful.* [Ger. *wunderlich.*]

wundorlice (70), *wondrously.* [Cf. Chaucer, *Prol.* 84.]

wundrian (118), *wonder.* [Ger. *wundern.*]

wunian (118), *dwell, remain, live.*
[Ger. *wohnen;* cf. Chaucer, *Prol.*
388, Spenser, *F. Q.* 2. 1. 51.]

wunung (**51.** 3), *dwelling.* [Ger.
Wohnung; cf. Chaucer, *Prol.*
606, Spenser, *F. Q.* 6. 5. 13.]

wurdon, see **weorðan.**

wuton. see **uton.**

wyllan. see **willan.**

wylm, see **wielm.**

wyn-sum (**57, 146**), *winsome,
pleasant.* [Ger. *wonnesam.*]

wyn-sumlice (**70**), *winsomely.*

wyrcean (**114; 161; 184.** *a*),
*work; do; construct, make,
build; yield.* [Cf. Ger. *wirken,*
and Chaucer, *Knight's Tale*
1901.]

wyrhta (**53**), *craftsman, work-
man, maker.* [Cf. **wyrcean;**
Mod. Eng. *-wright* (see Chaucer,
Prol. 614).]

wyrm (**43**), *worm.* [Ger. *Wurm.*]

wyrm-cynn (**47**), *kind of worms.*

wyrt (**51.** 1), *herb.* [Mod. Eng.
wort; cf. Ger. *Wurz, Wurzel,
Gewürz,* and Chaucer, *Nun's
Priest's Tale* 401.]

wyrt-ge-mang (**47**), *spice.*

wyrt-ge-męngnes (**51.** 5; **147**),
spice.

wȳscan (**113**), *wish.* [Ger. *wün-
schen.*]

Y.

ȳcan, see **īecan.** [*übel.*]

yfel (57), *evil, wicked, bad.* [Ger.

yfel (**47**), *evil.*

yfele (**70**), *evil, wrongly.*

ymb(e), *about.*

ymb- (**142**).

ymb-clyppan (**113**), *embrace.*

ymb-hōn (R. **110**), *surround.*

ymb-hwyrft (**43**), *compass, circuit; orbit.*

ymb-hycgean (**124**), *consider.*

ymb-sęllan (**114**), *envelop; beset.*

ymb-sittan (V. **106, 142**), *sit
around.*

ymb-trymman (**115.** *a*), *surround.*

ymb-ūtan, *about, around.*

yrre, see **ierre.**

ȳð (**51.** *b*; **30**), *wave, billow, flood.*
[Cf. Lat. *unda,* and **30.**]

ȳð-bord (**47**), *ship ?*

ȳð-lād (**51.** *b*; **215**), *billow-road.*

ȳð-lid (**47, 215**), *ship.*

NOTE. — The EWS. forms of s**ǣ** (p. 310) are: sing. nom. s**ǣ**, gen.
s**ǣ**s, dat. s**ǣ**, acc. s**ǣ**. Other forms are: sing. gen. dat. s**ǣ**we; plur.
nom. acc. s**ǣ**s, s**ǣ**, dat. s**ǣ**um, s**ǣ**wum.

ANNOUNCEMENTS

ALBION SERIES OF ANGLO-SAXON AND MIDDLE ENGLISH POETRY

Under the general editorship of JAMES WILSON BRIGHT, Professor of English Literature in Johns Hopkins University, and GEORGE LYMAN KITTREDGE, Professor of English in Harvard University

---

THIS series is intended to be exhaustive for the Anglo-Saxon period, and will include the best portion of Middle English poetry up to (but not including) Chaucer. The texts have been critically edited with introductions, explanatory notes, and glossaries that adapt them to the practical needs of the classroom.

THE CHRIST OF CYNEWULF. A Poem in Three Parts: The Advent, The Ascension, and The Last Judgment. Edited by ALBERT S. COOK, Professor of the English Language and Literature in Yale University. 8vo, cloth, ciii + 294 pages, $2.50.

THE SQUYR OF LOWE DEGRE. Edited by WILLIAM E. MEAD, Professor of the English Language in Wesleyan University, Middletown, Conn. 8vo, cloth, lxxxv + 111 pages, $1.25.

ANDREAS AND THE FATES OF THE APOSTLES. Edited by GEORGE PHILIP KRAPP, recently Professor of the English Language and Literature, University of Cincinnati. 8vo, cloth, lxxxi + 238 pages, $2.00.

THE SEVEN SAGES OF ROME. Edited by KILLIS CAMPBELL, Adjunct Professor of English in the University of Texas. 8vo, cloth, cxiv + 217 pages, $2.25.

THE RIDDLES OF THE EXETER BOOK. By FREDERICK TUPPER, Jr., Professor of the English Language and Literature, University of Vermont. 8vo, cloth, cxi + 292 pages, $2.50.

The following volumes are in preparation: the Cædmonian " Christ and Satan," edited by Professor E. M. Brown, of the University of Cincinnati; the Cædmonian " Exodus," edited by Professor James W. Bright, with a Glossary by Professor Morgan Callaway, Jr., of the University of Texas; the Cædmonian "Genesis," edited by Professor F. A. Blackburn, of the University of Chicago; the Middle English " Harrowing of Hell," edited by Professor W. H. Hulme, of the Western Reserve University; the Cynewulfian " Elene," edited by Professor Frederick Klaeber, of the University of Minnesota; the Middle English " Pearl," edited by Professor O. F. Emerson, of the Western Reserve University.

48

GINN AND COMPANY PUBLISHERS

BOOKS ON
OLD AND MIDDLE ENGLISH

GINN AND COMPANY Publishers

BOOKS ON HIGHER ENGLISH

Edited by ALBERT S. COOK

Professor of the English Language and Literature in Yale University

---

ADDISON'S CRITICISMS ON PARADISE LOST. 12mo, cloth, xxiv + 200 pages, $1.00.

ASSER'S LIFE OF KING ALFRED. Translated with Notes from the text of Stevenson's edition. 12mo, cloth, 83 pages, 50 cents.

BACON'S ADVANCEMENT OF LEARNING, Book I. 12mo, cloth, lvii + 145 pages, 75 cents.

CARDINAL NEWMAN'S ESSAY ON POETRY. With reference to Aristotle's Poetics. 8vo, flexible cloth, x + 36 pages, 30 cents.

LEIGH HUNT'S ANSWER TO THE QUESTION "WHAT IS POETRY?" Including remarks on Versification. 12mo, cloth, vi + 98 pages, 50 cents.

SHELLEY'S DEFENSE OF POETRY. 12mo, cloth, xxvi + 86 pages, 50 cents.

SIDNEY'S DEFENSE OF POESY. 12mo, cloth, xlv + 103 pages, 65 cents

THE ART OF POETRY. The Poetical Treatises of Horace, Vida, Boileau, with the translations by Howes, Pitt, and Soame. 12mo, cloth, lviii + 303 pages, $1.12.

TENNYSON'S THE PRINCESS. 16mo, semiflexible cloth, xlvi + 187 pages, 30 cents.

EDMUND CLARENCE STEDMAN, Author of "Victorian Poets," "Poets of America," "The Nature and Elements of Poetry," etc.

More than once of late, when asked to name for some friend or correspondent a course of reading upon the spirit and structure of poetry, I have at once recommended Professor Albert S. Cook's series, and have been grateful to him for his admirable labors. He could have made no better choice of treatises to edit: Sidney, Shelley, Addison, Hunt, and Newman have had no better editor — so far as their exquisite essays upon the divine art are concerned. Professor Cook's notes are the fruit of sympathetic taste and liberal scholarship. The books, in fact, are models as handbooks, upon an ideal subject, designed for practical use.

GINN AND COMPANY Publishers

THE
NEW HUDSON SHAKESPEARE

Introduction and Notes by HENRY HUDSON. Edited and Revised
by E. CHARLTON BLACK, Professor of English Literature in Boston
University, with the coöperation of ANDREW J. GEORGE, late of the
Department of English in the High School, Newton, Mass., and M.
GRANT DANIELL, late Principal of Chauncy-Hall School, Boston

D R. HUDSON'S great work as a Shakespeare editor and interpreter still remains, in all t' e elements of æsthetic criticism, the most significant yet prod ced in America. Since his time, however, there have been interesting and significant developments in the study of Elizabethan 'erature, language, and prosody; and the careful research of scholars in Europe and America has made available much new and important matter bearing directly upon Shakespeare criticism and comment.

In the New Hudson Shakespeare the results of the latest research and scholarship are incorporated with the introductions, notes, and critical apparatus which have given the old edition its commanding place. The following distinctive features characterize the new edition:

1. A new text, based directly upon that of the First Folio.

2. The modernization of the spelling and punctuation of the text.

3. Two sets of notes at the foot of page, — one giving textual variants, and the other a brief philologi 1l explanation of unusual words and constructions.

4. A brief essay on versification and an analysis of the dramatic construction of each play.

5. An authentic portrait of a facsimile of an important page of a Quarto or a Folio to illustrate each play.

6. The insertion of line num'ers and the giving of the names of the characters everywhere in full.

7. A chronological chart.

8. Large, clear type from new plates.

We shall be glad to send to any address a descriptive pamphlet giving sample pages and further information relating to this new edition.

GINN AND COMPANY PUBLISHERS